The Book of Skin

Image opposite: A real 'Book of Skin': the record of the 1821 trial, conviction and execution of the murderer John Horwood, bound in his skin (removed during his medical dissection). The inscription reads 'Cutis Vera Johannis Horwood'.

The Book of Skin

Steven Connor

REAKTION BOOKS

Published by Reaktion Books Ltd
79 Farringdon Road
London EC1M 3JU, UK

www.reaktionbooks.co.uk

First published 2004

Printed and bound in Great Britain
by Biddles Ltd, Guildford and King's Lynn

British Library Cataloguing in Publication Data
Connor, Steven
   The book of skin
   1. Skin 2. Skin - Symbolic aspects
   I. Title
   612.7'9

ISBN 1 86189 193 8

Contents

NOTE ON EDITIONS AND TRANSLATIONS

References to works by Chaucer are to the *The Riverside Chaucer*, 3rd edn, ed. Larry D. Benson (Oxford, 1988).

References to works by Shakespeare are to *The Arden Shakespeare Complete Works*, ed. Richard Proudfoot, Ann Thompson and David Scott Kastan (Walton-on-Thames, 1998).

Biblical references are to the Revised Standard Version unless stated otherwise.

Where no indication of translator is given, translations are my own.

ACKNOWLEDGEMENTS

I am very grateful to the Arts and Humanities Research Board and the Leverhulme Trust, awards from whom made the completion of this book possible.

PHOTO ACKNOWLEDGEMENTS

The author and publishers wish to express their thanks to the below sources of illustrative material and/or permission to reproduce it:

Photos courtesy of Bristol Record Office: pp. 2, 43; photos British Library Reproductions: pp. 16, 17, 127, 130, 151; photos courtesy of the artist (Cheryl Casteen): pp. 263, 266, 275; property of the artist (Michael Clark), care of Marlborough Fine Art, London (photo Prudence Cuming Associates, courtesy of the artist): p. 61; photo courtesy of the artist (Brooke Davis): p. 261; photos Medical Photographic Library: pp. 13, 14, 15, 18 25, 26, 44, 77, 132 (right), 162, 228; photo courtesy of the artist (Tamara Sadlo): p. 264; photos courtesy of the artist (Lisa Deanne Smith): pp. 81, 131, 258, 259; photo Statens Konstmuseer/Erik Cornelius: p. 160.

Pregression:
A Skin That Walks

MAN is alone, desperately scraping out the music of his own skeleton, without father, mother, family, love, god or society.

And no living being to accompany him. And the skeleton is not of bone but of skin, like a skin that walks.[1]

The skins were no longer living but I had perfected a process which would ensure they could be conserved indefinitely, losing none of their original suppleness or velvety texture. I hung these tapestries up in my house; they solicited touch and made me dream of what a tactile art might be. The idea came to me of draping myself in one of them, looking at myself in the mirror, trying on others. Some of them suited me very well. A cry came from me: 'What a fine funeral outfit.'

I had found a last use for them. Like a tailor, I cut out these portions of cutaneous tissue into a suit of clothes. I adjusted the front, the back, the arms, the legs until it was a single sheath which could envelop me completely, head, feet, hands and all. Carefully disguised zip fastenings allowed me to slip into it easily. The Egyptians wrapped the mummified bodies of their rulers in bandages. I will need no sarcophagus. To bear on my dying flesh this second incorruptible skin, drawn from the multitude of people I have known and who will accompany me for ever, will be for me sufficient shroud. This mantle of suppleness, beauty and warmth will lap me in its illusion for the long passage into eternity.[2]

1 Complexion

If the skin has always been pressing, it has never been so much in evidence as it seems to be today. The skin is pervasive not only in critical and cultural theory but also in contemporary life. Everywhere, the skin, normally as little apparent as the page upon which is displayed the words we read, is becoming visible on its own account; not only in the obsessive display of its surfaces and forms in cinema and photography, in the massive efforts to control and manipulate its appearance by means of cosmetics and plastic surgery, and the extraordinary investment in the skin in practices and representations associated with fetishism and sadomasochism, but also in the anxious concern with the abject frailty and vulnerability of the skin, and the destructive rage against it exercised in violent fantasies and representations of all kinds. All of this appears to bear out the judgement of James Joyce that 'modern man has an epidermis rather than a soul'.[1] It gives the strange effect of a cultural literalization of a figure, the further desublimation of the idea of skin-as-surface whose primary purpose was always anyway to substitute apparition for appearance, ostension for the theatrics of figure or allegory. This book enquires in part into this ubiquitous ostension of the skin, and the contemporary fascination with the powers of the skin, as substance, vehicle and metaphor.

One might say that the language of critical and cultural theory has correspondingly been full of the presence and pressure of the skin, were it not that the specific compulsion of the skin as a surface disallowed so voluminous a figure. The skin asserts itself in the erotics of texture, tissue and tegument played out through the work of Roland Barthes; in the concern of Emmanuel Levinas with the exposed skin of the face, as the sign of essential ethical nudity before the other; the ghostly drama of the trace and the drama of its inscriptions on various kinds of surface bequeathed by Levinas to Derrida and others; the extraordinary elaborations of the play of bodily surfaces, volumes and membranes in Derrida's concepts of double invagination, the hymen and the sexual dynamics of the pen and the web-sail-paper it punctuates; the concept of the fold in the rethinking of subjective and philosophical depth in the work of Gilles Deleuze; the fascination with the intrigues of the surface in the work of Baudrillard; and the abiding presence of skin in the work of Jean-François

Lyotard, from the arresting evocation of the opened-out skin of the planar body at the beginning of his *Libidinal Economy* through to the Levinasian emphasis on the annunciatory powers of skin at moments through *The Inhuman*. Most strikingly of all and, as far as this book is concerned, most fruitfully, there has been the prominence of the skin in the meditations on place, shape and the 'mixed body' of Michel Serres. Across all this work, as ubiquitously in modern experience, the skin insists.

This visibility has taken a surprisingly long time to come about. There is very little specific attention paid to the skin in early medical conceptions of the body. For many early civilizations, the skin is understood primarily in its role as a covering that keeps the body inviolate. The practices of embalming in ancient Egypt indicate some considerable familiarity with the workings of the inside of the body, but even here the practices of the embalmer and the incisor, the one who made the first breach in the body, seem to have been kept separate: an embalmer could only work with a body in which an incision had already been made by another. Diodorus Siculus reports that once the παρασχίστης (*paraschistes*) or 'slitter' has opened up the body, 'he at once takes to flight on the run, while those present set out after him, pelting him with stones, heaping curses on him, and trying, as it were, to turn the profanation on his head; for in their eyes everyone is an object of general hatred who applies violence to the body of a man of the same tribe or wounds him'.[2] Where it is the function of the skin in life to maintain the integrity of the body, embalming removes the putrescent viscera of the body in order to preserve the integrity of the skin. Thus the skin that has protected the body in life must be protected from it after death. So even after the separation of the inside and the outside of the body, the role of the skin is to maintain the integrity of the soul – to be, as it were, the soul's body.

Despite wide acquaintance with the wounded and dismembered body in experience and representation, classical Greece seems similarly to have maintained a strong conception of the inviolability of the body, as guaranteed by the smooth and immaculate skin. The flayed or abstracted skin was the object of fascinated attention for the Greeks, and was often the bearer of specific powers. The skin was not the principle of identity, so much as that of entirety. You could be made more entire, more yourself, by taking on another's skin. Heracles wears the skin of the Nemean lion and so, ridiculously, does the figure of Dionysus in Aristophanes' *Clouds*: Athena wears the aegis, which is the skin of the giant Pallas, or of the Medusa.

One of the distinctive features of the skin in the Greek and Roman worlds is the variety of different words there are to name its different forms and aspects. χρώς (*chros*) is a common name for the skin in Greek, though it can also mean the whole of the body. Often, too, it expresses the idea of proximity: ἐν χρῷ (*enchroi*) means right up close to the skin. It can also refer to the colour or complexion of the skin, sometimes, as in the word ὁμοχροία (*homochroia*), signifying evenness of colour. The reference to colour involves a reference to the whole of the body, since, as we will see, the colour of the skin was held to

Hercules threatens Cerberus, dressed in the skin of the Nemean lion. A detail of a Corinthian vase in the Musée du Louvre, Paris.

be the expression of the way in which the entire body was knitted together. The Greek word for hide was δέρμα (*derma*). A range of other words might also be used for the skin, corresponding to English words like surface, rind and cortex.

Latin did not have a single, all-purpose word for the skin either. The two principal words in use in Latin were *cutis*, which signified the living skin, the skin that protects, that expresses and arouses and that is the subject of care and beautifying attention. *Pellis*, by contrast, is the dead, the flayed skin. It is the word used for animal skins, and evokes disgust, disgrace and horror. Once scoured away from the body, the human or animal skin becomes simply a hide, deader than a corpse, a corpse's remnant, the corpse of a corpse. A certain unsteadiness in the ways in which the skin is referred to in medical language is the legacy of this duality. The science of the skin is called 'dermatology', but early hospitals for diseases of the skin would more commonly refer to 'cutaneous' diseases. It would be right to see this in one sense as a sign of the complexity or polymorphousness of the skin in the ancient world. It is also a sign of the relative invisibility of the skin in itself. In a sense, we might say that the different words that we might translate with the word 'skin' are not yet joined together on a single plane, as they are for us. Although the skin conferred and confirmed entirety, it had none of its own.

If the skin was in one sense idealized in classical Greek culture, there are also signs that it was regarded as a kind of excrescence, which could protect the integrity of the body precisely because it is not wholly of it. Aristotle's explanation of the formation of the skin sees it as a kind of after-effect, brought about by the actions of drying and hardening. The skin is formed, he says, 'by the drying of the flesh, like the scum upon boiled substances; it is so formed not only because it is on the outside, but also because what is glutinous, being unable to evaporate, remains on the surface.'[3] Here, the skin is not just the medium of excretion, it is itself the product of it. This unflattering account of the formation of the skin is repeated for centuries. In his *Book of Treasures*, the Syrian philosopher Job of Edessa (or Job al-Abrash) who wrote and taught in Baghdad in the early decades of the ninth century, similarly accounts for skin as the result of congelation:

> The skin came into existence in an outside position because, when the humidity of the outside portion met the air, the latter destroyed the thinness which it possessed, and it thickened; and as a result its parts came together, solidified, and became skin. The same thing happens when we cook grains of wheat, or other things; after they have dissolved and become chyle, if we leave them a short time exposed to air in a vessel or plate, the humidity rises above them and forms a skin in an outside position, in such a way that we can take it with our hands.[4]

The Paduan anatomist Alessandro Benedetti was still following Aristotle in his *Anatomicae: sive historia corporis humani* of 1497, in which he wrote that '[t]he skin is formed by the drying flesh as (according to Aristotle) the crust is formed in polenta. For when the sticky matter cannot evaporate it settles down since it is fat and viscous'.[5] The belief that the skin is formed last of all in the developing organism, rather than being present from the beginning, would take centuries to be displaced.

Of course, this metaphor of curdling need not always represent the denigration of the skin. It seems to have a positive inflexion in Job's cry to the Lord: 'Didst thou not pour me out like milk and curdle me like cheese? Thou didst clothe me with skin and flesh, and knit me together with bones and sinews' (Job 10:10–11). But the Lord God is about to allow Satan to wreak havoc on Job's skin, and the early Christian tradition developed a decidedly ambivalent attitude towards the skin, often continuing to regard it as an accessory substance or even an excrement of the body rather than an organ. Despite the assurance in Luke (12:7) that even the hairs of the head are all numbered by the Lord, Aquinas was of the opinion that the hair and the nails would not rise again, since they were waste products of the body like urine and sweat.[6] St Augustine was worried that animals seemed to have a power of moving their skins autonomously, to twitch away a fly or other irritation, for example, which human beings did not, and attributed this immovability to the Fall: 'Man could once have received from his lower members an obedience which he lost by his own disobedience'.[7] The horror at the skin survives both in the word 'horror' itself, which signified in Latin the lifting or horripilation of the skin, and in the allusion to the hide which may linger in the word 'hideous'.

The continuing taboo on cutting or breaking open the skin to investigate the body's interior inhibited studies of human anatomy both in the classical world and in Christian Europe. However, this taboo was not absolute and seems to

have been relaxed sufficiently by the third century BC to allow dissection of dead bodies to take place at the famed medical school in Alexandria. But even as anatomy began to increase in importance in the early Christian era, the skin continued to feature in that anatomy only as that which is to be breached in order to gain access to the hidden innards of the human body. Even Galen, who insisted on the importance of anatomy, though he seems to have derived much of his knowledge about the structure of the human body from the dissection of animals, seems curiously inattentive to the skin which it was necessary for the anatomist to enter in order to conduct his enquiries. In his *De anatomiciis administrationibus*, Galen laid down the order in which the student should learn about the human body. First of all come the bones, which constitute the form of the body. The student is advised to move on after that to the muscles, and then the veins, arteries and nerves. After that, it does not appear to matter where one turns: to the internal organs, or the intestines, fat and glands. In other words, Galen recommends moving from what is the innermost level of the body to the outermost – except that there is no mention of the skin. The skin – whether of ape or man – is that which it is necessary to part or perforate in order to begin anatomical investigation, not itself the subject of such investigation. Galen's concern with the skin is restricted to the technical problem of how it may best be removed without damaging underlying nerves and membranes.[8]

The eleventh-century Arabic natural philosopher Avicenna orders the anatomical portions of his encyclopaedic *Al-Qanun fi al-Tibb* or *Canon of Medicine* in the same way, treating of bones, then muscles, then nerves, veins and viscera.[9] When dissection and anatomy were revived in Europe, the relative inattention to the skin continued. Guy de Chauliac, one of the most important physicians of the late medieval period, says promisingly that he intends 'to bygynne atte pe skyn for it renneþ first in makynge of the Anothomye', but in fact then notes only that the skin is the covering of the body before moving to other topics.[10] Despite the many innovations and revelations of his magnificent

Male figure holding open the skin of his trunk, from Jacopo Berengario da Carpi, *Anatomia* (Bologna, 1521).

The flayed skin suspended from a triumphal arch. Frontispiece to Nathaniel Highmore, *Corporis humani disquisitio anatomica* (The Hague, 1651).

and influential *De humani corporis fabrica* (1543), Vesalius also sticks to the Galenian scheme of working outwards from the bones through the muscles to the nerves and arteries. The fact that so many of the illustrations of Vesalius and his anatomical followers seem to draw playful attention to the skin, which is peeled back, lifted like an apron, held daintily aside, or hangs in flaps from wrists and ankles, is misleading, since the point of such illustrations seems to be to guide us to what is really essential, namely the interior organs and bodily systems. (In fact, some later anatomical texts would play with the cutaneous suggestions of the book's binding and pages. Thomas Bartholin's *Anatomia reformata* of 1651 had its title inscribed upon a human skin stretched upon a frame, while Johann Remmelin's *Catoptron Microcosmicum*, first published in 1639, provided anatomical illustrations with cut-out panels to enable the reader to see below the surface of the body.)[11] The skin is discussed only briefly, in chapters 5 and 6 of the second book of *De humanis corporis fabrica*, on the muscles and ligaments. Vesalius' principal contribution is to distinguish four distinct layers 'that always surround the entire human body' and through which one must pass in order to reach the bones, muscles and organs. They are the cuticle (or epidermis), the derma, the fat, in variable thickness, and finally the stronger and thicker layer of what he calls the *panniculus carnosus*, or 'fleshy

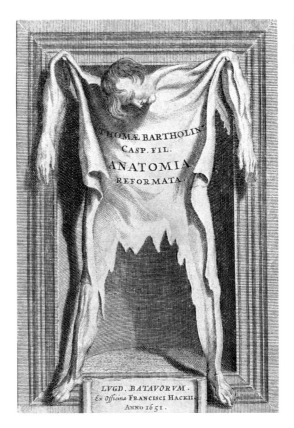

rag', a membrane which, Vesalius maintained against 'the most distinguished physicians of our age', extends over the whole interior of the body.[12] Thereafter, the attention that Vesalius pays to the skin is mostly, like Galen, in terms of the techniques of incision and retraction required to get past it into the body.

Another sign of the 'thin' rather than 'thick' understanding of the skin in medical terms is the longevity of the curious belief, articulated by Aristotle, that the skin cannot feel.[13] This judgement is articulated, for example, by Alessandro Benedetti, who wrote in 1497 that 'By means of [the skin] as a temperament we judge with the sense of touch, therefore it is itself without sensation'.[14] Vesalius writes as though against a prevailing opinion when he affirms in 1543 that 'Aristotle must certainly be disregarded when he deprives the skin of sensation as if its sense of touch came only from the flesh beneath the skin; for we discover from dissection that a definite series of nerves belonging specifically to the skin extends to the skin [sic]'.[15] The understanding that the outside of the skin is directly rather than mediately involved in the apprehension of touch (though one doubts that non-medical people ever entertained any doubts of this) was an important stage in bringing the skin to life.

Although the actuality of the skin may have been invisible to the anatomist, or interesting only as impediment, a formal idea of the skin began to play an

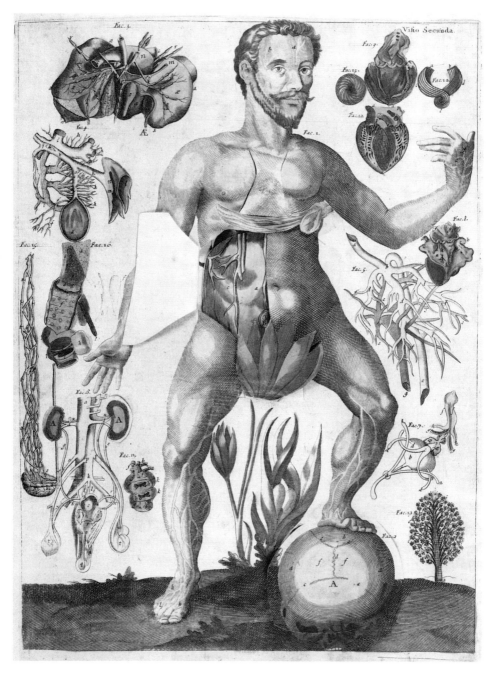

Male figure with fold-out flaps, Johann Remmelin, *A Survey of the Microcosme: or, The Anatomy of the Bodies of Man and Woman* (London, 1695).

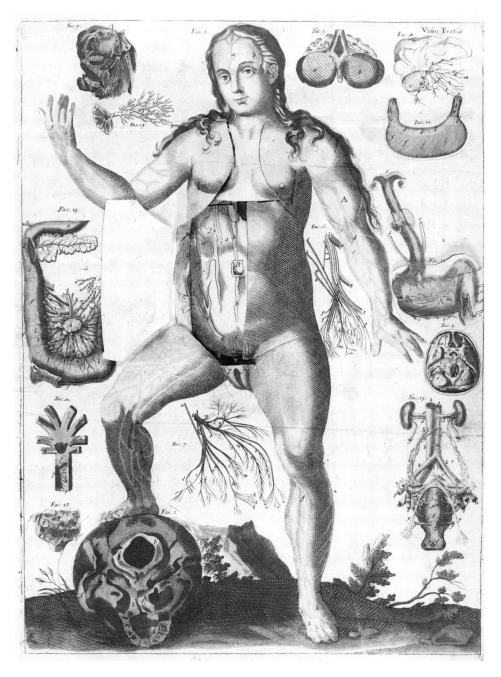

Female figure with fold-out flaps, from Remmelin, *A Survey of the Microcosme*.

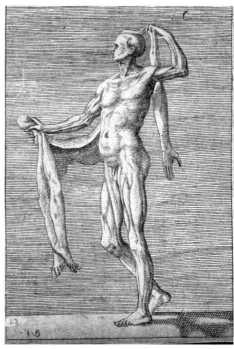

TAB. XIII.

(left) An *écorché* holding his skin, from William Cowper, *Myotomia reformata: or, an Anatomical Treatise on the Muscles of the Human Body . . .* (London, 1724).

(right) A sixteenth-century engraving by Giulio Bonasone of a male *écorché* figure holding the skin of his legs in his right hand and the skin of his arms in his left hand.

important structural role in maintaining the relations between the body and the world. Marie-Christine Pouchelle has pointed out that medieval physicians regarded the body as a series of nested or concentric enclosures, each bounded by its own membrane or tunic. The skin bounds the body, which is divided by the diaphragm between its upper, spiritual and intellectual organs (lungs and brain) and its lower nutritive and generative organs. Springing from the membrane, there are the linings of the lungs and the heart. The belly too, was thought of as enclosed in several layers of skin. This nesting involution of the body duplicates the relation of the body as microcosm to the macrocosm of the natural world, the universe being articulated by an endless series of such enclosures of the same within the same.[16] Although these membranes do not form the subject of extended analysis or description, the conception of the skin as that which lies between areas that are both kept distinct and kept in contact with each other, is indispensable to this concentric view of the body within the universe.

The skin had more salience in the physiological understanding of the body's workings, which, from Hippocrates through Galen and until some considerable way into the eighteenth century, was dominated by the humoral theory developed in the Hippocratic Corpus of writings on the island of Kos between 600 and 400 BC. According to this theory, the four elements of earth, water, air and fire corresponded to the four bodily fluids of black bile, phlegm, blood and yellow bile. Yellow bile was thought to be hot and dry; black bile cold and dry, phlegm cold and moist and blood hot and moist. The longevity of humoral theory, and its wide distribution over the world – Indian and Chinese medicine employs variants of it and it can be found in Latin America too[17] – is surely due to the complexity and limitless adaptability of the scheme to different circumstances. There are few diseases or treatments for which, suitably adjusted, refined or enlarged, humoral theory could not account. This is perhaps because its endlessly enlargeable scheme of parallel quaternaries offers so many opportunities for the elaboration of the mythical logic of homology (as a is to b, so x is to y) elaborated by Lévi-Strauss and structural anthropology. Humoral theory allowed for the detailed integration or nesting of human life in the cosmos. Thus the fourfold scheme of the humours acquired seasonal and astrological correlatives; in spring, blood and Jupiter predominated; in summer, yellow bile and Mars; in autumn, black bile and Saturn and in winter, phlegm and the moon.[18]

Most importantly for our purposes, humoral theory allowed one to categorize not just disease, but human characters and dispositions. Each person's physiological make-up was thought to be constituted from the particular ratio maintained in them between the four humours or vital fluids, and the balance of the qualities of heat and cold, dryness and moistness that they connoted. Women were thought to be temperamentally cold and moist, men hot and dry; within these broad categories, characters could be choleric, phlegmatic, melancholy or sanguine.

The term used in Latin and medieval English to designate this ratio was 'complexion', from Latin *con*, with or together, and *plectare*, to plait or twine. The fortunes of this word will allow us to trace the thickening into visibility of the skin. In its uses in the earlier Middle Ages, 'complexion' nearly always refers to the particular combination of qualities and humours determining the nature or condition of an individual body. This is the sense in which it is used in John Gower's discussion of the 'Complexions foure and nomo' in his *Confessio Amantis*.[19] It was sometimes also used in the fifteenth century to mean the intertwining of two bodies in sexual embrace, a usage that enlivens the chapter on diphthongs in Ben Jonson's *English Grammar* of 1640, which begins with the statement that '*Diphthongs* are the complexions, or couplings of *Vowells*'.[20] The term also began to be used to refer to a bodily constitution or condition more generally, or even the condition of particular parts of the body, for example the tongue, head or womb. Chaucer uses the word in the sense of disposition when he writes of the sinner who excuses himself with the protest that his 'compleccioun is so corageous that he may nat for bere' (584, p. 307). The use of the term 'complexion' to signify the colour, texture or condition of the skin, rather than the skin being used as an indicator of the body's complexion, seems not to have been common in England before about the middle of the sixteenth century. Henry Wotton's claim, in 1578, that painters 'cannot imitate, neyther subiect vnto their pensell, the fashions, graces, maners, & spiritual complexios, which either laudable or vitious do cleare or darken beautie' makes a clear distinction between outward appearance and inward, or 'spiritual' complexion.[21]

Gradually, during the later medieval period, the skin came to be taken as the most direct and easily legible manifestation of the way in which these different elements were 'folded together' in the implicate order of the individual.[22] The prominence given to the colours red, white, black and yellow in the thermochro-matic palette of humoral theory made the colour of the skin particularly import-ant. By the end of the sixteenth century the word 'complexion' was being used most of the time to designate the skin rather than the temperament it indicated.

Shakespeare's uses of the word, of which there are more than forty ex-amples, illustrate this transition very well. In *Love's Labour's Lost*, Moth under-stands and uses the term in the traditional sense in his discussion of a woman with Adriano de Armado. Asked 'Of what complexion?', he replies 'Of all the four, or the three, or the two, or one of the four' (*LLL*, I. ii. 77–9, p. 746). When Hamlet says 'Methinks it is very sultry and hot for my complexion' (*Hamlet*, V. ii. 99–100, p. 328), he is concerned about more than the condition of his skin. The sermon which Duke Vincentio delivers to Claudio in *Measure for Measure* includes the advice that 'Thou art not certain;/For thy complexion shifts to strange effects/After the moon' (*Measure for Measure*, III. i. 23–5, p. 812), and here the word again suggests a general mutability of condition rather than (just) a variable appearance.

For the most part, however, Shakespeare's uses of the word signify not inner nature but outer appearance, as when, a little later in the same scene, the Duke praises Isabella by saying 'The hand that hath made you fair hath made you good … grace, being the soul of your complexion, shall keep the body of it ever fair' (*Measure for Measure*, III. i. 179–82, p. 814). The Prince of Morocco is clearly referring specifically to the colour of his skin when he says in *The Merchant of Venice*, 'Mislike me not for my complexion,/The shadowed livery of the bur-nish'd sun,/To whom I am a neighbour and near bred' (*Merchant*, II. i. 1–3, p. 835). The word is again clearly used to indicate appearance when, hatching her plot against Malvolio with Sir Toby Belch in *Twelfth Night*, Maria proposes to trick Malvolio into seeing himself 'feelingly personated' in descriptions of 'the colour of his beard, the shape of his leg, the manner of his gait, the expressure of his eye, forehead, and complexion' (*Twelfth Night*, II. iii. 156, 153–5, p. 1198).

There are occasional uses in which the figural and the physiognomic blend. Scroope seems to have composition as well as colour in mind when he says in *Richard II* that 'Men judge by the complexion of the sky/The state and inclina-tion of the day (*Richard II*, III. ii. 194–5, p. 686). Reluctantly admitting his weariness to Poins, Prince Hal says that 'it discolours the complexion of my greatness to acknowledge it' (*2 Henry IV*, II. ii. 4–5, p. 402). The word seems to summon the suggestion of skin disease for Hamlet when he refers to the gen-eral contamination that can spread in an otherwise unspoiled character from 'some vicious mole of nature' (though the word 'mole' could mean a blemish or spot in general, it did at this point also have a specifically epidermal applica-tion) and 'the o'ergrowth of some complexion,/Oft breaking down the pales and forts of reason' (*Hamlet*, I. iv. 24, 27–8, p. 299).

By 1601, the word was becoming so identified with the skin that it could also mean a false or cosmetic skin. As a gloss on the word '*Fukes*' (cosmetics) includ-ed in his 1601 translation of Pliny's *Natural History*, Philémon Holland wrote: 'They are called at this day complexions, whereas they bee cleane contrarie: for the complexion is naturall, and these altogether artificiall'.[23] The religious writer William Sclater gave the cosmetic term a moral overlay when he complained in 1619 'Complexion-makers wee have, not onely for withered faces of over-worne strumpets; but for ugliest and most deformed sinnes, to give them countenance of vertues'.[24] By the middle of the seventeenth century, the usual meaning of complexion was the colour of the skin. Margaret Cavendish observes of the inhabitants of the Blazing World, in the utopian fantasy of the same name she published in 1666, that they 'were of several complexions; not white, black, tawny, olive or ash-coloured; but some appeared of an azure, some of a deep purple, some of a grass-green, some of a scarlet, some of an orange-colour, etc.'.[25] Interestingly, as humoral theory began to lose its hold during the second half of the eighteenth century the word began to widen its application once more. Nowadays, in cosmetic advertising and the culture of skincare in which it predominates, the word 'complexion' signifies not so much the colour as the texture and condition of the skin, once again with a strong sense that these are indicators of more general conditions of health, vigour and age.

As humoral theory was refined and ramified over the two thousand years during which it held sway in Europe, the skin started to have a functional as well as a symptomatic role. Hippocratic texts had emphasized the role of the skin in expelling wastes and poisons, and the pores of the skin had provided an important principle of physiological functioning. The exudation of moisture through the pores of the skin was taken to provide a model for how the fluids moved from one part of the body to another. As well as travelling along ducts and canals, and being gathered in bags and membranes, fluids were secreted through the skins of organs. The condition of the pores that enabled this process of secretion was therefore important in maintaining balanced relations: both contraction and excessive dilation of the body's pores were regarded as undesirable. It was in terms of this metaphor that the skin came to be understood by the end of the eighteenth century. First of all a pure and inviolable covering, and then an expressive screen, the skin began through the medieval period to be thought of more and more as an organ of interchange, or permeable membrane, traversable in two directions, this function of the skin being regarded as crucial for the maintenance of the body's well-being through the exhalation of sweat and other excrementitious humours.

Barbara Duden's work on the casebooks of Johannes Storch, a doctor practising in the central German town of Eisenach in the 1730s, presents evidence of the move towards this newly dominant metaphor of the skin as membrane. Storch's work is seen against the background of a traditional understanding in which the skin is not thought of as bounding or closing off, but rather guaranteeing continuous interchanges of substance between the body and its environment:

The skin itself seems made to be permeable from the inside; it has 'sweat holes' which heat could open to allow the discharge of humidity, bloody matter, and impurities. A swelling, a boil on the skin, was a sign for [sic] some matter that was pushing toward the periphery in search of an outlet

. . . The skin does not appear as a material seal shutting the inside off from the outside. Instead it was a collection of real, minute orifices – the pores – and potential larger openings, especially when the skin was delicate.[26]

However, Duden finds in Dr Storch's treatments and casenotes the evidence of a transition from an older order of the body, in which '[t]he permeable boundaries between the body and the environment served the fruitful metamorphosis in both directions' and in which patients experienced themselves 'as multidimensional vectors, as bundles of constantly shifting but directed forms', to a newer economy, in which the older open systems had progressively to be channelled and rationalized.[27] This results in an intensifying ideal of continence, in which the skin functions as the body's principle of self-possession, keeping it from dissipating its resources wastefully. But it also encourages an obsessive effort to drain the body of its toxins and impurities. In both cases, the aim seems to have been to achieve a static condition of closure, rather than a 'multidimensional' traffic of substances and qualities. Although this history of the arrival of the possessive, disciplined and neurotically privatized and possessive individual out of a glamorous condition of rich and vital relatedness is a little too neat and familiar, it may help explain the undoubted prominence in early accounts of the metaphor of skin as membrane, and the growing emphasis, from the late medieval period onwards, on its capacity to expel and excrete rather than to absorb or exchange.

The theory of the excremental function of the skin is accompanied and reinforced by an extraordinarily intense concern with the skin as regulator of temperature. This is verified by the link between the word 'temperature' itself and 'temper', which for a long time occupied a similar semantic field to the word 'complexion', and still signifies the degree of one's composure. Keeping your temper meant keeping a balance of hot and cold as well as keeping the different humours in balance with each other. The belief in the intricately thermal body of the humours survives in the belief that survives, unaccountably but stubbornly, everywhere in the modern world, in the malignancy of draughts and the power of 'chills' to disturb the economy of the body.[28]

The dominance of the theory of the skin as membrane accompanies a general defensive closing of the pores that took place across Europe from the end of the medieval period until the nineteenth century. This is the period in which bathing, which had flourished in the classical world and, after dying out with the shrinking of the Roman Empire, had become popular again during the thirteenth and fourteenth centuries, became a source of acute anxiety and regulatory concern. The suspicion of bathing probably has a great deal to do with the catastrophic epidemics which swept across Europe – of bubonic plague, at the end of the fourteenth century, and of syphilis during the sixteenth. Public bathing was periodically revived, for example in the form of vapour baths, for which travellers to the Middle East in the eleventh century developed a fondness, and periodically suppressed, often because of its association with prostitution and promiscuous sex.[29]

The revival of bathing which took place in the growth of spa-resorts during the eighteenth century and the growth of private bathing and sea-bathing in the nineteenth century was accompanied by much debate about the strengthening and weakening effect of exposure to different temperatures, for different constitutions, at different ages and times of the day. The Hippocratic doctrine that taking a bath that was hotter than the body's temperature had a weakening effect on the constitution survived well into the nineteenth century and beyond.

This concern with the regulation of the body's temperature was accompanied by a newly intense concern with the operation of perspiration. Observing that in each square inch of skin there exists the equivalent of 73 feet of drainage in the form of sweat glands, John Dowson's 1857 book on the dangers and benefits of bathing quoted this warning from the leading dermatological writer in nineteenth-century England, Erasmus Darwin: 'Surely such an amount of drainage as 73 feet in every square inch of skin, assuming this to be an average for the whole body, is somewhat wonderful, and the thought naturally intrudes itself; *what if this drainage were obstructed?*'[30] The blocking of perspiration was sometimes blamed for the many distensive and dropsical conditions that seemed to have flourished during the later eighteenth century.

The great age of thermodynamic science and technology brought an equivalent attention to the economies of energy involved in the skin's temperature exchanges. This gave the skin a new function, not only as a thermodynamic engine, but also as a reserve and restorer of nervous energy. Thus the skin began also to be associated with the temper of the mind, though now not according to the analogical thinking of humoral theory, but following a form of mechanical thinking preoccupied with the distribution and conservation of energies. Philip Myers, who, as proprietor of the Pelham Street Baths in Nottingham was not exactly a neutral commentator, wrote in 1836 that

[I]n the large and afflicting class of Nervous and Mental diseases attention to the skin becomes therefore almost a sine qua non of successful treatment. In most nervous ailments, languor and inaction of the skin shew themselves simultaneously with the earliest dawn of mental uneasiness, and often attract notice before the morbid feelings of the mind have acquired either permanence or strength.[31]

Although the awareness of the homeostatic functions of the skin represents a considerable advance on the conception of the skin as a mere envelope or integument, it means that the skin could continue to be taken as a synecdoche for the body as a whole. This has the advantage that diseases such as syphilis or leprosy could be understood as arising from deeper and more systemic disorderings of the body, despite the fact that their manifestations were primarily on the skin. But it has the disadvantage that conditions that are disturbances of the economy of the skin itself could neither easily be recognized nor understood.

The first book devoted to the skin published in Europe was Girolamo Mercurialis's *De morbis cutaneis*, which appeared in 1572.[32] This was a synoptic work, that usefully gathered together the ideas and arguments about the skin of over seventy ancient and modern medical writers. The book is thoroughly Galenic in its elaboration of terms and distinctions and its focus on the skin's excremental and evacuating functions. No more significant works on the skin appeared for nearly two hundred years. The first work on the skin in English was Daniel Turner's *De morbis cutaneis*, which was an odd and idiosyncratic mix of observation, surgical advice and wild anecdote. Its celebrity was to be mostly as a result of the debate it sparked about the doctrine of maternal impressions, which will be discussed in detail in chapter 4 below.[33] Turner was followed by two other dermatologists later in the century. The Galenic tradition was maintained in Anne Charles Lorry's *Tractatus de morbis cutaneis* of 1777, which emphasized the many different influences on the skin, like diet, climate, exercise, sleep, but was casual and imprecise when it came to the description or analysis of skin disease. Like so many others during this period, he seems obsessed with the skin's function as a vehicle for carrying away malignancy, waste and toxins.[34]

The first attempt to classify skin diseases systematically came from Joseph Plenck, a Viennese military surgeon, who broke with the inherited practice of treating skin diseases according to the part of the body where they appeared and classified some 114 skin diseases on the basis of their characteristic lesions. Here at last was an attempt to understand the workings of the skin as such and in something like its own terms.[35] Thereafter and in parallel with the process in which, in eighteenth-century anatomies, 'the idealized body of the Baroque era dissolved into its constituent parts'[36] the skin started to be considered as an organ in itself, with its own structure and functions. Inspired by the classifications of the vegetable kingdom produced by Carl Linnaeus from the 1730s to the 1750s, the Edinburgh physician Robert Willan followed Plenck in classifying skin diseases by their lesions, though he reduced the number of categories of lesions or 'efflorescences' of the skin from 14 to 10: scurf, scale, scab, stigma, papula, rash, macula, tubercle, vesicle and pustule. This morphological exercise allowed him to define, name and classify a range of skin diseases. He presented his results in the first volume of a book entitled *On Cutaneous Diseases*, but died before he could complete the second volume.[37] This work passed across to his pupil and associate, Thomas Bateman, and was completed in 1813, with the appearance of his *Practical Synopsis of Cutaneous Diseases*. This was followed in 1817 by his *Delineations of Cutaneous Diseases*, which, joining Willan's plates with his own, formed the first usable atlas of skin complaints.[38]

The Willanist paradigm came up against a rival system in Paris, where Jean-Louis-Marc Alibert had founded the Hôpital Saint Louis in 1802. Alibert had his own, much more elaborate idea of how to classify skin diseases. In 1829, he was stung into mounting a public challenge to the Willanist system by the defection to it of his trusted colleague Laurent Biett. Instead of the simple, plane projection of skin diseases found in Willan and Bateman, Alibert devel-

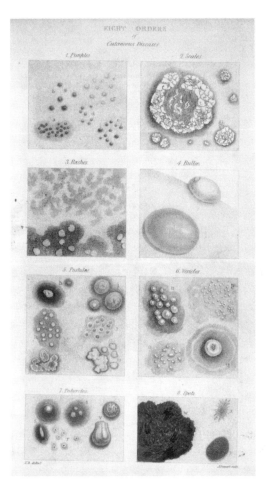

'Eight Orders of
Cutaneous Diseases',
lithograph from
Thomas Bateman,
*A Practical Synopsis
of Cutaneous
Diseases* (London,
1813).

oped an impressive, but in the end unfeasibly complex 'tree of dermatoses'. But his system did not survive the savaging it received in reply from Biett and thereafter French dermatology for the first fifty years of the nineteenth century was dominated by the Willan/Bateman system, as was the American dermatology that sprang from it, through the mediation of Noah Worcester, whose synoptic book on diseases of the skin appeared in 1845.[39]

If the separation of the skin from the rest of the body were necessary to make dermatology possible, developments during the next most important phase of dermatological history, in the second half of the nineteenth century, would to some degree restore the systemic view that had dominated until the eighteenth century. Its most dominant figure was the Austrian Ferdinand Hebra, Professor of Dermatology at the University of Vienna. Advances in bacteriology, mycology and histopathology (the study of tissues or cells arranged in layers) made it possible to classify skin diseases on the basis of general pathology, now released from the humoral paradigm. Armed with a

Jean-Louis-Marc Alibert, 'The Tree of Dermatology', a family tree of skin diseases. c. 1835, coloured engraving.

much richer understanding of the different agents and causes responsible for skin disease, Hebra's clinic was able to develop much more effective therapies.

So, if one were to read the cultural history of the skin solely in medical terms, there would be three stages to be distinguished. For the classical and medieval worlds, the skin was everything and nothing. As the guarantee of the wholeness of the body, the skin was not itself a part of the body. This perhaps accounts for the simultaneous glorification and disposability of the skin in the ancient world. Like a universal currency, the skin could underpin every value while having none itself. As that which made the wholeness of the physical being present, and that which made disease visible, the skin was itself invisible, like a screen. The skin was that unseen through which the body must be seen, the ground against which the body figured. Gradually, the functions of the skin as integument and screen, covering the body and expressing the complexion of the soul, began to give way to a second phase, a more mechanical conception of the skin as a membrane, concerned principally with the elimination of wastes. This very narrowing of the understanding of the skin made it possible for Willanist dermatology to begin to understand the skin in its own terms, detaching the skin from overtotalized humoral understandings. In the third phase, the more general functions and connections of the skin are restored. But the skin does not vanish into its ubiquity once again. Rather its functions multiply, and multiply beyond the merely medical understanding. First a screen, then a membrane, and finally, this book will assume, what Michel Serres calls a milieu: the skin becomes a place of minglings, a mingling of places.

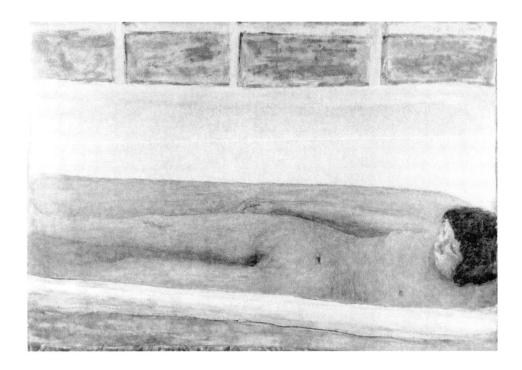

MILIEU

The skin has a special place in Michel Serres' philosophy of the senses. This is because it is the most widely distributed and the most various of the organs of the body. Unlike the other organs, it is not concentrated in one portion of the body. Indeed, the skin is the ground against which the other senses figure: it is their milieu. If all the senses are milieux, or midplaces where inside and outside meet and meld, then the skin is the global integral of these local area networks, the milieu of these milieux: 'The skin forms the variety of our mixed senses.'[40] Serres uses Bonnard's paintings of nudes to evoke the mutual implication of painter and model in the space of the representation. In seeing and painting his model, the painter reproduces the way she sees and paints herself, tattooing her own skin with make-up in precisely the way the painter will render her. Painter and subject enclose and environ each other. As she applies her cosmetics and ornaments she draws a map of her own sensory receptivity, highlighting ears, lips and eyes. This 'cosmetography' underlines the etymological link between the cosmetic and the cosmic, for her skin becomes a meeting place for her different senses: 'The tattooed nude, chaotic and noisy, bears on herself the shared and immediate place of her own sensorium, plains and risings in which mingle the flows which come from or are drawn to the organs of hearing, sight, taste, smell, variegated skin where touch summarises the sensible' (35–6). Serres begins mapping the senses with the skin because it is the milieu of the senses, a kind of

Pierre Bonnard, *La Baignoire*, 1925, oil on canvas. Tate Modern, London.

'common sense'. But he does so indirectly, tacking left to move to the right, by looking at a painter's act of looking, in order to show how 'the eye loses its pre-eminence in the very domain of its domination, painting' (40). This painting is already an amalgam or mediation of seeing and touching. Serres suggests that Bonnard's paintings can be seen as simulacra, not in the Baudrillardean sense, but according to the Epicurean doctrine that sight, like all the senses, works through being touched by simulacra, the fragile films of atoms which are stripped off bodies and fly to other bodies. This idea will be treated at length in chapter 4. Bonnard's canvases are simulacra, not just because they produce semblance or resemblance, but also because 'parting from the skin of the painter and the subtle envelope of things, the veil of one meets the veil of the others', forming 'a simultaneous simulacrum' (41).

Serres rejects the predominating metaphor of the skin as a surface, membrane or interface. The skin is an entire environment. Nodding towards Paul Valéry's judgement in his *L'idée fixe* of 1933 that 'Nothing is deeper in man than his skin', Serres writes 'Nothing goes down so far as makeup, nothing extends as far as the skin, ornament has the dimensions of the world' (34).[41] The skin is the meeting, not just of the senses, but of world and body: 'through the skin, the world and the body touch, defining their common border. Contingency means mutual touching: world and body meet and caress in the skin' (97). Serres would see the body as a milieu, were it not that this would seem to mark it off too exclusively from the world of milieux or minglings in which it has its place:

> I do not like to speak of the place where my body exists as a milieu, preferring rather to say that things mingle among themselves and that I am no exception to this, that I mingle with the world which mingles itself in me. The skin intervenes in the things of the world and brings about their mingling. (97)

If the skin mediates the world by mingling with it, this may be because the world itself may be apprehended as a kind of flesh, or what biologists aptly call 'tissue'. If 'the world is a mass of laundry', then we might expect that, reciprocally, '[t]issue, textile and fabric provide excellent models of knowledge, excellent quasi-abstract objects' (100–101). The object of thought seems to prescribe the manner of its being thought.

NINE LIVES

Skin has come to mean the body itself; it has become the definite article, the 'the' of the body. But skin is not the body. I have even come to think, and aim to bring you to agree, that the skin is really *not even a part of the body*. Skin is not a part of the body not because it is separate from it but, surprisingly, because it cannot come apart from it. Unlike a member, or an organ, or a nail-clipping, the skin is not detachable in such a way that the detached part would remain recognizable or that the body left behind would remain recognizably a body: a body *minus*. The skinned body is less a body even than a skeleton, which we find it easier to reclothe in flesh (there are plenty of dancing skeletons in story and ritual, but very few skinned bodies). The skin always takes the body with it. The skin is, so to speak, the body's face, the face of its bodiliness. The skinned body is formless, faceless, its face having been taken off with its skin. Where a leg, or a liver or a heart remain what they are once removed from the body and may be imagined as continuing to function apart from the body which has formed them, the skin itself is no longer a skin once it is detached. By being peeled away from the body, it has ceased to be itself. The skin cannot easily be thought of as a part of the body because, despite the fact that it has its obvious, specialized functions, its principal function is to manifest the complex, cooperative, partitive complexion of the body.

We can go further along this improbable path. Precisely because it is not separable from the body, the skin is always being imagined as breaking from it, in magical flights, excursions and exfoliations. The skin is not a part of the body, because it is the body's twin, or shadow, that part of the body which, cleaving ever so tightly to it, is able also to take leave of it, but taking the whole of the body with it, as in so-called 'out-of-body experiences'. The very wholeness that the skin possesses and preserves, its capacity to resume and summarize the whole body, means that it is always in excess of, out in front of the body, but *as another body*. The skin is thus always in part immaterial, ideal, ecstatic, a skin that walks.

We invent with our bodies, and thereby reinvent those bodies. Unlike other animals, we have a relation to our bodies, a relation that we invent, and a relation that is our bodies. Our bodies are the kind that are always in question, or transition, are always work in progress. For the Quakers and Camisards and Shakers and other ecstatic sects of the seventeenth and eighteenth centuries, the body is taken to be, even lived as if it were, already raised, already glorified, perfected. Lately, we have been made accustomed to think the opposite, that the body is everywhere subject to discursive regulation. Of course, a languaged body is subjected to the orders of discourse. A languaged body can be regimented, cabined, confined, abjected, insulted by language. But never wholly so. The novice who bows her head, the squaddie who stiffens in salute, have another body beside, just to the side of the statue they have become: a subjunctive, a possibled body, an imposture alongside the imposed posture.

Michel Serres has spoken of the sense of soul which resides in the fingers' ends. This is because, for Serres, the soul is not something sequestered or inhumed in the body, but that which comes into being in contact, in activities of reaching, stretching, doubling, magnification. The soul is neither the body's position, nor that object or new position for which it reaches. It is the reaching itself, what Serres calls the *tiers-instruit*, the body instructed in its thirdness, between here and there, this posture and that other posture, that the body teaches itself, and is taught by: 'Let us call the soul the kind of space and time that can be expanded from its natal position toward all exposures.'[42] It is what lies just beyond the fingers' ends, as when you reach for a key or coin in a narrow aperture, and, even as you elongate yourself to your fullest extent, must consult your own body inwardly for the knowledge of whether you can stretch to it, must imagine your reach, reach for the image of clasping your object, in order to reach it in actuality. Primates, for whom hand and eye are so intricately wired together, will always see that shimmer of possibility at the fingers' ends, will recurrently dream we see that shimmer take on an embodied form – in the idea of the aura, or nimbus, that tremulous, cutaneous body-soul, soul-body. Not for nothing did the New Testament Hemorrhissa, the woman with an issue of blood, touch the hem of Christ's robe – presumably the tassel or *tzitzik* worn by all devout Jews – to be healed. As we will see repeatedly in what is to follow, power is indeed concentrated at the fringe, or the outermost edge of things. The sunderings and propagations of the skin are not always dramatic, and do not always involve ordeal and trauma. I will be drawn throughout this book, and especially in my final chapters, to the experiences of lightness, thinness, subtlety and insubstantiality which flutter at the fringes.

It is the second nature of the skin to go beyond itself. Our skin outdoes us, it is the means of our self-undoing and outgoing. I am driven by a curiosity about why it is that so many figurings of the skin emphasize not the coming home to oneself, to that condition known in French as being *heureux dans son peau*, but of passage, from hand to hand, body to body, time to time and state to state, a passage that seems to involve walking in particular. I am interested in the coming together and coming apart of assumption and appropriation in figurings of a skin that walks.

Nothing is deader than a skin, peeled, shucked or sloughed. And yet skins are often imagined as containing or preserving life and therefore having the power to restore it, as, for example, in the Brothers Grimm story of 'The Three Snake Leaves'. In this, a king unwisely gives his bride a promise that he will be buried with her if she dies before him. She does and he duly takes up his vigil in her tomb. A snake comes out of a hole and is about to begin gnawing at the body, when the king hews it into three pieces. Another snake appears, bearing three leaves, which it applies to the cuts in the snake's body, restoring it to life. The king applies the leaves to the eyes and mouth of his wife, restoring her too to life. In the second half of the story, the king is himself killed by his wife, who has ungratefully conceived an adulterous passion for the captain of the ship on which they are sailing. The king's servant applies the leaves to him in the same way as he has previously used them.[43]

Flaying is always, it seems, accompanied or followed by the possibility of a re-assumption: either the assumption of another skin, or the resumption of one's own skin (through healing). The skin therefore provides a model of the

Michelangelo, Piero Aretino holding the flayed skin of St Bartholomew, with the artist's own face; a detail from *The Last Judgment*, 1537–41, fresco. Sistine Chapel, Vatican City.

self preserved against change, and also reborn through change.[44] The aegis passes from Zeus' goat-nurse Amaltheia to Zeus and then, metaphorically to Zeus' daughter Athena, who uses it in her battle against the giant Pallas, whose skin she strips off for her aegis. The power of the aegis passes to Perseus, in the form of the bronze shield with which he deflects the gaze of the Gorgon, before decapitating it and fixing it to Athena's aegis, to increase its power even more. At each stage, the aegis becomes more itself, its power generalized and concentrated even as it is shared.

Marina Warner's novel *The Leto Bundle* (2001) has as its centre and its self-image a bundle of artefacts and clothes, themselves made up of stories and incantations, attached to the mummified body of a woman.[45] The woman, whose diasporic story is told in a number of different ways throughout the novel, may be the avatar of the Titan Leto, lover of Zeus, who is taken to be a new spirit of the exiled, the driven-out, the self-transforming. At the centre of the novel is a play in the idea of the mummy-cloth. On the one hand, it signals preservation, the product of the desire that what should remain of us should not be what lies deep within us – heart or viscera, or bones – but the most inessential part, the skin. On the other, the skin is the sign of our transformability, our *alentity*, so to speak, or ability to become other, as well as our identity, our ability to persist and survive in that becoming other. This is why the gift of skin, to furnish disguise or transformation, is also so often a means of preservation.

What characterizes most of the walking dead, in all the films, in Michael Jackson's *Thriller* video which recapitulates so many of them? They are in rags. In our mortuary imaginations, the dead are not absent or decomposed. The dead are *ragged*. They are held together by shreds and patches, shreds and patches that are themselves perhaps only held together by our idea of them. Rags promise transformation – *rags to riches*. But this is because rags *are* riches: because there is such a strange, vagrant, second life, even Herrick's 'wild civility', amid the degradation of rags. For Yeats, the greatest poet of the ragged, so far, there is also a sexual allure in rags. The English song of *The Raggle-Taggle Gypsies*, who steal the hearts of your ladies-o, hints at this randiness of rags.

Perhaps the libidinal charge of rags has something to do with the sense that rags are a compromise between skin and fur, or, more particularly, hair. Hair is immensely important as a way of focusing and amplifying skin sensation. Long, tangled hair, like ragged clothes, seems to signify (in fact, as always with the avatars of the skin, to do more than signify), a body alert or awoken to touch, a body not intact, but a 'tangle of tatters'[46] – tactile, tangible, touched, torn, touching itself, soliciting touch. So the ragged dead are scary partly because of the unnatural life that resides in their raggedness. It is as though the swarming attentions of the worms and flies had brought their skins to life. Rags are perhaps the busy life of decomposition, a dying that walks.

What is a ghost? A ghost, as opposed to a spirit, or Spirit, is always a kind of body. In fact, *ghosts are crustacean*, for they tend to take the form of a vapour inside a shell: encased in armour, or, as Mummy and Invisible Man, held together by the cerements that they themselves hold up. In both cases, it is a matter of filling out, and creating uprightness (the opposite of the flat or recumbent life in which the skin is also so often implicated). Carriage and collapse distinguish the two forms of the skin signalled in the two words that Latin uses for it, *cutis* and *pellis*. We carry our skins, which account for around 11 per cent of an adult's body weight. But, in its role as taut support, our skins also help form our carriage. Ghosts, similarly and definitionally, walk. They rise in order to walk. They are a skin that walks.

Michelangelo shows himself awaiting resurrection, not as a body, but as the flayed skin of St Bartholomew. It is usual for resurrection to be imaged as the gathering together and reanimation of the dry bones of the skeleton, but there are phantasms of the resurrected skin too. The resurrection of the body is sometimes imaged in the grotesque idea of the skin itself standing up and walking. Writing of the importance of clothing in artistic depictions of the crucifixion and its aftermath, Ewa Kuryluk says that 'As skin dies, cloth may come alive and replace the body. When the body falls, garments fly up'.[47] Christ's actual resurrection was followed shortly afterwards by his disappearance from the earth, but the visible evidence of his being was maintained by the various miraculous cloths, whether *sudarii* (sweat cloths) like that offered to him on the road to Calvary by Veronica, or his burial shroud, on which his image was thought to have been impressed. Some of these fabrics were credited with incorruptibility and the power to effect miracles, and even themselves to undergo resurrection. There seems to have been a number of such cloths in Constantinople in the early thirteenth century, and one report, by one of the soldiers gathered together for the Fourth Crusade in 1203, shortly before they sacked the city, is given in an intriguing form:

> there was another of the churches which they called My Lady St Mary of Blachernae, where was kept the sydoine in which Our Lord had been wrapped, which stood up straight every Friday so that the features of Our Lord could be plainly seen there.[48]

The skin must rise before it can walk. Faces are 'lifted', we tell each other, not merely tightened. Flags seem to be a promise of the resurrection of the skin. The flag of the United States must never be allowed to touch the ground, and the meaning of a flag is that it should never in fact flag (the *OED* suggests that this is from *flaccus*) – that it should fly. Of course, there is phallic application in this; but it is not the male organ which determines the conditions of the flag's condition, and we should not mistake the flagpole for the flag. When a flag flies it keeps itself clear of the ground by being stretched out. The flag lifted in and engorged by the wind is in fact stretched out flat. The skin is the model for this vital, emblematic tension. The flag can only be stretched out by the wind because it would otherwise fall limply, because it can so easily flag. The stars and stripes planted by Neil Armstrong on the surface of the moon had to be artificially rigid in the absence of air and seemed spectral and deathly as a result. The flag flaps as it flies, like a wind or a sail; its tension is periodic, its flagging drawn into the tensorial rhythm.

SHAPE OF SHAPE

The skin is often associated with wholeness and entirety. The skin, after all, is not located at any one point in the body, like the other sense organs. Indeed, the skin provides the medium in which the other sense organs are located, and the element of which we feel they are largely made. The other sense organs exist as particular kinds of convolutions or complications in the skin, the labyrinthine turning inward to produce certain kinds of sensitivity – the scooping out of the mouth, the whorling of the ear, the knotting of the sphincter. The skin provides the means whereby the different senses can be connected, can cooperate with and mirror each other. The vulnerability of the human skin to cutting, tearing and abrasion makes the care for the entirety of the skin fundamental in human beings. The skin connects, and connects with everything. When the skin itself is seen, separated from what it covers, protects and connects, it risks being seen as something flayed, flaccid, dead, *skinny*. This is why partial, or emptied skins – the flayed skin of the *écorché*, a discarded sock, the hinge of skin hanging off after a finger has been cut, strike us as so pitiful, so inhuman, so painful, so disgusting.

But it is precisely for this reason, the fact that it is so bound up with everything, and binds everything together, that the skin is also by its nature intermittent. Although it seems vitally necessary for the skin to be kept entire, and experienced as entire, one cannot ever feel the whole of one's skin all at once. Even the skin of another is never the whole skin. We may see the merest portion of the skin – the face, hands, or neck – and therefore not see the skin itself, but rather the body part that it covers and displays. And when we see the skin, even if we see the whole of one surface, or see it in the round, by the use of mirrors, as in the device inherited by pornography from painterly set-ups like that in Velázquez's 'Rokeby Venus', the fact that we are only seeing the skin, rather than being in tactile contact with it, means that we are deprived of a vital dimension. Perceiving the whole of the skin of another all at once would mean being able to be at once pressed up against it, and far enough away to get a visual impression of it. And even when we do have this kind of close-up perception of the skin, it is often hard to see what is nevertheless in front of our eyes. The well-known difficulty of determining and representing the colour of the skin is an effect not of the intrinsic complexity of what is seen, as of the unseeability of skin which is known and recognized or identified with.

Furthermore, as Paul Schilder has observed, 'the distinct surface of our skin is perceived only when we are in touch with reality and its objects'.[49] Feeling the wind on my face, my face starts into sensitivity; lowering my weight into a chair, I feel the length and curvature of my thighs and lower back. Resting my elbows on a desk, I feel the two knobs of my elbows. The world presented to my touch imprints itself on me, in impermanent shapes that are homeomorphic

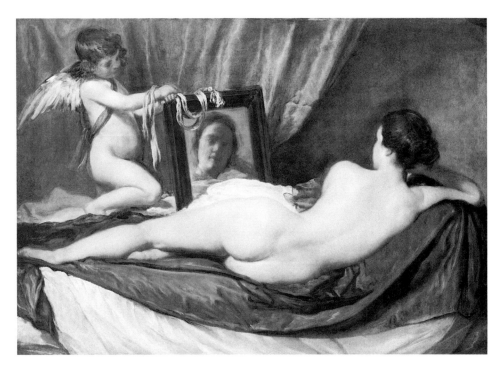

Diego Velázquez, *The Toilet of Venus* ('The Rokeby Venus'), 1647–51, oil on canvas. National Gallery, London.

with the shapes of the surfaces that I present to it. These imprintings bring about curious repercussions and permeations: 'body and world are continually interchanged', as Schilder observes.[50] As I touch objects in the world, they seem to rise to their own surfaces, to meet me in the shape that I present to them: a brick wall offers me a patch of roughness exactly coincident with the back of my hand. Indeed, it seems possible that, inasmuch as the world is presented to us primarily as actual or implied surface, we experience that world as a single, intermittent skin, which mirrors and gives rise to our own single, but inter-mittent skins. Because we encounter the world so regularly through our hands, the world seems to put on its own gloves to touch us back. If I am struck, by a fist, by a buffet of wind, by the branch of a tree, by the handle of a rake, the object that has struck me leaves its mark in a painful residue that lingers on my skin in just the same way as an image persists on the retina after its visual source is removed. We take our own print from the print of objects upon us. Some of the masochistic pleasure in being spanked, whipped, and even tickled into a condition of helplessness may sometimes, as is often suggested, come from the sensation of shapedness, boundedness and entirety that it may give to a person with an insecure sense of their own body image and boundaries. In such circumstances, which are only the intensified form of a large range of ordinary experiences – swimming, lying down in bed, being embraced – we experience a donation of our own wholeness and shape from the outside. We then return our own relation of impressibility and imprintedness to the world in all the many ways in which we seek to make our mark on it, to make permanently visible our touching of the world, in all the arts of printing, stamping, sealing, embossing, engraving and incising. We depend upon the world to give us the shape which we present to it, in order to feel it. Since the first shape presented to us in the world may be the rapturously entire – but probably also painfully intermittent – shape of the parent's body, or so it insistently seems to us, since we only begin to encounter the hardness, edgedness and roughness of the nonhuman surfaces after our shape has been formed in the interchange with other human bodies, we will find it hard not to experience the world when we do finally encounter and explore it, in terms of that primary touching, retouching, touching-back.

There seems to be a literal sense in which the skin gives us both the shape of the world and our shape in it. In mammals, the abrasion experienced by the skin during its passage through the birth canal in vaginal delivery stimulates the action of breathing. In foals, calves and young chimpanzees, this process is prolonged and reinforced by licking immediately after birth, in the absence of which the animals will often fail to thrive, or even survive. Similarly, there is a marked increase in the tendency to apnoea and brachycardia in human babies delivered by Caesarean section. This process may even begin before birth, since the rippling movements of the womb prior to labour known as Braxton-Hicks contractions appear to stimulate the foetus to inhale and exhale the amniotic fluid. This uterine massage prepares the skin for the abrasions or writing of the world which it will receive upon its surface and thus be awoken as a being with a surface. From the very beginning, or perhaps before it, the skin is the tablet on which the world is writing the shape that the individual will take. This seems to offer some confirmation for the belief maintained by Pliny and still widespread in the early modern world, that a bearcub was, as Samuel Butler puts it 'Whelped without form, until the Dam/Have lickt him into shape and frame'.[51]

The extreme arduousness, joy and beauty involved in trying to make a shape or space which will encompass all the different shapes or spaces of the skin come from the fact that the skin is itself the generator of such shapes and spaces in the first place – the skin being indeed the first of all first places. The skin is nothing less than the shape of shape. The aspiration of this book is to point beyond the skin's limited, necessarily cartographic condition, to something like what Didier Houzel has called a 'non-orientable manifold'.[52] Houzel means by this a three-dimensional version of the Möbius strip, in which different faces or aspects of a solid shape are imagined as connecting with each other. Rather than sticking together the upper and lower surfaces of a two-dimensional strip, one would achieve a non-orientable manifold by sticking together the faces of a three-dimensional object, for example, the top and bottom faces and the right and left faces of a cube. Of course, such a shape is imaginary, if one means by that a shape which cannot be represented in three-dimensional terms and that therefore must be imagined rather than being simply and straightforwardly presentable to the eye. A Möbius strip can only be visualized in a three-dimensional world with difficulty and with the supplementation of, as it were, mental hands and fingers. More complex manifolds can only be visualized in a world possessing more dimensions than three. Perhaps one begins to mean by this, that the skin is a topology rather than a topography, a shape which does not present itself all at once to the eye, but emerges, like the gathering of a wave, or the piling of a cloud, through the passage of time, whose shape it itself comes to be.

In fact, for Didier Houzel, the non-orientable manifold is in no sense a desirable or healthy condition. It typifies the experience of the autistic child, whose life is the enactment of an unmasterable internal turbulence. Faced with such an extreme and paradoxical involution, the success of psychoanalysis would depend upon 'the analyst's capacity to allow himself to be drawn, without losing himself, into the whirling autistic world, and little by little to give meaning to the child's anxieties, which would have the effect of opening up the psychic envelope and giving it an orientation, so that an inside/outside distinction becomes possible.'[53] But one need not limit the conception of the non-orientable manifold to the experience of the autistic child as imagined by psychoanalysis, for there are other ways in which to read out this figure. The distinguishing feature of such a shape is the multiplicity of the ways in which it touches on and joins up with itself, when subject to investigation. One may perhaps think of the skin as just such a manifold, for it is the skin which allows us to keep in touch with ourselves in so many different ways – touching ourselves up, touching ourselves off, living hand to mouth. Rather than reading it as a figure of withdrawal, disconnection and disorientation, one may find in the skin an image of abundant connections, of plenteous and unpredictable unfolding. Rather than seeing the skin as possessing an inside which is on the other side of its outside, one might begin to imagine it, as it has in fact been drawn in imagination, drawn into imagination, drawn out in imagination, in many places and at many times, as a complex manifold, which is hugely impoverished by a scheme which depends upon the simple alternatives of inside and outside.

The sequence of my discussions in this book should not be thought of as a simple tally or telling off of the functions of the skin. It is to be thought of as a topology or phase-space – what Houzel calls a 'compacity' – which the different functions of the skin scoop out, as a river procures for itself the shape of the valley, the wind sculpts a cliff face, as a way of smiling or frowning incises its traces in the skin of the face.[54] Thus, the most important and telling moments in my account of the skin are those that mark the ways in which different functions of the skin cross or fold on each other. The shape of the skin is in fact not a sculptured shape made of planes, lines and masses, but a morphology as of smoke. The work offered in this book does not describe (draw lines around, contain) the structures and movements that are its subject; it follows them out, in the sense in which the finger follows the contours of a substance or a solid object. It uses the skin's own mode of touching on things. If I were a Jungian, I might say that the task of this analysis is not to rouse a dream or slumber into wakefulness, but to dream the dream of the skin out.

If there were one function of the skin that might seem to unite or underlie all the others, it would be that of providing a background. Like the cinema screen upon which images play, the canvas on which paint is laid, or the paper on which words are scrawled or stamped, the skin is always in the background. One of the commonest and most spontaneous ways of thinking of the skin is as a surface, something stretched on top of things; but its more fundamental condition is to be that on top of which things occur, develop or are disclosed. The skin is the ground for every figure. Perhaps the skin means, more than anything else in particular, the necessity for there to be a ground, a setting, a frame, an horizon, a stage, a before, a behind, an underneath. The hypothesis (literally, the 'putting underneath') of the skin makes for the duplicity of anything which becomes apparent to us, in that it must stand out against a background that is not itself, or not at that moment, in view. As soon as that background comes into view, is given the name of 'the unconscious', for example, it ceases to be a background, and itself comes to rest upon another background, or is fitted inside a newly-invisible frame of its own. Didier Anzieu has an interesting passage in which he speculates about the possibility of an origin for this sense of the duplicity of space:

> Before it becomes a setting that contains objects, space is not differentiated from the objects that occupy it. Even the expression 'from the objects that occupy it' has no meaning. This lack of differentiation between an object and the place occupied by it in space is the cause of one of the most archaic anxieties that the mind has to face – the anxiety of seeing an object that moves tear out the part of space in which it was located, take it with it, and encounter other objects into which it crashes, destroying their place.[55]

Of course, there is a primal scene at work here, since this undifferentiated space is clearly that dyadic unity of mother and child, skin against skin, which becomes apparent to the child only when it is torn apart. Another way of understanding this ontogenetic creation myth is as the bursting in of time upon space, the temporal dimension that allows the same space to be occupied by different objects at different times, and one object to occupy successively different places. With the birth of time (the birth into time), and the irruption into self-sufficient space of the possibility of change of place, it becomes impossible to maintain inviolate the link between objects and the matrices they occupy. The only way to maintain the shape of this diagram of the world is through a more abstract conception of space, as the outside of every outside, which has no shape of its own (otherwise it would have an outside, and so would itself be inside another space). This abstract space is able to contain bodies in movement, without having to be identified with them, and therefore be at risk of being torn apart by their movement. Space therefore becomes the support, or cure for the disease of place. Space is always whole, because it is never in any particular place. Different experiences of *fit*, of being at home, or fully in place, settling into a favourite pair of shoes, hearing a particular musical phrase forming at just the right tempo and intensity, seeing a joke, arriving at an apprehension of a complex mathematical proof: all these can, perhaps, be seen as miraculous restorations of Anzieu's archaic unity of apprehension, of a foreground so thoroughly accommodated by its background as momentarily to have dissolved into it. Needless to say, such a condition is as temporary and illusory as the very notion that there could be a 'before' to ideas of space and place. The very idea of a nonduplicitous space, the idea that there could ever be or have been any other way of being in time and space than that of being torn between the place I presently occupy and those other places I might and must come to occupy, is itself only possible to imagine within the terms of such a 'fallen' perspectival economy, in which what I see and where I am is always folded within what I do not see and the places I am not.

It will be hard to investigate the effects of this apprehension of spatial duplicity without seeming to be identifying the skin, as Anzieu tends to do, as the ground of grounds, or the form of forms, from which all conceptions and transformations of space, place and shape derive, and to which they all invariably devolve. Under such conditions, when everything is the skin, and the skin is everything, when, in short, there is no alternative to or outside to the experience of skin, there would be little point in undertaking the work of differentiating its functions. If the skin were really the everything in general and nothing in particular that made every difference possible, there would be no way of thinking or writing about it that could make any interesting difference to the monism of its manifold.

However, the suggestion of this book is that determinate points or passages in this indeterminate landscape of palimpsests and enfoldings may be made out. For if there are no particular ways in which the weather must necessarily turn out, there are particular meteorological phenomena which may hold our interest, and, in what follows, it will, I think, be apparent, that there is a particular kind of climatic condition that interests me recurrently in the weather of the skin. This is the moment of umbilical inclension and involution, folding-over, or falling-inward, in which an epidermal surface or matrix suddenly becomes apparent as something disclosed against another surface or matrix, and an outside suddenly proves to be an inside. When the cinema screen displays itself, when a literary text like *Tristram Shandy* figures the very page on which it rests, when a tattoo incises the image of a second skin (an armouring, a scroll, another body) on top of the skin, the invisible and indi-visible background formed by the skin of the world suddenly becomes visible. It is to such moments of intrication (literally, knitting inwards), when fore-ground and background change places, and when the skin or one of its many masks or avatars touches on itself, complies with itself, that this work will find itself drawn time and again. The idea of the division between inside and outside is not itself the ground against which these figures can be seen or displayed. Rather than being a primary or absolute condition, the invariant outside of the play of intrication, the division between inner and outer is just a tactic, a way of getting us to the apprehension we need. A column of smoke possesses no simple inside or outside, but the supposition of interiority and exteriority, repeatedly insurgent and abandoned, helps us to see it feelingly.

MATERIAL IMAGINATION

The transformability of the skin is much more versatile than is traditionally imagined. As Michel Serres has suggested, understanding the skin as a milieu requires a physics of the imagination that lies between the conditions of liquid and solid. In *Atlas*, one of a series of books from the 1990s in which he attempts to map the world of global media communications, Serres proposes that philosophy might find in textiles a different, intermediary sort of 'metaphorical matter' of which, and with which, to think:

> [B]etween the so-called rigorous hardness of crystal, geometrically configured, and the fluidity of soft and sliding molecules, there is an intermediary material which tradition leaves to the female, and is thus thought little of by philosophers, with the exception perhaps of Lucretius: veil, canvas, tissue, chiffon, fabric, goatskin and sheepskin, known as parchment, the flayed hide of a calf, known as vellum, paper, supple and fragile, linens and silks, all the forms of planes or twists in space, bodily envelopes or writing supports, able to flutter like a curtain, neither liquid nor solid, to be sure, but participating in both conditions. Pliable, tearable, stretchable . . . topological.[56]

We habitually envisage that in-betweenness in terms of membranes, borders, boundaries. But these are themselves abstracted forms of the skin, the skin emblazoned, stretched out, explicated. The implicative capacity of the skin – its capacity to be folded in upon itself – means that it is involved in other, much more mobile and ambivalent substances too, substances and forms which do not have simple superficiality or absolute homogeneity, but in which, so to speak, the surface turns on itself, goes all the way down: smoke; clouds; dust; sand; foam.

This is why the kinds of entering into skin undertaken through this book often require exercises and investigations of the material imagination. I draw this phrase from the work of Gaston Bachelard, for whom it describes two intersecting things: firstly, the ways in which the material world is imagined by everyone, all the time, not just scientists, but also poets, children, cultural analysts, cabdrivers, medics and Mad Hatters – the 'material imagination' as the imagination of matter. However, there is no way of imagining the nature of the material world which does not draw on and operate in terms of that material world. So imagination is itself always implicated in the world that it attempts to imagine, made up, like the gingerbreadman enquiring into his dough, of what it makes out. This is not least because the merely visual or image-making faculty suggested by the word 'imagination' is always toned and textured by the other senses. Imagine a muddy field, or a clear sky. Is it possible not to imagine such things in a muscular fashion, in terms of the resistance or release that we would feel in encountering them, in other words in terms of the theories of the nature of such material forms that are embodied in our habitual or learned comportments towards them and our likely or possible bodily interactions with them? The image in each case would be much more than something merely seen; it would be, it must be, not only image but also usage. So the phrase 'material imagination' must signify the materiality of imagining as well as the imagination of the material.

Consider a simple example of the materiality of our theories of materiality. When we think about thinking, most of us have in our minds (and so necessarily also in our mouths and at the tips of our tongues), an idea that thinking is an altogether more airy and gaseous affair than the objects to which it attends. Objects are, we dream, solid, stony, densely insensate, resistant, extended, but also determined in space and time. Thoughts, signs, representations, by contrast, are ghostly, feathery, insubstantial, at best a soft, sifting sort of mist that settles on things. Maxwell's demon, the imaginary creature who might inhabit the threshold between matter and thought, form and information, who by sorting molecules might create energy, adumbrates a world on which matter, or our account of matter, might itself have softened and diffused. Here is an implicit theory of matter which must change the nature of what we think thinking might be. There is no account of the operations of thought, and therefore, perhaps, no experience of the operations of thought, no epistemology or thinking about thinking, which does not operate in terms of embedded experiences and expectations of the nature of matter.

(It may be as well to be clear from the start that I am only in the flimsiest and most preliminary sense offering 'Bachelardian' readings. Bachelard's work on the imagination of matter is in varying degrees unanalytic, archetypalist, aestheticist, ahistorical, idealist, self-indulgent, masculinist, rhapsodic, pottering and just plain soppy. So I am not suggesting that one use Bachelard's alchemical model of the elements to programme a new form of cultural analysis.)

The skin provides a good opportunity for enquiring into the material imagination because it is bilateral, both matter and image, stuff and sign. If you touch your skin – and think how hard it is to think without touching your skin, forefinger to lip, say – then you feel yourself and you feel yourself feeling. You are simultaneously an object in the world and a subject giving rise to itself as it advances to meet the world in that object. The skin is an organ, but, unlike the other organs, also has many other functions in maintaining the definition, uprightness and continuing life of the body it demarcates. However wrapped in thought, the skin is also the sensible form of our corporeal being. The skin, in all its many allotropes, seems to be the stuff, or the emblem of the stuff, of which we are composed, the model for many of the ways in which we meet with the material world, and shape it to our ends or to its: as clay, fabric, membrane, armour, powder, breath, light.

VOLUMES

In stigmata, in acupuncture, in body-piercing, in other kinds of needlework, whether applied to the body or to body-substitutes, like tapestries (Philomela, Persephone), screens and samplers, the skin is reperceived through an activity not of folding, but of pricking and threading. What matters here is not the folding-together of planes, but the reorientation of the skin through points, usually points of particular sensitivity. The skin is reimagined as a new topology of coordinates and faces. The cardinal points of the body, hands, feet, nipples, nose, lips, ears, genitals, become the foci of a new rotation of planes and volumes. The points are distinguished from and spread out from each other on the body's natural surface, but also communicate with each other according to alternative and shifting body-images.

One image is perhaps that of the body not spread out like a page or a map, but rolled or compacted, like a scroll or a book; a needle entering such a volume at a particular point will traverse several planes. If the book is imagined as a line, tape, or surface that unrolls from its beginning to its end, the gatherings of the book mean that points that are widely separated – even hundreds of pages apart – in Euclidean reading-space are also only millimetres apart, and sometimes only the infinitesimal antipodes of a recto and verso. The binder's needle and bookworm alike experience the space of the book in this manner as well as in the consecutive manner of ordinary reading. One does not need to look to hypertext for an image of this, for anyone who has ever read a book with one finger or a bookmark keeping the place of the endnotes, or moved between the index and the text, has already inhabited this space. This communication between points gives the body depth and voluminousness. Most importantly, it allows the body to be experienced in more than one format or articulation; to be apprehended in folio, quarto, duodecimo. There is thus an important imaginative link between the point and the thread; between drawn-together structures, like books, and structures that are more loosely articulated by means of wires – mobiles, sailing ships, puppets, kites and the like. The points in a hypertext that allow one to replace one text with another, the words which 'yield' (to borrow Michael Joyce's word) or give way to other words, are not experienced as simple doorways.[57] For we have decided to call them *links* or lines (*liens* in French), a notion that preserves and extends the memory of the bookbinder's or sailmaker's needle. But links are also microcosms; as in a Mandelbrot set, the whole of the target document is resumed or condensed in the piece of text or image that constitutes the link. Links are both buttonholes and mis-en-abîmes; an entire other garment is fitted into the buttonhole. What links the idea of the buttonhole and the fractal replication is the knot or stitch: in making a knot, an entire length or volume is passed through itself. The implication of the skin in the idea of the book is more than a metaphor. For centuries of manuscript and book production, books were primarily things of skin. The most authoritative and evocative binding for a book is still leather. After Alfred Corder, the convicted murderer of Maria Marten, had been hanged and dissected, his tanned skin was used to bind a presentation copy of an account of his crimes which still resides in Moyses Hall Museum, Bury St Edmunds, England.[58]

The shock value of a book such as Alfred Corder's depends on its rarity, its obscenity. But books bound in human skin have, in a minor sort of way, abounded in the last two centuries. It is an odd fact that, although binding in

Double gallows motif embossed on the reverse of the record of the 1821 trial, conviction and execution of murderer John Horwood, bound in his skin.

skin is often thought of as a kind of atavistic barbarity, the practice does not, according to Lawrence Thompson at least, seem to have been known before the eighteenth century.[59] The long-established popularity of the genre of gallows confessions combined with the fact that, during the eighteenth and nineteenth centuries, the bodies of executed criminals were regularly made available for posthumous dissection, suggests the aptness of binding criminal testaments in the skin of the reprobate. A volume in the Bristol Records Office giving details of the arrest, trial and execution of a young man called John Horwood, who was hanged in 1821 for the murder of Eliza Balsum, is similarly bound in the culprit's skin. When a criminal's skin is used to bind the book in which he appears to give his own admonitory account of his wicked life and deserved death, the anthropodermic binding enables a kind of graphical ventriloquism, a garbing of the book in the body of the criminal that corresponds to the garbling appropriation of his tongue. As a mute affidavit of the authenticity of the account it encloses, the skin binding provides the same kind of bodily countersign as the cross or thumbprint by means of which the illiterate may make their attesting marks in legal documents. Normally, it is the legal document that is binding upon the bodies it concerns; here the body's own binding seems to underwrite and circumscribe the power of the official record. The rumour that the skin of executed French aristocrats was used in Revolutionary France to bind official state publications and texts such as Rousseau's *The Social Contract* seems to illustrate a similar principle.

Medical books have often been bound in skin in the pursuit of a similar iconic aptness. According to Lawrence Thompson, a copy of the 1568 edition of

Ce curieux petit livre sur la Virginité et les fonctions génératrices féminines me paraissant mériter une reliure congruente au sujet est revêtu d'un morceau de peau de femme tanné par moi-même avec du sumac.

Dr L. Bouland

Vesalius's *De humani corporis fabrica* in the possession of a Mr William Easton Louttit Jr of Providence, Rhode Island, bears a leather label reading 'humana cute vestitutus liber' (Thompson, 147). Walter Hart Blumenthal alludes to a series of 3 quarto volumes on anatomy, all bound in skin from the same black person's body,[60] the first of which, held by the Lane Medical Library of Stanford University, contains the 1737 essay by Bernhard Albinus on human skin pigmentation, the *Dissertatio secunda de sede et caussa coloris aethiopum et caeterorum hominum* (Leiden, 1737). The College of Physicians in Philadelphia owns a copy of Joseph Leidy's personal copy of his own *Elementary Treatise on Anatomy* (Philadelphia, 1861), which bears an inscription asserting that it is made from the skin of a Civil War soldier. The Wellcome Library in London has a copy of Severin Pineau's book on virginity, *De integritatis et corruptionis virginum notis* (Amsterdam, 1663), which a previous owner, Dr Ludovic Bouland, had bound in the skin of a woman which he had himself tanned. A note added by Bouland on a flyleaf of the book reads: 'As this curious book on Virginity and the female reproductive functions seemed to me to deserve a binding appropriate to its subject, it is bound in a piece of female skin, which I myself tanned with sumac.' Dr Bouland knew what he was doing. Sumac is derived from the leaves of plants of the genus Rhus, of which some examples can cause intense itching and burning reactions. It was at one time valued as a tanning agent by bookbinders because it produced a light and supple leather, which did not darken on exposure to light.

It is often the case that the corporeal countersign provided by the skin may not be enough on its own. Books bound in human skin (which after tanning may look and feel much like the leather derived from other creatures) tend themselves to be subject to validation, for example in the gilded inscription 'Cutis Vera Johannis Horwood' which decorates the Horwood volume. The skin validates the book, but the text must reach outside itself to give its authenticating stamp to the mute skin that confines and confirms it.

The epidermal imprimatur has not always been given unwillingly. George Walton, a New England highwayman, ended his days in the Massachussetts state prison in 1837, at the beginning of a twenty-year sentence to which he had been sentenced for the robbery of a man named John Fenno. Before he died, he asked that an account of his exploits, entitled *Narrative of the Life of James Allen, alias George Walton, alias Jonas Pierce, alias James H. York, alias Burley Grove, the Highwayman. Being His Deathbed Confession to the Warden of the Massachusetts State Prison*, be presented to the victim of his last robbery, John Fenno, and that it be bound in his own skin, as a token of admiration and respect for the resistance his victim put up during the crime. It now forms part of the library of the Boston Athenaeum. Like John Horwood's binding, Walton's also carries an inscription, the words 'Hic Liber Waltonis Cutis Compactus Est' being embossed in the cover. This bit of performance art seems to make good the boast Walton made during his life in a note left after one of his many jailbreaks, that he was 'master of his own skin' (Blumenthal, 76). Walton answers the *habemus corpus* of the legal text with his own countervailing act of self-curation.

Lovers have also sometimes been voluntary donors of their skin for the adornment of books. A nineteenth-century Russian poet unusually contrived to see his own skin performing its bibliodermic office by directing that skin from his own leg, which was to be amputated after an accident, be used to bind a collection of his sonnets for his mistress.[61] Blumenthal tells another story of a woman who used the skin of her deceased as a binding for a memorial book of poems. The memorial did not inhibit her from taking a new husband, and Blumenthal imagines him pondering his predecessor between the sheets and wondering how he might look as volume two (81–2).

The best-known instance of this kind of gift concerns the late-nineteenth-century popular astronomer and writer on spiritualism, Camille Flammarion. The story is that a young French Countess secretly fell in love with Flammarion while reading his work. When she was dying of tuberculosis, she asked Flammarion to see her, and told him that, after her death, she intended to send him a gift that he would be compelled to accept. She ordained that, after her death, a large piece of skin be cut from her shoulders and sent to the object of her adoration to serve as a binding for one of his books. Her doctor duly conveyed a rolled-up sheet of skin to Flammarion, who complied with her wishes by having a copy of his book *Les terres du ciel* (Paris, 1877) bound in it. The gilt inscription on the front cover of the book – 'Exécution pieuse d'un voeu anonyme. Reliure en peau humaine (femme) 1882' (Pious Fulfillment of an Anonymous Wish, Binding in Human Skin (Woman) 1882) – seems to make it clear that the act is a response to a request that is itself experienced as a binding one (Blumenthal, 85–9, Thompson, 144–5).

We have seen earlier in this chapter how early anatomical illustrations played on the analogy of the skin and the page. This has its electronic form in the National Library of Medicine's Visible Human Project, in which the bodies of a man (in accordance with well-established tradition, the body of an executed criminal) and a woman were sliced into thin leaves or cross-sections. It is possible to take an animated 'fly-through' trip from the top of the head down to the toes, in just the way a flip-book allows one to make and display amateur animations. The idea of the bibliomorphic body was dramatized in the arrangements made by an American named Keith Smith for the disposal of his remains. He asked that the cadaver be sliced vertically into one-inch thick sections, and then each of the fifteen sections sealed between plate glass. His instructions continue: 'Each of the fifteen sections should be placed in order, hinged one to the next along the back side. The "book" should be stood in the corner, slightly opened, in the entrance room to my house, to be renamed the Keith Smith Memorial Library.'[62] All of these examples of books of skin suggest the versatile substitutability of the bound volumes of book and body.

Books, which endlessly reconfigure the spaces and volumes they occupy, go beyond themselves into other kinds of bodily self-transformation. All the arts of what Mr. Micawber calls 'personal contortion', whether comic (upendings, pratfalls, tumblings, 'girning', or facemaking), heroic (cartwheels, somersaults, trapezes and balancing acts, acrobatics), or supernatural (yoga, levitation, the Indian rope-trick, ectoplasmic extrusion, stigmata), along with their many miniaturized forms like puppetry and card-tricks, in which the hand summarizes and impersonates the body, or displaced forms like pottery and balloon-sculpture, can be seen as attempts to fit out new (and old) extravagant body-images and body-volumes, topologies moulded in mid-air and mind-time by our phantasmal pellicular skins. They are all attempts to jump out of your skin. And what would happen if you did such a thing? Since only living beings, which is to say beings still provided with skins, are able to do this, even in imagination, you would have to bring your skin with you even as you jumped out of it. Even if jumping out of your skin were taken to mean jumping into a new one, this would have to be done *through* your old one, in the way that clowns (those complexly voluminous creatures), in my day, and perhaps somewhere still, would jump through paper hoops. You can only jump out of your skin by taking up a stitch in yourself, by tying a knot in yourself. Many art forms allow the body to be drawn out of itself; but only the pellicular imagination allows the body to be drawn through itself in this way. It is no surprise then that the arts of animation which allow us at last to see living bodies stretched, twisted, flattened, blown up (but never, ever atomized) should have had to wait for the development of film, the embodiment *par excellence* of the pellicular imagination.

Much cultural history, in these zealously moralized academic times, sees itself still as cultural critique, and critique etymologically signifies a cutting off, or excision. Such critique requires you to peel away, to unpick yourself from, the past. But there is a choice between cutting and darning. The black art of Atropos, giving birth by cutting the cord, so history can be over and done with; and the art of Philomela, darning up her ablated tongue in her tapestry. Where conventional cultural history aims never to miss a trick (*tricoter*, to knit or knot

together, and thus to deceive, riddle), I want to be able to follow out (and follow others in following out) the intrigues (from that same root, *tricoter*), the
knitting, the sifting, the inriddling of history. History, despite its sociable
reputation and self-image, tries to keep itself to itself. It needs to prevent itself
from going native, and usually expends much effort in keeping itself, in all
senses, in the clear: clear thought, clear skin, clear conscience. I expect to end
up materially implicated, perhaps incriminated in the things I am up to here,
with the skin. History, even that congenial cousin that calls itself cultural history, has had much to do with revealing, unmasking, stripping away disguises,
making the past give up the truth it was, but did not know. I am to be found
writing here, though, not as the skin's inquisitor but its amanuensis.

Although the skin as milieu represents the last of my medical epochs of the
skin, this is not a medical history of the skin, partly because dermatological history has been so well served, by John Thorne Crissey, Lawrence Charles Parrish,
Karl Holubar and others.[63] This is also why it is not organized in chronological
slices matching the broad epochs of screen, membrane and milieu. At every
stage in its history, different models contribute in varying degrees to the way in
which the skin is understood, experienced and itself drawn on as metaphor.
Indeed, the model of history the book assumes and attempts to substantiate is
not that of a steadily rolling river but rather the kind of voluminous surface
evoked by Michel Serres in his conversations with Bruno Latour:

> If you take a handkerchief and spread it out in order to iron it, you can see
> in it certain fixed distances and proximities. If you sketch a circle in one
> area, you can mark out nearby points and measure far-off distances. Then
> take the same handkerchief and crumple it, by putting it in your pocket.
> Two distant points suddenly are close, even superimposed. If, further, you
> tear it in certain places, two points that were close can become very distant
> … As we experience time – as much in our inner senses as externally in
> nature, as much *le temps* of history as *le temps* of weather – it resembles this
> crumpled version much more than the flat, overly simplified one.[64]

Serres' skin-like handkerchief provides a model for the tumblings and
crumplings of the history of the skin and the skin in history. At every stage the
skin will be both early and late, always in, yet never quite on time.

The chapters in the first part of the book will consider the various forms of
the skin's visibility, first of all in a range of contemporary forms of assault and
mortification of the skin, and then in the history of the reading of skin markings,
from legal brandings through to the miraculous and medical stigmata of the
nineteenth and twentieth centuries. Each of my discussions will show how
complex topological conceptions of the skin unfold from or are folded within
more geometrical attempts to figure or explicate the skin.

This will lead me in the second part of the book to discussions of aspects of
the skin which do not begin or end with the skin's appearance. Just as the skin
itself convenes or enfolds all the other sense organs as convolutions of its

surface, so in these later chapters I take the measure of the skin in terms of senses and sensations than the visual. In chapter 6, I consider the colour of the skin in terms of a certain material imagination of luminosity; a thickening of light into substance and texture. Thereafter, successive chapters explore the history of the allure and disgust attached to the practices of oiling and anointing the skin, the aroma of the skin and the difficult, delicious, intermittent history of the sensation of itch. Microscopy and the apprehension of littleness will come to seem increasingly important through these chapters, for microscopy both acquainted the eye with its ordinary limits, and taught it new ways of seeing feelingly. My final chapter concerns a different aspect of the minimal or minia-ture skin, in the imagination of delicacy. These chapters complete the trajec-tory of the book from the exposures, adversities and assaults to which the skin has so often been heir, especially in contemporary experiences and representa-tions, to the subtler, more fugitive modes and manners of 'the light touch'.

In moving away from the thematics of the cut, in moving from duress to finesse, I hope to make out a rather different, and necessarily rather more dif-fusive concern with the skin. It is not only individual psychological life but also cultural life that is lived at the level of, and through the intercession of, the skin, and its many actual and imaginary doublings and multiplications. I enquire into the kinds of sense we make of the skin, and the kinds of sense we make of the world and each other with it, which is to say, through the action of various kinds of epidermal shape, story, device and figure. I am trying to make a begin-ning not so much for a cultural history as an historical poetics of the skin, which would follow out the ways in which ideas of the skin are multiplied not just in the social history of the body – in medicine and combat and sexuality and religion, for example – and in the usual range of picturings and cultural representations (pictures, stories, statues and organized sounds), but also in milieux such as textiles, photography, cookery, law and alchemy. It would require a joining of the abstract mathematics of topology, the kind we properly and emblematically call 'mindbending', to the groping, wattle-and-daub dumb-show, the mudpie mentality of the toddler in the garden. My emphasis could be said to be on the two senses of the phrase 'making sense': the making of the various kinds of sensory beauty, intricacy and delight which human culture makes possible and of which it largely consists; and the forms of enquiry, knowledge and understanding that can be yielded through this way of thinking through things.

2 Exposition

It is a striking coincidence that so much of the pioneering work in dermato-logy should have taken place in Vienna during the years in which Freud began to develop the theory of psychoanalysis. At Charcot's clinic in Paris and then in Freud's consulting room and in hospitals in which soldiers were treated for nervous diseases, the skin began to be seen as a sensitive expression, not just of the body's, but also of the mind's complexion. A psychosomatic understanding of the skin grows through the twentieth century, reaching its culmination in the extraordinary work of Didier Anzieu on the relations between the experi-ence of the skin and the formation and sustaining of the ego.

Anzieu's *The Skin Ego* offers a paradigm for understanding the nature of the self which is both powerfully simple, and yet interpretatively versatile. Anzieu proposes that 'the ego is the projection on the psyche of the surface of the body',[1] and defines the skin ego as 'a mental image of which the ego of the child makes use during the early phases of its development to represent itself as an ego con-taining psychical contents, on the basis of the experience of the surface of the body'.[2] Though Anzieu is attentive to the possibilities of psychosomatic relation-ships between the mind and the skin, his work goes in the direction specified by Ashley Montagu, who wrote in 1971 that 'the psychosomatic approach to the study of skin may be regarded as centrifugal; that is, it proceeds from the mind outwards to the skin', and recommended 'the opposite approach, namely from the skin to the mind; in other words, the centripetal approach'.[3] However, the skin does not give rise to the ego in one fashion only. It also fulfils an extraordinarily wide and diverse range of functions, with respect both to the body and to the ego. In the first edition of *The Skin Ego*, Anzieu distinguished nine: supporting; con-taining; shielding; individuating; connecting; sexualizing; recharging; signifying; and assaulting/destroying (*SE*, 98–108). The nine functions distinguished by Anzieu do not smoothly cooperate, or interconnect. In the terms of his own metaphor, they do not form a seamless whole or coherent volume, but rather a repertoire of different kinds of metaphorical enactment of skin function. In what follows, I will be drawing in particular upon the eighth and ninth functions, in which the skin becomes the bearer and container of meanings that are not endogenous, deriving from, or serving the purposes of the ego itself, but rather represent a certain kind of ego-reinforcing compromise between the ego and that which threatens to lacerate or destroy its fragile self-enclosure.

In later work, Anzieu has tended to regard the last, 'toxic' function as not properly a function of the skin ego at all, but rather the name for the work of the negative, the damage and danger in the service of Thanatos that lead to the skin ego's collapse. The second edition of Le moi-peau therefore removes the ninth function, leaving a roster of eight functions, which forms the basis of Anzieu's further speculations about the function of the skin in the work of thought.[4] The removal of the toxic or anti-skin from the repertoire of its functions may be an attempt on Anzieu's part to disambiguate the relation between the positive and negative functions of the skin. That he should feel the need to make the fabric of the skin consistent in its function of giving consistency is striking in the light of the fact that the ostension of the skin in recent years has so consistently and conspicuously taken the form of assault upon it. The rest of this chapter will track and account for different forms of this hostility, aiming to show that the simple separation of positive and negative, or therapeutic culturing of the negative into the positive may not be possible.

Anzieu's work is so compelling because it seems to address so directly and so resourcefully the single most striking contemporary feature of the skin. If the skin has become more than ever visible it is as the visible object of many different forms of imaginary and actual assault: tattooing, piercing, scarification, suntanning, bondage fashions that appear to cut into or segment the skin, images of calcified, metallized or mineralized skin, along with the infliction of various kinds of disfiguring marks, actual and cosmetic. This chapter and the next consider different forms of this assault, the different forms of exposure of the skin, and the different ways in which the skin is both made subject to the law and makes itself a law unto itself.

The most general and perhaps the subtlest form of assault to which the skin has been subject is an optical assault. The skin ego is formed from, and remains powerfully associated with, sensory impressions which are previsual or at best weakly visual. We may surmise that the skin ego comes into being in the infant's early attempts to perpetuate or recreate the conditions obtaining in the womb, in which its existence is organized almost wholly in terms of taste, touch and hearing, and in particular a powerful combination of the last two. This birth into difference accomplished in and through the skin is also a birth into vision, or the spatial matrix in which vision will operate, long before the refining of the actual organs of sight. The retreat to the taste-touch-hearing complex of the psychic envelope is necessitated by the irruption into it (except that the spatial conception of irruption is itself evidence that the irruption must already have taken place) of a sense of relative position which has begun to serve the purposes of the eye more than those of the ear and skin.

Precisely because of the omnipresence and unlocalized quality of the skin, it is also uniquely exposed to the operations of the other senses, and particularly those of the eye. The skin figures. It is what we see and know of others and ourselves. We show ourselves in and on our skins, and our skins figure out the things we are and mean: our health, youth, beauty, power, enjoyment, fear, fatigue, embarrassment or suffering. The skin is always written: it is legendary. More than the means of what we happen voluntarily or involuntarily to disclose to sight, it has become the proof of our exposure to visibility itself.

SCAR

As I began thinking about the meanings of skin I became curious about the concern of children, especially between the ages of about three and six, with scars, scratches and cuts, as well as their intense and abiding preoccupation with the uses of sticking-plaster. One might imagine that, at this early stage in the development of the child's sense of body-image, the lesion, tearing, or perforation of the epidermal envelope can be experienced as the threat of complete collapse, as though the child's skin were sustained by a pressure from within like a balloon and, once punctured, might be transformed into a slack and shapeless rag of flesh. However, children of this age have already learned about the skin's spontaneous capacity to repair itself after it has been damaged. The trick of sticking sellotape over two opposing points of a balloon's surface, to allow one to insert a knitting needle into one side and out the other side without bursting it, is experienced with corresponding awe and rapture by children. I believe that these observed physical processes of cutaneous regeneration are accompanied by the development of psychological resources of an equivalent kind. Starting from a consideration of the way a child makes sense of and incorporates into the structure of its own self the processes of cutaneous lesion, scarring and regeneration, I want to move towards a consideration of the relationship between the rent and reconstituted skin in adult experience, most specifically in some practices and fantasies associated with sadomasochism, but also with the cultural generalization of such image-dynamics.

Let us suppose that the child sees that the wound sustained by the skin, or through the skin, results in a mark, of abrasion, contusion, inflammation, or incision. Where 'the skin has been broken' (in that curious English idiom which suggests a desire to see the skin not as a fabric, of which we should say it is torn or ripped, but a hardened shell or membrane; the equivalent French expression, *entamer la peau*, does not have quite the primary associations of penetration through a hardened surface) the child learns to expect the formation of a scab. This scab is highly ambiguous. It is the perpetuation of the injury, to which the child pays close and repeated attention, each time experiencing a renewal, though with gradually diminishing intensity, of the shock of the injury to the skin, and the accompanying threat to the integrity of the secondary fabric of the ego-skin. But in marking the place of the injury, refusing to let it dissipate, the scab also transforms it. Since the scab is the mark of the injury, and not the injury itself, it transforms the injury *to* the skin into a mark left *on* the skin. A scab is a visual compromise between lesion and healing; it preserves the blemish or disfigurement to the smooth integrity of the skin's surface even as it affirms the skin's successful defence against puncturing or laceration. This is one reason, surely, for the fact that children are unable to resist picking scabs. A scab is different from a scar, since a scab will go away. A scar is an arrested scab. The scab thus offers the pleasure of an averted threat; by reopening the wound, the child may play with and master the trivial but symbolic (symbolic because it is trivial) risk to its psychic wholeness. Picking scabs is therefore in part to be understood as a variant of the *fort-da* procedure of playing with danger, absence or negativity in order to bind it into a kind of syntax. This gathering-together of the self is achieved, not in the face of potential loss or trauma, but through it. Such gathering-through-loss can be interpreted in terms also of the sublime, in which the dialectic of pain and pleasure is seen in terms of a threatened loss of proportion between the perceiving self and its environment (the loss of a relationship of adequation between the imaginary propriocentric volume of the individual body and the unencompassable hugeness of the sublime prospect), a potential loss against which one may defend by a defensive 'bracing' of the self, a congregation of the energies threatened with dissolution.

Very quickly, the transforming powers of the scab may get transferred to other injurious and non-injurious markings of the skin, and the pleasures of controlling the coming and going of the scab reappear in a more general eroticization of such markings. This surely explains the pleasures of the sticking-plaster, which allows the play of rending and suture with an artificial surface placed over the surface of a wound or, indeed, over a patch of uninjured skin. The important feature of the sticking-plaster is its edge, which both seams and seals the otherwise uninterrupted surface of the skin, marking the skin and then placing it 'under erasure'. It appears that the imaginatively erased wound or mark is more powerfully pleasurable than the merely virgin surface. For the child, as for Yeats's Crazy Jane, 'Nothing can be sole or whole/That has not been rent.'[5] The pleasure in the sticking-plaster makes some of the purposes of deliberate injuries to the skin in adult society intelligible. Among these we could enumerate ritual practices or scarification and their nonritual equivalents in the practices of self-laceration which have become so epidemic among both women and men, and body-piercing, the point of which is to enable the body to be marked, by a ring, stud, or other material substitute for the scar. It is worth observing how essential it seems to be that what is displayed in, or hung from the pierced skin should be some hard and inorganic substance, with a preference for metallic objects which recapitulate the act of piercing; few cultures seem very drawn to the use of fabrics or textiles in earrings. This is not to say that textiles are not sometimes implicated in the austere play between the organic and the inorganic. In sadomasochistic representations of piercing, both in pornographic images and in performance art like that of Ron Athey, the piercing of sensitive body portions, such as genitals and nipples, is very often supplemented by actions of binding: ringed nipples are drawn together by thread, labia are sewn up, and male genitals are folded inwards and sewn over. The combined action of needle and thread involves a bizarre cooperation of 'male' assault upon the skin, with the puncturing effects of the phallic stylus, and 'female' repair of that surface, the restoration of the skin as web, veil or text.

Such practices seem to make it clear that the desire to tear the skin is inseparable from the need to darn it, or make it whole. As we will see, tattooing is a particularly complex form of this interchange between the injury and the mark, since here the marking of the skin takes place through a puncturing of its surface. The play between openness and closure, the rending and repair of the epidermal surface, is displaced into

Corset-style body-piercing.

the dynamics of exposure and concealment in clothing. Roland Barthes famously derived the pleasure of the text from a further displacement of the gaping and concealment of the garment into the hermeneutic dynamics of disclosure and secrecy in texts.[6] Barthes is one of a number of theorists in the last twenty years who have run the skin-writing analogy backwards; rather than reading the meanings of skin in terms of the erotics of its markings, he reads writing itself in terms of a dermatological dynamic of abrasions, tears, lesions in imaginary veils and surfaces: 'what I enjoy in a narrative is not directly its content or even its structure, but rather the abrasions I impose upon the fine surface . . . Which has nothing to do with the deep laceration the text of bliss inflicts upon language itself . . .'.[7] In these figures and phantasms, the scar and the symbol of the scar are hard to distinguish, since a scar is always anyway a kind of symbol. The symbol of a scab or scar always recapitulates the manner in which scarring is itself already a transformation of injury into visual symbol. At the same time, the infliction of injury to the skin may also be an assault upon the signifying function of the skin. In that the scar signifies that something *real* – some exceeding of mere signification – has taken place, the scar can become the figure for the violent erasure of the epidermal grounding of figurality.

SKINSHINE

The libidinization of the scarified or inscribed skin may be associated with other forms of epidermal idealization through degradation, for example in the fantasy of toughened skin, whether in the form of scales, leather or metal, which seems designed to produce a reassuring condition of impenetrability. Associated with many of these forms of toughened or impermeable skin is the fascinating, seductive quality of reflectiveness or shine. The shiny skin, whether in the form of the latex or leather that clings tightly to the body of the fetishist, or in the anointed sheen of the bodybuilder, or in the frankly metallic gleam of the body-become-machine, as in films such as the *Terminator* and *Tetsuo* series, is the skin that resists penetration. It is invulnerable because it absorbs nothing, not even light. The fascinating sheen of shining skin, or luminous skin-substitutes reduces the voluminous body to the spill and shimmer of light across a surface and therefore immaterializes it. At the same time, however, the shiny skin metallizes or mineralizes the body in such a way as to display it wholly as an object. Epidermal lustre, whether in the form of synthetic second skins, such as latex and rubber, or in the flesh burnished to a semblance of such a second skin, is therefore at once substance and chimera. The shiny skin is skin that is no more than a skin, skin thinned to a sheen. The hardness of the shining skin is constituted out of this impossible compromise between the adamantine and the immaterial. A corresponding ambivalence results from the shiny skin's enigmatic hesitation between the possibility of moistness or oily lubrication, and the shell-like hardness of high polish. The lustre of the bodybuilder's musculature suggests organic softness and pliability, only to countermand it in the display of perdurability; the rubber fetishist's gear suggests the hardness and restraint of the inorganic, while displaying the contrary qualities of elasticity. The shining skin suggests a change of biological order – the human become mineral, reptile or mechanical. The hardened skin is a visual as well as a physical shield. Like the modernist building faced in mirror glass, the shining skin is able to hide in plain sight; hardened into pure objectivity, the shining skin eludes its own condition of objectivity by perplexing the act of looking that would make of it an object. The shine of the skin deflects and diffuses the perforative, punctual line of sight across the horizontality of the planar body. The shining body therefore aspires to that abolition of theatrical depth enacted in Lyotard's body spread into infinite, paradoxical surface. The skin borrows the mirror's depthlessness and invisibility (the mirror offers everything to the eye but itself, for you can only ever look *in* a mirror, never *at* it) while refusing its perspectival compliance. Like an ordinary mirror, the skin mirror effaces itself in the visibility it returns to the gaze, but also retains a certain opacity. The light of the skin mirror is neither wholly absorbed nor wholly returned to its source, but, as it were, captured, slowed and thickened. Is this one reason for the centrality of black in leather and rubber fetishism? Shining black allows the ambivalent exchange of light and its absence, reflection and absorption to an extreme degree.

The skin mirror is, ultimately, narcissistic. On the gleaming surface of the fetishist's second skin, or the burnished armature of the weightlifter, we see an eyeless light that is watching itself, neither accepting nor releasing light, an impossible 'flat depth' of viscous liquidity, a diffulgence that never divulges itself to the eye. One of the most frequently-remarked characteristics of skin is that it is susceptible to endogenous and exogenous sensation, that is, it can be felt both on the inside and the outside; one can feel one's skin as though it were another's, apprehending its softness, moistness, looseness and so on, from the outside, even as one feels *with* or *through* one's skin. You cannot taste your tongue, smell your nose or hear your ears in the same manner. (Though you can, of course, see your eye; this overlap may be involved in some of the insistent links between tactility and sight in the fantasy of shining skin.)

But the hardened skin, the skin that has become no more than the shell of its lustre, represents an exteriorization of tactility, which is to say, a concentration of sensation on the outside of the skin, with a diminution of sensation on the outside. The armoured skin is anaesthetized, and, in allowing no sensation through, severs that dual directionality characteristic of ordinary skin. In the

shining skin, the depth and ambivalence of the skin as epidermis thin and rigid-
ify into tegumental simplicity. The hardened, shining skin is no longer a medium
of passage and hymeneal exchange, but of division, separation and cleavage. The
uterine fantasy of pure interiority without exterior with which I began here
turns inside out – into the display of an exteriority without interior, a container without content. As such, we can perhaps connect the hardness of shining
skin to Klaus Theweleit's investigations of male fantasies (along with shared,
transferred and diffused fantasies *of* male fantasies) of a kind of hardness that
would enclose, canalize or otherwise discipline the threatening fluidity attributed to the female body, or the feminized interior of the male body. The shine
of the skin may therefore appear as the mark of its capacity to maintain the
divisions between hard and soft, outer and inner, ego and other, masculine and
feminine, in that fundamental split which Theweleit's work brings to visibility,
a split between 'an inner realm, concealing a "numbly glowing, fluid ocean"
and other dangers; and a restraining external shell, the muscle armor, which
contains the inner realm the way a cauldron contains boiling soup'.[8]

The essential feature of shining skin is its quality of uninterrupted surface.
The shining skin presents no impediment to the glissando of the eye across the
surface; indeed, in enforcing such a movement, it converts the body into an
imaginary geometry consisting wholly of vectors, planes and trajectories,
rather than points and lines. The shining body is phantasmally defended, not
only against perforation (from the outside or the inside), but against the
dimensionality of the edge, the line, the point in general. It is a kind of visual
immune system. It is surface without edge, area without perimeter, plane
without perpendicular, connectedness without articulation. This is to say that,
curiously, the hardened, armoured, helmeted body is an aphallic image, in its
resistance to the metaphor of the point; indeed, it borrows from an allegedly
female metaphorology of flow, movement and surface to enforce its per-
durable, phallic impenetrability. The folding-together of male and female
topologies is indicated by the evolution of the heroically mechanical termin-
ating robot in *Terminator I* into the polymorphous robot of *Terminator II*.
The Schwarzenegger robot belongs to the world of Newtonian mechanics, in
which the concussion of objects separated in space, and the conflict between
force (bullets) and resistance (the robot's toughened outer shell and
indestructible metallic skeleton) are powerfully operative. The robot is invulnerable because its inside is as tough as its outside. But the next generation terminator against which the Schwarzenegger version is pitted in *Terminator II* is not
less, but more superficial than the first, for it is, in a more radical way still, *all*
surface, surface all the way through, a surface that never bakes into a permanent
distinction between surface and interior, that can reform itself into any shape.

What, then, has the skin mirror to do with skin laceration? Klaus Theweleit's
account would suggest that they are unquiet opposites; the wounded,
lacerated flesh must be kept apart from the rigidified armature of the male
phantasmal body, or – not at all the same thing – the phantasmal male body.
The scarified skin is the very sign of spoiling and disfigurement, while the shiny

The male bodybuilder, pumped and lustrous.

skin is perfected and immaculate. But the skin mirror and the skin inscription are integrated, by the very function of integration that they both perform. The skin that holds itself together in and through its laceration has as its more than implied ideal the absolute invulnerability of the minero-mechanical integument. The interrelationship of the two modes in fetishistic and sado-masochistic imagery ought therefore to be unsurprising. The ideal of total envelopment indulged by the rubber or latex fetishist is rarely satisfying for long. When it is visualized, such envelopment must be subject to forms of *articulation*, which break into or across the non-differentiation of the shining surface, arresting the lateral skid of sight. Articulation can work in two dimensions: the skin can be written into, its surface penetrated vertically; or it can be written across, gridded, articulated, incised. The articulation of the skin is not simply the opponent of its shine. In fact, it intensifies shine, establishing lines of sight, even as it heightens the sense of the erotic slalom of sight and light across the skin's surface. In extreme cases, it can manifest itself in that desire to cut or mutilate the skin which, as we have seen, far from enacting a violent breakdown of body boundaries, is actually a means 'by which an individual endeavours to maintain body boundaries and self-cohesion'.[9] This argument has been confirmed by Armando A. Favazza, who writes that, far from causing inner self and outer world to collapse into each other, self-lacerators 'first are able to verify that they are alive, and then are able to focus attention on their skin border and to perceive the limits of their bodies'.[10]

The shiny skin is therefore textured with the articulation of the skin associated with the forms of skin inscription that I began by looking at: in fantasies of flagellation, laceration, incision, marking, as well as, more generally, the erotics of bondage, and the designed alternation of substances and textures in fetishistic clothing and images. This is particularly apparent in the imaging of weightlifting. Male bodybuilders rely on their extreme muscular development, and, to use that most telling of bodybuilding terms, 'definition', to bring about the play of surface and articulation across their own flesh. Their bodies are ribbed, ridged and written over with the obstructions to the slide of the eye over the lubricated flesh. Male bodybuilders, as it were, include the dimension of articulation on the surface of their skins; this kind of body wears its depth on its surface, folding out, in a kind of auto-écorché; the imaginary assaults upon the body, evidenced in the language of bodybuilding which will speak of well-defined muscle groups as 'rips', are turned into the very form of the body's defence. Mass becomes sublimated into the dimensionless play of light and shade: the gleam of the bodybuilder's body allows its symbolic wounding to be converted into the very image of unassailable impenetrability. To borrow and mix up the old soccer joke: the male bodybuilder has got its retaliation in first, on itself.

If the skin of the male weightlifter writes its articulation across itself, the skin of the female weightlifter needs to be articulated from outside or above, via the supplementation of clothing, props and lighting. This may connect with another interesting differentiation within bodybuilding images, namely a differentiation in the intensity of *shine*. The convention in most bodybuilding magazines is that male bodybuilders should reflect more light than female ones. The contrast here may be between the body seen as self-sufficient (invulnerable both because of its resistant, excluding shine, and because of its internalized control of its own articulation), and the body which is partial, impermanent, dependent. Presumably somewhere in this is the assumption that men should give out their own light in solar solitaire, while satellite females should derive their light from some other more primary source. An important constituent in this shine is the use of oil; I will return to the question of shine in a discussion of unguent illumination in chapter 7.

These images of burnished lustre also traffic with the powers of the photograph. Indeed, one might say that they establish a concord between the subject and the form of the photograph. If ours is a world in which skin surfaces of all kinds have multiplied, the first such surface was perhaps the photograph, in which a particularly pellucid relationship was established between touching and looking, skin and image. Photographs, we dream, the very word dreams, have been touched by the world's light, leaving its trace upon the surface of the photographic film. The photograph, as Roland Barthes has suggested, removes the eye from looking, and touches us: 'From a real body, which was there, proceed radiations which ultimately *touch* me, who am here . . . A sort of umbilical cord links the body or the photographed thing *to my gaze*: light, though impalpable, is here a carnal medium, a skin I share with anyone who has been photographed'.[11]

Far from spectralizing the world, putting it at a distance, the photograph is the modern embodiment of the contiguity between looking and grasping.

This is surely one reason for the continuing popularity of the glossy finish of the photograph. This sheen signifies the magical preciousness that we wish the photograph to retain, giving the eye notice that it is a tangible thing which looking is insufficient to encompass. The gloss is an ideal skin, flesh transfigured, but the ideality of that skin (its intangibility) is what seems to guarantee its quality of tenderness, that word that signifies both the quality of something touched and the manner of our touching. This image has been touched and can touch us back. Perhaps it is for this reason that we feel called to handle photographs, both to caress their glossy surfaces and occasionally, in sadness or anger, to gash and efface them. The gloss of the photograph signifies its more than human perfection, and therefore its vulnerability to the attentions of fingers, and the scratches, creases and corrupting smears of greasiness they can impart. This quality of the photograph is transmitted to the surfaces of other technological quasi-objects, such as the vinyl gramophone disc, tape (now boxed protectively in cassettes), and the CD, in the reverent kind of touch that it seems to teach us to use in handling it, a touch in which we keep the living, vulnerable surface of the object intact, instinctively preferring to hold it by its edges. When they first appeared, we were told that CDs were incorruptible; but nobody ever wanted to believe that, and we were glad when we discovered that, like living beings, they were indeed vulnerable to erosion and to the damage wrought by our tactile attentions. The practice of 'scratching', the manipulation in live performance of vinyl records, which grew up the club culture of the 1980s, at once rescued the possibility of damage in a world of incorruptible and immaterial data and preserved this ideal delicacy in our relationship to objects, drawing attention to the surface that would be as sensitive to our attentions as the skin of another person.

This ideal disembodied but quasi-bodily surface was rediscovered and extended in cinema, the most extraordinary feature of which was perhaps not so much its capacity to make moving images, as its capacity to move images anywhere, to project them in different places at different times, and thus to make the world newly intelligible as a series of screens or receptive surfaces. Whether this screen-creating capacity repeats the experience of the primal screen of the mother's breast, as implied by Bertram Lewin's arguments about the 'dream screen', or whether the mother's skin is in fact hereby being retroactively cinematized, will not need to be in question here.[12] But the concept of the dream screen teaches us that the projected image always implies and as it were supplies itself with its own immanent screen, implicit within the image at its own focal length, on which the image will be able to come to rest. The projected images of cinema are shadowed by the techniques of reproduction and enlargement that have made the living environments of the twentieth century a phantasmagoria of signifying surfaces. If anything and everything can become a screen, then everything has the capacity to bear faces and exposed bodies. The harsh banality of brick and metal, the sides of buildings, cars and buses, are capable of being made the vehicle for visible flesh. Anything can assume a mask of light; anything can become a *front*.

Like the life-size images of photographs that we pass from hand to hand, these cinematized public images have a tactile kind of radiance. All this visible skin, the skin of these models advertising sports shoes, ice creams, mascara and brassieres, and the secondary skins of the objects they wear, hold, caress, ingest, or recline in, all this skin *glows*, as if with its own serene, interior illumination. Touch continues to be implicated in this radiance (and it is perhaps one of the functions or effects of the ubiquity of skin to ensure the tangibility of the visible). The flesh displayed in posters and magazines, and in the electronic screens that are more and more a feature of public space, looks touchable, caressable, for what is to be impressed upon our eyes is the way that it has been touched by light; but we know that its touchability is of a higher order than the ordinary touchability of skin, the grasping touch which advertising also encourages, reaffirming constantly the association between envy and the evil eye, *invidia* and vision. Envy seems an appropriate relationship to the advertisement, rather than lust or desire, since we are encouraged to want something that we should not want, and cannot ever really have. Odourless and textureless, these skins nevertheless acquaint us with a kind of higher touching, an immaculate, intactile, imperishable touch of the eye. Whenever we look at a poster or a projection on an impersonal surface, we are looking at such an idealized, generalized human skin.

But there is another kind of touch, the expression of another, harsher, kind of optics. The ideal untouchability of the image ensures that, when we can get our hands on it, we will take the opportunity to penetrate, tear and deface, as the bathing beauty in the poster advertising 'Sunny Prestatyn' is torn and defaced in Philip Larkin's poem:

A couple of weeks and her face
Was snaggle-toothed and boss-eyed;
Huge tits and a fissured crotch
Were scored well in . . .

Someone had used a knife
Or something to stab right through
The moustached lips of her smile.[13]

Pornography brings to light the two kinds of tactile looking offered in Larkin's poem – the ideal, unbroken smoothness of the body as scene, incorruptible because untouchable, and the availability of this surface for sadistic defacement. Sadomasochistic pornography in particular combines the two modes of touching, absorbing defacement into the face. It shows the skin itself already shadowed by its disfiguration – tightly bound, caged and barred by fetishistic clothing, menaced by blade, stiletto or whip, or indeed actually bearing the marks of punishment. The last ten years have seen a steady increase in the

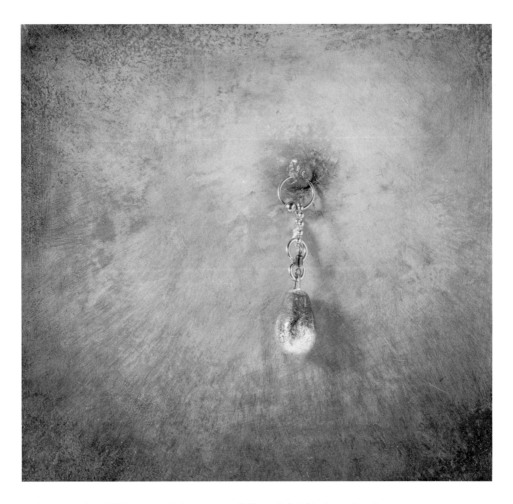

visibility and solidification of the respectability of fetishistic and sado-masochistic imagery, in piercing and tattooing, bondage fashions involving spikes, straps and constrictions of the flesh, and cosmetic styles that stripe and slash, intensifying the contrast between the surface of the skin and the markings applied to it. Such sadomasochistic imagery takes our revenge on itself. In the last chapter we encountered Michel Serres' suggestion that the application of make-up makes the sensorium visible, highlighting the organs of sense, and thus painting on to the skin the capacity to hear, see, taste and smell.[14] Sadomasochistic make-up reduces the skin to a dead, monochrome alternation of black on white, denying the display of sensitiveness, and marking the reduction of the skin to the condition of a surface to be marked. Are such assaults actual or imaginary, enacted or merely acted out? It may be suspected that this very numbing of the skin, the very playfulness or superficiality of sadomasochistic style, allows the intense libidinization of the surface itself, and our combined craving for and rage against it.

Michael Clark (piercing by Erdal Mehmet), *Wound with Lead Weight*, 1999–2002, oil, human organic material, surgical steel, lead, gold leaf on canvas.

(left) Tattoo: the imaged carapace 'skin' of an insect.

(right) Tattoo: the skin holds the image of the hypodermic that pierces it.

In taking our print, the skin also bears our weight. As the medium of making literal, the ground upon which every figure is inscribed, the skin is often now-adays concerned with the question of weight. In sadomasochistic practice and representation, for example, it is often as though the skin were dramatizing the primary significance of the word *bear*. In much sadomasochistic practice and imagery, there is an obsessive interplay between the attack on shape carried out through the use of weights, or objects hung from the skin in order to stretch and distort its contours, and the display of the skin's reassuring capacity to support weight. The skin bears weight as its owner bears suffering. In one ritual practised by masochistic performance artist Bob Flanagan, a third meaning was enacted; he hung plastic babies from hooks in his skin, as a way of demon-strating the enforced bearing of children.[15] Hanging objects from one's skin seems to reduce one's skin to an object, mere fleshly stuff to be played with at will and without mercy. But to hang yourself from your skin, or, as we might say, in a significant little prepositional shift, *by* your skin, as practised, for example by the self-modifying performance artist Stelarc, who hung himself high in the air through hooks in his skin, is to reduce *yourself* to the condition of object, or mere mass or weight. The hung person is of course reduced to an object, a mere carcass. They are wholly vulnerable and available. But they are also supported, borne up by the mortification they elect to have to bear. Suspension gives a curious compensatory sense of protection, as though one were lapped in one's own skin as in a hammock. Language gives us another literalization here; of the person in this appalling condition it must be said that they literally depend upon their own skin. This can be confirmed in the obsess-ive drive for symmetry or visible shape often evidenced in the way victims are hung or bound in sadomasochistic imagery. Like many other assaults on the skin, in weight-training, diet restriction, body-sculpture and self-modification through mortification, the point seems to be to *keep in shape*.

The ambivalent interchange of surface and articulation of the surface is also, most remarkably, evident in the practice and display of tattooing. The tattoo

Tattoo: the internal workings of the arm displayed on its surface.

uniquely combines vertical with horizontal incision, or articulation. It turns the vulnerability of the body, its exposure to penetration, into a flaunted surface. Tattoos often play with the alternation of soft and hard, displaying images of reptiles, shields or metal to suggest a kind of cicatrization, a toughening through the ordeal of exposure. The tattoo substitutes a surface for the actual surface of the skin: but it does so in a way that plays with the knowledge that the skin has been penetrated, since the technique of tattooing in fact requires pigment to be injected *beneath* the surface of the skin. Thus what appears to lie on top of the skin, in fact lies below it. The body flaunts the surface that it has taken into itself as a secondary interiority. The fact that the tattoo is irremovable involves a similarly ambivalent play between injury and self-defence. Once marked, the skin can never again recapture its infantile immaculacy and clarity. But the very permanence of the blemish-ornament can then make it a guarantee of continuity, or preemption of assault from the outside, as well as an imaginary stay against the wearing, sagging and wrinkling of the skin in the process of aging. A tattoo is for life, indeed: it is both a lethal assault upon the skin, and a means of cryogenic survival.

The complex of affects attaching to the marked skin may have a bearing upon contemporary concerns about suntanning. It has proved difficult to persuade inveterate sunbathers in Australia, the US and Europe of the dangers of prolonged exposure to the sun. The reason for this is that the sunbather is wedded to a fantasy of sunbathing as the construction of protective second skin. In English, sunbathing results in a 'tan', the word disclosing the association between a change of colour and a change of substance, in the passage from living tissue to the ambivalent rigidity of leather. In French, in which the word for suntanning is *bronzage*, the fantasized process and outcome seem markedly more metallurgical. The metaphorical association between the change in colour and the change in texture rests upon the larger association between marking, scarification and sheen: the endogenous change of pigmentation and the fantasy of a shield placed over the skin from the outside. The difficulty of persuading people to refrain from sunbathing may be in part that it is experienced as a prophylactic, as a way of making yourself safe from the sun, as well as from light, from eyes, from pain. The suntan is in fact the very best kind of reconstituted skin, in that it is both a scarring – the sign of a secondary shield or integument formed in response to a traumatic assault upon the skin – and a reassertion of the skin's smooth, shining integrity. The association of suntan with sheen completes the reassuring but paradoxical link between exposure and protection.

There is perhaps enough in what I have already said to indicate that the intense libidinization of the skin in contemporary cultural practices and representations is inseparable from a desire for psychic integration, or, as it might be put, integumentation, through the skin. (The words *integrity* and *integument* are etymologically less close than one might at first suspect. *Integument* comes from Latin, *tegere*, to cover; *integrity*, meaning the condition of being a singular integer, comes from the Latin *integer*, from *tangere*, to touch, meaning entire in the sense of untouched. But it is hard to resist the notion of a backformed etymological link between covering, touch and entirety.)

EXPOSURE

If we can see an increase in the intensity and frequency of processes designed to promote or supplement the process of psychic integumentation, then it seems appropriate to ask what are the cultural, as opposed to purely medical conditions to which this is a response. What, in Didier Anzieu's phrase, might be the terms of 'pathogenic impingement by the environment on the skin ego' which leads to the formation of these second skins?[16] While I am impressed by the implications of psychoanalytic accounts of the importance of the supportive and arousing tactile environment provided for the child in early life, I do not find it plausible to derive the sense of the vulnerability of the skin from the mother's or caregiver's failures of caressing technique or the monotonousness of their voice. I am inclined to wonder instead what might be the contemporary conditions of exposure to which the investment in the skin might be a response.

One kind of answer might be suggested by a discussion of the aesthetic theory of Walter Benjamin by Susan Buck-Morss, in which she emphasizes the close relations in modernity between the aesthetic, the late nineteenth-century cult of neurasthenia, and the techniques of anaesthesia. Assailed routinely by shock and sensory discomfiture of every kind, she argues, a modern subjectivity comes to be organized around the imperative need to filter, screen and block out excitations.[17] In the light of this, Freud's famous evocation of the origins of the ego in defensiveness may itself be read historically as a response to the same distinctively modern conditions of assault and saturation. To this might be added a prescient remark made by Marshall McLuhan in the course of a more recent discussion of the extending, exteriorizing effects of the modern communicative and reproductive media: 'In the electric age', he writes, 'we wear all mankind as our skin.'[18] In the first industrial revolution, the human body was extended and amplified, mostly for the enlargement of its locomotor apparatus. In the twentieth century and beyond, it is the nervous system rather than the arm or leg that is enhanced by technology, and therefore in the process transformed. In the epoch of electronic media, the actual skin that bounds us within our individual selves is dissolved away and replaced by a polymorphous, infinitely mobile and extensible skin of secondary simulations and stimulations, which both makes us more versatile by enlarging our psychic surface area, exposing us to more and different kinds of experience, and also numbs us, precisely because of the dazing overload of sensations which this synthetic pseudo-skin conducts.

If the skin is a screen and a filter, it is also the medium of passage and exchange, with the attendant possibility of violent reversal or rupture. The skin is the vulnerable, unreliable boundary between inner and outer conditions and the proof of their frightening, fascinating intimate contiguity. Thus, the threat of 'pathogenic impingement' from the outside is matched, as some have noticed, by an apparently new fear and fascination regarding the interior body, as expressed in fantasies of various kinds of eruption through or perforation of the skin from the inside. The skin has become intensely vulnerable and thoroughly unreliable in its combined incapacity to resist external threats and its tendency to harbour (but then to release) internal threats. In films such as *Videodrome* and the *Alien* series, the skin betrays what it is its function to guarantee, the integrity of the distinctions between internal and external, depth and surface, self and other, and the regulation of the passages between these regions. When, in contemporary horror fiction and films, the frail containing envelope of the skin is torn, dissolved, melted and lacerated, this is perhaps an apprehension in a violent mode of the growing fluidity of relations

between the self and its contexts and secondary instruments, a condition in which the skin is no longer primarily a membrane of separation, but a medium of connection or greatly intensified semiotic permeability, of codes, signs, images, forms, desires. In the reforming, infinitely reformable contemporary sensorium, the associations of the skin with transmission, passage and connection become more emphatic than its functions of screening, or separation. We start to learn to live, not so much with the famous body-without-organs of Deleuze and Guattari, but with the transbodily hyperorgan that the skin has become.

The increasing fear of skin cancer consequent upon the dramatic erosion of the ozone layer may be understood partly in the light of a certain doubling of the experience of skin, in its conjoined capacity to contain and to expose, in our relations to the earth itself. The flaying away of the ozone layer – from the inside out, we should note – results in a generalized vulnerability to the harmful rays of the sun, the fragility of the earth's protective shield stripping us all of a vital second skin. The exhortation to 'Practise Safe Sun' offered by one advertisement for suncream a few years back, trips a switch between openness to infection and vulnerability to sunburn, a switch which perhaps depends at some level on the association between AIDS and Kaposi's sarcoma, the previously rare form of skin cancer to which AIDS sufferers become vulnerable and which was indeed the first form in which the AIDS epidemic manifested itself in the US.[19] It also suggests and supplies a phantasmal identification between sunblock and the protective second skin of the condom. The condom protects against the ecstatic passage of bodily fluids, maintaining manageable distinctions between the inside and outside. The phallic, invasive sun is made safe by establishing a quasi-epidermal block or filter against its penetrating rays. No doubt there might be more to be said on the fear of light as sexual violation; such an enquiry would proceed via the myth of the flaying of Marsyas by Apollo, Daniel Schreber's paranoia about the punishing sun and Bataille's exploration of solar erotics. What may seem new is the actualized fear of a violation of the skin by the light that had previously been believed to nourish and sustain it. The flaying of the body by light and the compensatory fantasy of the body turned into a kind of light via libidinized glow or shine are brought together in the complex of the inscriptive-mirror I have described.

Another way of putting this might be to say that the skin becomes recruited to experiences that are more auditory than visual, insofar as the auditory involves the sharing or transmission of impulses rather than their localization. Indeed, McLuhan's remark may be an instance of an idealizing protective response to this condition of permeability and contingency, in its metaphorizing of the skin as a visualizable envelope or membrane. Modernity set visuality against the various ecstatic enlargements and invasions of modern auditory technologies, allowing the visual to retain its customary sensory privilege; one defining moment here might be the coming of sound to the movies in 1926, which bound the errant, unlocalized, and permeating voices of electronic technology (telephone, radio) into synchronicity. Not long afterwards, in *Brave New World*, Aldous Huxley was imagining a similar cinematic binding of other kinds of sensory impulse, in the idea of the 'feelies'. Though in one sense the digital technologies of postmodernity offer a mere actualization of the modern dream of the artificially reconstructed and unified sensorium – the psyche as prosthetic *Gesamtkunstwerk* – in practice the networks of sensory linkage, exchange and mutual transformation mean that the visual is no longer the master sense, providing the stable scene or frame within which auditory, olfactory, and tactile phenomena can be recombined. The immaculate modernist grid of manipulable, permutable possibilities suggested by the 'desktop' metaphor that has become universal in the operating systems of computers belies the fact that the screen has entered the consciousness of its users, and that its function as separating membrane, screening out unwanted stimulus, and marking the point of defining interface between the user and his or her object, is yielding to a much more complex interimplication of the user and the used. The screen was the privileged modernist form of mediated encounter or interface between the self and the world, imagined as these are as surfaces or membranes; the move away from the keyboard to the mouse, the touch screen, the voice command, and even the immediate control of screens by the control of brain impulses, along with the abandonment of the screen altogether implied by such developments as intelligent buildings and the implantation of information and communications technology, makes the screen only one switch in an infinity of possible sensory configurations and reconfigurations.

Though it makes little attempt to connect the psychological and the technological, contemporary psychoanalytic theory and therapy based upon the concept of 'psychic envelopment', such as that evidenced in the work of Didier Anzieu, Claudie Cachard, and others, might suggest that the sensory euphoria of postmodernity also gives rise to an agoraphobic exposure, and need for defence. But the very idea of exposure implies a certain visual consolation that may not be easily available in the emerging conditions I am evoking. Exposure suggests the condition of being reduced to an object for sight. The objectifying power of sight, which comes from its unique reliance on distance and separation, is capable of separating me from myself, of painfully dissociating the visualizable portion of me from the rest. But this very dissociation is what allows me to dissociate myself in turn from this dissociation of myself, allows recourse to what one can call recursive reparation: as the involvement of the eye in masochistic fantasy suggests, you can always watch yourself being watched. Vision is the most *ironic* sense.

It appears that the other senses, sometimes called the proximity senses because, unlike vision, they require some kind of contact, or even intermingling of substance, between the senser and the sensed, do not allow for such perspectival control. Paul Virilio has spoken of the new era of 'tactile telepresence' in which the old oppositions between the proximate and the remote, the present and the absent, will no longer obtain.[20] This would be an era in which everything distant would be capable of coming close, and the most intimate sensations would be capable of being abstracted and distanced from us.

All these developments leave the body – or the self's relation to its body and its newly dissolving limits – not merely exposed and open to the gaze, but unvisualizable. This is the particular nature of the epidermal jeopardy being mimicked and responded to in so many different contemporary forms of assault upon and reparation of the vanishing skin. The terror of skinlessness evoked by Gilles Deleuze in his characterization of the schizophrenic seems to match this experience:

> [T]here is not , there is no longer, any surface . . . The first schizophrenic evidence is that the surface has split open. Things and propositions no longer have any frontier between them, precisely because bodies have no surface.

The primary aspect of the schizophrenic body is that it is a sort of body-sieve. Freud emphasized this aptitude of the schizophrenic to grasp the surface and the skin as if they were punctured by an infinite number of little holes. The consequence of this is that the entire body is no longer anything but depth – it carries along and snaps up everything into this gaping depth which represents a fundamental involution. Everything is body and corporeal. Everything is a mixture of bodies, and inside the body, interlocking and penetration.[21]

There is an odd cooperation between the 'collapse of the surface'[22] evoked in the world of the schizophrenic and the euphoric projection of depth into surface found in Lyotard's *Libidinal Economy* and currently being lived out in the cultivation of fetishism, as practice and obsession in cultural-critical discourse. What is lost in both is what Lyotard calls the 'theatrical' configuration of surface with depth. Both characterize current anxieties about the loss of coherent body-image, or the possibility of effecting a spatio-temporal coincidence between the individual body, and the multiple simulation-body of transmitted affects. What both Deleuze and Lyotard miss is the necessity of a compromise between membrane and envelope; between the body-without-organs, or the body-as-infinite-surface and the various imaginary enclosures necessary to health and productivity. In this sense the grotesque mingling of masculine assault upon the skin and female repair of it imagined in Thomas Harris's *The Silence of the Lambs* is a perfect enactment of this contemporary predicament, and an instructive complication of the unilateral model of male violence proposed by Theweleit's account. In the context of the vanishing skin, the forms of dermographic assault upon the skin are essentially attempts at grafting the skin back on. The knife, the needle, the stylus, the pen, the whip, the eye, that perforate the skin, are currently also at work binding it together. We will see if we are going to turn out to be creatures capable of imagining less fetishized, petrifying and toxic forms of self-securing and self-envelopment.

A sizeable literature has established the connections between the violent mode of a modern epistemology, and the defacing encounter between surface and marker. In *Spurs*, Jacques Derrida suggests that philosophical style itself is nothing but this resumed meeting of female fabric and male stylus:

> In the question of style there is always the weight or *examen* of some pointed object. At times this object might only be a quill or a stylus. But it could just as easily be a stiletto, or even a rapier. Such objects might be used in a vicious attack against what philosophy appeals to in the name of matter or matrix, an attack whose thrust could not but leave its mark, could not but inscribe there some imprint or form. But they might also be used as protection against the threat of such an attack.[23]

Where Derrida sees an originary agony in all stylistics, Friedrich Kittler sees a more systematic, and historical, escalation of violence in modernist technologies of automated writing, with the displacement of the pen by the typewriter, and then by the typewriter's analogues, phonograph, telephone and cinema. Where the pen inscribes, the typewriter impacts. In the 'discourse network' that was already in place by 1900, the intimate economy of brain, hand, eye, line and paper is replaced by the violent, blind, tactile concussion of surfaces. 'All that remains of the real is a contact surface or skin, where something writes on something else', Kittler tells us.[24]

Perhaps one reason for our current, continuing interest in hysteria, and perhaps also the recent revival of the concept of trauma, is surely that we so envy the symptoms which we do not have. Indeed, perhaps what we mourn and covet is symptomatology itself: the lost apparition of the symptom. This hysteria-envy surfaces clearly in Paul Virilio's recent analysis of the universal conditions of technological 'telecontact', in which everything can touch everything else, at a distance. As in the coming of the typewriter, as explicated by Friedrich Kittler, with its splitting apart of the coordination of hand, eye and paper, everything takes place at a remove from the actual individual sensorium: but this general mediation produces an overwhelming sense of the intolerable immediacy and proximity of everything, in which nothing is in fact sufficiently apart from the self or from any other thing to allow it either to exist, in the Heideggerian sense of 'standing clear' or 'standing out' against some background, or to communicate, in the sense of a making common of what is separate:

> beyond the confines of proximity as we know it, prospective **telepresence** – and shared **tele-existence** with it – not only eliminate the 'line' of the visible horizon in favour of the linelessness of a deep and imaginary horizon. They also once again undermine the very notion of **relief**, with touch and **tactile telepresence at a distance** now seriously muddying not only the distinction between the 'real' and the 'virtual', as Cybersurfers currently define it, but also the very reality of the *near* and the *far*, thus casting doubt on our presence *here* and *now* and so dismantling the necessary conditions for sensory experience.[25]

This is hysterical writing in a literal sense, which is to say, a writing that finds a certain relief in the elaborate exhibition of the typographically impassioned surface which it is telling us has vanished; bold, italic and inverted commas seem to insist on the truth of its terms, a truth that is made to seem so inescapably and self-announcingly apparent that it has gouged its way into the page we are reading, or risen up dermographically from within it.

Virilio articulates (articulates against) the nausea of edgeless exposure that follows from having broken out of our skin. There is the dread of there being no inviolate, therefore violable, surfaces any more, no possibility any more of contact or contingency, as the modernist world of traumatic impact, concussion and repercussion gives way to interfaces, interactivity and the volatile coalescence of bodies. We may read this as a nostalgia for the palpable in a world in which palpability has evaporated into discourse and signification; and as approximations to the essentially skinless propinquity and immediatization of contemporary media.

The term 'immediatization' appears, attributed to Rémy Auxerre, a media analyst with certain resemblances to a Jean Baudrillard, in Salman Rushdie's *The Ground Beneath Her Feet*, a novel in which reflections on the traumatic breaking through of worlds into another is accompanied by forebodings of the loss of skin.[26] Whether in earthquake, that governing metaphor for the 'tectonic contradictoriness' of the contemporary self, or, in the remarkable chapter entitled 'Membranes', in the natal passage from East to West, accomplished through a 'tear in the sky', which allows the musician Ormus Cama, flying from Bombay to London, to glimpse 'miracles through the gash', the novel is full of the rapture of epidermal rupture.[27] But there is also apprehension about this failure of the skin. The rock-god Ormus Cama writes: '*My greatest concern is that I feel the fragility of our space and time. I feel its growing attenuation.*'[28] The narrator suggests that this attenuation encourages a primitivist return to the skin: 'It looks like it's scared us so profoundly, this fracturing, this tumbling of walls, this forgodsake freedom, that at top speed we're rushing back into our skins and war paint, postmodern into premodern, back to the future.'[29]

In Rushdie's novel, the narrator of which is a photographer, and is as much concerned with photography as with the seismic powers of mass media and rock and roll, the gash in the skin is always a figured gash, even as it seems to be an assault on figurality itself, a denial of figure's ground. This may then seem to demand a further act of tearing open, or stripping away, even if this threatens the loss of skin. The alternatives of tearing and binding are not recto and verso; rather, in the Möbian topology of contemporary epidermal culture, in which everything has been turned to the front, they form a continuous surface, since what is at stake in them is the continuity of surface itself.

So we are seeing that, alongside and within the intense longing for a scene on which to represent and make reparation for the loss of shape and surface, there is a longing for an assault upon the surface that will leave no mark, for a disfiguration that will erase – but visibly erase – the apparatus of figurality itself. Literature, performance and psychosis twist grotesquely together. The speaker in Samuel Beckett's *The Unnamable* grimly imagines himself as an organless, featureless egg in an extreme of defacement.[30] A patient known as Mr H went as far as cutting off his entire face with fragments of a mirror.[31] The face is both what is written on the face, and the faciality of the skin itself, the availability of the skin to bear inscriptions. It seemed not to be enough to remove the features of the face; the faciality of the face had to bear the brunt of the annihilating attack. But the stripping away of the features seems to reveal, even to be designed to reveal, the invariant ground of faciality, the face beneath the face, the unfigurable support of figurality.

Antonin Artaud, mistrusting his own body, colonized and infected as he felt it to be by God, language and history, just as the possessed of earlier ages may have felt their bodies to be the haunt of demons and agencies of putrefaction, sought a body remade in the immediacy of cry and gesture, a body mutilated into clamorous muteness. As Jacques Derrida has shown, this mutilation is in fact a blow against articulation, against the possibility of repetition in time and space, perhaps against the possibility of time and space as such, in so far as these are marked out on the originary ground or skin of the body. 'The body', Derrida suggests, 'must be autarchic . . . remade of a single piece.'[32] Artaud thought he had discovered the condition of radical, spiritual and bodily self-making in the drug-induced Peyote ritual practised by the Tarahumara people of Mexico, with whom he spent some months in 1936. In a note added in 1947 to the narrative of his experiences, which he wrote while incarcerated in the asylum at Rodez, Artaud seizes on the skin as the principle of autarchic uprightness:

> with Peyote MAN is alone, desperately scraping out the music of his own skeleton, without father, mother, family, love, god, or society.

> And no living being to accompany him. And the skeleton is not of bone but of skin, like a skin that walks. And one walks from the equinox to the solstice, buckling on one's own humanity.[33]

Here, Artaud rejects not only the spatial partition of organs across the skin, but also the top-to-bottom stratification of the body. The reimagined body of the Peyote ritual has its skin on the inside, and wears its skeleton like a second skin, or armour. This unthinkable body, at once flayed and reskinned, in which the skin bears the weight of intrinsic being rather than the traces of extrinsic meaning, allows one to be made from the inside out rather than the outside in.

The scarifier, the lacerator, the self-abuser, the piercer, all seek, like Artaud, to do violence to the primary violence that deprives me of my body, the violence of representation, naming, abstraction, the alienation of the body into significance. Theirs is an assault that goes beyond the attempt to efface and rewrite what is written on the skin: it is an assault upon the skin as the bearer or scene of meaning. It is an assault upon the apparatus of figuration, of which the skin is the privileged sign or locale. The skin is made to show, not appearance, but *apparition*, that which is immediately visible and readable, that which is, to remember the impressive, and instantly duplicable, self-mutilating performance of Richey Edwards, lead singer of the Manic Street Preachers, shortly before his own disappearance, '4 REAL'.[34] But all of this is, at the same time, also a rage against the loss of scene consequent upon a culture of tele-contact. Hence the melodramatic excess of figurings of the skin; melodrama is nostalgic, it forces the skin into presence by forcing it back in time, as in the rituals of the Modern Primitives, seeming to testify to the fact that the skin is always out of time.[35]

3 Disfiguring

Most cultures seem to have a myth of the primal marking of the skin; whether it is a story of the inauguration of rivalry and blood-guilt into the world, as with Cain's slaying of Abel, or the distribution of the animals of creation into their different habitats and functions, as indicated by the markings of their skins. Many such mythologies begin with the idea of a primal indifference: a generalized formlessness, the undifferentiated totality of a kind of white light. The beginning of time, the beginning of culture, the beginning of sin, the beginning of difference, the beginning of mixture, the beginning of death: all these may be imagined in terms of the marking of a previously immaculate surface. Time leaves its mark. There can be no time without deviation and difference, and no deviation or difference that is unmarked.

The marking of skin is the arrival of accident and contingency. Whatever it may be, the first, arbitrary, unnecessary event is a marring, a maculation. Behind every myth of the coming of writing lies a myth of the marking of bodies or faces previously dreamed perfect, by the traces of injury and death, by the lines of age.

But perhaps this story of immaculacy followed by marking is an illusion. Perhaps the very order of succession which enables the story of the making of marks, this marring of the countenance of things, to be recounted, is a secondary effect of this order of marking. Perhaps there only ever was contingency, and the unmarked skin merely the not-yet-marked skin. Perhaps it was inevitable that creatures who had evolved such hairless, vulnerable skins, which bore little in the way of permanent markings, but whose skins had so striking a capacity to take and bear marks of all kinds, would live in time, in the exposure to what happens to happen, in a way that creatures with less changeable skins would not.

Contingency is the absence of law. In a contingent world, there is no necessity for me to live this life rather than some other life. In a contingent world, there is no essential way in which things must inevitably turn out, only the contingent pressures of the accidental things that just happen. But there is a higher, or prior lawfulness in this subjection to the lawless contingency. The making of a mark breaks into the seamless continuity of things, and may often appear as an infraction of a law. Before the violent marking of a difference in things, there was no law that such a thing had in the end to happen. But after that violence has happened, it will – suddenly, but then irrevocably – always have been on the cards. The first mark is always utterly without precedent or preparation and, in that blinding instant, also long overdue. In reality, it is the evidence that there will always in the end have been a break in the fabric of time. As long as time somewhere has a beginning, it will have lurked as a possibility, like a virus dormant in eternity, for all time, which will then have been waiting for time to happen. The first crime is an infraction of a law that does not yet exist, since, without the possibility of crime, it does not yet need to exist. The first crime – the murder of Abel by Cain – can then fall under the sway of the law that it makes necessary, a law which by the same token is unjust, since it is applied retrospectively, to the one who committed a crime which did not yet exist. Time is crime. And time means matter too, bodies living in time, which is to say, bodies being marked with decay. Time is marked in bodies, and all bodies mark time.

In the order of marks, contingency and necessity continually change places. The law of the contingency of things is continually being rewritten as the law of the necessity of the contingency of things. The immaculate countenance of the earth is spoiled by some accident or injury. The mark of that injury then signifies that the countenance was never really clear or innocent of marks, but was always shadowed by the necessity of the accident that would come to mark it, to subject it thereafter to the law of marks. The law will attempt to harness the power that accrues to the mark. In penal branding, whipping, in the making of marks that are meant to last for life, the law mimics the prior law of liability, the law lurking in the undifferentiated primal mass of things that there would one day be a mark. You will not only always henceforth be marked as a felon; your mark will show that you were always going to be so marked.

If law is to bear down upon the body, then the skin is the medium or locale for this encounter. Inscribing its text on the body, law makes the body, and more specifically its skin, bear witness. In the penal marking of the body, the law is not only done, it is seen to be done; and this seeing-to-be-done is no mere reflection or re-echoing of the operations of punishment; rather, it is the nature and reach of the doing itself. In the mark incised or pricked or burned upon the body of the criminal, the law precipitates a lasting sign of its action, the letter of the law made actual and present in a continuing here and now. Whatever its primary meaning, this unfading mark connotes a secondary meaning, of the enduringness of the law, the law of marks, the letter of the law, the time of the law that is brought to bear upon the merely mortal time of the body.

The law enacts itself through markings, but we can posit that there is a higher or more primary lawfulness that manifests itself in markings. This higher law is called upon to some degree in every kind of spontaneous or immediate manifestation of a mark: the handprint which signs the cave-painting, the writing on the wall at Belshazzar's feast, the miraculous images deposited on the handkerchief of Veronica, or the Shroud of Turin, the burning handprints of devils and damned souls found in cloth, books and and tables,[1] the medium's planchette suddenly filled with writing, the fingerprint of the burglar, the silhouettes seared upon the wall at Hiroshima, and even the signature coiled in my DNA. This higher, lower law can perhaps be stated thus, and in the teeth of Yeats's 'things fall apart': *things come together*. Things of the world and beyond it sign themselves through the contact, impact, or printing of their surface upon another surface. The signing of a contract (that which is drawn together in the act) brings about a binding agreement that is also called a 'compact'. This mode of manifestation is immediate, faster than thought or even perception. It requires and allows no transcoding, no transliteration, no selection, no compression. What signs in this spontaneous impression, this sigillating impingement of things one upon another, is not a proposition, or a proper name, but the all-at-once, *tout d'un coup* here-and-now haecceitas of the very gesture of the signature. One must sign quickly, after all, without pausing for thought; and how hard it is to do that consciously, for example when we strive to replicate it under a suspicious eye or when we are required to sign a new credit card, occasions when we must ensure that the signature be like itself, which is to say unfalsifiably spontaneous,. Forging a signature, or imitating one's own, cannot be done letter by letter or word by word, for a signature belongs to a different order from writing: the immediate law or order of marks. A signature is therefore not to be inscribed, but stamped.

CAPITAL PUNISHMENT

Prisoners and slaves were marked with the signs of their condition, which often meant signs denoting their owners. But they were also frequently marked with what appears to be their own signs. In a mime by Herodas from the second century BC, a slave is threatened by his mistress with a whipping and a tattooing, which will mean that he 'will soon know himself when he has this inscription on his forehead'.[2] The reference is to the famous proverb 'Know Thyself'. The oracle at Delphi was inscribed with a siglum 'E', which was sometimes interpreted as standing for 'Know Thyself'. There seems to be the possibility that the slave would be tattooed, not just with the details of his crime, but with the injunction 'Know Thyself' itself. Other penal markings in the ancient world marked ownership and subordination by making subjects display marks signifying their own identities, rather than those of others. Plutarch relates that Athenians tattooed their Samian prisoners with a representation of the representative ship, the *samaina*, while Athenian prisoners were reciprocally tattooed with their symbol of the owl.[3] It may at first seem odd that the two sides should use each other's emblem to mark their prisoners, but it is not necessarily more plausible that prisoners would be marked with signs denoting their owners. If this kind of marking is seen as a degradation, then one might expect uneasiness about the master implicating their own signs in the degradation. To make the one marked bear their own sign, to show forth as literally as possible their own character, is at once to reduce them to the condition of a sign, and to degrade their sign to the condition of a body.

Law has often sought to identify itself with the law of marks. Slaves were branded in Greece with the character D, for δοῦλος (*doulos*), slave. Judicial branding and marking flourished in Europe during the eighteenth and nineteenth century especially for purposes of military discipline. Until the mid-nineteenth century, deserters from the British army might be branded on the forehead with the letter D, the brand being effected by an instrument that not only burned the flesh but crudely tattooed it by piercing it with needles arranged in the shape of the letter and rubbing gunpowder into the holes. The marking of the body with single letters is commonplace at various times: the letter K, for *kalumnia*, was used to mark bearers of false witness; Hester Prynne's letter A in Hawthorne's *The Scarlet Letter* refers back to this tradition. The great twentieth-century fabulist of judicial stigmatization, Franz Kafka had an abhorrence of the letter K, but adopted it nevertheless as his siglum. The mark of Cain is sometimes supposed to have been a single Hebrew character, *ot*, a character that came to have the meaning of 'a character' or 'sign' itself. The fact that the word 'character' means a stamped impression implies a link between having a self and being marked in this single way. The one marked, whether with a D, a K or an A, is marked for life. His life becomes a mere punctuation mark in time; he becomes characterized, stigmatized, for ever, unchangeably. The law takes him out of his own time, and submits him to its durance. He is made to mark time.

A signature appears different from a mark: it is the illiterate peasant who, presenting himself to perform an act of witness, makes his mark, his handprint, his thumbprint, or a cross, instead of forming a sequence of letters – the joined-up writing that marks the successful passage into literacy. But the peasant's incompetence also gives him access to a force, a force of necessity that bursts through the line of script, a force that is incommensurable with, perpendicular to writing. Marking literally cuts across writing, which makes it appropriate that it should traditionally be the cross that is made by the illiterate. Marking has as its basic form the chiasmus, the imposition rather than the juxtaposition. In handwriting, a cursive loop recoils upon itself in order the better to spring forward. The form of the cross, one line, crossed or crossed out by another, signifies the refusal of advance, reduces to the point of intersection, impact, incision. For Christians, the cross is the sign and the site of incarnation, the X which marks the spot, because it is where heaven and earth, the divine and the human orders, painfully intersect. Christ is nailed to the cross as the cross is nailed to itself. The sign of the cross always implicates the body in writing; it marks the inflicting of the law of absolute identity between Christ and man in the phenomenon of the stigmata. Thinking of the signature affixed about the cross, *Iesus Nazarethi Rex Judaeis*, Joyce's Leopold Bloom intuits the capital logic of its inuring mark: 'Iron Nails Ran In'.[4] In reading records of trials in the British Public Records Office, one will sometimes come across the mark of a red cross of St Andrew next to a name, to signify that the person has been executed. The signs of the cross stamped at intervals in the printed

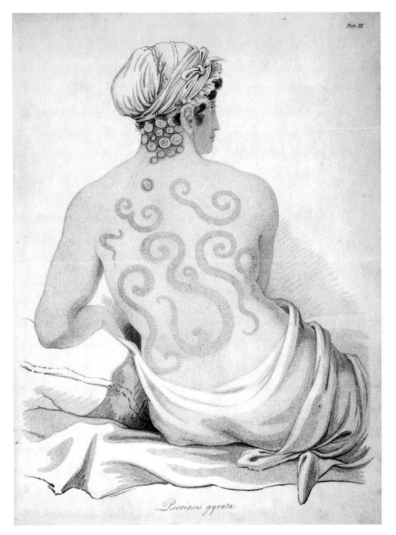

liturgy mark the points at which the priest must make the consecrating sign of
the cross, the temporal sequence of the spoken words being suspended, or rolled
up on itself for the period of the gesture. The cross, the mark, is the skewering
of syntax. This is why stamping is a warrant rather than a claim, and embodies
rather than merely signifies authority; absolute, entire and uninflected.

   In the West, penal or judicial marking of the skin appears later than the
ornamental marking of the body. The practice of ornamental tattooing seems
to have been unknown among Greeks and Romans, though the branding and
tattooing of slaves and criminals was common from 500 BC onwards. Indeed, it
is perhaps the very reservation of marking for these classes of person that made
ornamental marking unappealing. In fact, penal marking often marks a difference between the civilized, or law-governed peoples and those peoples they

Tattoo: a convoluted dragon.

stigmatize as savage, lawless and, as proof of this, self-stigmatizing. So the law of marks marks a break as well as a convergence; it marks the absolute coincidence of law and the body, but also marks an absolute break between an epoch of law and an epoch of wanton decoration.

One might even see this temporal break enacted spatially in the play of the two dimensions of physical letters: the vertical and the horizontal, or the line and the loop. The vertical suggests that letters are impressed or incised into their surfaces. Cuneiform scripts preserve the memory of the resistance of the clay or the stone, schooling the stylus to rectangles and chevrons formed from separate straight lines. The fantastic arabesques which are characteristic of many tattooing and skin-marking practices, especially among groups like the Picts and other similarly daubed and pictured peoples, make the body into a temporal topology, folding time into the skin, unfurling the skin into time, tempting and drawing the eye to follow the complexity of their lines. Curves and crossings-over suggest a medium that allows the stylus to slip and slide across its surfaces, multiplying forms, allowing individuality, accident, improvisation and signature: style, in fact. When the surface is not incised, the lines need not be broken up, and so can bend over themselves. Law, or its phantasm, looks to the first mode or dimension of writing. Something like literature will be coming about in the swirls and coils that move across the surface, bewildering and perfecting the letter in self-touchings.

A single letter stands for ornament bent to meaningfulness, the searing noontime of the law rather than the twilit twinings of scrolls, vines, serpents and leaves. Penal and punitive markings, the markings of law, may borrow these efflorescent effects, but aim to temper and discipline them. The branding iron scorches its mark in a moment, and is meant to be read instantaneously. It knits together into its tight nub of *fiat* the diffuse, tangled, procrastinating, indolent time extravasating across the skins of backward peoples. Ornamental tattooing borrows, extends, conjugates and populates the body. Penal marking, by contrast, confiscates, limits and divides it. The letter replaces the complex, iterated chromo-thermodynamics of flesh and image, line and colour, with the absolute hot-cold, hard-soft of inscription. The ornamental tattoo preserves and awakens the repetitive movements of hands over the body, the fecundity of the caress: the brand or penal tattoo suggests the once-and-for-all application of an instrument.

Not all penal markings involve single characters, and in Greece some slaves and captives were tattooed with lines of poetry as well as single characters. As late as 836, Saints Theodorus and Theophanes were punished for their venera-tion of images by being scourged and having twelve lines of verse cut into their flesh, leading them to be known as γράπτοι (graptoi), written on. However, a magic potency does seem to attach to a single initial when it is stamped or incised. For a single character is a double violence, a reduction of the reduction that is language itself: it is language reduced to absolute picture, sealed or sutured into ideogrammic instantaneity. The initial letter therefore borrows from the pictoriality it is meant to replace. The fact that such characters are also often credited with magical powers to protect, heal, or transform is the reflex of this power of gathering or arresting the living body. Coptic fellahin considered the sign of the cross tattooed upon their wrists to be a protection against disease and ill spirits.[5] Occult and medical texts of the early modern period also provide evidence for the inscription of the body with marks and symbols for magical purposes. So the letter can give life as well as kill. Just as the body may be subdued by being reduced to the condition of a sign, so magical inscriptions – the characters inscribed upon the fragment inserted under the tongue of the Golem, for instance – have the power to give speech or movement to an inanimate body.

OVERWRITING

From the very beginning of judicial marking, the trade in the removal or mod-ification of the tattoo or brand has flourished. There are two ways in which a disfiguring bodily mark can be removed. One is through effacement, for exam-ple by razing or cauterizing, a further disfiguring of the disfiguring mark. But the skin is a thing of time, which means that it can never suffer revocation, but only revision. Something will always remain of the first defacement and deci-sion, the first excision of the body's immaculate autonomy. The fact that many judicial systems forbid the tattooing of minors embodies the belief that those who are unable to make irreversible decisions on their own behalf not only do not own their own persons, but have not advanced into irreversibility itself, have not crossed the line into the irreversible time of decision and incision. The other, subtler and less drastic way of removing a mark from the skin is to subject it to overwriting or extrapolation. Athenaeus, writing around AD 200 of the cruelty of the Scythians, records the following method employed by their Thracian vic-tims for displacing the figures traced on their skin by the Scythians' buckles:

[M]any years afterwards, the wives of the Thracians who had been treated in this manner effaced this disgrace in a peculiar manner of their own, tattooing also all the rest of their skin all over, in order that by this means the brand of disgrace and insult which was imprinted on their bodies, being multiplied in so various a manner, might efface the reproach by being called an ornament.[6]

The shaming 'A' which Hester Prynne is made to wear in Nathaniel Hawthorne's *The Scarlet Letter* is never revoked, but is transformed, by extension and extrapolation. Eventually, the badge of shame which is intended to maintain the absolute hold of the past over the present, comes to signify the revisability of the past and the present. Hester Prynne is not only an adulteress, but a seamstress, and the implicature of the needle is oblique to the caricature of the brand. The full stop of her shame is taken up into the variorum of her life's work.

Not surprisingly, the law has practised its own brand of overwriting. For the law can carry the making of marks to the point where it destroys signification itself; and for human beings, the possibility of signification is always dependent upon some thought of the skin. The revolting and extreme practices of military discipline that took a grip in Europe during the period of colonialism and slavery represent an attempt to take into law the orgiastic practices of scourging and flagellation of previous eras. When 200 lashes were comfortably enough to induce death through sepsis or shock, punishments of 1000 lashes were designed, not to mark the body of the offender so much as to destroy its capacity to bear marks. Under these circumstances, the only point of the neat and decimalized systems of counting, with their divisions of 25, 50 and 100, along with the ledgers in which such punishments were recorded, was to degrade the body into arithmetic. The law here is concerned not with appropriate penalties, not with establishing exact and measured retribution, but with the denial that there could be anything other than law, here made identical with the establishing of quantitative equivalence, ever. Law will be exacted *exactly*, to the letter. Perhaps the spectacle of punishment, like the extremities of hanging, drawing and quartering of an earlier age, was also designed to bring about a sort of higher body, a general military corporality, bracing together the ship, the regiment in its remorselessness.

And yet bodily markings can also act to hold or contain this absolute dissolution of the surface. It was believed that a tattoo of a crucifix offered some protection against the pain of a flogging. The Australian convict John McCarthy, who was subject to floggings of almost unbelievable severity, had a tattoo on his chest of the crucified Saviour bleeding, and an angel catching his blood in a cup, which has allowed Hamish Maxwell-Stewart and Ian Duffield to reflect on the interchange between the figurative and the literal:

On every occasion, the assembled convicts would have seen two passions. First, there was McCarthy hanging limp from the triangle, his 'Back like a

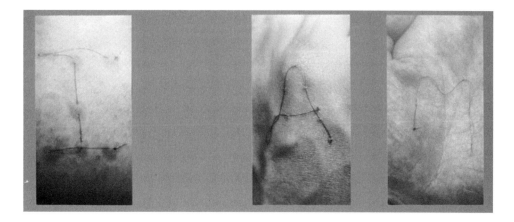

Bullocks liver and . . . his shoes full of Blood'. Secondly, there was the passion pricked out on his blood-splattered chest: 'Crucifix Our Saviour bleeding on it [and] an angel with a cup catching the blood.'[7]

The point of such floggings seems to have visibly to annihilate the skin's power of holding, of bearing marks intact. Here, the savage and remorseless overwriting of the skin reduces it to a kind of bloody nothing, an invisibility in plain view. Even the implements with which such floggings were effected seem designed to erase the possibility of leaving legible traces, in their own kind of overwriting. Although the infamous cat-o'-nine-tails may have retained some reference to the sacred or consecrating powers of the three times three, its real point was to allow the widest possible area of flesh to be tortured with each lash. Images such as those borne by McCarthy provide a picture of religious suffering which holds suffering together with meaning (the etymological meaning of the word 'religion' is a binding).

Historians of tattooing have frequently observed a duality acted out through the marking of the skin. The skin provides the means for the law to enact itself upon the flesh of transgressors, bringing together the penalty and the meaning of the penalty, making, as we say, the punishment fit the crime. As I observed in chapter 1, the word 'fit' often brings with it an epidermal idea of a match, a hand-in-glove coincidence of inner and outer, a body and its skin. But the power that is displayed in and through the body of the one whose body becomes pure signification can be captured and reorientated. The abolition of compulsory tattooing of prisoners in the French penal service during the nineteenth century was followed by a huge increase in the activity of voluntary tattooing.

The Judaeo-Christian law of marks is enacted between the alternatives of Leviticus 19:28 – 'Ye shall not make any cuttings in your flesh for the dead, nor print any marks upon you: I am the Lord' – and Galatians 6:17, in which Paul declares 'From henceforth let no man trouble me: for I bear branded on my body the marks of Jesus.' These two texts mark the polarity of the mark as the sign of discredit and sin, and the mark as the guarantee of salvation. Leviticus

Lisa Deanne Smith, detail of "I AM" from *I AM EXTREMELY RATIONAL*, 1996, print of letters sewn into human skin with hair found in public places.

both prohibits marking – in the chapter which also forbids the cutting of the corners of the field and of the beard – and also enjoins the act of cutting involved in circumcision. Circumcision is circumspect cutting, a mutilation hemmed in with rules and rituals, which takes extreme care, or exhibits the signs of taking care, to be as close as it can be to a non-touch. Marking is at the heart of Judaic religious thought. A marked man is one who is a target (a mark means a target). But a marked man is also a protected, reserved man, for God is the source of all markings. Even the mark of Cain, spoken of very obliquely in Genesis, is intended not to mark him out, but to protect him from being slain: 'And the Lord appointed a sign for Cain, lest any finding him should smite him.' This apotropaic mark reappears in chapter 9 of Ezekiel, which describes a vision of God taking vengeance upon the corrupt city of Jerusalem. He first of all commands a man clothed in linen and equipped with a writer's inkhorn to go through the city, 'and set a mark upon the foreheads of the men that sigh and that cry for all the abominations that be done in the midst thereof' (Ezekiel 9:4). Six armed men are subsequently sent through Jerusalem to slay all those who are unmarked. This recalls other instances of protective markings, notably the marking of their doorposts with paschal blood to protect their firstborn from the Angel of Death (Exodus 12:21–8). Paul may be recalling this story of the mark in Galatians 6:17. His comments occur at the end of a discussion of the idea of rebirth, and contrast this branding with the now empty rite of circumcision: 'For neither is circumcision anything, nor uncircumcision, but a new creature.' (Galatians 6:15).

On the one hand, then, there is the mark of the sinner, mark of the beast, disfigurement of the body formed in the image of the Lord. On the other, there is the mark of salvation, the mark as the sign of the body reborn, redeemed, a new creature. On the one hand, the outsider, the lawless pagan: on the other, the circumcised, the one knowing and known to the law, marked out for redemption. Law will make use of both modalities of marking.

INURING

In marking the skin, part of the point is to set the skin at naught, to treat it, not as the outward part of a living being, but as an object. And yet the skin itself is indispensable to that process; the living quality of the skin, the *cutis*, is necessary to the process whereby it is made two-dimensional, reduced to a *pellis*, pelt or pall. Writing instantiates a play between hard and soft, durable and malleable, mineral and organic. When the stylus writes in the soft clay, it is hard to its soft. But when the clay bakes hard, it arrests the nervous fluidity of the writing hand. This commerce of hard and soft is accompanied and interpreted by an exchange between wet and dry. The drier and less organic the surface which receives writing, as with the baked tablets of the Sumerians, the more permanently signs can be fixed. For Europeans, Latin, the language of law, learning and authority, always contains an implicit visualization as public inscription or prescription (set, as we say, in stone), on a column or a monument, or set in

Black Letter. But, when it comes to paper, the more desiccated the surface, the more easily it will absorb the ink deposited upon it. However, if that surface is too absorbent, as in blotting paper, there is nothing to fix or arrest the ink, which then flows away from the nib. Wet or greasy paper, by contrast, repels the ink.

In marking the flesh, the law indicates that it is harder, more enduring, than the soft, vulnerable flesh. The flesh, by contrast, can grow back around its wound, borrowing the hardness of the wound. When we say that someone has become 'inured' to pain, we are borrowing a metaphor from the Latin *inurere*, to incise by burning, or to brand. When someone is given the law, they are given something of the law's insensitivity, the coldness of the decree that is joined to the vengeful burning of the brand. The flesh can become harder than that which marks it, can give itself coldness and hardness. If the living mobility of the sinuous is often involved in tattoos, they also often assume the images of cold-blooded and shell-covered creatures, like lizards and snakes. The past participle of *iurere* is *iustum*, coinciding therefore with the word for the law of the social body in Latin, the *ius*, as opposed to the *lex* of statute law, or the *fas* of divine law. It is necessary for the surface to yield to the iron or stylus that marks it; but, if the mark is not to dissipate, if the action of marking is not to destroy itself, then it is the surface, not the centre, which must *hold*.

The act of writing has been so closely linked to the hand that all these abstract possibilities have bodily and sensory correlatives. The hard is that which resists the hand, forcing it to cramp and concentrate its movements. The warm and the soft – wax, clay – are a kind of reciprocal, emollient flesh, which soften the hand and finger. When wax or clay dries, it seems to form a scar or cicatrice, which seals in the meaning, as though a skin had formed over it, protecting it from degradation and change. It is the body that writes, and in writing, discovers, or bestows a skin wherever in the world it writes.

The practice of sealing – from Latin *sigillum* – concentrates together the impressing of a mark or visible form and the closure of a surface. The signet ring stamps its authorizing mark in the formless wax, and the resulting device then forms a seal for an envelope or a document. The seal, with its mark, first breaks and then completes and guarantees the epidermal integrity of the object that is sealed. The incising of solemn marks always has this symbolic reference to the body, the integrity of which is first violated, and then restored in a new form, that pretends to be original.

Writing is painless. But the fact that writing seems to have an ineliminable reference to the skin, as its ideal ground or surface, implies hurt and injury as the counterpart of law. If letters are imagined, not as resting on a surface, but as being incised into it, then that surface cannot be imagined except as patient but suffering, passive yet impassioned by the signifying touch. Writing awakens its mute, receptive surface into life, by constituting it as a surface. For beings in whom the reddening and darkening of the flesh is both signification of stimulus and itself stimulating (at once designating and transmitting alarm, fear, pleasure, arousal), the making of marks is an intense affair. We speak of 'angry' marks left in the skin of the victims of violence, or 'livid' marks, where lividness is also the sign of anger. The anger of the oppressor has been caught and pre-served in their skin, becoming their skin's anger at its own violation. The skin's capacity to bear and retain marks is also a capacity to transfer affect from body to body.

In penal marking, the hard appears to impose itself relentlessly and unbendingly upon the soft. This is in violent contradiction to the alternative trajectory which Michel Serres has made out in the history of culture, in which energy is gathered up as information, the obdurateness of inhuman nature is taken up more and more into the softness of signs, codes and culture.[8] Certainly the physical embodiments of writing seem to have undergone this passage from the hard to the soft, from the tablets of the law through to the virtuality of digital lexis, in which words are at once permanent and erasable, absolute and abstract. In digital text, both the surface and that which is inscribed upon it have dissolved. Or perhaps we should say that digital writing has taken the play of surface and stylus up into itself, as so many designs on the skin, mermaid, crab, dragon, incorporate secondary, represented skins of their own. Nowhere is this allegorized more obviously than in the ubiquity of the word 'brand' itself, which has been in use since the early 1800s to signify a particular company or product line, which takes itself to market in the form of a mark. The brand here is no longer literal, but aims to purloin some of the enigma of the literal. The production of a brand is the display of the mark of a necessity, an essence. The real, it may seem, is what hurts. And yet the age of digital writing, of ubiquitous signification, seems to have brought about a nostalgic return of the bracing encounter of the hard and the soft, in the imagery and practices of contemporary skin marking.

MARKING TIME

The two kinds of skin markings, letter and picture, discourse and figure, encode absolute and empty time. The law that exacts its everlasting marks is a law of vengeance, measure and ordeal, enacted in linear time. The marks of law mark the entry of law into time. This is the law of the line, the line to which time is reduced, and the line that divides different times absolutely one from another. This is why the coming of the law often involves the forbidding of marking. *Tattoo* is close to *taboo*. When the savage judicial marking of human bodies began to pass away from the penal systems of Europe (passing across into colonial locations), the second half of the nineteenth century saw a fascination with a different kind of marking: the taxonomic attention to and ordering of self-markings among the poor, the mad, the criminal and the deviant. During the nineteenth century, the word 'stigmata' began to be used by medical writers to signify the essential characteristics of conditions such as hysteria, degeneration and criminality, often in distinction from the 'accidents' which signified non-essential features of these conditions.

The assumption grew in the literature on tattooing that, far from being a punishment to be feared, self-marking was an innate degenerative tendency, which was likely to appear under conditions of boredom and underemployment. Convict ships in particular were thought to breed epidemics of body-marking. This is the resurgence again of a kind of waste time; arrested on the body are the marks of what overflows this schedule, the eddying indolence, the entropic, infantile shilly-shally of self-attention. Self-marking, as in Joyce's evocation of the masturbatory writer Shem in *Finnegans Wake*, covering his own body in excremental daubings, like the self-mutilations so endemic in prisons, is the sign of the refusal to 'do time'. As we will see in the chapter that follows, hysterics were similarly thought to be marked with the unmistakable – but so easy to mistake – marks of simulation and malingering.

Whether it is an exhibition of a penalty or a redemption, marking is a making good, in which the exhibition of the mark is part of the equation. This is an equation that aims either to refuse or to reverse time. It borrows and transforms the skin's tendency to gather and retain the marks of injury and accident. It trammels up accident and change in representation. Marking is re-marking. The marked skin allows the past and present to communicate, easily, running backwards and forwards. The mark in my skin is a destiny, a portent of what I may become, as in the explication of moles, or birthmarks, or chiromancy. Thus what I will have become is that which I will always have been meant to have been. Marks in the body are foldings of time, bookmarks that look forward to the future that will loop back to them, the body made pluperfect.

The order of marks is the order of identity, of immediate resemblance, in which everything can be the image of everything else, because everything can both make its mark and be made to bear the mark of everything else. The law of marks, the law enjoining conjunction, the principle I enunciated earlier that *things come together*, strives against all differentiations of time, place, person and form, all the aching space and difference between things. It dreams of a primal and a final compaction, in which every offprint will be returned to its source, every simulacrum will fly back to its original, every coin to its matrix, every petal to its bud and flame to its spark; a Big Crunch in which time and space themselves will be slammed tightly together like the pages of an unopened book.

Because of this, the law of marks has hitherto always been rare and absolute. It represents the occasional, redemptive irruption into successive time of a folded-together, instantaneous time. It is precisely because of this power that the making of marks has been associated with the extension and distribution of power, with the replications and repetitions of mass communications. They have their beginnings, not with the technologies of phonography, photography or even printing, but with numismatics and the practices of sealing and the casting of metals from moulds. They represent the extension into mortal, linear time of the logic of the mark, the attempt to deflect the singular event of the mark into the general logic of writing.

We have perhaps arrived at the beginning of an age in which the logic of the mark has been finally captured within mortal time. As Michel Serres has recently suggested in his *Hominescence*, we live at the threshold of an era in which there will no longer be any distinction possible between the model and the copy, the code and its embodiment, theory and the world.[9] Genetic research has revealed coding to be the very stuff or flesh of things. In such a period, it is not the copy, but the experience of the 'live' – mediated, yet immediate, which predominates. Photography presented itself to Walter Benjamin as a powerful irruption of the previously unapprehensible instant into ordinary time and perception – 'the dynamite of the tenth of a second'. Paul Virilio points to the acceleration and generalization of the photograph as an image of what he calls the 'over-exposure' of the contemporary world, in which there is no longer any delay or gap between originals and images. The intervals and extensions, both temporal and spatial, of a previous era yield place to a continuous interface. The law of marks was once powerful because, unlike everything else, which occupied space and took time, it testified to an instantaneity. But a world run at maximal speed, with communications which operate literally at the speed of light, is a world which operationalizes the law of marks, or self-impressing signatures. We are seeing, says Virilio, 'the emergence of a new conception of time, which is no longer exclusively the time of classic chronological *succession*, but now a time of (chronoscopic) *exposure* of the duration of events at the speed of light'. We must look forward to living in 'an *intensive present*, spawned by the limit-speed of electromagnetic waves and no longer registered in chronological time – past-present-future – but in chronoscopic time: underexposed-exposed-overexposed.'[10] Once rare and redemptive, the law of marks seems to have become routine and ubiquitous.

At such a time, the desire for a return of the lost rarity of the law of marks may be seen; whether it is in the desire for a model of the self based upon trauma, or in the politics of lines drawn in the sand, or the practices of piercing, marking and punctuating ordeal applied to the body. I am about to suggest that the epidermal justice-machine of Kafka's 'In The Penal Settlement' anticipates our nostalgia for this law of marks.

PRESCRIPTION

What makes the marking of the skin different from marking paper, what seems in fact to make it the origin or model of the marking of paper, is its reference to time. The marked skin means memory, means never being able or willing to forget.

The mark of law is enacted both in absolute linearity and in absolute reversibility. Law is a system for making the past and the present commensurate, the present and the future in balance. Without penalty, law would always be owing. Law aims for absolute equality between a deed and the penalty, crime and retribution. It is because law ranges time in a line, or irreversible sequence, that it can give itself the power of folding time over on itself, in exact equivalence. We have seen that, as retribution, law must not only come last (the last judgement), it must come first; for there to have been crime, there must have been law to be broken. The marked body is the sign of this meeting and marrying of disjunct times. As I wondered earlier in this chapter, Cain kills Abel, but what law does he break? The law that his own act institutes as prior to it; thus Cain is marked with the primal mark. Cain is marked with the sign of the deserter; but, like certain Greek slaves who, according to one ancient commentator, were marked, like an *ex libris* plate, with the words, *kateche me, pheugo: stop me, I'm a runaway*,[11] he is marked in order that he can never desert, that he will always be at home in his wanderings.

Kafka's 'In The Penal Settlement' is the story of an explorer who is the guest of the commandant of a prison camp. The commandant shows him a machine of execution known as the Harrow, which kills its victim by slowly pricking the details of his crime into his flesh by needles.[12] Kafka's hideous writing machine cannot now not be read as the direct, unconscious inscription of such processes of inscription. In this self-explicating allegory, the story imprints itself as forcefully and corporeally as the very process of inscribing the law which it presents. Like the body of the condemned prisoner, the story seems to have no interiority, no curiosity or secret, no concealed or implicit backside. Law, like psychoanalysis and the other privileged expressions of the discourse network, bypasses consciousness and is made to appear directly on the body of the subject (the subject here being literally, in this story in which everything is done to the letter, the one who lies underneath, the support, the platen, the receiving bed). The text which shows all this seems itself to be inscribed by the truth it inscribes, locked between the recto and verso of its pages as immovably as the condemned man is inserted between the Designer and the Bed.

But the machine (or perhaps we should say the two machines, the device written of in Kafka's story and the machinery of that writing itself) goes wrong. Realizing that the explorer, to whom he has been explicating the glories and mysteries of the machine, is not convinced of the justice of the old way of execution, the officer takes the place of the condemned man under the Harrow. And then the machine appallingly, absurdly begins to destroy itself, vomiting up its own mechanical innards in place of the human body that it ought to deliver, just in time, at the fulfilment of its sentence, and in the demonstration of the demonstration, to its ready-made grave. There is a horror and a violence in everything being brought to the surface, in everything being made a matter of surface, in the way of the old law. But the story itself seems not to be able to articulate the nature of the different horror, when the defining, violent encounter between the surface and the inscribing force fails. Does the machine of Kafka's own allegorical demonstration itself fail as a result? Or is its aim to open up a gap between itself and the mode of law's inscription? Does it know its meaning, or is its meaning written involuntarily through it? The story might be available to be read, not only as the figuration of a traumatic assault on a surface, but also as the dread of a failure of the surface, the giving way of embodiment.

In his remarkable meditation on Kafka's story, Jean-François Lyotard marks out in it a conflict between two modes or moments of touching. For Lyotard, Kafka writes of the violent touch of the law, which demands to be written directly on the body, rather than merely being applied to it. Lyotard's concern is with the topography and the temporality of this typography. On what, and in what time, does the law inscribe itself? The law wants to impose its violent figuring touch upon what at first and in the end must slip through its fingers, namely an experience of an indeterminate preconceptual 'here and now' of the body that can be in no way prefigured or prescribed. This 'infant' body knows nothing of law or language, for it has not yet received their touch or taken their print. Lyotard identifies this groundless, lawless being in the here and now of corporeal experience, in which one is 'exposed in space-time and to the space-time of something that touches before any concept and even any representation', with the aesthetic:

> To be aesthetically (in the sense of the first Kantian *Critique*) is to be there (*être-là*) here and now . . . This *before* is not known, obviously, because it is there before we are. It is something like birth and infancy (Latin *in-fans*) – there before we are. The *there* in question is called the body. It is not I who am born, who is given birth to. I will be born afterwards, with language, precisely in leaving infancy. My affairs will have been handled and decided before I can answer for them – and once and for all: this infancy, this body, this unconscious remaining there my entire life. When the law comes, with my self and language, it is too late. Things will already have taken a turn. And the law in its turn will not manage to efface the first turn, this first *touch*. Aesthetics has to do with this first touch, which touched me when I was not there.[13]

What matters most about Lyotard's autistic aesthetic of self-touching is that it leaves no mark, because there is not yet a ground or surface in place to retain the trace. It is this which makes the temporality of this primal touch, the temporality upon which we must make it rest to conceive it at all, so complex. For temporality works through the making and retaining of marks and is therefore of the order of inscription. To see this first touch as *at first* – first a surface, then what comes to mark it – is mistakenly to have preinscribed it with its place in that order of temporal succession.

When it is a question of an art that would manage an encounter with this primary corporeal aesthetics, Lyotard's account has a more austere and destructive character. Discussing musical experimentation, for example, he writes of a writing that would not merely apply itself to a given surface (the blank slate of the medium, or of cultural tradition), but would scour or scratch away the surface of the inscription: 'I'd like to falsify the value of the prefix 'e' to hear in *écriture* something like a 'scratching' – the old meaning of the root *scri* – *outside of*, outside any support, any apparatus of resonance and reiteration, any concept and pre-inscribed form. But first of all *outside any support*.'[14] The avant-garde art which would make contact with that which has no concept is characterized no longer by the lightest of caresses, but by the incendiary destruction of contact itself:

There would not first be a surface (the whole tradition, heritage, memory) and then this stroke coming to mark it. This mark, if this is the case, will only be remark. And I know that this is how things always are, for the mind which ties times to each other and to itself, making itself the *support of every inscription*. No, it would rather be the flame, the enigma of flame itself. It indicates its support in destroying it. It belies its form. It escapes its resemblance with itself.[15]

The primary touch of the infant aesthetic as conceived by Lyotard has certain resemblances to what Levinas thematizes as the ethical condition of proximity, which Levinas regularly represents as a pure touch or contact without mark, residue or inscription. Where, for Lyotard, the aesthetic is the traceless touching that leaves no trace, for Levinas, the ethical relation is characterized by a contact that is too immediate to be susceptible to representation. But, like Lyotard, Levinas nevertheless characterizes this immediacy of contact as a rupture:

> The *ethical* . . . indicates a reversal of the subjectivity which is *open upon* beings and always in some measure represents them to itself, positing them and taking them to be such or such (whatever be the quality, axiological, practical, or logical, of the thesis that posits them), into a subjectivity that enters *into contact* with a singularity, excluding identification in the ideal, excluding thematization and representation – an absolute singularity, as such unrepresentable. This is the original language, the foundation of the other one. The precise point at which this mutation of the intentional into the ethical occurs, and occurs continually, at which the approach *breaks through* consciousness, is the human skin and face. Contact is tenderness and responsibility.[16]

What matters, in such contact between self and other, is not meaning or understanding. As with Kafka's writing machine, there is nothing but the contact itself: 'This utterance of the contact says and learns only this very fact of saying and learning – here again, like a caress.'[17]

Both Lyotard and Levinas seek from the skin figurations of the nonfigural: the image of a touching without marking, a writing without residue, a weightlessness, nearness and immediacy. The skin is now reserved as that which eludes visibility, the ground on which the visible is written and which itself can thus be seen only in intimate revelatory flashes: 'The law takes a grip . . . Features have to be deciphered, read and understood like ideograms. Only the hair, and the light that emanates from the skin escape its discipline.'[18] This is perhaps why both Levinas and Lyotard are reluctant to thematize the skin; they want the skin to remain invisible, unfigured, and yet able to touch and be touched through the blind palpations of metaphor, the nudgings and insurgences of touch into discourse.

And yet, writing's element is time. When a mark is made, it is made, as a sound is uttered, at a certain time, and in a certain place. But the time of writing, as we have by now been so thoroughly taught, is the time, or the unpredictable many times, of its revisitations. Writing writes in anticipation of these revenances, it is pitted by the impact of all these foreseen, unforeknown futures.

Time is therefore written into writing with invisible ink. According to a traditional metaphor, the skin is written by time in just the same way as time is written into writing, its lines and furrows being said to be the work of time's pen, or chisel or plough. Time's writing on the skin, or the concealment of that writing through cosmetics or cosmetic surgery, is our meaning: but it is a meaning that was never meant, or intended, in the way that a written mark inscribed on a surface represents a decision. It is the way we come to mean, the meaning we come to have, through time. In this sense, the figure of time writing on the skin is itself a protective anthropomorphism, which projects a scene of here-and-now writing on a here-and-now surface – as though time could gather to a point and make its mark at a moment *in time* – to make sense of a writing of time that is really a writing through time.

If time writes the skin, then the skin can also be thought of as writing time. Assailed by marks, the skin possesses the capacity to regenerate itself, to grow out of, as well as into disfigurement. The skin marks time partly by effacement: by the healing of lesions, and the reassertion of the surface against every assault. The skin's way of writing time is indeed to write it out. The skin is a soft clock, which we wind up whenever we mark it; for when we mark the skin, and await its healing, we can make time run backwards. No other feature of our physical lives offers so magical a promise of reversibility. When we attempt to countermand time by artificially effacing its writing, smoothing out wrinkles with emollients, hitching up the face and the breasts, sucking out the adipose tissue from thighs and belly, we attempt to mimic the skin's own powers over time. So the skin *is* nothing but time, and yet, because the skin marks time, and can even reverse it, it can sometimes seem, like us, to be at odds with time, and therefore on our side against it.

It is for this reason that the mortified skin comes forward so insistently in the contemporary world, in which time, no less than place, has become multiplied and immaterialized. Mortification used to be a making visible of the here and now of the body, of the body *as* the here and now, in order to point away from it, to a longer, or different temporality. The purulence, the corruption, the visible suffering of the body, were all to be testimony to its subsequent redemption. Christ's suffering body on the cross was itself an earnest of its glorification to come, just as the breaking of the bread was the necessary part of its transfiguration into Christ's already transfigured body. In Christian traditions of mortification, disfiguration is a necessary prerequisite for transfiguration.

Contemporary mortification borrows from this history, but to very different effect. Contemporary mortification does not aim to put the body in proleptic memory of its death, but to transfix the body in its presence. Medieval mortification attempted to transport the body into its redemption by accelerating its decay and death; contemporary mortification attempts to transport the body into its suffering, transfigured, ceaseless being. The body is indispensable to transcendence, for now our need is for a transcendence of the body in the body. This is not simply the replacement of a spiritual with a corporeal logic, since, to be sure, the latter is already operational in medieval mysticism, as Piero Camporesi and recent feminist explorations of female corporeal mysticism have shown.[19] But in earlier periods, the body was capable of being thought of as plus and minus sign simultaneously, as the intersection of mortal and eternal time. For us, for whom there is only mortal time, and an immediatized present, mortification must mean a negation of the difference between the plus and the minus sign, not their aggregation, or the intensification of their difference.

For there is an intrinsic difficulty in placing or dating the time of the skin, since its function for us is to be anachronistic, or partly out of time; as the Modern Primitives movement may attest, there is a desire for the skin to figure as archaic survival, as a reminder of a different, lost way of being in one's skin. It is for this reason above all that the drive to mark the body cannot be separated from a desire to assault the very medium and apparatus of epidermal figurality, since this apparatus is temporal as well as inscriptive. By assaulting the skin, one assaults time, or the ravages inflicted on it, on us, by time.

The medical history of the skin might confirm what the analysis of the ubiquitous imaginary assaults upon the skin would seem over and over to have suggested: namely, that the new multiplicitousness of the skin is intolerable, so intolerable that relief is sought in a recursion to archaic experiences and conceptions of the skin, as ideal envelope, primal barrier. At this point, however, the history of the skin has turned over on itself. The new skin is the old skin, as the skin restores and renews itself through exposure to primitive kinds of suffering and jeopardy. The aim of this book is to show that the time of the skin is always in fact folded-over or complex. For one thing, the multiplicitousness of the skin is not in fact without historical precedent, for the skin has been lived and figured and imagined in a rich variety of ways that cannot be reduced to or neatly synchronized with the history of the medical understanding of the skin I have sketched out. It is necessary to emphasize this point, because the multiplicitousness of the skin as milieu seems to have encouraged a defensive retreat to what is a too narrowly medical view of the skin as poised between healthy wholeness and pathological damage. The arguments and examples assembled in the last chapter and this could easily suggest that the skin is understood almost universally as in jeopardy. But it is in jeopardy not just from actual material causes, pollution and poisoning of the environment, the depletion of the ozone layer, but also from the very cultural transformations it is undergoing. Faced with the prospect of its multiplication, the skin seems to have taken refuge in phantasms of suffering and cure.

SCISSORS, STONE, PAPER

The arguments I have developed have fitted Didier Anzieu's psychoanalytic theory of the skin to some of the many enactments of the skin's jeopardy and reparation to be found in contemporary culture. I want in the last part of this chapter to haggle a little at that correspondence, to pick at the seams of that fit. For the principal difference between Anzieu's conception of the skin, as it is shared with those in his group, and the conception of the skin found in this book, is that between a therapeutic discourse – albeit one in which experiences of collectivity are very important – and a cultural-poetic one. Anzieu is fundamentally concerned with the defects and deficits of the skin ego, or ego-skin, endured by his patients, and with the ways in which therapy and analysis can repair them. Not surprisingly, this brings the thematic of suffering to the fore in his work and tends to stretch it out between the alternatives of damage and healing. Much of the work on culture which Anzieu's work has recently suggested similarly reproduces this twin emphasis on the impairment of the skin and the efforts to recover its wholeness.[20]

But the model of the skin as case or container and the therapeutic narrative which it subserves is just not extensive or various enough to account for the psychosocial life, or lives of the skin. As François Dagognet has written: 'The skin deserves more than to be taken as a simple defensive enclosure: it should not be reduced to a sack'.[21] For the suffering transexuals of whom Jay Prosser writes so powerfully, as for other kinds of sufferer from dysmorphic maladjustment to their bodies, the loss or lack of the skin becomes all-consuming – becomes, in fact, a kind of carapace or false skin of loss. The fact that many people suffer from an acute sense of the lack or loss of a continuous, positive proprioception need not imply that other people who are not similarly tormented, or not all the time at least, actually have what is felt to be missing. For such conditions of raw deprivation are indeed aberrations, malfunctionings, cases where something has gone wrong. What is pathological about this form of suffering is not merely the impairment of the sense of the body as containment, it is the shrinking of the skin to this function of containment alone. To be happy in one's own skin is not to be contained, grounded or bounded, or not this alone. It is also to be able to live the skin's multiplicity – its many-foldedness. The multiply-lived skin is not a clear, coherent and positive integrity, not an integument, that can be seen and held together all at once, but an untegument, which only appears 'fragmented' from the perspective of lack. Health is not integrity, it is resource and possibility. To the one who lacks it, integrity appears like everything; it is not.

Lyotard writes of the struggle of the law to prescribe, predicate or otherwise come before and mark the body before it comes to itself. The desire for integumentation of which Anzieu's work provides such a compelling exposition attempts by contrast to make the body come before the letter of the law. The second skin of the transexual is a thrusting off of a dead, indifferent or damaged skin in order to reinstate a first lost, primordial skin. Michel Serres offers us another, more irenic meaning of the word prescription. In his *Le tiers-instruit*, translated as *The Troubadour of Knowledge*, Serres protests against the ideal of just reason based upon equilibrium:

Here is the immobile motor of our movements, reason in the world and in history, the twin of vengeance, imitating its compensations or reparations ... Vengeance and its apparent justice, founding the eternal return, keep the complete memory of exact reason intact, through reversible and cyclical time.[22]

However, the passage of time opens up lack or non-equivalence in these vengeful equilibria of reason. The word prescription, which in French signifies something like the English statute of limitations, prescribes the time after which the grip of law lapses. Prescription is the law given to law, the law of fading, forgetting.

On the one hand, therefore, there is Lyotard's greedy prescription, in the desire of the law to come before every other marking, to put itself in the place of the first touch of the flesh. On the other, there is Serres' 'natural law', the law of the fading of every law, a law which the law can and should give itself, in the name of a reason which knows how to limit itself.

But there is another possibility. The skin marks and holds another time, an embodied temporality that is a third element, between the law and the flesh, which, we will see, disturbs their settled compact. The skin may be something else, a third thing, between the alternatives of a screen that lets things through, or a slate on which things may be deposited. It might be, as it in fact is, a temporizing volume, a milieu, an environment, a multiplicity, a depth, an archipelago or Northwest Passage. The law of marks imposed upon the body, either as expression or as accident, is a positive law, which erases the possibility of loss, or erasure, or approximation. The life of the skin is probabilistic, an unfolding between the alternatives of the family face, with its bags and folds and wrinkles buried in the genes, and the tannings, softenings, emaciations and alimentations to which it is heir in time. The idea of marking the skin aims to hold it suspended between the alternatives of figure and ground, accident and intention. But the mark on the skin in fact marks out the subjection, not to the positive law of visibility and making good, but the subjection to the invisible and imperfectly calculable space of competing probabilities. Freckles and acne come and go. The mole may or may not develop into melanoma, which may or may not be malignant. The skin is more like a sea than a screen, more like a mobile sky of shifting cloud and sun than the punctual night sky.

We have seen that law and the body therefore change places with each other; the body becomes inured with law's hardness to the injustice and the cruelty of law. The game of vengeance and retribution played out between the law and the body through the law of marks endlessly presents a hard thing with a harder thing, and in which only hardness, coldness and endurance can win. It is like the game of scissors-paper-stone flattened out, or reduced to a linear series driven by the endlessly reconstituted binary of hard and less hard. If the flesh is not grass, but paper, and the operations of penalty and retribution are the scissors, then the stone may appear as the impassive, enduring, inured law, against which even penalty blunts its edge. Sharpness wins against softness, and hardness wins against sharpness.

But, as we know, the elements in this game are not ranged in a simple ascending series, from hard to less hard. For there are not only two possibilities, of winning or losing, depending on one's antagonist, dependent on one's degree of hardness relative to that of one's opponent, literally, that which you come up against (scissors win against paper, but lose against stone); there are also two ways of winning or losing. Stone either wins because it is harder, or loses because it is harder, depending on whether it meets something which is softer (scissors) or something which is even softer (paper).

So this marking out of the relations simultaneously and all in one go, on a single plane or surface, does not complete the picture, precisely because it renders it as a picture, a something that might be apprehended by the eye, held in the hand. What is the space in which the permutative series of this game is enacted or exhibited? It cannot be grasped, held all at once, or maintained in a now, a *maintenant*, because it includes and is caught up in the action of grasping. Each of the vectors in fact involves a change of value; scissors beat paper by cutting it; but stone beats scissors by blunting them; and paper beats stone by enfolding it (which is a way of blunting weight). The game is a phase-space, an ambidextrous topology that requires the repeated protean contest of hands, a battle played out as a Klein bottle. Serres' prescription involves the subjection of the law, not to a greater and more remorseless hardness, but to an inescapable liability, a subjection to the softening and diffusing influences of time. Serres' prescription, like the paper-scissors-stone game, requires of the law that it do time.

So there is a law that comes before and after the law of marks. There is the law of the scar, the tattoo; and there is the law of the scar's preordained (prescribed) subjection to time. Herodotus tells us that Xerxes commanded the waters of the Hellespont, which had impeded the progress of his army, to be given 300 lashes, and then threw a pair of manacles into the waters.[23] Iron beats flesh, but water's irony melts iron. There is the law of memory, equilibrium and retribution, kept radiantly in sight and in mind; and there is another law enjoining on us eventual recall of the forgetfulness of time. Amnesia is a slower, surer bomb than the dynamite of the tenth of a second. The skin can be forced to remember: but it will always harbour a longer intimation, that it cannot but forget.

4 Impression

If the skin is adored and idealized in many cultures, if the marked and decaying skin prompts the immemorial dream of its immaculacy, the skin is also made to bear the blame for guilt, time, history, death. Innocence is unthinkable without the thought of an unmarked skin. Since human beings have their skins on display, and since their skins display so openly and copiously the signs of their health or disease, it is no surprise that there are strong negative as well as positive feelings attaching to the visible condition of the skin. The skin can come to signify not just beauty and security, but value as such. It is for this reason that law, medicine and religion bend their attentions to the skin.

It seems that at certain periods the dichotomous feelings towards the skin can be greatly intensified. According to Barbara Maria Stafford, the Enlightenment was one such period. The remarkable chapter entitled 'Marking' in her book *Body Criticism* outlines in detail the fascinated disgust with the pathological skin which reigned in Europe from the late seventeenth to the early nineteenth centuries. The 'aesthetic of immaculateness' of the eighteenth century, with the smooth, white complexions of its ladies, the dazzling white lines of its neo-classical sculpture and architecture and the sumptuously bland sheen of its portraits and landscapes, was, she argues, a panicky and unstable response to the nauseating phantasmagoria of rotting, eruptive and squamous skins that constituted the actual bodyscape in the eighteenth century.[1]

For thousands of years, up until the beginnings of modern medical science in the eighteenth century, the skin has provided most of the signs and symptoms of the diseases suffered by human beings. It is for this reason that diseases such as leprosy and syphilis were so regularly mistaken for each other and regarded for so long as primarily skin complaints. We have seen that a recognizable science of dermatology, built on an awareness of what was specific to the skin rather than the expression on the skin of other complaints, could only form once larger and more plausible explanations based on the new sciences of anatomy began to be developed

When it was the skin that would display the first signs of serious illnesses, such as syphilis, bubonic plague and smallpox, it is not surprising that it should have been regarded as, in the most general sense, ominous, full of import and portent. This extended beyond a purely medical attention to the skin. The arts of palmistry, and the feelings of premonition attached in European folklore to sensations of itch and shivering are part of this cultural watchfulness, as are games like the buttercup test employed by children, in which the flower is held to the skin of the neck to see if it is greasy enough to reflect the yellow, and thereby determine whether the subject likes butter.

The most important feature of skin markings is that they are both mute and blatant. The word 'blatant' comes from the now obsolete verb 'to blatter', from Latin *blattire*, meaning to prattle or blabber. The word seems to have been coined by Edmund Spenser who used it to describe the 'blattant beast' with a thousand tongues.[2] That which is blatant, speaks out openly and excessively. Gradually the word has lost its specifically verbal associations, and has come to be used of an offence or enormity that flames into view, flaunting itself glaringly to vision without need of words, but also, and more importantly, without confessing itself in words. A blatant offence thus 'speaks' while pretending to be mute, its pretended muteness compounding the offensiveness. Skin markings, especially when they are associated with disease, have the flagrancy of the blatant; they blurt out what the tongue might prefer to keep decently veiled. They are shameful and disgusting, not only because they inspire fear, but also because they are shameless.

Among the commonest but most enigmatic and fascinating markings of the skin were moles and birthmarks. As we will see a little later, a specific explanation based upon the power of the mother's imagination during pregnancy existed for birthmarks. Rarely was such an explanation extended to moles, perhaps because, though they are much less ephemeral than boils and pustules, they are not as permanent, nor as originary as birthmarks. Moles meet the conditions for successful divination. First of all, they are largely inconspicuous, and, to an untrained eye, exhibit little obvious variation. They can be found in any part of the body, though they also have a tendency to gather in certain places, being common on the neck and face, but less common on the feet. Moles are eminently interpretable because of the fact of these minor variations against a background of near-uniform randomness.

Evidence for the divinatory function of moles abounds in popular fortune-telling books and pamphlets from the sixteenth century onwards, and probably points to the widespread existence of such beliefs much earlier. Almanacs, manuals of advice on common ailments and remedies, and fortune-telling books written for young girls and women, to enable them to distinguish good from bad sweethearts, would often include a section on the significance of moles, often in close proximity to sections on the interpretation of dreams. Like popular ballads, these books were frequently reprinted. One such general guide book, *A Book of Knowledge*, published in 1696, promised information about 'the Nature of Astrology, by the Celestial Signs and Planets', 'Divers things necessary for Trade and Dealing', 'the manner of resolving doubtful questions relating to Love, Business, &c', along with 'Moles and marks in the body, their signification' and 'Dreams, and their interpretation'.[3]

The reading of moles is done in broadly the same terms as the reading of the lines of the palm. What seems to weigh most heavily is the position of the mole. '[F]rom their colour nothing material can be gathered', we are assured by one writer, 'that arising from the complexion of the body, and is not at all to be minded; the situation being the basis on which we must gather what will befall us.'[4] Sometimes this can be explained by simple symbolism. 'A mole on the belly, denotes whoredome, luxury, and gluttony', according to the *Book of Knowledge*.[5] *The Spaewife, or Universal Fortune-Teller* of 1845 says that the bearer of a mole on the belly will be 'addicted to sloth and gluttony; selfish in almost all articles, and seldom inclined to be nice or careful in points of dress'.[6] Moles near the neck had uncomfortable associations. 'A mole on the side of the neck, shows that the person will narrowly escape suffocation', said *A Book of Knowledge*.[7] Another book warned that 'A mole on the throat, threatens the party with diseases, such as the strangury, quinzey, &c.'[8] Readers of *Love's True Oracle* (1810?) learned that 'A mole on the throat, threatens the person with hanging, or some violent death.'[9] Somewhat surprisingly, moles near the heart were not generally regarded as benign: 'Any one having a mole near unto the heart, shews them malicious.'[10] Perhaps the logic here is that a mole in this position represents a spoiling or blemish on the heart.

The reading of moles was also significantly inflected by the opposition of left and right, and by the top-to-bottom orientation of the body. Moles on the right hand or arm are often considered 'an infallible token of good luck'.[11] The heraldic bar sinister, the diagonal stripe passing from top right to bottom left to signify illegitimacy, may have had some influence in the judgement that 'A mole on the left side of the mouth, denotes vanity and pride, and an unlawful offspring to provide for.'[12] *The Golden Dreamer* says that 'A mole on the right breast, denotes riches and prosperity', while warning, somewhat mysteriously, that 'A mole on the left cheek, causeth a man molestations.'[13]

Another important inflector of the meanings of moles was male and female difference, which could override or significantly modify the evidence of position. According to *Dreams and Moles*, 'He that has one on his upper lip, will have exceeding good fortune; but a woman will be debauched.'[14] *A Book of Knowledge* claimed that 'A Mole on the shoulder of a man, promiseth troubles and sorrows, and an unfortunate end. A woman having a Mole on the same place, it betokeneth much outward happiness, she will be fruitful, honourable, in goods and chattels abounding.'[15]

Given the background of whim and invention, some of the consistencies in the reading of moles appear striking, for example the fact that moles on either ankle signified the inversion of sexual qualities. 'A man having a mole on the ancle, it bespeaks him to take on him the woman's part of an hen huswife: if a woman, that she shall wear the breeches,' declares *A Book of Knowledge*.[16] *Partridge and Flamsted's New and Well Experienced Fortune-Book* agrees that a mole on a man's ankle 'shows him effeminate, and to act the part of a woman, like Sardanapalus at the spinning-wheel', while 'a woman having the like, she shall lord it over her husband'.[17] *The Spaewife* repeats this judgement in 1845:

'A mole on either ankle, denotes a man to be inclined to effeminacy and elegance of dress; a woman to be courageous, active and industrious.'[18]

Moles in certain positions were regarded as having an ambivalent significations, or promising good fortune followed by bad: 'A mole on the outside corner of either eye, denotes the person to be of a steady, sober, and sedate disposition, but liable to a violent death', we are warned.[19] Similarly, 'A Mole on the hand, or wrist, of a man or woman, doth speak them to be very much afflicted in their latter days; beginning their days in Joy, but ending their days in Poverty, increasing in children.'[20]

Moles were sometimes regarded as paired. Thomas Borman's oracle book explained that

> there is such a comfort and harmony between the parts, that feeling one mole, you thence conclude where the party hath another; thus a mole on the nose or lip of a man or woman, denotes another on the privates. A mole on the nape of the neck, another on the buttocks, and if it be on the neck, another on the belly. A mole on the forehead, another on the breast. A mole on the eye-brow, another on the navel; and this seldom fails.[21]

Not all manuals arranged correspondences in this way, but most agreed at least on the correspondence between the nose and the genitals. Indeed, moles in general seemed to signify the display of lubricious markings that ought to be kept hidden. One to one correspondences spread out and divided the surface of the body into different divinatory zones; territories; these odd conjunctions of body parts then suggested the ways in which the body might be knotted together, literally as a 'complexion', or augural origami.

The reading of moles belongs to a divinatory sensibility that is no longer precisely our own, though the reading of bodily marks has not been so much superseded as vastly generalized – and the increase in skin cancer has, of course, given moles a new ominousness.[22] The reading of moles does not seem to have rested on a very strong or explicit theory. The author of *Dreams and Moles* began his account of the subject by saying that

> It is confessed by most modern authors that as the wise architect of this spacious globe thought fit most gloriously in his own image to make man the sole ruler on earth; so he imprinted on him many bits of history, that thereby he might read some events which will befal him in the series of his life. Now these historical bits are no more than spots in the flesh, commonly called Moles, which, as their situation is various, so they differ much in nature and quality.[23]

Thomas Borman hinted at an astrological determinant for the distribution and relationship of moles. 'MOLES', he wrote, ' are certain remarks imprinted on several parts of the body, as the planets in every one's birth happen to be placed, according to whose natures they denote good and evil.'[24] Neither

Borman nor any other source that I have found elaborated these astrological correspondences in any systematic way, though their divinatory practice is surely governed by the general principle of the mirroring of the large in the small in the universe, and the foreshadowing of large purposes in insignificant phenomena. The astrological reading of moles seems to be another aspect of the analogy between skin and sky which takes so many different forms. Moles are thought of as fleshly or terrene stars, seemingly sprinkled at random when considered one by one, but orderly and comprehensible once their configurations and conjunctions are mapped.

In showing that moles imprinted in human skin are not merely arbitrary, but 'bits of history', the interpreters of moles rescued these particular blemishes from the arbitrariness that attached to meaningless or disorderly markings, especially dots and spots.[25] It was believed that the heavens, being perfect, were free of such blemishes, so the astrological analogy may have the all-too-human imperfections of the human complexion on to the clear composition of the sky.

THINKING SKIN

I suggested in my opening chapter that there is a close relation between the skin and the activity of thought. Thinking of the skin is complicated because to some considerable degree the skin is what we think with; thinking through the skin, in the sense of getting straight about the skin, is always going to be difficult because, as the later work of Didier Anzieu makes clear, all thinking is a form of thinking through the skin, the skin being literally implicated in thought. The skin is a thinking organ and a form of thought.

This idea is clearly illustrated in contemporary theories of the involuntary expressiveness of the skin. There is a strongly held prejudice in favour of seeing the skin as the part of the body most likely to register emotions and states, such as shock, trauma, grief, fear, anxiety and shame, in which the reasoning subject appears to be, if only momentarily, taken over or set aside. Psychoanalytic theory sometimes goes further, seeing the skin as capable of expressing not only states and feelings in which the subject is not quite in control, but also states and feelings of which the subject is not conscious. Thus not only may one blush when an embarrassing thought enters one's mind unbidden; but an attack of eczema or dermatitis may be construed as an expression of thoughts and feelings which are not consciously in mind at all. It might be thought that this body of opinion concerns the expressive rather than the ratiocinative powers of the skin, and that the skin is taken in such accounts merely to be the vehicle of feelings rather than the form or process of thought. But such a distinction cannot easily be secured. Expressing a state of mind or a feeling means formulating an attitude, and in the process forming a relation to that attitude. All feeling involves some element of comportment towards the world and the self, which is to say, some measure of taking thought. There is no state of feeling, however apparently raw or spontaneous it might appear to be, that does not constitute a judgement about the world and our relation to it. Above all, the expressive skin always also shows the effects of meaning or figuration. Expressing something on the skin, especially the propositional kinds of feelings and ideas which attract psychoanalytic attention – 'I have no shape,' 'My skin is a wall,' 'My skin cannot hold in my guilt' – involves the translation of otherwise inchoate states and feelings into epidermal terms. The acts of translation which psychoanalysis is apt to engage in claim to be no more than doublings or underwritings of the original translation effected by and on the skin, articulations of the figural thought, or predication through bodily images, that the endlessly versatile skin makes possible.

It is generally easy to agree with specialists in psychosomatic dermatology that, as the most important expressive organ of the body, the skin is a sensitive marker of different mental and physical states. What is less easy to accept, or even perhaps to understand, is the claim that the skin allows the more or less direct picturing of those mental states, as images or allegories. The argument that the daughter of a Holocaust survivor images her guilt at her family's survival by developing a patch of eczema in precisely the place where her mother had her identifying tattoo erased literalizes the idea of the mind's power to write on the skin, or the skin's power to change its own form. It is one thing for a patient to entertain fantasies and delusions about his or her skin – that it has turned to glass, that it is leaking, or infested with worms, that it is too tight and is suffocating him – but quite another for the skin literally to change its form or appearance to act out these figures or beliefs. It is the difference between the skin's powers to express and its powers to formulate. In the one case, the skin is involuntarily emitting signs – pallor, rash, flush, pruritis – that may certainly be read in various ways but only have the status of signs for their interpreters; in the other, the skin is regarded as forming, indeed in some way consciously forming, signs, and thereby both declaring and interpreting itself. Another way of seeing this is as a distinction between indexical signs, which are phenomena that may come to be associated by convention with certain mental or physical states, and phenomena that display an iconic resemblance to what they figure forth. In one case physical and mental states are transposed into an epidermal register; in the other, the skin starts to speak another language than its own.

And yet stories persist of marks forming on the skin which are not only tokens of a general excitation or suffering, such as the eczemas or erythemas affecting many people in states of anxiety, but specific picturings or enactments of events. One such experience is described in the biography of Chris Sizemore, whose experiences as a sufferer from multiple personality disorder were the basis for the film *The Three Faces of Eve*. One evening, Chris Sizemore suddenly underwent a flashback to an experience of being burned in a fire which she had had as a three-year-old child. Not only does her voice change into the piping cry of a child, but her skin manifests the physical signs of the heat that she is seemingly suffering in recall:

> Bobby ran for his mother's robe, and the two teenage boys held her still and covered her naked body while Tiny brought a wet towel from the bathroom.

She and Don put the towel on Chris's upper right arm, the one containing the puckered scar from that old burn more than forty-six years before. The arm and scar now burned an angry, fiery red. As the wet towel touched the arm, Chris eased her tossing and screaming and grew quiet, lying on the floor wet and spent with sweat, as one might whose excruciating pain had been touched and soothed by morphine. When Don removed the towel from her arm, he and Tiny stared at each other over the small square of terrycloth. It was steaming and burning hot to the touch, and the arm that it had just covered and that had shortly been so red and burning itself, was now white and cool to the touch.[26]

This kind of marking is at the opposite extreme from judicial or penal branding. Here the endogenously self-marking skin apparently produces the forms of its own subjection from within itself. The rest of this chapter will explore the beginnings of this belief in the active powers of the skin not only to bear out meanings but also participatively to shape thought, feeling and desire.

SPOTS AND MARKS

Despite its Latin title, Daniel Turner's *De morbis cutaneis* was the first book on diseases of the skin to be published in English. Considered strictly as a contribution to dermatology, it does not have very much claim to distinction. Its interest and importance come rather from its odd twelfth chapter, which is entitled 'Of Spots and marks of a Diverse Resemblance, imprest upon the Skin of the Foetus by the Force of the Mother's Fancy: With some Things premis'd of the strange and almost incredible Power of Imagination, more especially in Pregnant Women'.[27] The chapter is really an anthology of anecdotes, drawn from a variety of classical and contemporary sources, including Aristotle, Hippocrates, Pliny, Plutarch, Aelian, Ficino, Paracelsus, Cornelius Agrippa, Coelius Rhodoginus, Aelian and St Augustine. The most fertile modern source upon which Turner draws is a book published in 1608 by Thomas Fienus on the power of the imagination,[28] which is itself full of stories concerning the alteration of 'the Lineaments of the *Embryo* or *Foetus*, with the various Stigmata, if I may so call them, imprest upon the Body, at the Time of Conception, as well as afterwards, by the sole Vertue of the Mother's *Phansy*' (*De morbis cutaneis*, 107). Turner's chapter included the story of a woman who, after a vivid dream of the Three Kings, bore triplets, one of whom was black, and the story of a boy born with his viscera hanging out after his mother had been 'forced by some Souldiers to be present at the killing of a Calf; at the Opening of which she felt an extraordinary Motion in her Self, when she saw how the Bowels came tumbling out from the Belly' (*De morbis cutaneis*, 114–15).

Turner's book was successful enough to be reprinted with enlargements and revisions in 1723 and 1726. It was thus still current in 1727 when a book appeared entitled *The Strength of Imagination in Pregnant Women Examin'd*. The book was by a fellow-member of the Royal College of Physicians, James Blondel, though his identity would not be known to Turner for some time. It attacked the 'vulgar error' of Turner's work head-on.[29] Turner replied with a defence of his twelfth chapter in 1729.[30] Blondel, now writing in his own name, was quick to issue his response to Turner's response, giving it a title – *The Power of the Mother's Imagination Over the Foetus Examin'd* – which was confusingly similar to that of his first text.[31] Turner issued a third and final defence of his position in 1730, in which he announced that he had no intention of engaging in further public debate on the matter.[32]

Although they aimed and affected to reply point by point to each other's arguments, not much ground was made intellectually or medically. Blondel just went on insisting that there could be no physical explanation for how these effects were produced, Turner kept on telling and retelling the same stories of incredible markings and deformities; in fact, his final contribution in 1730, *The Force of the Mother's Imagination*, concludes by reprinting in its entirety and almost unchanged the infamous twelfth chapter of *De morbis cutaneis* which had provided Blondel with his initial target.

The argument between Turner and Blondel was obviously a high profile affair, and might even be seen as a defining intellectual encounter between medicine and miracle. But the debate was no simple watershed, for there was no simple, or decisive victory for Blondel. This is not just because of the many scientific weaknesses of his position, most notably his denial of any physical communication between the mother and the foetus. The argument over maternal impressions looks forward as well as backward, for it anticipates movements of feeling and belief that would develop at the end of the nineteenth century concerning the powers of the mind over the body in the hysteric. At both these periods, as we shall see, the marking of the skin plays a particularly important part.[33]

Psychoanalytic theories of the displacement of affects and ideas on to the skin have an ancestor and correlative in the widely held belief in the power of the mother's imagination over the developing form of her child. Many cultures seem to have theories about the damaging effects of maternal shock or upset on the developing child; J. W. Ballantyne, a late nineteenth-century gynaecologist who assiduously gathered evidence of the history of this belief, recorded instances across Asia, America, Africa and among the Eskimo.[34] Like many such beliefs, they provide an acting out of the feeling of closeness and interconnectedness with their children experienced by mothers, an enactment which, however grossly mistaken it may be in its details, is sure and exact in its fundamental apprehension of the intimate and physical intertwining of lives involved in pregnancy. Awareness of the dramatic changes in form undergone by the developing foetus, combined with a shaky grasp of the precise stages of that development, has regularly secured the belief in the extreme susceptibility of the child to any kind of disturbance or accident, especially those involving fright or desire.

Beliefs of this kind obviously form part of the larger network of theories of influence and susceptibility that determine the forms taken by religion, politics, psychology, medicine and science in any culture. What is striking about what became known as the theory of 'maternal impressions' is that it centres on the idea of the direct contact between the mental condition of the mother and the skin of her developing foetus. It is as though the mother's skin – which itself undergoes striking changes in form, colour and condition during pregnancy – became a kind of stencil, blueprint or photographic plate for the child's skin. An alternative name for the action of maternal impressions, 'psychic imprinting', makes the link between the mental, the maternal and the epidermal even clearer.

Influences on the mother have been believed to imprint themselves for two contrasting reasons: as the effect of sudden fright, and as the effect of immoderate, baulked longing. A mother terrified by a fish or lobster may produce a scaly child; alarm caused by a bear or an ape may produce unnaturally shaggy offspring. A minor form of this belief sees the foetus duplicating forms of contact experienced by the mother; thus a woman who has port wine spilled over her may give birth to a child bearing the characteristic birthmark known as a 'portwine stain'. This kind of vascular naevus might also be blamed on a corrupting admixture of menstrual fluid with the semen in the work of conception. Direct contact with the skins of animals was sometimes believed to produce similar markings or distortions. Turner tells the stories of a woman who played with an ape while pregnant and produced a child of ape-like appearance and of a woman who had a lizard jump into her bosom while pregnant, who 'after brought forth her Child, having a fleshy Excrescence growing out of the Breast, exactly resembling the Lizard, which had the Head fixed into the Child's Flesh, as if it had hidden therein, whilst the Rest of the Body hung forth' (De morbis cutaneis, p. 118). He derives a similar story from one of the most widely read anthologies of stories of monsters and prodigies, Ambroise Paré's Des monstres et prodiges. A woman suffering from a fever was advised to hold a live frog in her hand until it died. Retiring to bed with the frog and submitting to the embraces of her husband with the frog still tightly grasped caused the birth nine months later of a baby with the face of a frog.[35] Fish and aquatic animals seemed to give rise to particularly intense fears. Turner reproduces an account from Fienus of a woman 'complete in the rest of her Body, but without a Head: Instead of which was joined to her Neck the Likeness of a Shell Fish, having two Valves which shut and opened'. This inconvenient condition was occasioned by the fact that, when pregnant, her mother 'had a strong Desire after some Mussles she beheld in the Market, but could not procure at that instant'. The child lived until the age of eleven, until, losing her temper one day while being fed, she bit the spoon, cracked her 'testaceous Valves' and died shortly afterwards (De morbis cutaneis, 117).

In the case just cited it is the mother's desire rather than her alarm which leaves its mark on her infant. In the forming of this kind of maternal impression, it is usually not direct skin-contact that produces the effect. In the case of a so-called 'longing-mark' (an English expression approximating the French word envie, which can mean both desire and a birthmark), what causes the damage is something seen and desired at a distance rather than something felt on the skin. There are many stories of erotic fixation on pictures of persons of a different skin colour producing children of that same colour; one widely-reported story was that Hippocrates testified at the trial of a Greek woman who had given birth to a black-skinned child that this could be innocently explained as the effect of a picture of an Ethiopian which had hung in her bedchamber and much admired. Similarly, a craving for strawberries or pineapples is believed to leave its imprint in birthmarks in the shape of those fruits on the skin of the child. In fact, the craving for fruit seems to have featured with particular frequency in explanations of birthmarks during the seventeenth and eighteenth centuries; it appears that the desire for coffee and chocolate began to displace this predilection, at least in France, during the eighteenth century.[36] In his *A Discourse Concerning Gleets* Turner tells the story of a woman whose baby was unluckily marked by an another, more robustly English craving:

> I hear a Gentlewoman of good Report tell me that some Months past, and before she was brought to Bed, sitting in her Parlour, a Footman carried up a Slice of *Plum-Cake* to a *Lodger* in the House, after which she had a more than usual Desire, but through Shame, she said, she at that time conceal'd it till her Husband came in, and having discover'd the Matter to him, he went immediately in quest thereof, when the Cake was eaten, and she would not suffer him to enquire farther, or to endeavour the procuring more of the same, notwithstanding she could not keep it for long time after out of her mind, the Consequence was this; her Child (whom I have seen also) came into the World with the exact Resemblance of a *Slice of Cake*, the Currants interspersed, and regularly depicted, the compass of a Palm, upon its Shoulder.[37]

EXPLICATIONS

Much of the debate between Blondel and Turner concerned the mechanism whereby maternal impressions were transmitted to the child. In response to Blondel's repeated demands that he specify precisely how these dramatic lesions were produced in the bodies of babies in the womb, Turner responded by frankly acknowledging that he did not know, but continued to insist that the evidence of the effect was nevertheless overwhelming and unmistakable. The nearest he comes to an explanation is at the beginning of his twelfth chapter, in which he suggests that the skin is a boundary which both marks and displays two fundamental movements of the animal spirits in the organism. These are the movement of 'irradiation', or movement of the soul towards some pleasing object, causing 'the Eyes, Face, Hands and all the Members to shine and leap for Joy' and the recoil of the spirits away from something ugly or frightening, leaving the countenance 'pale and sad' (*De morbis cutaneis*, 106, 102). It is these excursive and retractive movements that have the power, in an organism in which the lineaments are less fixed and more vulnerable, to leave permanent marks.

At work in this kind of superstition is a long-established idea of the epidermal nature and effects of sight. What one sees or, less often, hears, it is believed, can pass straight through the skin, to the heart and soul. John Maubray, the credulous and bullying author of *The Female Physician* (1724) warns against the effects of sight and touch together in terms that suggest that the latter is merely the former intensified:

> Whence is it then that we have so many *deform'd Persons, crooked Bodies, ugly Aspects, distorted Mouths, wry Noses*, and the like, in all Countries; but from the IMAGINATION of the *Mother*; while she either conceives such shapeless *Phantasms* in her *Mind*, or while she frequently and intently fixes her Eyes upon such *deform'd Persons* or disagreeable OBJECTS? Wherefore it is very wrong, and highly imprudent in *Women* that have conceived, to please themselves so much in playing with *Dogs, Squirrels, Apes*, &c. carrying them in their *Laps* or *Bosoms*, and feeding, kissing, or hugging them, as I have both often heard, and seen with my own Eyes.[38]

There is an interesting ambivalence in the way in which the mother's skin is held to be related to that of her foetus. On the one hand, her skin appears to be thought of as particularly sensitive during pregnancy, and she particularly prone to shocks delivered to her own skin through sudden touches, like that of an animal. On the other hand, her susceptibility is such as to transmit the shock directly to her infant, which, as many explain, has a skin which is less hardy and defended against injury, and will therefore be more susceptible to being marked. Medieval writings about pregnant women emphasize their characteristic permeability. Albertus Magnus' *On the Secrets of Women* has nothing to say about the marking effects of fright on pregnant women, but he does suggest that the foetus can be killed by thunder and lightning, 'by the shock which penetrates to the interior, destroying and consuming it, though no external sign of the burning is apparent, due to the subtlety of that vapour'.[39]

This view of the mother as passive, transparent transmitter of shock to her foetus is slightly complicated by a belief recorded by Levinus Lemnius in his *Secret Miracles of Nature* of 1658, and widely distributed across Europe and Asia:

> [I]f a Mouse, a Cat, a Weasel, leap suddenly on a Woman, or Strawberries, Cornel-berries, Cherries, Grape-stones, fall on any part of the body, they presently leave their mark, and the print of the thing will be printed on that limb, unlesse the woman at the same time that these things happen to her body, do presently wipe the part, and put her hand behind her back, or on some remoter part of her body. For so the mischief is suddenly cured, or the mark is made on that part she touched, all her Imagination and natural faculty being turn'd thither.[40]

Lemnius's words are reproduced almost exactly in Maubray's *Female Physician*.[41] Here the aspect of the mother's skin that differentiates it from that of the foetus is not the degree of its susceptibility, its greater permeability or its greater power to resist damage. Rather it is its two-sidedness, or capacity to touch as well as to be touched. The procedure of touching oneself seems to mean the taking in hand of aversion to allow the danger to be averted. The hand acts as a kind of tactile mirror, which captures the optical shock and, having turned vision into touch, proceeds to turn the touch aside to some safer or more discreet portion. This superstition also highlights the importance of orientation. Where the child is nothing but a receptive surface, with no back or front, the hand signifies the mother's distribution into front and back, allowing the buttocks to be substituted for the face. A mark always puts the face in doubt, literally defacing, or giving the body a rival face; conducting the force of the shock with the hand to the buttocks, removes the rivalrous quasi-faciality of the mark to the other, invisible extreme of the body, and to the body's other side which, because it is normally concealed under clothing, is like folding it away inside. As the active power of the skin, the hand represents the power of the skin not just to brace itself against disruptive threat, but also to reorganize itself. The hand can deflect because it can reinflect.

However, the special power of the hand, as the active or formative faculty of the skin, implies dangers of its own: in one story, reported in the nineteenth century, a woman feared that her action of involuntarily covering her face with her hands at the sight of her husband's chest wound would produce a child with the marks of a bloodied face.[42] James Blondel reproduced from Johannes Swammerdam's *Uteri mulieribus fabrica* (1672) an extravagant version of this sort of emergency apotropaism in order to mock it:

> A certain Woman at *Utrecht*, being with Child, was frighted with the Sight of a *Negroe*, and apprehended to be delivered of a perfect *Black*; but at last recollecting her self, she made Use of a second *Imagination* to prevent the Danger from the first; for she washed her self from Head to Foot with hot Water, to clear the Child from Blackness. The Time of her Delivery being come, the Child was born with all his *Teeth*, and appeared perfectly white, except those Places, the hot Water did not reach in the Body of the Mother, as the Interstices of the Fingers and Face, which still retained some sign of *Blackness*.[43]

Among the things that Blondel found it hardest to accept in Turner's account was that the mother's imagination had the power, not only to leave impressions on the skin of the foetus, but actually to rupture that skin, and, ultimately 'to ruin and demolish the human Structure' (*De morbis cutaneis*, 107). This belief seems to have been connected with a more radical notion of the power of the imagination than that it merely disrupted the development of the organism. Believers in maternal impression seem often to have accepted the classical view that the formation of the foetus requires the exercise of imagination.

The Aristotelian explanation for the relative uniformity of animal offspring as opposed to the variousness and unpredictability of human offspring is that human beings have more various and unpredictable thoughts and images passing through their minds at the time of conception. The most well-known lampooning of this belief is in Laurence Sterne's *Tristram Shandy*, in which Mrs Shandy's interruption of the work of coitus by her enquiry about winding the clock is held responsible for all the constitutional formlessness both of Tristram's physical person and his book. The informing power was sometimes thought of as the impressing of a shape into the surface of some semi-amorphous substance, along the lines of a seal impressed into wax, and sometimes as the giving of shape and form – or, in other words, the giving of an integument – to that substance. The skin is therefore, as so often, on the borderline between form and substance. In the light of all this, the duty of mothers and fathers is to maintain the orderly and comely complexion of their thoughts, in order that the bodies of their children be formed in the same manner. When he invented the word 'esemplastic' to characterize the unifying and informing power of the imagination in *Biographia Litteraria*, Coleridge connects with the tradition of thinking about the imagination as giving things their unity by moulding them from the outside.[44]

That the skin participates in the formative power of the imagination, as well as being its object, is indicated by some of the more extravagant claims about maternal markings. These are sometimes said to be, not just flat depictions of objects and animals, but voluminous masses growing out from the skin. Robert Plot reported that skin markings caused by fright are 'many times more than Skin deep', and describes 'a *Gentlewoman* I once saw at *London* that had the *figure* of a *Mouse* on her *cheek* standing fourth [sic] protuberant *in mezzo relievo* with the furr on, given her by her mother upon a *fright* she received from that *Animal*'.[45] The most extraordinary thing about these masses is that they seem to share some substance with their originals. Turner reports on fruit markings which enlarge at the season of the fruit's ripening, and, when describing surgical techniques for removing 'Currans, Cherry, Raspberry, Mulberry or Similitudes of the lesser Fruits', recommends that '[t]he Time of Extirpation is the Season when they look palest, lye flattest and softest, and are least troublesome: For some of these, like the Fruits they resemble, have their Times of blossom, ripening and languishing, tho' never quite dying or falling of themselves' (*De Morbis Cutaneis*, 123). This phenomenon was still being described as late as 1862, when it was reported in the French newspaper *Le Siècle* that a woman had given birth to twins both carrying the mark of a beet on their skins. The article went on to report what 'science tells us' of such birthmarks, namely that the mark goes through the same cycles of maturation as the plant it resembles, ultimately, as the beet dies, becoming dull and grey, with the danger that it will rot and infect other portions of the skin if it is not cauterized.[46]

The ultimate threat was a pregnancy in which there was no evidence of the informing power at all. Seventeenth- and eighteenth-century manuals of childbirth often included, alongside discussions of maternal impressions, accounts of the particular kinds of imperfect conception known as 'moles'. Now known as hydatiform moles, these are tumours or masses of tissue which form (in about 1 out of every 1000 pregnancies in the UK) in the uterus. Francis Mauriceau's *Accomplisht Midwife* of 1673 described a mole as 'nothing else but a fleshy substance, without bones, joynts, or distinction of members; without form or figure, regulated and determined'.[47] John Maubray described the Mole as a 'praeternatural body', formed as a result of 'the *Superfluity* of Matter, and the *infirmity* of the *forming* Faculty'.[48] Moles were often supposed to be formed from an excess of menstrual blood, as a result of lustful intercourse during menstruation. Maubray believed that Dutch women were particularly prone to the production of moles, and that

> The *MOLES* generally conceived there, are very different from Others commonly conceived in *other Parts*: Insomuch that *Those* are of a strange, astonishing, deformed *Shape*, having (as it were) something in them like the *Rudiments* of a *Work imperfectly begun*; such a *Piece*, as for Example, a *Limner* may draw out at the first *Draught*, with a rude *Pencil*; together with something of both *Life* and *Motion*: LIVING however only (as it were) *Vitâ Plantae*, and moving but by *Palpitation*; as I have also seen and observ'd this *Body* to contract it self sensibly at the *Touch*, and immediately again dilate it self perceptibly. In the *interim* I must further observe in this Place, that most commonly NATURE ejects these *Bodies* happily about the *fourth Month*; however yet, not always *all* at once, but most frequently by *Peice-Meal* and in *Heaps*, not unlike as the PUMP does the *Bildge-Water* out of the Ship.[49]

Such growths were called 'moon-calves' and were caused, Maubray believed, by the disruptive effect of living so close to the sea

> whose bellowing Waves and tumultuous Surges, are not only obvious to their Eyes all day, but obnoxious also to their Ears all Night long; as they continually beat upon their Coasts, and sometimes too mar their very Doors: From whence these Women cannot but be much affected and disturbed, if not also frighted in their very Embraces.[50]

Here, the moon-calf mole is imagined as something more than just a lumpy mass. It is a sort of protozoic creature of skin, having no other senses than that of touch. It is, as it were, the form of the formless, the nauseating surge and plunge of the sea enclosed in a minimal epidermal contour. It too seems to belong and contribute to the imagination of the skin's powers not just to bear marks, but to form and sustain its own life.

SUBTLE FINGERS OF LIGHT

The modern career of the belief in maternal impressions can be measured in some part by the success of a long poem in Latin published by Claude Quillet in 1655, entitled *Callipaedia: seu de pulchrae prolis habendae rationae* ('The Way to Beget Comely Offspring').[51] The poem was a kind of versified vade mecum for midwives, which used a mixture of folk-belief, classical myth and contemporary science to convey advice about the nature of generation and pregnancy, and the care of infants. Like many guidebooks of this time, the most notorious being the ubiquitous *Aristotle's Masterpiece*, it is a mixture of common sense (expectant mothers are advised to eat a varied diet and keep active while cutting back a bit on the dancing) and wild fantasy. The book seems to have found a huge readership, particularly among English readers; at the beginning of the eighteenth century, three separate translations of the book appeared within the space of as many years.[52] It certainly helped form a climate in which the fierce argument between Daniel Turner and James Blondel could blow up.

One of the striking features of the poem is the care that Quillet takes in explaining the physical process whereby the damaging impression is conveyed from the object of the mother's fear or desire to the skin of her child. Quillet declares himself opposed to Aristotelian ideas about the nature of generation, turning instead to the rival atomist theory of Epicurus as it was explicated by his contemporary Pierre Gassendi. Aristotelian theory had suggested that all objects impressed their likenesses or species on their environments, in obedience to the general natural law that like strove to join with and propagate like. Aristotle had conceived this, not as a physical process, but as the actualization of a potential.[53] Gassendi, who had been devoting himself since the 1630s to the development of mechanist theories of natural phenomena and the senses, found in Epicurus a physical basis for this process. The striking feature of this theory is that it not only emphasizes the closeness of sight to touch, it also speculates that the objects of sight are themselves subtle skins, scoured or scaled away from the surface of visible objects:

> *In primis magno in munde aspectabile quidquid*
> *Oppositosque ferit sensus, corpuscula quaedam,*
> *Subtiles tanquam exuvias, hinc inde fluore*
> *Continuo, circumfusas dispergit in auras:*
> *Atque haec cunctarum rerum simulacra vocantur.*

> First of all, whatever there is of visible aspect in the whole world that strikes up against the sense is made of subtle skins of atoms stripped off from the surface of things and thence diffused through the air in a continuous stream; and these are known as the simulacra of all things.[54]

The visible aspects of things consist of these tenuously particulated skins, which are shed by or stripped off from their outer surfaces and yet retain their shape. Quillet's word for these subtle skins – 'exuvias' – derives from Latin *exuere*, to strip or slough off, and can mean the cast of an animal or spoil of snake. The skin metaphor remains only implicit in Epicurus' word εἴδωλον (*eidolon*). The literalization of this conception as a skin seems to derive from the versified explication of Epicurean theory of vision in Book IV of the *De rerum natura* of Lucretius:

> *Principio quoniam mittunt in rebus apertis*
> *corpora res multae, partim diffusa solute,*
> *robora ceu fumum mittunt ignesque vaporem.*
> *et partim contexta magis condensaque, ut olim*
> *cum teretes ponunt tunicas aestate cicadae,*
> *et vituli cum membranas de corpore summo*
> *nascentes mittunt, et item cum lubrica serpens*
> *exuit in spinis vestem; nam saepe videmus*
> *illorum spoliis vepris volitantibus auctas.*
> *quae quoniam fiunt, tenuis quoque debet imago*
> *ab rebus mitti summo de corpore rerum.*

First of all, since among things clear to see many things give off bodies, in part scattered loosely abroad, even as wood gives off smoke and fires heat, and in part more closely knit and packed together, as when now and then grasshoppers lay aside their smooth coats in summer, and when calves at their birth give off cauls from their outermost body, and likewise when the slippery serpent rubs off its vesture on the thorns; for often we see the brambles laden with wind-blown spoils from snakes. And since these things come to pass, a thin image from things too must needs be given off from the outermost body of things.[55]

The theory of atomic discharge does little on its own to explain the operation of sight; the crucial feature of Lucretius' explication is the phrase 'contexta magis condensaque' which evokes the way in which, despite their immense speed, the atoms remain laterally bound together, as a plate, or skin. The snake-skin metaphor is also taken up by Gassendi, in his *Animadversiones in decimum librum Diogenis Laerti* (1649). This book had appeared in an influential (partial) translation into English, entitled *Physiologia Epicuro-Gassendo-Carltoniana*, by Gassendi's disciple, the Royalist physician Walter Charleton, in the year before the appearance of Quillet's poem. Gassendi uses Lucretius much more explicitly and extensively than Charleton, who buries his Lucretian allusions in his text; nevertheless the effect of Lucretian metaphor is manifest in both.[56] Charleton's treatment of vision begins by setting out the principle that 'in the University of Nature are certain most tenuous Concretions, or subtle Contextures, holding an exquisite analogy to solid bodies'. These images, 'the same that the Grecian philosophers call εἴδωλα and the Latin *Imagines, Spectra, Simulachra, Effigies*, and most frequently *Species Intentionales*' are 'direpted from the extreams of solid bodies' and have the singular properties that they 'conserve in their separated state the same order and position of parts that they had during their united', and fly off from objects through the air with 'insuperable *Pernicity*' on account of their '*Tenuity* or *Exility*'.[57] They are described more particularly as

Excortications, or a kind of most thin Films, by the subtle fingers of Light, stript off from the superficial extremes of Bodies; for Alexander himself calls them . . . *Pelliculae* and *Membranulae*, and *Apuleius Exuviae*, because as the slough or spoil of a Snake, is but a thin integument blancht off the new skin, and yet representing the various Spots, Scales, Magnitude, Figure &c thereof: so likewise do the Visible Species, being meer Decortications, or *Sloughs* blancht off from Bodies, carry an exact resemblance of all Lineaments and Colours in the Exteriours thereof.[58]

David Sedley has recently argued that the biological metaphors of simulacra as bark, scale or skin in Lucretius belong to an earlier stage of the writing of his poem, and that the later drafts place less emphasis on them.[59] Nevertheless, the odd but stubbornly biological conception of things wearing and radiating their visibility as a skin continued to prove useful and attractive for those, like Gassendi, Quillet and Charleton, interested in corporealized theories of vision. Their stubbornly tactile sense of the operations of vision accords with the folk-philosophy of the doctrine of maternal impressions, which testifies to an equally strong desire to understand sense and sensation as essentially operations of touch, applied or impressed directly upon various kinds of receiving surface.

One of the most difficult problems for the Epicurean theory of sight was how the life-size facsimiles exuded or streaming from objects were shrunk down in order to fit through the pupil of the eye. The conclusion to which the theory really seems to tend, without ever being able to become explicit, is that the body may actually receive visual impressions through all of its exposed surfaces. Quillet is less than precise about the actual mechanism whereby images impress the sense:

Quae simul impigris pennis, motuque volucri
Praedita, vel minimos gaudent penetrare meatus,
Implicitisque atomis sensoria quaque pererrant

Endowed with swift flight and winged motion, these [simulacra] gladly enter the smallest channels, and penetrate the senses with dissolving atoms.[60]

The English translations of Quillet's text respond specifically, even extravagantly, to his suggestions of an epidermis irradiated by simulacra. The Oldesworth translation of 1710 renders the lines just quoted with

they [simulacra] convey around
The Taste, the Shape, the Odour and the Sound:
Through every Pore they pass and every Vein,
And bear the Image to the active Brain.[61]

Rowe's translation of the same passage is much more economical, giving 'These with swift violent motion wander o'er/Each Sense, and penetrate the smallest Pore'.[62] The word 'pore' had a more general application in the eighteenth century, and could apply to tiny gaps or apertures in surfaces other than living skin. Nevertheless the specific application of the idea that the images are imagined as streaming through the skin is also to be found in the other, anonymous translation of 1710. Clumsily, but intriguingly, this translation enlarges over six lines the suggestion that the skin apprehends the atoms in ways that pass under the threshold of visibility:

> About they in Successive Order fly.
> And pierce the Pores, but 'scape the searching Eye;
> Yet imperceptible affect the Sight,
> Mix with the Rays, and flow around with Light.
> From thence the Eye no pow'rful Atoms brings,
> But what the Image forms with rapid Wings . . .[63]

Something is seen – imperceptibly affects the sight – even though it escapes the eye. It is as though vision had a tactile dimension which acted directly upon the organism (and on other senses than vision), rather than through the eye, which can respond only to the form of what is seen, rather than its substance.

What happens to the simulacra once they penetrate through the pores in the skin? Two explanations are conceivable. One is that the image or 'contexture' maintains its integrity inside the body, until it is somewhere impressed or arrested, for example in the still malleable flesh of the foetus, which, like a photographic plate, sensitively yet insensately receives and records the impression striking upon it. Another is that the impressions are thinned down in order to be channelled through the nerves or veins to the brain, whence they are reflected or rechannelled to the foetus in the womb via other nerves and veins.

There is another ambivalence in the explanations offered of why the child is vulnerable to impressions that leave the mother unharmed. We have seen that the commonest explanation is that the mother's frame is firmer and fully formed, unlike the child's flesh which is soft and yielding, and therefore more apt to retain impressions, as the dough is shaped by the baker. At the same time, of course, the mother proves more penetrable; the fact that her flesh cannot be harmed by the corpuscular images which stream at her, means that she transmits their force intact (literally untouched), rather than deflecting them. So, like glass, her skin is both tough and transparent. The soft and mutable flesh of the foetus, by contrast, may be intensely vulnerable to the shock of the image, but it is also capable of absorbing and arresting its force. It is as though the skin of the foetus were ductile but opaque, like putty, and thus provided a crumple zone for the speeding atom-skin. I have not encountered the suggestion anywhere that simulacra might continue on their path after penetrating the foetus, though there is nothing in the theory as commonly stated to prevent this. Indeed it might seem to follow naturally from the explanations given that somebody standing behind a woman at the moment when she receives the shock would be at risk of being marked.

Atomism is important to the skin – and a conception of the skin is intrinsic to atomism – because of the importance of touch in it. Gassendi argues against the Cartesian separation of body and mind, for example, on the grounds that such a separation allows for no possibility of effective contact: 'How can there be contact without a body', he asks in his *Disquisitio Metaphysica* of 1644, 'when, as is so clear to the natural light of reason, "no thing can touch or be touched without a body"?'[64] The last words quote from *De rerum natura*, Bk I, 304 – 'tangere enim et tangi, nisi corpus, nulla potest res', 'for, if it be not body, nothing can touch and be touched' – a phrase that concludes a passage in which Lucretius is arguing for the corporeal nature of invisible things such as heat and fragrance.[65] It is the theory of atoms which allows Gassendi to mount his materialist argument against Descartes' view of the incorporeality of soul; soul is opposed to body, not as the incorporeal to the corporeal, but rather as the subtly to the grossly corporeal. '[W]hen you concede that "it is certain that you are truly distinct from your body," it will be granted you; but it need not be granted therefore that you are incorporeal, and not rather a kind of very subtle body distinct from your coarser body.'[66] Atomic theory allows the distinction between matter and spirit to be represented as a division within matter itself (or, rather, a continuity, since there is no fundamental change in nature between a subtle and a gross body). The outside or other of matter is, so to speak, blent back into it. Skin provides a favoured metaphor for this, for it too is a materialization of the immaterial, the making literal or material of the borderline – or the abstract idea of the borderline – between matter and form, *res* and *species*, a thing and its figure.

A conception of surface or contact is also important to atomism because of its inclusion – intolerable to its Aristotelian opponents – of the idea of the void. Indeed, the theory requires the existence of void, otherwise the atoms of which everything is made up would have no medium in which to move. This means that everything in the universe apart from individual atoms must include absolute void as part of its composition. But if this is the case, what is the nature of the contact between an atom and the void that it occupies? If the atom is a determinate body, with shape and extension, albeit one of unimaginably small dimensions, then it must have a surface, and this surface must form a contact with the void. But if the void is entirely nonbodily, as it must be, how can it form any kind of contact with the bodily matter of the atom? Thus the Cartesian problem of the nature of the contact between mind and body seems not to be solved definitively by atomic theory, but only deferred, or, better perhaps, driven inwards to the heart of matter.

COMPASSION IN BODIES

The Epicurean simulacrum theory focuses attention on the processes whereby the woman is penetrated by the images of her fear or anguished longing. Another, rival theory focused on the processes occurring within the mother which allowed the image to be imprinted on her baby. This theory is enlarged most clearly in some early chapters of Nicolas Malebranche's *Search After Truth* (1674). Malebranche tells the stories of two effects of maternal imagination. One concerns a woman who saw a criminal being broken upon the wheel and gave birth to a child with similarly smashed limbs, the other a woman who gazed intently at a portrait of St Pius and subsequently was delivered of a child resembling the saint's portrait – with the face of an old man, and growths of skin on his shoulders resembling an inverted mitre.

Malebranche's explanation depends, not upon the direct and unmediated imprinting of images on the mind, but upon the mediating work of the animal spirits. Malebranche assumes that the brain and the exterior portions of the body are joined by a taut network of nerves, which he thinks of as hollow canals filled with animal spirits. '[O]ur sense organs are composed of tiny fibres that on the one hand terminate in the external parts of the body and skin, and on the other lead to the center of the brain.'[67] Sensory impressions cause agitation in the animal spirits at the outside edges of the body, which is transmitted at great speed through the nerves to the brain. When the subject is awake and alert, these nerves are stretched out. Skin and brain are imagined as two parallel impressionable surfaces, kept taut like a tent, sail or drumskin by the tension exacted by the nerves. Malebranche seems to imagine this as a kind of phonographic apparatus, in which impressions are transmitted along the nerves as a stretched string transmits sound ('just as one part of a taut string cannot be moved without the other being disturbed', 49), and then etched directly into the brain, 'just as the breadth, depth, and clarity of the strokes of an engraving depend upon the pressure applied to the burin, and the pliancy of the copper, so the depth and clarity of the traces in the imagination depend upon the animal spirits' (89). The impulses scored on the exterior skin are reinscribed on the brain, which is clearly being imagined at this point as an interior skin. Since the brain is the point of mediation between the body and the soul, one can perhaps assume – though Malebranche himself never puts it exactly like this – that the brain is to the soul as the skin is to the brain: in short, that the brain is the tympanum of the soul (49). Malebranche's solution to the problem of how mind and body can connect with and act on each other seems to be to imagine sense, brain, imagination, soul, arranged as a series of reverberating skins.

Forms, impulses and ideas can be transmitted in either direction, from outside to inside, or, as in the case of imagination, from inside to outside. What makes the soul able to distinguish between sense and imagination, i.e. impressions originating from the outside and from the inside, is not any essential difference in quality between them, but rather the depth of the impressions they leave, or the intensity of the touch they effect. Real objects make deeper impressions on the brain; ordinarily, 'if the internal fibres are only lightly disturbed by the flow of animal spirits, or in some other way, then the soul imagines, and judges, that what it imagines is not outside, but inside the brain' (88). Malebranche insists that, just as sense impressions impart a direct pressure and agitation on the brain, so that the soul itself experiences sense images through contact and impact, so the soul can in its turn imprint its imaginary conceptions on the brain: 'Since the imagination consists only in the soul's power to form images of objects by imprinting them, so to speak, in the fibers of the brain, the greater and more distinct the traces of the animal spirits, which are the strokes of these images, the more strongly and distinctly the soul will imagine these objects' (89).

This reverberant reversibility of sight and imagination underlies the explanation Malebranche gives in his seventh chapter of the influence of maternal impressions on the body of the child in the womb. Malebranche first of all asserts the principle of physical sympathy between different beings – what he calls 'compassion in bodies'. He means something surprisingly literal by this. To see somebody wounded is to be correspondingly wounded oneself:

> [T]he transport of spirits in the parts of our bodies that correspond to those parts one sees injured in others causes an acute impression in sensitive people with a vivid imagination and very soft and tender flesh . . . the sensible sight of the wound a person receives produces another wound in those who see it that is greater in proportion as they are weaker and more delicate. (114)

For Malebranche, vision is not the searching, analytic, discriminating sense: seeing something involves making oneself over to it, a yearning towards the object of sight and a merging of seer and seen.

Malebranche follows tradition in seeing women as softer and more impressionable than men. This may make women more sensitive and tactful in their perceptions and judgements, but only because they are experts in reading the surfaces of things: 'normally they are incapable of penetrating to truths that are slightly difficult to discover . . . They cannot use their imagination for working out complex and tangled questions. They consider only the surface of things, and their imagination has insufficient strength and insight to pierce it to the heart' (130).

But, despite the mother's impressionability and concentration on the surface of things, her outward form is fixed and stable enough to resist the repercussions of the animal spirits from her brain which are agitated by the sight of a powerful stimulus. It is a different matter for the child in her womb. Since it sees what its mother sees and feels what she feels, the child will suffer the same agitations of animal spirits in its brain, and will transmit them, like its mother, to the outward portions of its body. Malebranche's claim is that the child's body, being softer, cannot resist the impact of the spirits that its mother can. In the case of the woman watching the execution

> All the blows given to this miserable creature forcefully struck the imagination of this mother and by a sort of counterblow, the tender and delicate brain of her child . . . At the sight of this execution, so capable of frightening a woman, the violent flow of the mother's animal spirits passed very forcefully from her brain to all the parts of her body corresponding to those of

the criminal, and the same thing happened to the child. But because the mother's bones were capable of resisting the violence of these spirits, they were not wounded by them . . . But this rapid flow of the spirits was capable of sweeping away the soft and tender parts of the child's bones. (115–16)

So, in this explanation, the mother does not transmit the images directly and, so to speak, indexically; but rather acts as a receiver. It is as though her soul, and the soul's outer cortex, the brain, brooding on the shock that it has received, conserve, amplify, and internally broadcast the image to the foetus. Malebranche brings forward the same explanation for the fact that the child can be deformed as much by the mother's desire – especially for things she would like to eat, but cannot – as by her fear:

If the mother imagines and strongly desires to eat pears, for example, the unborn, if the fetus is alive, imagines them and desires them just as ardently: and whether the fetus be alive or not, the flow of spirits excited by the image of the desired fruit, expanding rapidly in a tiny body, is capable of changing its shape because of its softness. These unfortunate infants thus become like the things they desire too ardently. But the mother does not suffer from it, because her body is not soft enough to take on the figure of the things she imagines, and so she cannot imitate them or make herself entirely like to them. (117)

It is less easy to understand why desire should produce the impulse to mimetic identification in the same way as the spectacle of pain. In the case of witnessed pain, sympathy is at work, a mechanism that Malebranche regards as a normal and natural way of maintaining the bonds between living creatures. But Malebranche neglects to explain why intense desire for an object can induce a desire to imitate it. Perhaps the idea is that an imaginative incorporation of the object takes the place of a physical incorporation of it, and that imitating is regarded as a form of imaginative incorporation; *that which is denied me, I will instead become.*

Similar explanations to Malebranche's were offered to English readers in Kenelm Digby's *On the Nature of Bodies* (1643). Digby first of all considers the question of how imagination might affect the shape of a child during the act of conception. His explanation depends on animal spirits as the means of transmitting visual *species*. During sexual intercourse

aboundance of animal spirits do then part from the head, and descend into those partes which are the instruments of generation. Wherefore, if there be aboundance of specieses of any one kind of object then strong in the imagination, it must of necessity be carried downe together with the spirits into the seede: and by consequence, when the seede infected with this nature, beginneth to separate and distribute it selfe, to the forming of the severall parts of the Embryon, the spirits which do resort into the braine of the child (as to their proper Element) and from thence do finish all the outward cast of the body (in such sort as we have above described) do sometimes happen to fill certain places of the childes body, with the infection and tincture of this object; and that according to the impression with which they were in the mother's fantasy.[68]

As in Malebranche, the impression or species is not stamped directly upon the body of the child, but rather transmitted to the animal spirits, which then relay the species to the brain of the child, which in its turn forms the body of the child according to this impressed image. In the absence of any idea of the genetic encoding of form, Digby can offer no better explanation than Malebranche of how it is that the animal spirits preserve the shape which they transmit – his rather feeble explanation is that 'thinges which come together into the fantasy, do naturally sticke together in the animall spirits' – hence his wobbling between words like 'impression' and 'infection'[69]

Later in his treatise, Digby reverts to the question of maternal impressions, or 'longing-marks'. Here he relies less upon the rushing hydraulics of animal spirits than upon a notion of universal sympathy to explain the imparting of marks from mother to child. Because the child and the mother are 'one continuate piece', and the child is so finely 'well tuned to the fantasy of the mother', it is impossible that there should be any 'motion or trembling' in the mother's body that is not reduplicated in that of the child:

> Now as we see when one blusheth, the bloud cometh into his face, so the bloud runneth in the mother to a certaine place, where she is strucken by the thing longed for: and the like happening to the childe, the violence of that suddaine motion, dyeth the marke or print of the thing in the tender skinne of it: the bloud in some measure piercing the skinne, and not returning wholly into its naturall course: which effect is not permanent in the mother, because her skinne, being harder, doth not receive the bloud into it, but sendeth it backe againe, without receiving a tincture from it.[70]

The pregnant woman is important because she is herself regarded, not as a receptacle, but as an interface. She is an outside that contains another outside (the skin of the foetus) inside itself. Her skin is a meeting place for the different possibilities or natures of the skin; as point of contact or exposure; as medium of transmission or permeation.

We can see enacted in the debate about maternal impressions during the eighteenth century the encounter of the two orders of marking encountered in chapter 3. One is the absolute law of marks, which resolves that the skin must and will bear out the nature of a being. The law attempts to usurp and occupy the place of this primary self-evidence. The other is the law of contingent marks, the law determining that beings will come to bear the marks of what happens to happen to them. According to one law of marks, or as I designated it earlier, order of prescription, marks occur in a nondurational instant, and are therefore out of time. According to the other law of marks, no mark and no law is immune to the operations of time, which, subtly or violently as it may be, can intercept and complicate the primary encounter of law and its object. The law of beings is subject to the accident of adversity, which is its own prior law.

The doctrines of sympathetic impression and repercussion depend upon the idea that skin is not simply a boundary or interface. The arguments and explanations that cluster round the idea of the maternally marked skin lead to complications and convolutions in the idea of the surface and the envelope. Skin becomes more than the compliant wax in which passion and dread score their traces; instead, the skin begins to wake and wander, an actively unfolding and self-forming organism rather than merely passive stuff.

5 Stigmata

Jean-Martin Charcot liked to encourage his students at the Salpêtrière hospital to set aside the unfortunate gynaecological connotations of the word 'hysteria', partly because he thought it blurred observation and thinking, blocking awareness, for example, of the fact that hysteria was as much a problem of men as of women. An important part of his effort to get the disease of hysteria on to a firmer clinical footing was the generation of a new medical vocabulary, which would make the various afflictions traditionally grouped together under the rubric of hysteria interpretable in terms of the work beginning to be done in psychology and neurology.

This was necessary since, as Elizabeth Bronfen observes in her book *The Knotted Subject*, the disease had been defined at least since Hippocrates as most characteristically the disease without a lesion.[1] Bronfen evokes the navel as the mark of the elusive 'wound that is not one' that lies at the origin of hysteria. It is also the bodily mark that allows hysteria to lurk in plain view: it is a symbol and a visible anchor-point for a disease that is otherwise so prodigal and promiscuous of symptoms. Adopting the navel as the absent centre of this worryingly now-you-see-it-now-you-don't ailment also allows everyone to be regarded as prone to hysteria: who has not been torn into life in the manner to which the navel testifies, who has not suffered the primal wounding which makes every subject incomplete?

Bronfen's adoption of the navel as her characteristic blazon may also be regarded as a particularly skilful compromise formation. For Bronfen seems otherwise to do everything she needs to in order to show that hysteria indeed does not exist, except as a set of mutually confirming expectations and suppositions circulating between doctor and patient. This is not to say that none of the symptoms displayed by patients said to be hysterics were real; it seems quite clear that most of Charcot's patients and a good few of Freud's were suffering from substantial neurological complaints, quite apart from forms of mental distress that were resulting in palpable physical symptoms. But it is to say that the aggregation of those symptoms into the syndrome bearing the name of 'hysteria' is and always was an error, and sometimes a rather foolish one. In this sense, hysteria not only no longer exists, but never has existed. It has always been 'hysteria' – the grouping and ordering of symptoms according to the aetiology and explanatory framework implied by this name – rather than hysteria.

Bronfen goes all the way down this line, right up to the point where it would become impossible for her to write about hysteria at all, except as the history of a particularly tenacious medical hallucination or as the very loosest of designations for any illness with a psychological component. But then, just when the bottom appears to be about to fall out of the whole hysteria business, she finds in the very fact that hysteria may be founded on nothing a saving principle:

> If traditional notions of hysteria, in the absence of organic lesion, kept returning to the image of much ado about nothing, I want to take seriously and literally this *nothing* and its resilience of self-representations engendered by the hysterical performance. I argue that the traumatic impact, itself a figuration of nothing, can be located as the indeterminable lesion at the core of hysteria.[2]

It is this nothing that is nevertheless so full of itself that is to be imaged in the navel. This is a move at once of great subtlety and breathtaking *chutzpah*. The navel is the guarantee that all these puzzlingly various manifestations of illness are in fact the dissimulations of a single disease. The very fact that hysteria does not exist, in the vulgarly palpable senses in which stroke or influenza or depression exist, is in fact its most mysterious and defining characteristic, that makes it possible to continue discussing it as a substantial entity on its own terms. For hysteria is now defined as a special way of being nothing or relating to nothingness, while the navel becomes the symbol of the shattering awareness of mortality. For Bronfen, the navel is what links us to our losses, signifying our simultaneous apprehension and forgetting of the fact that we all emerge out of mortality, lack and the death of the mother. The tomb of hysteria can then safely be revealed to be empty because hysteria has in fact risen again, reborn – but with all the same characters and plots – as the complex and dissimulated response to this traumatically buried awareness.

My purpose here is not to enter detailed objections to Bronfen's argument or procedure. Instead, I want to try to see whether there is not some connection between her effort to find a mark where there is none to correspond to this 'malady which is not one, even as it is' ('qui n'en est pas une, tout en l'étant')[3] and earlier attempts to make sense of hysteria, to find a mark, or set of marks to bear it out, and to see what kind of law of marks is in operation in these attempts.

STIGMATA DIABOLI

As part of his effort to put the understanding of hysteria on a clear and evidential basis, Jean-Martin Charcot introduced the word 'stigmata' to signify the permanent and unchanging features of hysteria, as distinguished from its 'accidents', or more mobile and transitory features. This word established a relation between the hysteric patients in Charcot's care and the hysterics of earlier ages, in whom Charcot and his associates had a sustained interest: witches, sorcerers,

Giotto, *St Francis Receiving His Stigmata*, 1312, tempera on panel. Musée du Louvre, Paris.

saints, the possessed, and the stigmatics. Charcot's team produced many articles and books about outbreaks of hysteria in the past. The *Iconographie de la Salpêtrière* and the *Nouvelle iconographie de la Salpêtrière*, the two series of publications devoted to the work at the hospital, mixed with its contemporary case histories reports of possession cases from the past, such as those at Louviers and at the convent of Loudun in the 1630s and the miraculous cures of the sick and other miraculous phenomena associated with the 'convulsionaries' at the tomb of St Medard in Paris in the early 1700s. Désiré Bourneville, one of Charcot's leading associates and most energetic publicizers, seemed to have a particular mission to reveal the hysterical basis for the stories of saints, sorcerers and the possessed of previous ages, and took a leading role in a series called the *Bibliothèque diabolique* published by the medical journal *Progrès medicale*. Most of the books in the series were annotated reprints of documents relating to historical cases of the past, one of the most notable of these being the autobiography of Soeur Jeanne des Anges, the mother superior who originated the accusations of sorcery that led to the burning of Urbain Grandier at Loudun in 1634.[4] The two *Iconographies* also reflected the personal interest that Charcot had in the representation of religious passion, suffering and ecstasy in art, on which he himself published a book.[5]

In France as in England, the revival of interest in supernaturalism that had taken place in the middle of the century, with the crazes for mesmerism, seances and spiritualism, had moved into a second phase of modernized super-naturalism. This was characterized by energetic reinvention of occult tradition, centred on Madame Blavatsky's invention of Esoteric Buddhism, the growing association between supernaturalism and movements of political protest and reform, such as socialism, suffragism and the antivivisection movement, along with an uneasy rapprochement between science and the supernatural, of which the most important symbol was the establishment of the Society for Psychical Research in England in 1882. The interest of the Salpêtrière in the miracles and mysticism of the past was part of this movement of defining negotiation between science and the supernatural.

Stigmatization appeared late in the history of the Christian Church. The first stigmatic was St Francis of Assisi, who received his wounds in 1224, during a vision of a six-winged seraph, holding an image of the crucified Christ. In conventional representations of the scene, such as that by Giotto, the wounds in Francis's body are affected by rays emanating from the wounds in Christ's hands, feet and side. Francis kept the wounds throughout his life, though he took trouble to keep them covered. The wounds in his hands and feet had a unique feature, in that the congealed blood formed dark, hard lumps of tissue that struck witnesses as exactly like the heads of nails. Later stigmatics would tend to display lesions or hollows in the feet and hands, or even holes going straight through them, but few had these characteristic nail-formations. Most stigmatics since St Francis have been women, and most of these have exhibited a feature which was not apparent in his stigmata, namely periodic bleeding from the wounds. Where St Francis's wounds remained a fixed testimony to the instant of transformation, the wounds of many female saints and mystics show a pattern of reopening and healing, often over many years. Often the wounds will open and blood flow from them to coincide with particular festivals of the church; sometimes they will operate on a weekly cycle, reenacting the Passion and Resurrection from Friday to Sunday. Sometimes the wounds will appear slowly, over a period of years, and then vanish. For most stigmatics, in fact, the variability of the marks is the most distinctive and miraculous feature.

The Salpêtrière doctors also had opportunities to comment on contemporary cases. One of the features of the contemporary scene in France was a revival of stigmatizations. Marie-Julie Jahenny, a Breton peasant woman, developed her stigmatization in 1873. She exhibited wounds in her hands, feet and side, as well as, successively, the marks of a crown of thorns, a mark on her left shoulder as from carrying a cross, and weals as from scourging on her ankles and forearms. The most celebrated stigmatic of the second half of the nineteenth century was a Belgian girl called Louise Lateau, who began bleeding from hands, feet and side in 1868 and continued to have outbreaks of bleeding punctually every weekend until her death in 1883: in all there were claimed to have been over eight hundred repetitions of the cycle. Charcot's associate Bourneville was closely involved in examining and reporting on her case. Some of the long-term patients at the Salpêtrière identified strongly with Louise Lateau, one of them being Rosalie Leroux, who was admitted in 1846 suffering from epileptic seizures and remained a patient for forty years, her increasingly violent and spectacular seizures becoming the subject of intense scrutiny both by Charcot and Bourneville. Her adoption of rigid cruciform postures during her attacks led Bourneville to compare her repeatedly with Lateau.[6] Pierre Janet worked with a patient called Madeleine Lebouc at the Salpêtrière, who herself had 16 episodes of stigmatization between 1896 and 1899 and attracted a great deal of publicity.[7]

Although, as was to be expected, stigmatization was much commoner in Catholic countries, especially Italy, stigmatics were also appearing in England: Annie Girling became the first English stigmatic in 1864, and went on to found the People of God, a working-class religious movement. Teresa Higginson responded to the reports of Louise Lateau with her own stigmata and the acting out in her own person of the Passion in Bootle during the 1880s.[8]

All this makes the clinical term 'stigmata' an oddly specific word to use for the characteristic symptoms of hysteria, despite the fact that its physical signification seemed so thoroughly worn away or numbed off, so to speak. Pierre Janet's synoptic account of the stigmata of hysteria makes no explicit connection, for instance, between the conditions of hemianaesthesia and other occasional skin symptoms it associates with hysteria and the word that it is using to signify these marks.[9] And yet it is a metaphor which, as so often in matters of the skin, refuses to surrender its literality. Like the words 'trauma' and 'traumata', the word 'stigmata' seems to exercise its functions unacknowledged in writings about hysteria and allied conditions; the physical lesions implied but not stated in the literality of stigmata and traumata are disavowed, hidden in plain sight. William James brings the two ideas of trauma and stigma together very closely in a discussion of the process whereby certain psychological shocks passed through consciousness into unconscious memory: 'Certain reminiscences of the shock fall into the subliminal consciousness, where they can only be discovered in "hypnoid" states. If left there, they act as permanent "psychic traumata", thorns in the spirit, so to speak.'[10] Another term in the lexicon of hysteria which had an interesting and rarely acknowledged reference to stigmatization was the 'clou hystérique', the 'hysterical nail', which was used to describe headaches of piercing intensity. In his review of stigmatics in 1903, Maurice Apte scornfully described the rivalry between Franciscans and Dominicans in producing stigmatic symptoms: 'Every time a nun would have acne spots on her forehead, these would be the crown of thorns . . . If a monk had the "hysterical nail", the nail would be considered a thorn of the crown.'[11]

The word 'stigma' became the metaphor of choice for other conditions as well, particularly those believed to have a hereditary origin. Numerous articles and books appeared during the 1880s and 1890s about the 'stigmata' of degeneracy and criminality. The associations with religious stigmata became looser in the twentieth century, when the word 'stigmata' was progressively abandoned in favour of the word 'stigma', which shifts the reference from the crucifixion to the more distant and generalized myth of marking embodied in the mark of Cain.[12] Those who reflect nowadays on the problems of those enduring the 'stigma' of mental illness, AIDS, prostitution, suicide, poverty, divorce and mixed-race marriage, use the word to signify the effects of a generalized setting-apart, through the bearing of what is above all an *invisible* or wholly metaphorical mark.

There have been occasions, of course, when such metaphorical markings have erupted again into literalness, for example in Nazi efforts to make the insufficiently transpicuous self-evidence of the degeneracy of Jews, homosexuals and other social groups visible by various kinds of mark: the star of David, the pink triangle, the tattoo. There is always something awkward about this marking, for it needs to signify its redundancy; it needs to prove that Jews and others in fact bear the evidence of what they are in the whole of their appearance. The point of the stigma is precisely that it is not a point; in signifying the general degeneracy of the Jew, the Gypsy and the homosexual as such, it must aim not to draw attention to itself. It must melt or diffuse into the whole of the stigmatized subject's being. This is perhaps an instance of Lyotard's prescription: a law's desire to put itself in first place, by showing that the body marks itself. But the mark will always be too much and not enough, for the need to mark categories of person out physically will always also signify the worrying truth that they are not always and reliably distinguishable, do not carry their marks in their being and are not otherwise indistinguishable from their marks.[13]

It does appear as though the idea of the marking of the skin has a strangely indeterminate status in discussions of hysteria. Perhaps we might risk the suggestion that it is a disease, not of the womb, as so many have thought, nor of the imagination, as Freud declared, but a disease of marking. There must be visible marks, stigmata, to hold together the drift and appearances and simulations that constitute hysteria. Actual marks, however, would imply the possibility of error or arbitrariness, the possibility that the physician, or the analyst was merely marking their subject. The mark must come from without in such a way as to be seen to come spontaneously from within. So there cannot be anything as palpable and violent as a mark. And yet, all the same, there must be a mark.

All this gives the skin a particular importance in hysteria. Sander Gilman has shown how important skin conditions were in constructing and maintaining the visibility of the hysteric; eruptions on the skin may have seemed to be the most palpable and self-evident of evidences, and therefore ways of stabilizing this otherwise mysterious and chameleon-like disease.[14] But Gilman represents the bringing to visibility of the hysterical patient as a one-way and once-and-for-all objectification by and for the eye. The problem of hysteria, as instanced particularly in the cutaneous stigmata apparently presented for all to see on the outside of the body, is not that it hides from the eye, but that it complicates visibility. Like the *stigmata diaboli* after which, as we will shortly see, they were named, the hysteric's stigmata marked places of invisibility, marked the places where they could not be seen. The body of the hysteric is an episodic body, in which symptoms come and go. The flash of the photograph fixes the skin like a second stigmatization, but in doing so lets slip the intermittence that the body is borrowing from its skin. Doctors took stigmata as an image of the fixation of ideas in the skin, but in fact the skin displayed frequency rather than fixation, patterned dispersal, both in space and time, rather than permanent marks.

In 1909, Thomas Savill, an English doctor who specialized in the treatment both of nervous diseases and of diseases of the skin, proposed that the link between hysteria and the skin was more than contingent. The link between the skin and the brain (or, more strictly, the solar plexus, which Savill called 'the brain of the sympathetic system generally') was provided by the vaso-motor or circulatory system, of which the skin was the most obvious mirror: 'You have only', he wrote, 'to stand and watch some of these hysterical persons for a time and observe the alternation of flushing and pallor of their skin to be assured of the paroxysmal variations which occur in their vaso-motor systems from minute to minute and from hour to hour.'[15] Savill thought that these displays corresponded to two kinds of morbid episode in the vascular system, which he called 'syncopal' and 'congestive'. The former involved the sudden lowering of blood flow, causing numbness of the skin, fainting, weakness and confusion, and the latter sudden inundations of blood, causing 'flush-storms' (especially in female patients), hypersensitivity, irritation and excitability. 'Fugitive patches' of erythema, or reddening of the skin, such as those in a female patient he illustrated, constituted 'an infallible sign or stigma of the hysterical diathesis' (118). Savill was inclined to blame weakness of the brain and central nervous system for the psychological dimensions of hysteria. He had little time for the psychogenic theories of hysteria, and blamed writers like Janet and Freud for paying too little attention to the 'veritable signs' displayed so openly to view on the bodies of their patients (114).

The mysteriously unlocatable lesion responsible for hysteria was therefore apparent to the eye, for anyone who could see. Savill allowed himself to relish the irony:

> Strange, gentlemen, that we should have before our eyes, in the skin, the very lesion we have been looking for all these years. In the skin, the solid protective covering of the body, slight pallor or congestion or rapid changes do not do much damage, but consider what a disturbance these same changes can create in the delicate, sensitive tissues of the brain, spinal cord, sympathetic ganglia, or peripheral nerves! (139–40)

Skin conditions indeed bulked large in the massive encyclopaedias of hysteria-symptoms that were so painstakingly assembled by Charcot's followers in the last two decades of the nineteenth century, Richer, Pitres, Gilles de La Tourette and Janet. There were two classes of symptoms on the skin, according to which the hysteric was either unnaturally hot or unnaturally cold; unnaturally sensitive or unnaturally insensitive. One involved intensely visible manifestations of swelling and tenderness (oedema), irritation (urticaria) or even spontaneous bleeding and eruption. A hysteric displaying this class of symptom had a skin of unusual susceptibility and sensitivity. His or her skin was indeed a living register, both thermometer and chart, of fluctuating states of feeling and excitement. It was indeed as though the operations of the nervous system were being projected on the skin, in something of the way T. S. Eliot imagined in 'The Love Song of J. Alfred Prufrock' – 'as if a magic lantern threw the nerves in patterns on a screen'.[16] Evidence was brought forward regularly of the capacity of particularly sensitive subjects to produce inflamed or blistered skin, or even haemorrhage through the skin as a result of hypnotic suggestion. According to the Salpêtrière doctors, stigmatics were examples of persons whose state of religious mania had switched them permanently over to this eruptive mode of manifestation.

But there was another, opposite class of symptoms that were much more stable and reliable. Time and again writers on hysteria insisted on the tenacity of phenomena of anaesthesia in hysterical patients. Patients were squeezed and pricked systematically to reveal areas of insensibility, and this insensibility was itself subdivided, into insensibility to pain, heat and pressure; a patient might be insensible to pain while retaining the capacity to feel touch and heat, for example. It was these anaesthetic phenomena, rather than the contractions, the fits, the catatonic episodes and other evanescent 'accidents', which were identified as the 'permanent stigmata' of the disease. Oddly, having established anaesthesia as a fundamental and infallible sign of the hysteric, Charcot's associates also began to experiment with the production of variations in it. Following Charcot's interest in the work of Victor Burq, who had published a book in 1853 on the applications of metallotherapy, Salpêtrière doctors started to combine hypnotism and the application of certain substances to insensible areas of skin in patients.[17] Paul Richer reported that the application of a metal to an insensible area could temporarily restore feeling in that area, but only if a corresponding area on the other side of the body became anaesthetized.[18] Patterns of complementarity began to emerge, confirming and refining the symmetrical maps of body-sensitivity drawn in articles and books.

The symptoms of anaesthesia maintained their special status among the permanent stigmata of hysteria not just because they happened to correspond to the metaphor of marks more closely than other such permanent signs, but also because they were often not apparent to the patient. Patients would present themselves with localized symptoms of numbness or pain in one part of the body, and be amazed to discover that large areas of their body were lacking in sensation. For writers such as Pierre Janet, who became convinced that hysteria provided evidence of areas of personality that had become autonomous from consciousness, they provided a perfect metaphor for the gaps in consciousness. An insensible patch of skin could be seen perfectly well by the patient, but would nevertheless not be part of their picture of themselves, the coenesthetic integument which subtended and held together the self they felt themselves to be.

Despite the fact that anaesthesia constituted the leading form of hysterical 'stigmata', there was some disagreement as to whether it really was an invariant symptom. Reviewing the evidence for localized anaesthesia in a doctoral thesis in 1873, Gustave Alquier distinguished between the permanent areas of loss of sensation which were the indication of a determinate physical cause and the more variable patterns of anaesthesia:

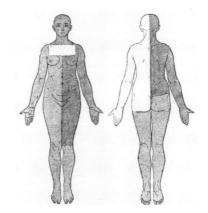

Skin anaesthesia, irregularly distributed, from Gilles de la Tourette, *Traité clinique et thérapeutique de l'hystérie d'après l'enseignement de la Salpêtrière* (Paris, 1891).

Just as anaesthesia resultant upon a material lesion is persistent, regular and, up to a certain point, predictable in its course and duration, so it is variable, irregular and, so to speak, capricious, in certain other affections of which it is a symptom, like mental illnesses, neuroses, etc; this has great diagnostic value.[19]

By the following decade, more sustained investigation had tended to cast doubt upon this distinction, and it was the very variations in the sensibility of the skin, as carefully established by the various investigative methods developed at the Salpêtrière, which came to be regarded as a sort of invariant, the firmament against the background of which other symptoms would come and go.

The analogies with earlier investigations of cutaneous anaesthesia were not lost on doctors who cultivated an interest in the history of witchcraft, sorcery and possession. Gilles de la Tourette began the chapter on cutaneous anaesthesia in his two-volume study of hysteria with a discussion of the *stigmata diaboli*, or Devil's marks. These were spots of numbness, which could only be detected by agonizing probings with needles, and were believed by sixteenth- and seventeenth-century exorcists to provide infallible proof of concourse with the Devil.[20] Tourette discussed in particular the outbreaks of possession at Louviers and Loudun in 1634. Despite the fact that the Parliament at Paris had actually forbidden the 'épreuve de la piqûre' in 1603, the process was employed during the investigation in 1610–11 of Lewis Gaufridy, who was alleged to have been a sorcerer and to have caused the possession of two girls by Beelzebub in Louviers. Tourette alludes to a treatise written by one of those involved in the investigation of the case, which deals explicitly with the question of the *stigmata diaboli*. Jacques Fontaine's *Des marques des sorciers* (1611) insists, against the arguments of sceptics, that patches of insensitivity in the body are an infallible and sufficient sign of confederacy with the Devil. Gaufridy had protested that, if he had such marks, they had been inflicted without his knowledge, but Fontaine chillingly rejects this argument simply on the grounds that God would never allow such a thing to happen. They therefore cannot have been made without the consent of the one so marked.[21] Indeed, the totalitarian Fontaine has an explanation ready of why it is that the marks would be denied; Satan makes these marks not just as a formal covenant of a bond between him and his servants, but in order to make the diabolical pact undeniable, especially in timid spirits who might otherwise be liable to backtrack. Only a few pages later, Fontaine reverses his argument, when considering the marks found on the two feet and in the breast of Gaufridy's principal accuser, Magdaleine de la Palud, marks which subsequently disappeared after his burning and her return to godliness. Fontaine concludes that the erasure of the Devil's marks cannot be a miracle, since the process was accompanied by pain, and God performs his miracles painlessly. On the other hand, it is possible for the Devil to remove his marks, and Fontaine inclines to the view that this is what must have happened in this case, since the Devil would not allow one quitting his service to continue to bear his marks (20).

The characteristics of the marked flesh are dryness, or absence of humour (there is no bleeding when the needle is removed) and absence of sensation: Gaufridy was found to have thirty places on his body – concentrated around the area of the kidneys – where the needle could be inserted to a depth of three fingers without signs of pain. (Traumatic shock reactions with accompanying endorphin production may explain some of this, though Gaufridy would have had to undergo great agonies before this endogenous anaesthesia would have begun to operate.) Fontaine maintained that the marked places on Gaufridy's body could be distinguished reliably from other marks such as birthmarks, citing the case of a man accused of sorcery who defended himself successfully against the charge with the explanation that a pig-shaped mark was imprinted on him by the desire of his mother for pork during pregnancy (14). Devil's marks, which Fontaine surmised are probably made with a red-hot iron, accompanied by some potent ointment, are distinctive in that they reduce the living skin to dead matter. Where such an ambivalence would not normally be allowed to survive for any period of time in nature, since either the living flesh would reanimate the dead portion, or the dead portion would corrupt the entire body, as in gangrene, the one marked by the Devil is kept in a condition of suspended (in)animation, carrying on his person regions from which the soul had entirely withdrawn (15).

Perhaps the most interesting part of Fontaine's awful pamphlet is his claim that the Devil is motivated to make his marks not just to establish ownership, or to betray his followers, but as an explicit mimicry of divine marking: 'The all-powerful God marks those who are of his company with holy and divine marks, which give the gift of eternal life. The evil spirit marks those whom he has taken captive with the marks of death' (6). It is not entirely clear what Fontaine has in mind when speaking of the holy marks of Christ; it is possible that he is thinking of the stigmata, or he may have in mind Paul's reference to the more metaphorical marks of his new life as a Christian (Galatians 6:17). So the mark which attempts to establish irrevocable and primary ownership is a doubled mark, which, in mimicking divine marking, also makes it possible for divine marking to be seen as a doubling of diabolical.

This ambivalence also comes to light in the outbreak of possession at the Ursuline convent of Loudun in 1634 in which the local priest Urbain Grandier

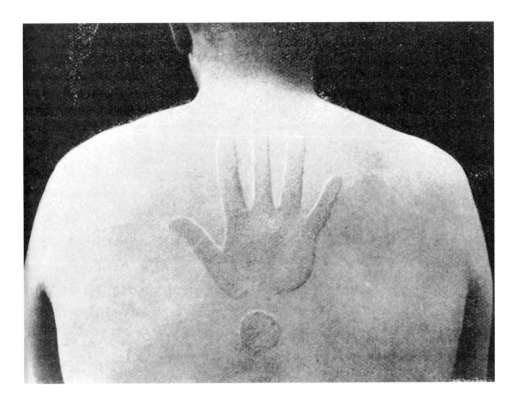

'The Sign of the Devil' from Jeremy Broome, 'Skin Writing', *Strand Magazine*, 14 (1897).

was similarly accused and in which the pricking test was again employed. Grandier was shaved, stripped and blindfolded in order to be subjected to the agonizing process of investigation, after Soeur Jeanne, the mother superior of the Ursuline convent at Loudun, had sworn that he bore five marks of the Devil. In Soeur Jeanne's testimony, these marks appeared to parody the five wounds of Christ's stigmata; the wound in the side was matched by a mark on Grandier's shoulder, the place where criminals were branded, while the marks in hands and feet were grotesquely matched by two marks on the buttocks, close to the anus, and the testicles. No doubt this testimony gave Soeur Jeanne the satisfaction of imagining the needle applied with particular zeal in those sensitive places.

Tourette is horrified at the credulity of accusers and exorcists in affirming that the *stigmata diaboli* were such an infallible sign of having given oneself over to Satan, but he himself regards such symptoms as a similarly infallible sign that the persons concerned were genuine hysterical subjects, and there is an uncomfortable rhyme between the investigative procedures used by the witchfinders and those employed at the Salpêtrière to map the sensitivity of the skin.

Of course the point about these infallible marks, whether diabolical or hysterical, is exactly that they are unmarked; they are apparent, but never visible. It might appear that this is in sharp contrast to the religious stigmatics who display their marks of identification with Christ so unignorably in their bloody exudations, but in fact stigmatics have also regularly asked for their

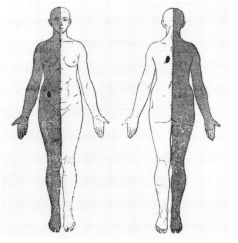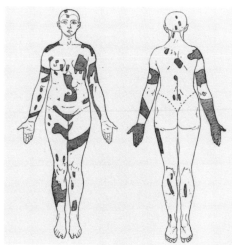

wounds to be kept or made invisible. The most famous case of invisible stigmata is that of Catherine of Siena, who, having received the five wounds in the spring of 1375, prayed that they would disappear, leaving her with the pain only. Fontaine claims that the Devil can mimic God in this respect as well, for he tricked his victim Gaufridy by promising to give him internal rather than external marks (12). The *stigmata diaboli* and the marks of hysteria are alike in that they are neither simply present nor absent; they are latent, waiting for the probing touch of the physician to be revealed. Where the arts of the dissection and anatomy sought to reveal what was happening beneath the screen of the skin, Charcot and his associates saw the visible and the invisible distributed across the skin. They formed a pattern which was a second skin, a motley, or parti-coloured skin which is draped on top of or is compact with the apparent skin.

These symptoms of the surface allow the hysteric to be thought of primarily not as a fractured, doubled, dispersed or even a knotted subject; but rather as a zoned subject. The idea of the zone – from the Greek for a belt or girdle – seems to contain a metaphorical association between the human body and the tropic earth, and the projected second earth of the heavens. The drawings which writers on hysteria produced resemble the astrological schemata of some Eastern physiologies. The belt or girdle connects the planar and the voluminous; it goes all the way round a spherical body, marking on it a region of adjacency.

The iconographical volumes of the Salpêtrière and other writings on hysteria abound with images which map the anaesthetic regions of the bodies of hysterical patients. Some patients exhibited strictly asymmetrical insensibility: others had clearly demarcated bands of insensible flesh; others displayed more chaotic spurts and sprinklings of insensibility. The skin of the hysteric was a map, a plane projection of an otherwise unrepresentable volume. Everything was projected outwards on to the flat screen of the skin, which then in turn became striated and furrowed, a landscape of cliffs and valleys, lakes, vortices and rivers.

Lisa Deanne Smith,
Untitled #2,
1994, dermographic
drawing.

The hysteric is an exotic hybrid, zebra and chameleon combined, its hide marked with fascinating and evanescent streaks, spots and patches. Michel Pastoureau has written of the dubious and exotic power of the idea of striped markings in European history, arguing that striped patterns regularly signify wildness, eccentricity and the condition of the outsider. At the same time, the stripe is, more than any other mark, a produced or purposive pattern, stripes being comparatively rare in nature. The stripe is distinguished in having no division between figure and ground; is a zebra a white animal with black markings, as white Europeans think, or a black animal with white markings, as black Africans think?[22] It is as though the skin of the hysteric faced at once inwards and outwards: some parts of it were so exquisitely sensitive they were like patches of mucous membrane rawly exposed to the air; others seemed so insensitive that it was as though they were turned inwards, away from the patient, or as though the patient had himself turned away from them. Everything could be found on the skin, even though the skin seemed to look elsewhere, away from itself, to some second skin.

DERMOGRAPHICS

There was one symptom in particular which seemed to draw together these two conditions of hyperaesthesia and anaesthesia. Dermographism or dermographia refers to an abnormal sensitivity of the skin which means that it reacts to the lightest pressure with swelling and weals. Words and images traced upon the skin of such patients may remain for 24 hours or longer. The process can sometimes cause pain, but does not invariably do so. Dermographia is, for much of the time, latent rather than manifest. One of the earliest dermographics was Soeur Jeanne of Loudun, who marked the expulsion of devils from her by the miraculous appearance of a cross upon her forehead and then of the word 'Joseph' upon her left forearm.

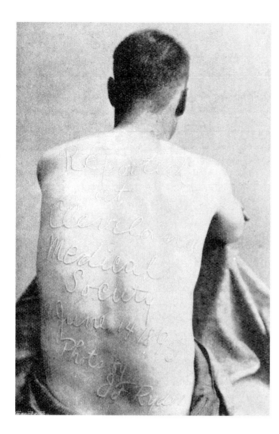

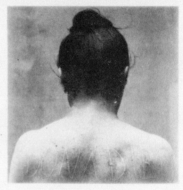

(left) John Miller, 'The Autographic Skin Man', a case of dermographism reported in Cleveland, Ohio, from Jeremy Broome, 'Skin Writing', *Strand Magazine*, 14 (1897).

(right) Dermographic patient with her name 'Angeline Donadieu' written on her front and back, from *Nouvelle Iconographie de la Salpêtrière*, vol. 14 (1901).

Dermographia exercised a particular hold upon the imaginations of medical writers in France, who treated it as a condition in itself, rather than as a mere accessory cause.[23] Janet Beizer has read this marking of the body as an allegory of what she calls the 'ventriloquized body' of the hysteric. Rather than bursting out spontaneously into her exotic and mysterious dance of symptoms, and rather than mounting a somatic protest to the authority of law, language and the father, as the romanticizers of hysteria, from André Breton to Hélène Cixous, have liked to think, the hysteric is, on Beizer's account, miserably written into the authoritative narrative of hysteria. 'In fact the body does not speak; it is spoken, ventriloquized by the master text that makes it signify.'[24] In the dermographic displays that were set up for the benefit of the camera, the capacity of the dermographic skin to fix and retain marks is used to get a fix on the 'impressionability' of the hysteric body (which could be male or female, but is always female even when it is male). In showing the law of the shifting instability of the impressionable body, impermanent as wax or water, it writes its own diagnostic law over it. Beizer sees this as a refusal of the mortality ultimately signified by the mutability of the body: 'clinicians and writers alike struggle to steal God's word, labor to inscribe on the hysterical body a new gospel, which would say: "And the flesh will be made word, will become the word of men."'[25]

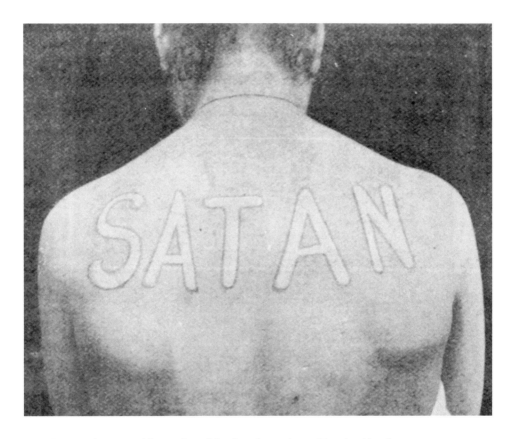

A dermographic inscription mimicking (imagined) 17th-century demonic skin-writing from Jeremy Broome, 'Skin Writing', *Strand Magazine*, 14 (1897).

Beizer sees dermographia as a sign of the shared attention paid to the skin of the hysteric by the writer and the physician, but another medium mediates the acts of writing, showing and knowing. The photographic process is no mere, mute witness to the fascination of the 'hysterical' skin, for which it furnishes both evidence and continuing occasion. These dermographic images testify to the immanence of the skin in photography as such. The backs and foreheads of the subjects of these photographs have been touched by the camera as surely as they bear the marks of the physician's fingernail. The photographs seem to suggest that the mere act of looking might be enough to bring to light these markings and the general state of impressionability they mark. They suggest the implication of the skin of the hysteric in the photographic apparatus, for this skin is a double of the photosensitive plate, and the process of taking the photograph seems to involve simply developing and fixing an image which has already been photographed on the body. One of the most dramatic of the Salpêtrière dermographic images, a woman who has had the word 'SATAN' dramatically (and unaccountably) etched across her shoulders, shows distinct signs of having been retouched. But the doubling of touch will always be at work in the process both of illustration and interpretation. Even the colouring of the front cover of Beizer's own book, which shows a dermographic photograph of the back of a woman inscribed with her own diagnosis, 'démence précoce', succeeds in making the letters much clearer than in the original.

I think that Janet Beizer is right to use the metaphor of the 'ventriloquized body', for dermographism indeed displays some of the dynamism of ventriloquism. The one who gives the Devil, or the trauma, a voice with which to speak, is in fact taking that voice as his own. The one who is marked is disfigured, but with a sign that strives to serve to indicate a more primary stigmatization, bringing to the surface a mark that is in fact originary and of a piece with the apparently blank and immaculate skin. It should not therefore be surprising to find that dermographism was also known as 'autographism'.

Late nineteenth-century medical writers saw it as their mission to explain supernatural or divine miracles such as the stigmata as the effect of hysteria or hypnotic suggestion or both. Since the 1840s, enquirers had been interested in the capacity of hysterics and others to bring about changes in the condition of their skin as a result of suggestion alone. One of these, Charles Baudouin, told the story of a woman who, shocked by the narrow escape of her child from guillotining with a heavy sliding door in front of the fireplace, developed suddenly 'a raised erythematous circle' about her neck, in just the position that was at risk in the child.[26] A story of even more miraculous dermographism was reported in France in November 1913. It concerned a twelve-year-old girl named Raymonde Bellard, who was puzzling over the solution to a sum in the village school of Bussus. Suddenly she felt an odd sensation in her arm and, lifting her sleeve, found the solution inscribed there in a raised welt. The girl was invited to repeat the feat with a sum involving division, an operation which she did not know how to perform. Again, the current answer started forth on her arm. Edmond Duchâtel and René Warcollier made the story a feature of the study they published in the following year of the 'plastic power of the will'.[27] Such stories and experimental scenarios recall closely the stories of images imprinted by shocked imagination on the body of the foetus. They suggest that the skin provided a particularly effective mediating screen for the double logic enacted in hypnotism, whereby a subject made passive in hypnotic trance develops powers beyond their ordinary subjective capacities, and in which the subject is simultaneously both less and more powerful than itself. Rational arguments for the role of autosuggestion in dermographic phenomena in fact explained as little as religious or supernatural accounts, in that neither explain precisely how the skin may be made to bear the print of fears or fixations.

The interest in dermography and other spontaneous markings of the skin registers the growing fascination with the arts and technologies of immediate contact during the later nineteenth century. Despite the similarities of their names, the telegraph and the photograph were on opposite sides of a division between mediate and immediate forms of representation. For all its miraculous speed, the telegraph required an operator at each end, to encode and decode the message. The photograph, by contrast, gave the image of a world now capable of writing or representing itself. The photograph ushered in a world of immediate and instantaneous representations, of autographic impressions. Compared to the world of slow and laborious translations, which had ruled hitherto, and constituted the distinctive work of culture, the modern world would be driven by technologies that would register rather than represent, would ventriloquize the world by allowing it to make its own mark. Such technologies were at once old and new. They evoked the crude mark-making of the illiterate, reviving the sense of the tactile where mass printing had abstracted and rationalized. But they also provoked the possibility of a world of self-report, of traces and signs and fingerprints which might come into being autonomously, according to their own laws of self-figuration, and untouched by human hand.

The most important point about such media was that they were precisely immediate, and in both senses: they were instantaneous, and they involved no intermediary process of translation, or not one that required the insertion of a reasoning human being into the apparatus. The spiritualist's planchette, which, rather than being slowly inscribed in the slow sequences of the ouija-board, would suddenly appear filled with writing, was the embodiment of the *tout-d'un-coup* contact or coming-together of worlds. The language of spiritualism and the occult, which is so full of evocations of the veil, of the other side, suggested that making contact would be a matter of immediate touch rather than a mediated, temporally extended process.

The process of deciphering the complex patterns of symptoms on and beneath the skins of Charcot's patients was certainly itself long and laborious, and some of the symptoms were strangely and puzzlingly various. But at the heart of the theory of hysteria is a conception of the body permanently marked in an instant, at the speed of light; by the flashpoint of trauma, or by the cataleptic fixation induced by sounds or sudden shocks. The skin is normally characterized by the slowness of its accretions. It develops and dissipates its characteristic mottlings, spots and wrinkles, little by little over time, like a cloud or a glacier. The skin exhibited by hysteria is immediate, discontinuous and spasmodic, like the modern world itself.

SECOND SKINS

In all the cases of marked skins that I have been considering – judicial, divinatory, maternal. morbid, ecstatic, ornamental – the mark on the outer surface of the body will be, and therefore partly signify, a doubling. Somewhere, in some other place, on some other, or some inner skin, there will have been a more primary mark, of which the manifest mark is a copy or trace. The mark of the law scorched or bored into the flesh will aim to mark the manner in which the criminal has already been marked from within by the destiny of their act. There will be a second skin of which the primary skin is an impression, and so is really a first. In the case of maternal impression, or some kinds of stigmata – the piercing of the heart from the burning spear suffered by St Teresa in her Transverberation, for example – the mark will pass through the first skin and take up residence in a second. In the case of other stigmatics, the skin of Christ provides an exterior model or template. The stigmatic's skin will willingly take the print of Christ's skin. The stigmata read the crucifixion as a flattening out; the crucified body becomes a single sheet of flesh, reduced to its recto and its verso. In the case of the hysteric, the first, or outer skin, its lesions flaring and fading, condensing and diffusing, gathering and spreading, seems like a duplicitous witness to the second or inner skin; but it may also be seen as an attempt to refold the outer skin in the image of that primary skin. And we can take that idiom 'in the image of' literally: the image is not followed or matched, but inhabited; the second skin is inside the contours of the first as a hand is in a glove. The skin is beginning to occupy and itself become a convoluted space.

Maternal impression and the kinds of dermographic effect allegedly brought about through hypnotic suggestion seem to offer a variant of the doubled skin. Here, the logic seems to be, not of one subject striving to match or rejoin two skins, but of two subjects conjoined in one skin: the mother and the skin of her child, the hypnotist and his subject collaborating on the work of marking the skin without laying a finger on it.

Writers on the occult also paid attention to stigmatization and other phenomena of skin-markings during the later nineteenth century. As one might expect, H. P. Blavatsky's *Isis Unveiled*, a massive compendium of stories and speculations about the supernatural, drawn promiscuously from every possible kind of source, had plenty to say about the subject of preternatural markings of the skin. Blavatsky was convinced that stigmata, along with birthmarks, were signs of the power of the directed or powerfully affected imagination over the body. Mixing references to Pythagoras and the seventeenth-century Neoplatonist Henry More with contemporary reports from *The Lancet*, Blavatsky argued that malformation and distinctive markings could be explained only by the influence of the imagination, which she saw as '*the plastic or creative power of the soul*'.[28]

In her elaborate explanation of how imagination is able to stamp its forms and images on the skin Blavatsky produces her own version of the doubled skin. At the heart of her scavenged and motley magical system is a conception of what she calls the triune nature of human and natural life. According to this, every visible, natural body has 'an invisible, indwelling, energizing nature, the exact model of the other and its vital principle', and a third, permanent and immortal spirit (II, 587). Blavatsky named the double of the mortal body its 'astral body', because she believed that it derived its form from the universal substance known as the ether, which shone in the form of astral light or electromagnetic radiation. This is not a theory of astrological influence, since Blavatsky held that electromagnetic radiations shone through rather than from the stars; among the many half-digested mystical ideas in her ramshackle system is the Paracelsian conception of the stars as a kind of outer shell or tegument for the earth (I, xxvi). Blavatsky found a great deal of evidence both in folklore and in contemporary spiritualist reports for the interaction of the mortal and the astral bodies, and the magical and mysterious marking of the skin provides particular evidence of what she calls 'repercussion', in which a blow aimed at the double or phantom of an absent living person can affect the person himself or herself in the corresponding portion, wherever they may be. Blavatsky has a marvellously complicated explanation of how this effect comes about in the case of markings caused by maternal impressions. She borrows the traditional account of the foetus as a malleable substance which is able to 'stamp with the effigies, or, as we might more properly call it, *astrograph*, of some object vividly presented to her imagination' (I, 385). Blavatsky means that the form comes, not directly from the mother's imagination, but from her astral double, or emanation (for sometimes the astral body is seen as a complete replica or *doppelgänger* of the body, and sometimes as a skin-like aura, emanation or atmosphere). The astral body both conserves and multiplies images, and Blavatsky extends her photographic metaphor with characteristic literalness in updating the Aristotelian explanation of the transmission of resemblance between generations:

> as each person's atmosphere in the astral light is peopled with the images of his or her immediate family, the sensitive surface of the foetus, which may almost be likened to the collodionized plate of a photograph, is as likely as not to be stamped with the image of a near or remote ancestor whom the mother never saw, but which, at some critical moment, came as it were into the focus of nature's camera. (I, 385)

A little later, she reports the case of a boy killed by a stroke of lightning, who was found to have an imprinted on his chest the image of a tree at which he had been looking when the lightning bolt struck. She suggests that this spontaneous photography provides a way of understanding how mental images of the mother are transmitted to the body of the child. Her explanation depends upon the principle that a pregnant woman is not only 'highly impressible', but also, so to speak, actively impressive:

> Her *pores* are opened; she exudes an *odic* emanation which is but another form of the *akasa*, the electricity, or life-principle, and which, according to Reichenbach, produces mesmeric sleep, and consequently is *magnetism*. Magnetic currents develop themselves into electricity upon their exit from the body. An object making a violent impression on the mother's mind, its image is instantly projected into the astral light, or the universal ether, which Jevons and Babbage, as well as the authors of the *Unseen Universe*, tell us is the repository of the *spiritual* images of all forms, and even human thoughts. Her magnetic emanations attract and unite themselves with the descending current which already bears the image upon it. It rebounds, and re-percussing more or less violently, impresses itself upon the foetus. (I, 395)

The emphasis here is not on the vulnerability of the pregnant woman to external influences, but on her heightened capacity for leaking or transmitting them. This seems both to redouble and amplify a power of spontaneous image-making in the astral sphere; quoting Fournié's *Physiologie du système nerveux* of 1872, Blavatsky assures her readers that "'Continual photographs of all occurrences are thus produced and retained. A large portion of the energy of the universe may thus be said to be invested in such pictures.'" (1, 398). It is therefore the interference of mental images with their ethereal doubles which seems to produce the amplifying recoil necessary to impress the form upon the astrographic skin-plate of the foetus.

It is hard to tell quite why Blavatsky sets so much store by these complex repercussion effects, when other writers had been content with the idea of the simple transmission of images directly from the mother, or from its source, to the body of the infant. Perhaps these repercussions and doublings between primary and astral bodies seem to explain the transmission of images from skin to skin better than other explanations. Perhaps Blavatsky's world is one in which the idea of an intervening network or 'exchange' has come to seem a familiar and necessary feature of the transmission of impacts and impressions. Blavatsky notes the relations between maternal impressions and the mimicry of the crucifixion involved in the stigmata, and records a story (from Catherine Crowe's well-known *Night-Side of Nature*) of the traumatic doubling of skin-impressions:

Two young ladies, in Poland, were standing by an open window during a storm; a flash of lightning fell near them, and the gold necklace on the neck of one of them was melted. A perfect image of it was impressed upon the skin, and remained throughout life. The other girl, appalled by the accident to her companion, stood transfixed with horror for several minutes, and then fainted away. Little by little, the same mark of a necklace as had been instantaneously imprinted upon her friend's body, appeared upon her own, and remained there for several years, when it gradually disappeared. (1, 398)

Despite the elaboration and idiosyncrasy of her explanations, it is possible to see some parallels between Blavatsky's astral body and neurological conceptions such as that of the cerebral homunculus. In both cases, the outer, visible skin shows the displaced effects of a second skin. Embryology and cerebral anatomy generated other ideas about the communication between inner and outer skins. Thomas Savill's *Lectures on Hysteria*, for example, drew on knowledge about the early development of the foetus for an explanation of the close relationship between the skin and the central nervous system he claimed to have found in hysteria. The first significant change in the embryo after fertilization, he explained, is the formation of three layers, the epiblast, medoblast and hypoblast. Only two structures evolve from the epiblast; it folds outwards to form the skin and its associated organs, while the central nervous system comes about 'solely by an infolding of the epiblast'. The reciprocity between skin and central nervous system is due to the fact that they are foldings in two dimensions of a common skin: 'just as the skin with its tactile corpuscles, the eyes and other external sense organs (also developed from the epiblast) represent the external projection of the sensorium, so does the central nervous system represent the internal projection of the sensorium' (139).

Charcot similarly sought to match the outer body with the inner body, though he thought this latter was inscribed in the motor-sensor homunculus of the cerebral cortex rather than in the central nervous system. The brain was beginning to be understood as a perverse twin of the skin, a flattened, but also twisted, pleated, stretched, folded-over plane projection of the body; the skin's anagram. Just as the crucifixion reduced the body to its cardinal points, hands, feet, breast and brow, so neurology sought to plot the cardinal points in the cortex which controlled movement and sensation. There were two stages to the work of careful, even obsessive observation of patients that took place at the Salpêtrière. The first was the registering of problems and idiosyncrasies, especially of movement, posture and sensation, in the living patient over a period of time. The second was the attempt, through autopsy, to correlate defects with observable lesions in the brain. Death provided the first opportunity to fold together these two disjoined membranes. Freud tells us of the clumsy servant whom Charcot kept in his employment, despite the broken plates and glasses it cost him until he was able to examine her brain after death.[29] The story perhaps tells us as much about Charcot's patience as it does about his charity.

For Charcot, hysteria was a disease of topology. Charcot's photographs, tables and diagrams, along with the various devices he invented for distinguishing and recording characteristic patterns of debility, tremor and numbness, were all accessory to his efforts to map this strange double topology. The wry lips and twisted limbs, the rigid 'corps-clichés', as Georges Didi-Huberman has described them,[30] of the passional postures he had photographed, were morphings or topological transformations of the alternative skin of the brain; tell-tale ripples in the secondary fabric which might reveal the weave and disposition of the brain's primary textile. Charcot was, as we might nowadays say, a decidedly 'hands-on' doctor. As well as pricking, pinching, tapping, stretching, squeezing and compressing the bodies of his patients, he would sketch them (he was a pretty accomplished artist) and plastically mould them in different positions. He recorded different styles of signature, to demonstrate the difference between different diseases; the delirium tremens of alcoholism would have a different 'signature', marked through or overlaid upon the actual signature, from, say, Parkinsonism.[31] He was also a good physical mimic, with a particular talent for imitating gait. He taught his students to listen for the characteristic shuffle and patter of the gaits arising from different conditions, and even devised a 'gait laboratory', in which he had patients dip their feet in ink and walk across long strips of paper, thus signing it with their characteristic movements, like parody Tinkerbells.[32] All of this provided evidence of the otherwise scattered, and always ideal inner skin of the patient's neurology. Charcot insisted that his terrain was not the higher (or in cerebral terms, 'deeper') cognitive functions, such as knowledge, memory and affect, but the sensory-motor functions, which were beginning so dramatically to be located in the brain. At Charcot's clinic, hysteria was understood as a deep superficiality. Charcot maintained that his techniques and treatment were focused only on the sensory-motor cortex, and not on the deeper and much more complex cognitive and affective operations buried deeper in the brain.

But Charcot also employed a different mode of touch. Although mesmerism was closely identified with the hand, with its repertoire of gestures and passes, mesmerists preferred to demonstrate their powers by operating at a distance from their subjects, rather than through the more direct laying on of hands. Earlier in the century, phrenomesmerists, who sought to combine the system of phrenology with the powers of mesmerism, would concentrate their movements on different parts of the skull, but usually without resort to the actual application of touch to it. The metaphor suggested here is not that of the psychic surgeon, seeking to locate and expunge some hidden lesion in a literal way, but that of the puppeteer. The mesmerist works with an imaginary apparatus of planes and strings. The hands smooth and caress the air, creating planes of smoothness and flatness; but they will also identify cardinal points in the body – the eyes, the hands, the knee joints, the feet – at which the mesmerist may tug at will, bringing the subject's body docilely behind it. Alison Winter has suggested that the figure of the mesmerist contributed to a growing nineteenth-century belief in the possibility of coordination and control not just of an individual body, but of the collective body of a crowd or social mass: the 'passes' of the mesmerist join with the conductor's baton that chops and shapes the air.[33] Mesmeric subjects, it seemed, required both to be diffused and concentrated, massaged into compliance, assuaged with an imaginary hand, all tensions diffused, and also brought to alert focus. Even when he was not engaged in mesmeric activity, Charcot was also involved in rearticulating the bodies of his patients, as a projection of points and zones.

The string puppet owes the illusion it can give of autonomous movement to the fact that it is not controlled directly by the hand, as is a glove puppet. The tension and looseness of the strings make the figure of the puppet seemingly the centre of a dynamic of contending forces, like a living body. But this is of course an illusion, and the nervous autonomy of the string puppet is in fact also largely due to the amplifying effect of the strings. The string puppet is not crudely identical with the hand as the glove puppet or the ventriloquist's dummy are, but is isomorphic with it, filled with its frail, excitable, nervous life. It appears alive because we attribute to it the sensitivity of the hand and fingers, the quivering of which run through it. Despite the fact that it is so obviously jointed, and moved part by part, it moves in complete gestures, like the hand that originates its movements. When two puppets meet, to collide or kiss, they do so as the secret, fluttering meeting of hands and fingers. The string puppet is not merely controlled by a hand; it is an amplified image of that hand, or the space it shapes, its tremor, its address, its attack. It is possible for us to see the body of the puppet as a hand, because we are so used to seeing the hand as a kind of body-double. The puppeteer first of all folds his whole body into his hand, like the painter or the pianist, then unfolds it into the secondary body of the puppet.

Michel Serres has written illuminatingly of this commerce between hand and body. The hand is not a mere part of the body; rather it represents the body as such, like a homunculus, for it is the body's capacity to reach out beyond itself, as well as transformingly towards itself. The hand is the body's possibility: '[W]hat is a hand? It is not an organ, it is a faculty, a capacity for doing, for becoming claw or paw, weapon or compendium. It is a naked faculty. A faculty is not special, it is never specific, it is the possibility of doing something in general.'[34]

This is to say that the hand (like the face) can be an alternative body, a second skin. It is the body reshaped, subject to topological transformation, or 'morphing'. This operation involves the changing of one shape into another without rupture or lesion of its surface – as when one stretches, twists and knots a bag, or, better still, a balloon, without tearing or bursting it. One turns the bag or balloon into a wholly different shape, without changing its original conformation. In this sense, topological transformation turns a shape into itself, into another shape that is still its own shape – an 'isotrope' of itself. In topology, the shape changes, but the skin remains entire and intact. The different kinds of puppet-show invented by Mesmer, Charcot and Freud were in fact different kinds of imaginary topology, involving the doubling of skins, the suturing of the outer skin with an imaginary second skin.

The ideal form of this suturing was absolutely isomorphic, in which symptom and cause would mirror each other as closely as the recto and verso of a sheet of paper. The charting of hysteria was, as Georges Didi-Hubermann has suggested, the effort to produce an ideal expressive flatness, or facies, which would exactly match its cortical inner lining.[35] But the mobile convolutions of the skin shaped a phase-space, a deep superficiality, which complicated this planar equivalence. Investigative and diagnostic procedures attempted to reduce hysterics to their skin, but, in the very attention they paid to the skin, they produced a body whose outer surface could assimilate and transform the whole of the body. In a sense, Charcot was bringing about the same kind of extraordinary interchange of inner and outer as were reported of St Francis, the original stigmatic, in which the skin formed the very nails that pierced his skin, or of St Clare of Montefalco, who announced on her deathbed 'in my very heart I have and hold Christ crucified'; the sequel is rendered with an exemplary mixture of credulity and grisliness by Montague Summers:

> The evening after her death . . . it was decided to extract and open the heart, and herein, in a concavity bisected by the razor of the operator, all wrought out of the flesh, filaments, muscles and nerves, were indeed discovered the Crucifix and other Instruments of the divine Passion. All these were modelled and ensculptured, clearly represented, by means of hard nerves of flesh, each in its own cellule. Thus in the moiety of the heart were contained the Crucifix, the three nails, the spear, and the reed with the sponge; in the other ventricle were the pillar of scourging, the scourge itself with five thongs, and the crown of thorns, all most plainly to be seen.[36]

Three gallstones were also apparently discovered, and 'the Commission appointed to inquire into this prodigy has no hesitation in acknowledging that the three spherical globes were emblematical of the Most Holy Trinity.'[37] Here, thickened and moulded into nerves and muscle, the skin trumps the very instruments of its tearing and torture by turning them into itself. As the image and principle of the body's shape, and no longer the dead, insensible and immovable carapace spoken of by St Thomas, the skin becomes a miraculous, polymorphous plasma, the shape of shape itself.

PRESSING CONCERNS

Charcot went along with his patients in somatizing the psychic, which is to say, tabulating symptoms in the form of a chart, and setting aside everything that could not be rendered in terms of the differentiae of movement, posture and sensation. Little of this passes across into Freud, who was determined to reverse the conversion process, and convert the somatic back into the psychic.

The story of how Freud shifted the study of hysteria away from its cruder and more dramatic outward manifestations, towards the subtler enigmas and agonies of the mind, is familiar. Psychoanalysis, we are told, would substitute intimate listening for public spectacle. It would abandon the suggestion that hysteria has a simple physical basis, and the notion of a one-to-one correspondence between damaged brain and damaged body. Born from the mistrust of the purely physical analysis of Charcot, psychoanalysis would nevertheless retain Charcot's sensitivity to the importance of sign and symptom; but it will see its patients as much more closely implicated in the production of these signs than Charcot ever did. There were those among Charcot's associates who themselves moved away from his mechanistic coupling of brain and body, in particular Pierre Janet, who argued that hysteria was the encysting in the body of *idées fixes*. But even Janet preserved a notion of the simple and unconscious imprinting of the conception upon the body. For Freud, there would be no such simple skin-to-skin impressing of brain upon body. Between them would come language, with all its powers to displace and simulate. Freud would attempt to restore the buffer, or intermediary zone of language, to a world of immediate contacts, of impacts and collisions and contingencies.

All of this makes psychoanalysis much less focused upon the skin and its symptoms than Charcot and his associates had been. Even in his earlier, pre-psychoanalytic writings on hysteria, Freud was much less concerned with tabulating the 'stigmata' of hysteria. There is no shared skin of hysteria for him. Freud's contributions to *Studies on Hysteria* imagine the hysterical cause not as an actual lesion on the cerebral cortex, but as an imaginary nucleus, buried like a carcinoma deeply within concentric circles of strata, and able to be reached only through complicated zigzag paths.

For Freud, the problem with hysteria was that it depended so much upon the bodily display which, while it sometimes delivered the hysteric up satisfactorily to the doctor's understanding and interpretation, also forced the doctor to play the game in the hysteric's own somatic register. By progressively removing his hands from the patient's person, Freud distanced himself from the theatrical mode of Charcot and Janet, and in the process erased the skin and its affections from his consideration. Like the psychic investigators who, at around the same time, were discreetly directing their attention away from the grosser and more ludicrous kinds of trickery in the séance – levitations, ghostly hands, full-body materializations and the like – towards phenomena like thought transference, Freud wanted to desomatize psychoanalysis. By the time of the Dora case history (1905), he was able explicitly to warn off readers looking for this kind of material:

> [N]othing will be found in the following pages on the subject of stigmata of cutaneous sensibility, limitation of the visual field, or similar matters. I may venture to remark, however, that all such collections of the strange and wonderful phenomena of hysteria have but slightly advanced our knowledge of a disease which still remains as great a puzzle as ever.[38]

Freud may have rejected the literality of symptoms, and the crudity of a model in which lesions on the outside corresponded to lesions on the inside, but he was never able to do without topology as such. Even where language and psyche mediate, there always remains in his thinking about the elements of the self and their ratios the guiding principle of a body-to-body contact in space. One of the reasons that Freudian psychoanalysis has occasionally seemed plausible and therapeutically effective is that it so congenially houses the self in a familiar kind of body or dimensional space – of layers, interiorities and depths. The skin will be implicated in the economic model of excitation which governs Freud's thinking from this moment onwards. For the skin is the barrier, the distributor of sensation, sometimes diffusing it, sometimes concentrating it, but always to the end of maintaining optimal levels of equilibrium, balancing the inside and the outside, the local and the global.

Freudian psychoanalysis does all it can to suggest the importance of depth; hysteria has a tendency to spread. One of the functions of the skin when it does come to occasional visibility in Freudian writings on hysteria is as a metaphor for the brain, now increasingly being understood in terms of networks, pathways and regions, organized not in masses, but in sheets or folds. In one of the essays he contributed to *Studies on Hysteria*, Breuer speaks of the normal levels of alertness and connection in an alert subject as an electrically charged network of wires, and uses an epidermal idea to evoke the displacement, or short-circuiting of insufficiently discharged affect, that brings about hysteria:

> If a stimulus of the mucous membrane of the nose fails for any reason to release this preformed reflex, a feeling of excitation and tension arises, as we all know. The excitation, which has been unable to flow off along motor paths, now, inhibiting all other activity, spreads over the brain.[39]

Freud shows in his concluding essay of *Studies on Hysteria* that same highly developed topological bent as is to be found in his later writings. But there is one feature of Freud's procedure that seems to imply a different, flatter topology. Freud writes in his account of Lucy R. of seeing Hippolyte Bernheim use the technique of pressing against the hypnotic subject's forehead in order to release memories (110). Freud dismisses this as 'a small technical device' (270) and by 1904 he was already eschewing touch in his consultations. Nevertheless, he does claim a great deal for its efficacy in overcoming the resistance of patients. 'In every fairly complicated analysis the work is carried on by the repeated, indeed continuous, use of this procedure of pressure on the forehead' (272). Because the technique has 'invariably achieved its aim', Freud writes that he 'can no longer do without it' (270).

Despite the talk of paths, tracks, threads and strata, Freud's patients were encouraged by the pressure technique to visualize ideas and memory-traces as inscribed on a surface, a cortical screen or tablet, hovering just above the eyes. Freud's technique offers to short-circuit the process of teasing-out, untangling and following through which governs his writing about the analysis of hysteria. Pressing his hand against the patient's forehead seems to give him direct access to the skin of the frontal cortex that lies beneath the skin of the forehead, allowing him to lift off a print or, so to speak, a cortograph. Freud offers a symbolic reading of the procedure, though without making it clear whether the symbolism is supposed to be operating for him or for his patient: 'The conclusion which I draw from the fact that what I am looking for always appears under the pressure of my hand is as follows. The pathogenic idea which has ostensibly been forgotten is always lying ready "close at hand"' (271). It may have been the very fact of its showy ancestry that caused Freud to drop this show-and-tell procedure in favour of a more strictly verbal talking cure. Nevertheless, there is a strange correlation between the technique of cerebral pressure and Charcot's extraordinary belief in 'hysterogenic zones', upon which pressure could be applied either to induce or to dissipate hysterical seizures. Charcot even devised an apparatus that would automatically apply pressure to the ovarian region.

Pressure does not release understanding straight away: Freud explicates the process of applying pressure as the production of images or ideas which must then be connected up and decoded, usually by being put into words. These images are the absent emblems or stigmata of the otherwise puzzlingly invisible illness of the neurotic patient. One patient in particular produced a number of images – a sun with golden rays, a triangle, a pile of writhing snakes – which he eventually realized 'were symbols of trains of thought influenced by the occult and were perhaps emblems from the title-pages of occult books' (278). The purpose of turning these images into words is not to make their meaning and significance clear, but to erase them. Thus, the more the patient says about the images, the dimmer they become: '*The patient is, as it were, getting rid of it by turning it into words*' (280). As long as any portion remains of the picture – a stigma, as it were lodged in the skin of the mind – there will be more talking to be done (281). In another patient, words were produced rather than images:

When I asked this lady whether she had seen anything or had any recollection under the pressure of my hand, she replied: 'Neither the one nor the other, but a word has suddenly occurred to me.' 'A single word?' 'Yes, but it sounds too silly.' 'Say it all the same.' 'Concierge.' 'Nothing else?' 'No.' I pressed a second time and once more an isolated word shot through her mind: 'Night-gown.' I saw now that this was a new method of answering, and by pressing repeatedly I brought out what seemed to be a meaningless series of words: 'Concierge' – 'night-gown' – 'bed' – 'town' – 'farm-cart'. (275–6)

Here, although the technique produces words rather than images, their cryptic nature means that they have the status of visual emblems – like the fragments of Sanskrit remembered by another patient – until they can be talked off. The hand thus signifies not only a kind of Veronican handkerchief which can carry away the 'vera icona' of the patient's obsession, but also a way of smoothing out the traces impressed cryptically on the brain. It is, in short, a version of the mystic writing pad to which Freud will later devote an essay, which can both transmit and erase traces. That little toy, with its arrangement of layers, celluloid outer 'screen', waxed paper, and wax slab, will later image to Freud how it is that perception and memory are both linked and separated in the laying down and erasure of memories.[40] This arrangement answers the difficulty first identified by Breuer in a footnote to his theoretical essay in *Studies on Hysteria*, that '[t]he mirror of a reflecting telescope cannot at the same time be a photographic plate' (189). The structure of the mystic writing pad, with one tough but permeable skin allowing impressions through to a more malleable skin that is nevertheless able to arrest and retain them as traces, is isomorphic with the model of maternal impressions maintained in the early modern period. The purpose of the skin has often been said to be that of defining the oneness and integrity of beings: for Freud, one skin is far from enough.

It is also important for Freud to defend himself from the thought that he might not be causing repressed material to come to the surface, or impressions to be lifted off from it, but rather pressing these thoughts in. He hides, not very convincingly, behind the assumption of infallibility. 'It is of course of great importance for the progress of the analysis that one should always turn out to be in the right *vis-à-vis* the patient, otherwise one would always be dependent on what he chose to tell one. It is therefore consoling to know that the pressure technique in fact never fails' (281). That must indeed have been a consolation. In order to fend off later doubting Thomases, Freud determines increasingly not to take the risk of handling his patients, and willingly surrenders the evidence of the palpable, the 'close-at-hand'; but here, as always, the skin seems to produce an infallible sign.

Freud recognized, as Charcot had not, that explication of the disease in terms of its physical signs and wonders would have only limited efficacy in maintaining the life of hysteria. Like the generations of psychoanalysts and psychoanalytically-inclined literary and cultural critics who have followed him, he realized that it was more important for its survival that hysteria should be a disease without lesions than that its characteristic marks should be once and for all mapped out. The secret of hysteria, that *it does not exist*, can be turned into a secret principle of strength; its unmarked nature, its non-evidence, is made into something occult and mysterious. Like Lacan's castration theory, as acidly described by Jacques Derrida, it is a lack that can never be lacking, a shortfall designed to ensure that hysteria will never run out: 'Something is missing from its place, but the lack is never missing from it. (*Quelque chose manque à sa place, mais le manque n'y manque jamais.*)'[41]

The bodily sigillae which froze time upon the skin must be turned into words; the apparitions, the instantaneous contacts and the automatic writings of the hysteric's stigmata must be made syntagmatic. Freud moved away from the skin to his vastly influential vision of the complex interior space of the mind, with its 'cliffs of fall/ Frightful, sheer, no-man-fathomed' (282) in order to reintroduce time to psychic functioning and the process of its analysis. The stopped clock of the stigmata had to be made to tick, if interminably.

Hysteria bears the impress of a more generalized law of marks based upon the idea of impression itself. Given the frequency with which hysterical patients were described as 'impressionable', Georges Didi-Hubermann's characterization of hysteria as '*une maladie du contact, de l'impression*' is apt.[42] This idea began to diversify into very different forms in the second half of the nineteenth century, as the making and taking of impressions which had first been developed in the processes of the printing press began to be generalized. 'Impressionism', which supplied the name for a particular form or ideal of immediacy in painting, and then writing, provides a name for this general mode of impressability, in which the skin, or the self imaged as such a skin, becomes not merely a register of scenes, events, feelings and ideas (themselves imaged increasingly as volatile skins, films, seals, stamps, plaques, plates and other forms of Epicurean eidola), but as their active acquirer, ever hungry for the touch of new impressions, like a photographic plate itching for the touch of light. The skin provides the metaphor for this impassioned passivity, but is transformed by it too, into an active enquirer after impressions. Even the relations of voice and ear have been reformed by this mobile order of exchanged touches, for now an 'impressionist' means, not an artist who captures a scene or feeling, but one who mimics another's voice. One still hears this mimicry described in British English as 'taking somebody off'. The fear of exposure in the doctrine of maternal impressions modulates into a more complex and general kind of touchiness, in the desire for and dependency on ever more subtle and fugitive forms of contact and impact, of making and taking of impressions.

One of the ways in which impressionist painters sought to convey the immediacy of their response to the world was to use dabs, slabs and streaks of colour in place of the enclosing lines and sculptured volumes of realist painting. Rather than being deposited once and for all on a receiving surface, the painting hovered as though in mid-air, waiting for the eye of the viewer to integrate its elements into an image. It was a virtual surface, concealed anamorphically at its focal length, like the cinema image that never comes together until it finds the screen or retina where it comes to rest. For Seurat and other painters, it was largely the dynamism of colour, unbounded by line and form, that allowed this hovering species without a superficies to persist. The next chapter will consider how these virtual skins of colour interact with the chromatography of the skin itself.

6 Off-Colour

THE COLOUR OF COLOUR

Why, it has many times been asked, should a man or woman suffer prejudice and discrimination merely because of the colour of their skin? The question implies an attitude that is worth wondering a little about. It implies that the colour of the skin is arbitrary. The injustice lies in this arbitrariness, in the fact of taking something so obviously superficial, so inessential, so little one's responsibility and therefore so little a part of what one is in oneself, as the basis for discrimination.

Why does the question ask itself in this way? For the association between skin and colour is not at all arbitrary. Colour is seen as inessential because it is thought of as a skin. To snip short the long story I am about to spin out, skin-colour cannot but be significant in human history (though, to be sure, in very different ways at different times and places) because colour *is* skin.

Sometime during the eighteenth century in Europe – certainly not very long before – the question of skin colour started to become what it had not previously been, the overwhelming discriminating factor in theories of racial difference. The discrimination of the colours in the spectrum of mankind began as mere emblems or blazons, to signal deeper differences of history, civilization and racial temperament, but progressively the colours themselves began to soak down into the discussion. It is not just that a matter of deploying the conventionally positive associations of whiteness – clarity, innocence, purity, power, beauty, truth, light – against those of blackness, or darkness – violence, ugliness, sin, ignorance, corruption, deceit. Red, yellow, brown, and the mixtures between them, all acquired specific and sometimes contradictory associations. A history of discrimination through skin colour must branch through a cultural history of colour and colours as such, though such a history is only just beginning to be formed.[1]

Our contemporary awareness of the massive historical overinvestment in the fact of skin colour in racism seems to require both acknowledgement and disavowal. It is necessary to acknowledge the division of the world in terms of the difference between black and white in order to expose and denounce it, in all its arbitrariness and vicious delusion, as quickly and unmistakably as possible. But, having once proclaimed that colour is the predominating racial category, we drain it away from our discussions, preferring to use only two colour terms, black and white, with a sort of willed indifference to the actuality of colour and an intolerance of any thought of mixture between them. To be black is to be not-white; to be white is to be not-black. These colour-terms are not in fact chromatic, but algebraic. They assert both the all-determining power of colour in certain instances and our present determination that it should no longer be so, since the actual colour or, of course, range of colours one may be, is as irrelevant to one's membership of an ethnic group as the colour of the political party one supports. Black and white must be seen as ethnic or political markers rather than physical designations; and should therefore have as little reference to the fact of colour as possible. This is given extra intensity by the fact that, in some cultural colour systems, black and white are not felt to belong to the spectrum of colours at all. They have also been described as being at a different level of colour awareness, according to the (highly controversial) model of colour-naming announced by Berlin and Kay in 1969, according to which there are six stages of colour awareness: 1) All cultures have words for white and black; 2) If there is a third colour term; it will be red; 3) If there is a fourth colour term, it will be yellow or green; 4) If there is a fifth colour term, it will be green or yellow; 5) If there is a sixth colour term, it will be blue; 6) If there is a seventh colour term, it will be brown.[2]

'Black' and 'white' signify their own arbitrariness, and are a deliberate way of maintaining and affirming a kind of colour-blindness. When I name myself or another as 'black' I mean 'one whom others regard as "black"'. I could not use the words 'red' or 'brown' or 'yellow' in the same way unless they too had a political profile, and summarized and signified the value and effect of a colour, rather than the colour itself. Black and white are therefore markers of 'chromaticity', so to speak, designators of attitudes towards colour, rather than colours themselves. In using the last phrase, I do not mean to imply a distinction between the conventional associations of colours and the physical facts of colours 'themselves', for what I mean by seeing colours as colours is precisely seeing the cultural meanings they carry. The distinction I imply between chromaticity and colours is not a distinction between culture and nature.

The saturation of the field of skin colour with black and white, which designate colour without properly being colours, creates an obstacle to the discussion of the cultural and political meanings of actual skin colours; that, indeed, is part of the point, for these terms are there, as I have said, in order to acknowledge the fact of colour prejudice while having nothing more to do with it. To enter once again into the particularized discussion of colours and their meanings, elaborating upon the historical meanings of the particular hues, shades and nuances of human colour, is to seem to linger on the objectionable surface of the history and the present of racial discrimination, replicating its fetishisms and obsessive distinctions: mixed-race, half-caste, mulatto, quadroon, octoroon. It is to take colour itself, rather than the history and fact of colour-prejudice, too seriously, and there is a long history of disapproval of this. Of course, it would be wrong to say that there have been no attempts to investigate the cultural meanings of different skin colours, though what work there has been tends to replicate our current dichromatism, and to be restricted to often rather predictable tottings-up of the positive and negative associations of whiteness and blackness.[3] So it is only with an uncomfortable sort of wrench and a sense of committing an indelicacy that one attempts, as I will here, to relate the history of skin colour back to the cultural history of colour as such. Such an attempt does not involve going behind or beyond the superficial phenomenon of colour, but rather going deeper into that surface.

One of the interesting and sometimes confusing features of the history of colour and colour terms is the natural tendency for colours to be identified with the particular objects they characterize: often these are natural objects, like plants or precious stones, but the same also applies to items of clothing and textiles. The colour moves from being a synecdoche or associated feature of the object to becoming the object's name, the most obvious example of this being gold, a colour which it is almost impossible to strip of its associations with the economic and symbolic value of the metal it characterizes. A less familiar example is the word 'puke', which in the early seventeenth century was the name for a woollen fabric, of a rather superior kind, used commonly in the making of gowns, which later came to signify the particular colour associated with this fabric – apparently a dark blue or inky black. Another case is the term 'isabelle', to signify a rather soiled-looking calico, in memory of the Infanta Isabella, daughter of Philip II of Spain, who vowed not to change her underwear until her forces had taken the city of Ostend. (The grubbiness of the shade they finally attained may be gauged from the fact that the siege lasted from 1601 to 1604.)

In such cases, and they are many, the colour as it were mingles with an object or substance, imparting its tincture to it, and receiving back its impress. The coloured object – gold, milk, sky, blood – gives rise to what we might call an object-colour, a colour with its own phantasmal form, texture and density. And then, since colours are by their nature transferable, for anything can in principle be of any colour, these object-colours can mingle with other objects. One of the reasons that the history of colour is so interfused with all aspects of social and cultural life is that it so intimately involved with the symbolic life of substances. No history of culture can well do without the philosophy of mixed bodies that colour comports. The most important of those reversible object-colours is the skin, and for a very particular reason: as we are about to see, of all the material associations of colour, the idea that colour itself is a kind of skin, or surface coating, is paramount.

David Batchelor has usefully explicated the meanings conventionally ascribed to colour in European history. On the one hand, colour represents the deceitful, superficial allure of sensuality, and is therefore infantile, exotic and feminine. Where whiteness means clarity of thought and purpose, colour signifies demonic perversion and delusion. In the West, writes Batchelor, colour has been 'systematically marginalized, reviled, diminished, and degraded'.[4]

Precisely because of this history of chromophobic, and sometimes uninhibit-edly chromoclastic, discredit, colour comes also to be associated in modernism with a utopia of the senses, and to be thought valuable for precisely the same reasons that it had been suspected by monochrome rationalists; because of its powers to enrapture, to intoxicate, and to exceed capture in definition, as it bursts or blooms out of the bony geometry of word and line and form.

Colour signifies materiality, the fall of the ideal into embodiment. Colour is accidental, not essential, and therefore belongs to the outside of things, as the body constitutes the mere casing or superficies of the soul. It is, as Batchelor says, 'added to the surface of things, and at the last moment. It does not have a place within things; it is an afterthought, it can be rubbed off'.[5] Discussing the understanding of colour in Plato, Jacqueline Lichtenstein has observed that colour has two distinct possibilities. On the one hand, colour can act to assist the sense of an object's distinct form, as the skin or outer surface of a body bounds and marks off its integrity. On the other hand, excess of colour or a perplexing medley of colours can blur the sense of an object's contours and interfere with the identification of distinct forms.[6]

The idea that colour is fundamentally superficial is found in the classical atomist theories we encountered in chapter 4. Lucretius, for example, draws on the experience of colour to convince his reader of his atomist theory of light and vision:

> For verily we see many things cast off and give out bodies in abundance, not only from deep beneath, as we said before, but often too from the surface, such as their own colour. And commonly this is done by awnings, yellow and red and purple, when stretched over great theatres they flap and flutter, spread everywhere on masts and beams. For there they tinge the assembly in the tiers beneath, and all the bravery of the stage and the gay-clad company of the elders, and constrain them to flutter in their colours. And the more closely are the hoardings of the theatre shut in all around, the more does all the scene within laugh, bathed in brightness, as the light of day is straitened. Since then the canvas gives out this hue from its surface, each several thing also must needs give out thin likenesses, since in either case they are throwing off from the surface.[7]

Those who, since Plato, have seen colour as an accidental feature rather than an essential quality of things in the world have been drawn to this metaphor of colour as a superficies. It is of course literally true that the colour of any object is the colour of its surface. But colour is also tightly bound to the idea of the flesh, as that which is unformed in bodily being. The formless matter present in bodies in the guise of flesh is the very matter manifest in painting in the guise of colour. 'It is color that renders flesh in painting . . . Color is to painting what flesh is to the body.'[8]

Just as all writing involves some reference to the making of marks upon the skin, so, too, all thinking about colour has an implicit relation to the pigmenting

'The Chameleon',
from Andrea Alciatus,
Emblemata (Antwerp,
1581).

of the skin. The word for colour derives, via the Latin *color*, from a Sanskrit word meaning the skin on the surface of the milk (an idea to which we will return at the end of this chapter). The word 'chromatic' derives from the Greek χρῶμα (*chroma*), colour of the skin, complexion, style. χρῶμα is related to χρώς (*chros*), skin, skin-colour, and to the verb χρώζειν (*chroizien*), to touch a surface or the skin, which in its turn derives from an Indo-European root *gheo*, meaning to abrade, or rub hard against.[9] Colour thus harbours the idea of something that both touches the skin, and is also itself, according to a curious logic of contagious replication, a kind of second skin, a layer, film or veil. The musical application of the metaphor in the chromatic scale perhaps draws out this idea. Where the diatonic scale is restricted to intervals of a full tone, the chromatic scale is coloured by the semitones that lie between these intervals, as it were, a fingertip or hair's-breadth away from the preceding or succeeding tone. The involvement of an idea of skin in the apprehension of colour is implied by words with tactile connotations. To say that something or somebody has a certain 'cast' – as when Hamlet speaks of 'the native hue of resolution/. . . sicklied o'er with the pale cast of thought' (*Hamlet*, III. i, 84–5, p. 309) – is to imply a dash or shading of colour, which may perhaps lean on the subsidiary meaning of 'cast' as something shed or thrown off, and specifically a shed skin, as of a snake, spider or caterpillar.

The fickle shiftiness of colour is frequently emblematized in the chameleon. Tertullian, who, as an African, might even have seen one of these little beasts and so should have known better, reported in his essay 'On the Ascetics' Mantle' of around AD 208 that the chameleon has no inner organs, but is 'a living pellicle' (*pellicula vivit*), the fact that it was also popularly believed to live on air contributing to this. For Tertullian, the chameleon is all appearance, not just the emblem of the flatterer or sycophant adjusting himself to prevailing opinions, but also the only animal to whom it has been given 'to sport with its hide' (*de corio suo ludere*).[10]

Shakespearean uses of the word 'complexion', discussed in chapter 1 above, indicate that by the end of the sixteenth century, this word was not only starting to signify the skin rather than the humoral disposition of a body, but also increasingly to have a chromatic cast. It seems to have been the colour of the skin which was most commonly implied in Shakespeare's uses of the word complexion, as when the failing sun is said to have 'his gold complexion dimmed' in Sonnet 18 (p. 21), or in Henry V's reference to the 'smirch'd complexion' of merciless war (*Henry V*, III. iii. 17, p. 443), or when, in *As You Like It*, Corin promises Celia 'a pageant truly play'd,/Between the pale complexion of true love/And the red glow of scorn and proud disdain' (*AYLI*, III. iv. 49–51, p. 179). A little later, after Rosalind has swooned at the story of Orlando's fight with a lioness, but then pretended it was a counterfeit, the disbelieving Oliver says ' there is too great testimony in your complexion that it was a passion of earnest' (*AYLI*, IV. iii. 169–71, p. 184). The bantering Beatrice says of Claudio in *Much Ado About Nothing* 'The Count is neither sad, nor sick, nor merry, nor well; but Civil count, civil as an orange, and something of that jealous complexion' (*Much Ado*, II. i. 275–7, p. 919, – orange and yellow vied with green at this point to signify the colour of jealousy.

Though the words 'tinge', 'tint' and 'tincture' all derive from *tingere*, to dye, and thus have no direct relation to the family of touchy words like 'tangent', 'intangible' and 'contingent', which all derive from the Latin *tangere*, to touch, the idea of touch seems nevertheless to have exercised an attraction on the words for colour. To be 'tinged' with a colour is to have the merest touch of it applied. But, perhaps because the efficacy of such a tangential touch implies a magnification of sensitivity, it can make this brushing, tangential touch seem essential. We have met this paradoxical power of the minimal in relation to skin or tactility before, and perhaps it is time it were given a name: let it be known as the principle of inverse efficacy. Thus, the tiny but significant difference produced in the word 'tint' when one adds a single letter to produce the word 'taint' suggests that purity is most at risk, not from the obvious disfigurations of daubing, but from the subtlest and most sinister kind of shading. The suggestive chiming of the French words *teindre*, to dye, and *feindre*, to counterfeit, upon which Michel Pastoureau remarks, is matched in English by that of *taint* and *feint*.[11] The word 'stain' is a shortening of the word *disteigner*, meaning to deprive of colour and is thus closely related to the word 'distain' and its later form 'disdain'.

A good example of the interchange between accident and essence is furnished by the fortunes of the word 'tincture'. The Middle English meaning of this word, formed from the past participle of Latin *tingere*, is a dyeing or a tinting. Gradually, it seems to have followed the cultural logic of diminishment attaching to colour in general, and come to mean a light tinge, shading or nuance of colour. The superficiality attaching to colour is highlighted in the idea of tincture, which enables it to suggest both a certain kind of delicate, evanescent beauty, typically the subtlety of the rosy blush spreading over the maiden's cheek, and the disgusting application of colour to disguise or deceive – 'false Die and lying Tincture on the Cheeks and Lips' as Benjamin Keach sternly put it in 1684.[12] Richard Brathwait described cosmetic paint as 'so odious a tincture to real beauty' in 1659, while the cosmetic ingredients employed by an aged aunt are cruelly disparaged in Thomas D'Urfey's comedy *The Virtuous Wife* (1680): '*Fucus, white Mercury*, Fat of Eeles, and *Jews Tincture*, with which she does so mortifie deformity, that her Face in a morning looks like an old Wall new plaister'd'.[13] Later on in the play, further sardonic insults are heaped upon attempts to improve upon nature:

> your Tawny, or Olive-colour'd skin would look better if it were White; Therefore White must be added: Then your pale dead Tallow Colour requires a Tincture, and it must have it, 'tis very necessary, and no more discredit to ye, then 'tis to wear a piece of thin Gold for the Kings Evil; or a row of Ivory Teeth, when your own have uncivilly left their habitations.[14]

'Tincture' thus became associated with more general kinds of hypocrisy; 'Hypocrisie in Church is Alchymie,/That casts a golden tincture upon brasse:/There is no essence in it', wrote Christopher Harvey, an imitator of Herbert.[15]

In alchemy, in which the colour and colouring of metals has great importance, the term 'tincture' originally referred to substances used to tinge or dye metals. Gradually, a distinction grew up between the superficial plating achievable by this means and a tincture that would effect real transmutation by penetrating through the substance of the metal. The word 'tincture' thus came to mean not a mere extract, quality or appearance of a substance, but rather its extractable essence. The tincture came to be identified with the transmuting elixir and stone themselves.[16] The dignity conferred on the term in alchemy probably encouraged those religious uses in which tincture is an expression of divine power. In a poem celebrating Charles II's power of healing scrofula by the 'King's Touch', a practice which had been recently revived, the ultra-Royalist poet Patrick Ker urges the praise of 'A *King* who's *Race* (unless experience lie)/Doth bear the Tincture, of a *Diety*'.[17] In a long mystical poem entitled *Mundorum Explicatio*, Samuel Pordage describes the condition of the soul in bliss in terms of a divine touch transmitting holy tincture, presumably identified in part with Christ's blood:

> Th' Anoynted's Hand which doth distempers heal,
> Upon him lay'd, he sensibly doth feel.
> The Tincture which doth from *Christ's* Body flow,
> With great delight he feels on his to grow[18]

Presumably, this flowing tincture is in part to be identified with Christ's blood, for, at the climax of the poem, we read of the soul

> Intoxicated, and o'returned quite
> With Love's exuberant delight:
> The burning *Tincture* of the Heart of God,
> Rol'd o're his Soul a most delightful Flood[19]

It is perhaps the combination of these two different meanings, of effulgent or exuberating power and superficial overlay, which suggests the common association of the word 'tincture' with poison, or mortifying quiddity transmitted through staining, contagion, or other contact of surfaces. 'Soules (they say) by our first touch, take in/The poysonous tincture of Originall sinne', writes John Donne.[20] A seventeenth-century collection of stories of murder and its consequences translated from French by one John Reynolds (who is described in most catalogues as simply 'a merchant of Exeter') contains a story of a girl treacherously poisoned by her sisters, and the colourful rebounding of the deed upon them: 'within lesse then sixe weeks after the deplorable death of *Iaquinta*, a sudden languishing sicknes oretakes and surpriseth *Babtistyna*, so as the white tincture of her face lookes yellow.'[21]

If colour is identified with the body, this makes it natural that colour should also be associated with disease. This is indeed borne out by the fact that so many diseases are identified by the chromatic changes they induce in the skin or bodily products; chlorosis, or green-sickness; yellow fever; scarlet fever; purpura, jaundice and the Black Death. Cholera preserves a reference to the Greek χολή (*chole*), or bile, one of the four humours of the medieval world, which came in yellow or black versions. Cirrhosis is from the Greek κιρρός (*kirros*), which denotes the tawny colour of the granulations found in the liver affected by it. Anthrax derives from the Greek ἄνθραξ, a coal or carbuncle. Candidiasis names a group of infections caused by the whitish, yeast-like fungus candida albicans, from the Latin *candidus*, white. Leukaemia is a disease of the white blood cells, from Greek λευκός (*leukos*) and melanoma, from Greek μέλας, black, names the black skin tumour of skin cancer. Cyanosis or 'blue jaundice' is from Greek κύανος, dark blue, and is a condition in which the skin becomes livid because of the circulation of imperfectly oxygenated blood. Porphyria is the name for a number of metabolic disorders characterized by the excretion of purplish pigments in the urine, from Greek πόρφυρος, purple. Greek γλαυκός, pearl-grey, gives us glaucoma, on account of the greyish coating on the surface of the eye to which it leads. Only very slowly did the predominantly chromatic body of the medieval world give way to the colourless, galvano-mechanic body of modern conception.

We have heard recently, hard on the heels of the news that the universe is flat, the Hitch-Hikerish revelation that, if one were to mix all the visible light in the universe together, its mean colour would come out as a rather subtle shade of turquoise.[22] In what follows I pose the following barmy riddle: if colour is a skin, what is the colour of that skin? And I offer a similarly touched answer: could it be – yellow?

DEPICTED IN LUMINOSITIES

There is a clear relation between the depiction of the skin in painting, and the cosmetic painting of the skin. Colour is applied to the skin, in the form of make-up, which accentuates, exaggerates or even replaces the natural colour of the skin. But the skin has two dimensions or forms of action with respect to colour. In the first place, it is a blank surface on which colour is applied, as a second skin. But by letting vision through without dimming it or letting it linger, makeup reveals the skin as a screen which lets out colour from within, especially, of course, the colour and the coursings of the blood. Such secondary coloration attempts to get under the skin, as a tattoo does, in order to suggest an endogenous colour radiating from within rather than being occasioned from without; it is a surface coating which simulates a 'surfacing' or breaking through from below. In the one case, the colour is correctly recognized as a superficial filter, which interrupts and masks off external light; in the other, it seems to be transmitting an inner light, that 'glow' beloved of art historians and fashion writers alike. This is why, as Jacqueline Lichtenstein has observed, makeup should ideally be transparent, for it should itself lie beneath the threshold of visibility: it 'must not be seen but must make its object visible, it must show without showing itself'.[23]

The relations between the skin and colour cannot be understood without taking the measure of this conception of the skin as a source of light. The only skins which literally are capable of generating, as opposed to reflecting light are the phosphorescent skins of glow-worms and certain marine creatures – though gangrene and other kinds of decomposition may also make the human skin phosphoresce for limited periods. Nevertheless, cosmetics, theology and aesthetic theory cohere in this quasi-conviction of the power of the skin to produce and give out its own light.

The lustre or glow of flesh implies and approximates to the eye, the moistest and most lustrous part of the outward appearance of a terrestrial creature. And perhaps the living glow or shine of the skin is fascinating partly because it has eyes for us, because it is all eyes. The living, luminous skin has something of the eye distributed across the skin, as in the myth of the ocular skin of the hundred-eyed Argus, employed by Hera to keep watch over Io. For centuries, followers of Plato accepted that the eye not only received and interpreted light, but also sent it out into the world. The patched or maculated skin, the skin mottled with vitiligo, or covered with scales, boils or pustules, is a coat of many colours, but colours which have been disfiguringly and meretriciously applied to the skin, obnubilating its light, and rendering it something to be looked at, rather than through or with; the consumer rather than the emitter of a radiance. The carbuncle, the name of a jewel traditionally believed to be capable of shining in the dark, is also the name for a particularly hard and concentrated kind of boil, often taken to be the harbinger of plague or cancer. Despite its parody of the eye, the carbuncle in the skin does not have its own light. The maculated skin, patched, pocked and socketed, is lunar rather than solar, it has had its eyes put out.

The cosmetic oscillation between radiant and absorbent bodies does indeed have a cosmological correlative, in debates about the spots to be found on the surface of the moon and, later on, the sun. Throughout the medieval period and into the seventeenth century, debate was renewed about whether celestial bodies, the sun, moon, planets and stars, were indeed, as Aristotle had suggested, perfect, smooth spheres, giving out light and formed not from a mixture of the four terrestrial elements but a fifth, a quintessential substance. As early as the first century AD, Plutarch had suggested in his dialogue 'De Facie in Orbe Lunae' that the obvious markings on the moon might indicate that it was formed of heterogeneous matter exhibiting the same irregular density and luminosity as that of the earth.[24] Few if any medieval philosophers knew this work of Plutarch's, and the majority attempted to develop explanations that would be compatible with Aristotle. Among these was the elaborate explanation put forward by Beatrice at the beginning of Dante's *Paradiso* that they were shadows cast on the otherwise immaculate surface of the moon by the earth.[25] A similar explanation was that the markings on the moon were reflections of the seas, mountains, land-masses and other features of the earth's surface. Both of these theories had difficulty in accounting for why the features projected on to or reflected back from the moon remained the same as the moon travelled across the sky. Many medieval philosophers followed the partial modification of Aristotelian cosmology offered by Averroës in his *In libris Aristotelis de caelo et mundo commentarii*, according to which the moon remained perfectly smooth, but exhibited variations in the density and rarity of its quintessential matter with corresponding variations in its capacity to absorb and project light. Leonardo was among the first to conclude that the spots on the moon were the marks of land and sea features like those of the earth, and thus that the moon was made of the four terrestrial elements.[26]

Religious thought and representation has been much taken up with phantasms of the radiant skin. Eve and woman are traditionally associated with the moon because the moon's light is corrupted, or imperfectly radiant. Adam, whose Hebrew name preserves a reference to blood and to the red earth, is promoted to solar glory in the apocryphal *Gospel of Bartholomew* (also known as *The Questions of Bartholomew*), which explains that the sun is bright 'according to the likeness of Adam'. The moon, by contrast, is 'full of clay' because of Eve's transgression:

> For God placed Adam in the east and Eve in the west, and he appointed the lights – that the sun should shine on Adam in the east with its fiery chariots, and the moon in the west should give light to Eve with a light like milk. And she defiled the commandment of the Lord. Therefore the moon was stained with clay and her light is not bright.[27]

As Ewa Kuryluk has observed, the frequent Biblical references to being clothed in light, radiance or splendour may derive partly from the fact that the Hebrew words for light and skin are very close to each other.[28]

Christian metaphorics and iconography took over and extended the Presocratic and Platonic conceptions of divine fire and light. This raised an aesthetic problem, which was a particularized version of the problem so fiercely debated during the Iconoclast controversy of the eighth century. How were the negative, light-filtering materials of coloured dye and pigment to be used to convey the dazzling emanations of light characteristic of the divine? In an epigram of the tenth century on an icon of the Virgin, Constantine of Rhodes protested that 'If one would paint thee, O Virgin, stars rather than colours would be needed, that Thou, the Gate of Light, shouldst be depicted in luminosities.'[29] One solution was to borrow the light of the world, especially that of gems and precious metals, for example in the elaborately ornamented covers for manuscripts like the Lindisfarne Gospels in the early Middle Ages, which incorporated gold, gemstones, ivory and enamel in abundance, or, of course, in the art of light developed in stained glass.

A visible emanation is an act of self-creation, imagined as a continuous phosphorescence, or solar radiance. According to this kind of luminiferous vitalism, all living things are characterized, not by the hoarding or holding in of their essences, but by their exuberant qualities of overflow. The essence of life is that it cannot remain with itself, but must ecstatically spill. To have life is always to have too much life. Kabbalistic writings, which are characterized by a suspicion not only of colour, but also of the dazzling deceptions of light itself, represent colour breaking out in creation as a result of the exteriorization of the will of the withdrawn, lightless principle of divinity known as the *En-sof* into the *Sefiroth*. The Kabbalistic Zohar describes the *En-sof* as emitting a 'dark flame':

> It was only when this flame took shape and extension that it broke out in gleaming colours. At the inner centre of this flame arose a source in which colours poured downwards, hidden the secret mysteries of *En-sof*. The source broke through and yet did not break through the surrounding ether, and became absolutely unrecognizable until the force of the break-through lit up the highest hidden power.[30]

These ideas are rearticulated in the *Naturphilosophie* or transcendental naturalism of Lorenz Oken, which regards the planets as 'coagulated colours':

> At that very distance from the sun, where light begins to grow dim, where, to speak in the Newtonian sense, it begins to refract, there planetary mass originates. The mass of the planet coagulates together around the sun, but not in an uniform manner like a mass of pulp, but in pauses of colours, exactly like a rainbow.[31]

The skin is on both sides of the coagulation of light. Light streams out from the outermost edge or surface of things, but is then slowed into manifestation as a second skin. This streaming is a kind of holy excrement, a doubling of the material skin by its shimmering sweat of light. The fact that the legends of the handkerchief of Veronica and the shroud of Turin involve the impressing of features on to a surface by means of sweat and blood implies that such substances may be thought of as secondary faces, or body images. But sweat, and the other things given out from or through the skin, ordinarily scatter, evaporate and are lost to the body. The logic of the aura is that what spills out from the skin is also retained by it; the aura forms a second skin, or series of such skins, which remains held in by and obedient to the contours of the first. The aura is an emanation which, like the *logos*, goes forth from and yet also remains, and remains in, itself; as the Zohar says, it breaks out and yet does not break out.

The idea of the human aura, which began to be popularized in theosophy, spiritualism and other forms of popular occultism of the late nineteenth century resembles the etheric or phantasmal body, versions of which are to be found in many mystical systems. But, where the etheric body is a second, as it were three-dimensional body which doubles the material body, the aura shadows this body and, like the shadow, it is conceived not as a separate entity that is capable of existence apart from the body (astral travelling and so forth), but as a doubling of an outline, a spiritual stammering of the body's lineaments. The etheric body dithers the body's volume; the auric body doubles the body's contour. It is the outside of the outside, the higher skin of the skin.

The halo probably derives from the convention, in both European and Asian artistic and religious traditions, of depicting sun-deities such as Apollo with rays streaming from them. This tradition was adapted in Rome for the representation of deceased, and then living Emperors; Egyptian and Syrian kings also had themselves represented with rayed haloes. These passed across into depictions of Christ and the Godhead in Christian art, helped by their correlation with scriptural references to various forms of divine radiance, and in particular the appearance of God as a glory of burning light wrapped in a cloud (Exodus 24:16–17); when Moses descends from his encounter with God, light is shining from his own face (Exodus 34:29). Classical gods share this capacity of being wrapped in light and radiating from concealment – 'nimbo effulgens', as we read of Tritonia in Virgil's *Aeneid*.[32] Indeed, the word 'nimbus' is related to the word 'nebula', and therefore implies the paradox of a cloud of light. Gradually, from the fifth century onwards, the use of the halo was extended to other saintly personages, though the square or four-cornered form was often used to distinguish living persons from those already in their station of bliss.[33]

The nimbus was usually a circular, or sun-like disc and its favoured colour was yellow, or, in mosaics, gold leaf, the luminosity of yellow no doubt contributing to its role in suggesting a light that leaps out and advances upon the viewer. It is the aureole or oval-shaped full-body emanation in which colour features most notably, and in which the idea of a rainbow of light, as it were decaying away from the luminous centre, features most strongly. It is this tradition that was drawn on in the great secularization of the divine that took place in the revival of magical thinking from the nineteenth century onwards, in which the fantasy of the human aura visible to the sensitive as a shimmering, shifting rainbow, has been a central feature. The interest in the human aura seems to have been formed at the end of the nineteenth century from a coalescence of Edward Babbitt's researches into chromotherapy with the interest in Eastern religious traditions.[34] Early writers on the subject were usually associated with or sympathetic to theosophy.[35] The late twentieth-century revival of interest in the aura seems to have been given great impetus by the development in 1939 of techniques for photographing high-frequency energy emissions by Semyon and Valentina Kirlian.[36]

The idea of an aura, or visible emanation of light, from divine or human creatures, may have received some impetus from Epicurean atomism; though atoms themselves were held to be colourless, we have seen that atomism imagines visible matter as what one sceptical commentator called 'fleeces of Atoms', which implied films of colour.[37] Certainly, the depiction of the glory, the halo, or the aura would require a representation of a radiance or emanation in forms and colours that will inevitably capture and delimit them, forms that, rather than impinging on the eye, would draw it in. The trope of a 'fall' from white light into colour as it has been imagined in religious and aesthetic thought is both confirmed and reversed in this casting out of second skins in a cadence of glory.

Miracles of religious stigmatization or marking, which, as we have said, also conform to the logic of an external mark making visible an internal condition, were sometimes believed to be accompanied by strange luminous emanations. One example of this was the stigmatic Louise Lateau, who underwent a month of 'living fire', during which, according to the enthusiastic report given by the writer J. K. Huysmans, 'light suddenly sprang from the two "wounds" in the palms of her hands, just as brilliant as the flash from a diamond, and which burnt for ten minutes.'[38]

The aim of painters through the ages has been to develop pigments and techniques that will allow the living glow of the flesh to be represented. There has been a particular closeness between the development of oil-based pigments, the discovery of which has often (but erroneously) been attributed to Jan van Eyck, and the realistic rendering of human flesh and skin tones. This may have to do with the quality of shine or luminousness that oil can give to a pigment. This chain of associations here is not particularly mysterious. Shiny things look moist, and moist skins look young; young skins are revered and infinitely desired. As I have already suggested, moistness also suggests the skin's *oeilladerie* or rolling eyes. Rather than merely covering or marking a surface, oil paints seem to mimic the living skin's capacity to glow. David Batchelor contrasts the 'atmospheric depth' of this kind of shine when it is found in traditional easel painting with the flatter shine of commercial paints and colour finishes, which latter have 'the double quality of the dead and the dynamic, the bland and the brilliant'. I am sure that Batchelor is right when he says that '[a] shiny surface gives depth to flatness at the same time as it emphasizes that flatness,' but I think that the distinction he is drawing between glow and gloss is one that is already a feature of traditional painting of the skin.[39] What appears to shine with its own unaided light in a painting is in fact the effect of a flat, or nearly flat sheen. However insubstantial the brush's touch, there will always be some opacity, some impasto, which is effecting the imposture of light. The ideal of glow depends upon the fascination of a skin that, while seeming to be transparent, in fact minimally dims and arrests the passage of the light from within.

Francisco de Zurburán, *Veil of St. Veronica*, 1631–6, oil on canvas. Nationalmuseum, Stockholm.

The myth of realistic flesh painting is a version of the myth of the ἀχειροποίητον (*acheiropoieton*), the miraculously marked skin or fabric, untouched by human hand, of which the veil of Veronica and the Shroud of Turin are the best-known examples. Since colour deposited on top of the skin is so associated with corruption and deceit, being both too speciously super-ficial and too pore-cloggingly piled, the painter of flesh must strive, through all the delicacy of his means and technique, to give the impression of a flesh which is in fact immaculate, untouched by human hand, and therefore illuminated by its own light and by radiant, rather than pigmented, colour. It is perhaps for this reason that the face and skin of Christ were often iconically represented by gold leaf, which was possessed of a luminosity not imparted to it by the colourist. If colour involves the reference to the touched skin, as the Indo-germanic *gheo* at the back of Greek *chroma* suggests, then the colour of the flesh must represent some form of higher, ocular touching, or even self-touching. This ethic of painting without the aid of hands or skin enjoins a similarly tactful kind of viewing (tactful here being precisely the right word to convey the touching without touch being imagined), as here articulated by Jacqueline Lichtenstein in her explication of the work of the seventeenth-century French writer on art, Roger de Piles. Painting demands

> to be 'touched' with the eyes – that is, from a distance; it requires a caressing way of touching the object without touching it, an analogical touch without contact, requiring great delicacy, infinite tact and finesse – a nontactile perception possible only when the gaze is really affected by what it sees. Touched by its desire.[40]

OFF-WHITE

We are accustomed to think of light as 'white', but many have observed the odd approximateness of this. At least since the sixteenth century, European women strove after the ideal of a pure white skin. Words like 'blank' and 'bland', which derive from the French 'blanc', evoke a skin which is both present and absent, in the field of vision, yet featureless, visible as invisible, and giving no hint of the slugs and snails that squirm behind it. The cosmetic ideal of white skin was the ideal of pure luminosity, of a skin so refined that it was itself vanishing from view, and letting through a light coming from within. The cosmetic paradox is that whiteness is actually one of the hardest skin colours to achieve, since it involves subtracting rather than applying colour. White colour applied to the face or skin, even for light-skinned or so-called 'white' races, always looks painted, and especially when it is done in painting. The aim of a lethal cosmetic like the arsenic-based white lead was to be a cloak of invisibility, to suggest whiteness as the absence of colour. The very fact that invisibility is itself so often imagined as a kind of cloak or skin-like integument suggests an important link between the skin and the ideal of transparency. This interchange between transparency and visible whiteness attains to a strange double-bluff in the Elizabethan practice of painting veins on the surface of the forehead, a practice visible in the engraving of Elizabeth I by William Rodgers.[41] The only way to thin the skin sufficiently is to thicken it with an extra layer.

The ideal of whiteness is an ideal of a thin or minimal skin. Its connotations are not only of purity and lucidity, but also of delicacy and sensitivity. White skin is two-sided. Racial theory always imagines black skin to be thickened or doubled, a bodily mask which impedes rather than assists the passage of light. The fixation upon the skin results in a view of black or coloured peoples as restricted to their skins. Frantz Fanon writes of the experience of 'corporeal malediction', in which, suddenly recognized in public as 'a Negro', the world-projecting being for-itself of his ordinary bodily awareness is replaced by a 'racial epidermal schema', and he shrivels into the shameful necessity of having to be all skin or nothing but skin.[42] But the ideal of skinlessness also has an ineliminable reference to the skin; the soul which shines through the skin as a window, as it was traditionally said to shine through the eyes, is detained at the level of the skin. So in fact both black and white have their souls upon their

John Boby, a
Kingston-born sufferer
from vitiligo, exhibited
himself as 'The
Wonderful Spotted
Indian' (etching,
1803).

The
WONDERFUL SPOTTED INDIAN,
John Boby;
Born at Kingston in Jamaica, & who exhibits himself in different parts of England & Scotland.
Pub.ᵈ by Alex.ʳ Hogg, at Paternoster row, Jan. 1803.

skins, but in opposite ways. For the racist European imagination, white skins embody the ideal of a skin pervaded or transpierced by soul; in those of black skin, soul seems suffocated or encrypted in a skin that will not let it out. The reversal of this stereotyping operates in the apprehension by some black peoples of white skin as a deathly carapace.

Whiteness is the absence of colour, or, what, given the close identification between colour and the skin, comes to the same thing, the thinning of the skin to translucency. But whiteness needs subtle tinctures to be white: cream needs its peach. Only another skin can perfect the skin. It is for this reason that whiteness can function, not only as glory, but also as the sign of decay and corruption. As we saw at the beginning of chapter 4, there was a particular horrified fascination during the eighteenth century with the mottled or variegated skin displayed by Africans or West Indians suffering from skin diseases such as vitiligo. Where horses and dogs might be bred specifically for such variations in their fur and hide, curiosities like John Boby, 'The Wonderful Spotted Indian', who exhibited his vitiligo-splashed skin, in all its patches and mottlings, across England and Scotland during the 1790s, had more disturbing suggestions of miscegenation.[43] Perhaps part of the fascination of mottled skins like that of

John Boby was that it suggested a reversibility of dark and light skin. If, on the one hand, the patches of unpigmented skin confirmed the idea that blackness was some secondary accretion, which could be stripped away to reveal the whiteness underneath, they also uncomfortably suggested that the patches of white had been applied, like some extra layer of pigment. It is the deathliness or death-in-life of a whited sepulchre, where whiteness has grotesquely become the colour of corruption. The reversibility of a skin which could be seen zebra-wise either as black on white, or as white on black, recapitulates an ambivalence within the idea of whiteness itself, according to which whiteness is both colour or light itself and a colour.

Such horror of white revives the fears of leprosy which bulk so large in Judaic culture and are to be found throughout the Bible. Leprosy has always represent-ed an incongruously white corruption. The Mishneh Torah of Moses Maimonides, a monumental 14-volume exposition and commentary on Biblical and Talmudic law written towards the end of the twelfth century, sets out in detail in its 'Book of Cleanness' the grades of whiteness afflicting sufferers from leprosy, in explication of the instructions to be found in Leviticus. The most distinctive and conclusive sign of uncleanness is the Bright Spot, 'an extreme whiteness, than which nothing is whiter, and which appears like snow on the skin of the flesh'.[44] Leprosy does not in fact produce white spots, which is one of the reasons that many have come to feel that this is not the disease being referred to in Leviticus.[45] Nevertheless, the lurid horror of leprous white has a long after-life, surfacing for example in 'the Night-mare LIFE-IN-DEATH' of Coleridge's Ancient Mariner, whose 'skin was as white as leprosy'.[46]

But it is in the colour that the medieval world regarded as the closest neigh-bour to white that this play between purity and discredit is enacted. Until Newton's distinguishing of the seven colours in the spectrum in the order Red, Orange, Yellow, Green, Blue, Indigo, Violet, the spectrum was organized rather differently. The dominant conception, at least until the fifteenth century, was of a spectrum of colours running from white and black, with the median colour being red. More subtle subdivisions added yellow, as white tending towards red; and then green and blue, which were placed between red and black. So compelling was this view of the internal ordering of colours that medieval trav-ellers were convinced that the offspring of white and black parents would either be streaked black and white, or be red.[47] The presence of yellow between white and red in the medieval spectrum helps make sense of Chaunticleer's descrip-tion in Chaucer's Nun's Priest's Tale of the colour of the alarming beast in his farmyard as 'bitwixe yelow and reed' (2902, p. 254); though this could mean that the beast's coat was streaked with both colours, a shade between these two colours would have made sense to an eye informed by the medieval spectrum.

The addition of yellow to the white-red-black scheme brings it into con-formity with the four colours or complexions of humoral theory, red blood, white phlegm, black and yellow bile. The Isagoge of Joannitius taught that the colours of the skin were due to excess or equality of the humours: 'from equality comes that tint which is composed of white and red; from irregularity proceed black, yellow, reddish (*rubeus*), greyish (*glaucus*), and white. The reddish, black and yellow set forth the ruling humour of the body'.[48] The colours of the hair were similarly divided into four: black, reddish, greyish and white. Black was due to an excess of overheated bile or blood; reddish to a superfluity of a rather lower kind of heat. These hair colours belonged to the vigour of youth, as opposed to greyish, which was due to an excess of black bile, and white, which was due to a deficiency of heat, and putrid phlegm. The striking thing about this spectrum is the absence in it of blue, though this may be due simply to the effort to get the white-red-black spectrum to conform to the palette furnished by humoral theory.

Michel Pastoureau has charted the growing eclipse of yellow between the twelfth and the fifteenth centuries in Europe, until it eventually became a colour associated with degradation and discredit.[49] In classical Greece, yellow was predominantly a bright and affirmative colour, associated with natural process. Already, however, in Roman culture, yellow was acquiring its unsavoury associations. I went to a Bluecoat school where the uniform consisted of knee-length breeches over yellow stockings. It was part of the mythology of the school that yellow had been chosen when the school was founded by Edward VI in 1552 because it repelled vermin. But this power to ward off dirt may have been the reflex of an association between yellow and dirt. The luminosity of yellow seems to mean that it has the quality both of standing out from its background and of invading other colours, making it liable to be regarded as both purgative and pollutant. Yellow is the colour of aging, particularly conspicuous in pale-skinned peoples, especially of skin tissues that have lost their living suppleness, like calluses on feet and hands, or hardened tissue like teeth and nails, both of which yellow with age. As the predominating colour of autumn in the arboreal countries of Europe, yellow can easily signify the deciduous quality of life itself, as it dries out in age, moving from the taut and moist condition of the *cutis* to the sagging, parched condition of the *pellis*. 'I have lived long enough. My way of life/Is fall'n into the sere, the yellow leaf', says Macbeth (*Macbeth*, V. iii, 22–3, p. 794). Yellow is mortuary; the newly dead white often acquire a characteristic yellow hue. It is excremental too, being the colour of many substances expelled or exuded from the body: earwax, mucous, pus, urine and faeces. This last-named may seem dubious to a modern reader, but a ballad like *The Yellow Sash: Or H[anover] Beshit* suggests that yellow encompassed the brown of faeces, or that faeces could be thought of as normatively yellow at least until a couple of centuries ago.[50]

Indeed, there is a close relationship between the most conspicuously yellow product of the body and the formulation of medieval colour awareness. This is due to the importance in the medieval world of uroscopy, or the art of analysing urine. Physicians paid close attention to the gradations of colours and textures in the urine flask. The flask was intended to provide a model of the condition of the urine in the bladder and, beyond even that, was treated as a kind of homunculus. Light and warm materials, such as air and froth, which floated to the top of the flask, gave clues as to the condition of the head and the airier regions of the body: the colder, darker and denser materials which gathered at the bottom of the flask helped the diagnosis of the lower organs. It was to aid the inspection of urine that the first spectrum of colours was devised in an anonymous fifteenth-century treatise on urine.[51] Robert Fludd was still using this spectrum in 1629, when he reproduced it in a chart in his *Medicina Catholica*. The chart shows the colour of the urine moving from 'pallida', through 'subpallida' to the bright yellow 'citrina', and thence via the orangey 'aura' and 'crocea' to the red of 'rubieunda', the grape-purple of 'vineta', and the green of 'virides' to 'nigra'.[52]

Despite, or perhaps because of, its subtlety and technical complexity, dyeing was regarded with a certain suspicion during the medieval period. The profession of the dyer involved the process of taking corrupted and mixed matter in order to form new skins from it. For the dyer, the metaphorical skin of colour is literally fixed in the second skin of the garment. Because of the materials with which they worked, dyeing works, like tanneries, usually produced strong and offensive reeks, and were often for this reason consigned to the outskirts of cities. As Manlio Brusatin suggests, this may partly have to do specifically with the fact that human bodily products were employed in the making of many colours, the fermented urine of a young boy or a man drunk on strong wine being particularly eligible. It was not until the thirteenth century that dubious and unstable biological substances like urine, earwax, saliva and blood gradually began to be replaced with purer and more enduring materials such as linseed or walnut oil.[53]

Urine was also used extensively in printing houses, its lightly acidic qualities making it ideal for the wiping down of the platen between impressions. Indeed the association between dyeing and printing extends also to their products. Papermakers, too, worked principally with rags and vegetable matter, miraculously raising new skins, smooth, blanched and immaculate, from the formless and mingled mulches with which they began. But the yellowing to which not only vellum but also the rag-based and woodpulp papers which succeeded it are subject helped to establish the poetic association between the leaves of trees and the leaves of books. Books decay into colour, and the colour of that decay is the yellow of aged skin. The associations of decay and deceit are brought together in many Celtic stories and songs, in which the untrustworthiness of dream and the insubstantiality of desire are signified by the motif of the withering of fairy gold into leaves upon return to the mortal world. Perhaps it is for this reason that yellow has such marked associations of threat and decay when associated with books, as we will see in the discussion of the 'Yellow Decade' of the 1890s.

Etymology hints at some suggestive filiations between the yellowness of the body and the values attached to the colour yellow. The word 'yellow' can be traced back through Old English *geolu*, Old Teutonic *gelwo* and Latin *helvus* to the Indo-European root *ghel*. This root also stands behind the English word 'gall', which was another name for bile, the bitter, yellowish substance excreted from the liver, as well as the similarly bitter substance exuded from the gall bladder. It therefore seems likely that gall is named for its colour. The bitterness of gall, and the fact that the word was also used to mean a poison, thus gives bitterness a yellowish cast and makes yellow bitter. A gall (from *galler*, to rub or scratch, which gives *la gale*, the French word for scabies) also means a sore raised on the skin by chafing or abrasion – a galling experience being one that rubs you up in this unpleasant way. The association with the bitter bile makes this word appropriate to name an envenomed sore. Gerard Manley Hopkins displays astonishing etymological erudition or intuition in his use of the word 'gall' in most of these senses in the last line of 'The Windhover', which makes us imagine the 'blue-bleak embers' of the earth turned over by the plough as they 'Fall, gall themselves, and gash gold-vermilion'.[54] Gall may also have been used to mean cholera, which we have seen also has a reference to the specifically yellow colour of bile. In this same family is the word 'felon', which is an obsolete name both for an abscess or inflamed sore (in fact, a gall), and for a wrongdoer, this latter a development from its primary meaning of one who is full of bitterness or venom. A further convergence of skin and the felony of yellow is provided by the adjective 'fell', which means evil, cruel, or dreadful, from the Latin *fellon* from which English 'felon' derives. A 'fell' is also the name for a skin or hide, though this derives separately from the Latin *pellis*. The queasy felony of yellow may be exerting its influence in Gonzalo's judgement of the boatswain during the opening storm in *The Tempest* that 'he hath no drowning mark upon him; his complexion is perfect gallows' (*Tempest*, I. i, 29–30, p. 1071). The logic that nags obliquely through these words is that wickedness and bitterness are of the skin, and that that skin has a yellow colour. The semi-rhyme between 'sallow' (related to French *sale*, dirty) and yellow, as well as the chain of echoes between surly, sullen and sullied (though they are etymologically unrelated) presumably also has an influence.

Of course, yellow retains some of the positive connotations that it had in the Greek world, though not for the most part (daffodils and standing corn aside), because of an association between yellow and earth. In Northern poetry, myth and ballad, the virtues of yellow hair are repeatedly assumed and asserted; and, as the most luminous colour, yellow approximates to gold. Alchemy, religion and economy all tend to identify gold as the single source of light and power, the power of giving without diminishment, yellow being the colour conventionally employed to represent the sun, and distinguish its effulgent light from the reflective gleam associated with the moon. And yet, as Michel Pastoureau indicates, yellow is an ambivalent friend to gold. The studies of heraldic colour and device undertaken by Pastoureau provide an index of the decline in the standing of yellow. Once thought of as the natural ally of gold, yellow gradually acquired the status of 'bad gold' between the twelfth and fifteenth centuries:

> From the statistical point of view, the frequency of gold (*or*) in blazons
> decreased steadily between these two dates, not only in actual, but also in
> imaginary armouries. In colour representations of armoury, gold began

correspondingly to be translated not by yellow, but by gilt. It would take at least a century longer for a similar substitution to be observed on any large scale with respect to the other heraldic metal, silver – silverplate as opposed to white. This chronological gap is highly significant: white retained all its semantic and aesthetic prestige during the 14th century, while yellow had lost this prestige. Yellow is no longer the colour of the sun, of wealth, of divine love. It has become above all the colour of lackeys, prostitutes, Jews and criminals.[55]

Yellow has a particular importance in Oken's cosmology. Yellow, in which 'the Earthy preponderates' is the colour of the planets closest to the sun, Mercury, Venus, the Earth and Mars, which are formed out of 'the first digression from Red' (the colour of absolute fire).[56] Yellow is not only the colour of first creation, but also the colour of sin and deception. As such, it is the joker in the pack of Oken's spiritual colour-scheme: 'Red is fire, love – Father. Blue is air, truth and belief – Son. Green is water, formation, hope – Ghost. These are the three cardinal virtues. Yellow is earth, the Immoveable, Inexorable, falsity the only vice – Satan. There are three virtues but only one vice.'[57]

As the vitiated state of gold, yellow is not just a drier and flatter condition of golden light; it also represents lustre thickened to a grotesquely parodic skin. The illumination provided in medieval books of hours was often supplied by actual gold, beaten into sublime thinness. Yellow is the quick light of that subtle, leastmost skin grown sick and slow, and loitering coarsely like a scurf or scum on the surface of things. If gold is an example of matter striving to attain the condition of light, yellow, we may say, is the colour of light that has curdled back into matter. Yellow, like pink, also has the power to tint vision. Somebody who has a jaundiced view of life sees it through a bilious screen of yellow. The new semi-transparent glass coming into use in bathrooms and elsewhere at the beginning of the eighteenth century became known for a while as 'jealous glass', presumably under the influence of French jalousie, window-blind, but there seems also to be a suggestion of a skin-like thickening into opacity in the word. The relation between yellow and gold is therefore closely equivalent to that between white, considered as a specific colour, and white as the colour of the light of day. The fact that the sun's light is often thought of as yellow (but why?) helps confirm this parallel between the powers and susceptibility to corruption of both yellow and white.

The suspicious condition of yellow is confirmed by another apparent pretender to the condition of gold, brass. Brass is an inferior version of gold, though it has the advantage of being a metal rather than a colour masquerading as one. Brass shares some of the opprobrium that attaches to yellow. Brass is a metal that tends to be used in plated form, and so it too is a dermic colour. Like yellow, it has associations with prostitution: indeed the British slang term 'brass' seems to be an indication that the colour referred to in the Australian term 'chroma', which also means a prostitute, might have a distinctively yellow cast.

But brass has a different set of connotations from yellow. For, while yellow appears as a dissimulating colour, brass is superficial without disguising the fact or pretending to be anything else. For this reason, brass has come to signify not just unashamed or brazen display (and shame is always a matter of the skin), but also a kind of candour (a word the original signification of which is radiant whiteness) and aggressively plain dealing. The brass band has become emblematic of the stubborn obduracy of the northern working class in Britain. St Paul's reference to brass in the King James Version has become proverbial for a sonorous, self-important vacuity: 'Though I speak with the tongues of men and of angels, and have not charity, I am become as sounding brass, or a tinkling cymbal' (1 Corinthians 13:1), though the positive associations both of the material and of its sound are retained in Revelation, where the Son of Man, speaking in a great voice like a trumpet, has 'feet like unto fine brass, as if they burned in a furnace; and his voice as the sound of many waters' (Revelation 1:15). The very fact that brass is not, like the gold it resembles, incorruptible, has a significance. The shine on a letterplate, doorknob or cap badge has been earned by the work of polishing, unlike the gleam of gold. So, for all its superficiality, brass appears like a deep or fundamental kind of superficies, a skin that acknowledges itself as such, for example in coming down to 'brass tacks'. And the link between gold and faeces is frankly reported in the idiom 'where there's muck there's brass'.

The increase, during the sixteenth century, in venereal disease, especially syphilis, thought of as a disease of the skin and associated with leprosy, gave an extra epidermal cast to the traditional metaphor of the false and superficial gilding of the prostitute's allure. When Shakespeare's Timon retires to the woods in search of roots and finds a stash of gold, his raging response elaborates the associations between gold, disease and deceit. The predominating conception in Timon's rage is that of foul or loathly skin made adorable by the power of gold, this colour that can invert all colours, 'make/Black white: foul fair' and (inverting this black-to-white inversion) 'Make the hoar leprosy ador'd' (*Timon of Athens*, IV. iii. 28–9, 36, p. 1112). The skin breaks through again into Timon's discourse a few lines later: 'She whom the spital-house and ulcerous sores/Would cast the gorge at, this embalms and spices/To th'April day again' (IV. iii. 40–2, p. 1112) It is duplicitous yellow, the 'Yellow, glittering, precious gold' (IV. iii. 26, p. 1112) decaying into 'This yellow slave' (IV. iii. 34, p. 1112), that governs the foul, epidermal slither of colours amid Timon's disgusted expectorations. The climax comes with the cramming together of the associations of putrefaction and prostitution in his mouth: 'Come, damn'd earth/Thou common whore of mankind' (IV. iii. 42–3, p. 1112). Paint, excrement, syphilis and the skin are smeared together again later in the scene when Timon is disbursing his gold to Phrynia and Timandra with instructions to spread as much disease and suffering as possible: 'whore still', he roars at them, 'Paint till a horse may mire upon your face:/A pox of wrinkles!' (IV. iii. 149–51, p. 1114).

As the fraud as well as the friend of gold, its lustre always close to glister, yellow became in the Middle Ages the colour of deceit, treachery, and false witness. It is also associated with apostasy, and with the proximate betrayal of the

heretic. (Cathars were forced to wear yellow crosses.) Judas was traditionally represented as wearing yellow, and with orange hair: Giotto's *The Kiss of Judas* in Padua shows the traitor drawing a yellow cloak over the body of Christ.[58] Yellow is the colour of the one who is almost but not quite flesh of your flesh, who is as close to you – but also as foreign to you – as your skin. All colours have a tendency to be regarded as 'meretricious' (having to do with prostitution, the seduction of the eye, the corruption of love through commerce), but the common association of yellow in particular with prostitutes in medieval Europe seems to make yellow the colour of colour – which is to say of veiling, dissimulation, decay – itself. In fact, it is never quite possible to secure the absolute signification of yellow. The sign of duplicity can become a duplicitous sign, which can both enhance and threaten its effectiveness.

The medieval spectrum running from white to black via yellow, red, green and blue has not entirely vanished. Yellow in fact is the colour towards which white tends in the range of shades we refer to as 'off-white'. No other colour has its shadow, or suspicious nuance signified in this way in English: though we can imagine similar nuancings for other colours, it is not immediately apparent, as it is in the case of off-white, in the direction of what other colour an 'off-red' or an 'off-blue' might be tending. When you are 'off-colour' you are likely to have a yellowish hue. Yellow is the sickly nuance of white. Some conditions, especially the pallor of nausea, might also seem to render someone 'green about the gills', but the effect of the Newtonian spectrum also seems to be exercising its effect here, in that yellow may be read as green; alternatively, the blue of the veins filtered by a yellowish skin may give this hint. It is as though yellow were being thought to be the colour of the skin when its colour has, as we say, 'gone off', started, like milk, to turn. White turns yellow, because it goes in the left-handed direction of time. Yellow is the colour of the skin corrupted; or of ideal whiteness corrupted into the condition of skin. When Julia Kristeva instances her loathing of the skin of the milk as a prime example of the phobic horror induced by the abject, by that which lies disgustingly on the boundary between self and other, she identifies the abject as a skin:

> When the eyes see or the lips touch that skin on the surface of milk – harmless, thin as a sheet of cigarette paper, pitiful as a nail paring – I experience a gagging sensation and, still farther down, spasms in the stomach, the belly; and all the organs shrivel up the body, provoke tears and bile, increase heartbeat, cause forehead and hands to perspire.[59]

For those of us brought up in Britain during the orgiastically lactic years that followed the Second World War, yellow has a very specific taste and a texture; it is that of custard, that magically aureate milk that is also inseparable from the thought of skin, to which one cannot ever be indifferent; you either prize or loathe the skin of the custard. The English 'custard' is in fact a corruption of the French *croutarde*, which signifies a pastry, or some confection with a crust or covering. At work in this corruption may have been the word 'curd' (according to the *OED*, traceable back as far as ME *crud* or *crod*, but no further), which signifies the fatty solid which coagulates in milk as a result of the action of acid, leaving the watery serum called 'whey'. The yellowish hue of curd suggests that milk is a mixture of colour and light, or skin and liquid; and that when liquid light thickens into colour, its colour is yellow.

THE BADGE OF YELLOW

Many of these associations are at work in one of the most conspicuous racial typings by colour, the compulsory wearing of yellow by Jews. Goethe's *Theory of Colours* has a remarkable passage connecting this colour and the stigmatizing of various outsiders, including Jews:

> When a yellow colour is communicated to dull and coarse surfaces, such as common cloth, felt, or the like, on which it does not appear with full energy, the disagreeable effect alluded to is apparent. By a slight and scarcely perceptible change, the beautiful impression of fire and gold is transformed into one not undeserving the epithet foul; and the colour of honour and joy reversed to that of ignominy and aversion. To this impression the yellow hats of bankrupts and the yellow circles on the mantles of Jews, may have owed their origin.[60]

The yellow badge has a long and rather complex history. It would not be true to say that yellow was specifically and without exception the colour assigned to Jews. The sumptuary laws of Europe between the thirteenth and eighteenth centuries assigned the wearing of various distinguishing colours to Jews; and some, like the sumptuary laws of Venice, also prescribed the wearing of yellow to prostitutes and courtesans. Nevertheless, the particular association of yellow with Jews gradually came to be formalized.

The regulation of colours and the wearing of distinctive marks is clearly a matter of the surface, and, like all such stigmatizations, involves a heightening of attention to the second skin. But there is another sense in which such stigmatization is skin-like. For it is a striking fact that such prescriptions of colours and forms is a feature both of persecuting authorities and of Jewish self-prescription, sometimes acting in close cooperation. The inside and the outside come together to regulate a shared skin. In a least one place in Europe, Germany, Jews were required to wear the pointed yellow hat as a con- scious and enforced return to a previously distinctive garb that had fallen into disuse. I said in chapter 3 that the logic of the mark is always that a mark is given to the skin from the outside which is meant to show the skin's own auto-inscription. It is equally desirable for both persecutor and persecuted, though for apparently opposite reasons, that mingling or assimilation be resisted. One recalls the fact that the mark of Cain was given by God to the first murderer, not in order to disgrace him, but in order to mark him out as God's and protect him from assault. Three days after Nazis rampaged through Jewish businesses in the spring of 1933, daubing yellow signs in their windows to encourage boycotts, Robert Weltsch published an article in the *Jüdische Rundschau* calling for Jews to see this as a sign of the impossibility of 'stealing away from the Community' and urging them to take in to themselves the sign which had been imposed upon them 'not as a matter of inner avowal . . . but by the impress of a red placard with a yellow patch', thus turning the dishonouring mark into a badge of pride.[61] The strange interplay between a mark that wounds and assaults and a mark that affords protection has been seen again in recent years. When the ruling Taliban issued a fatwa in May 2001 ordering members of the tiny Hindu minority in Afghanistan to wear a badge of yellow, the justification, apparently accepted by at least one Hindu religious leader, was that it would protect Hindus from punishment for infraction of Muslim law. The wearing of yellow seems to indicate that only a skin's width separates the insider from the outsider, the Jew from the Gentile, the off-white from the white. Add skin to skin, white to white, lucidity to lucidity and yellow is the result.

There are two further ways in which the yellowness of the Jewish badge is connected with the skin, and both of them also involve the convergence of Jewish self-prescription with regulatory markings imposed from the outside. The first has to do with the extreme sensitivity attaching to whiteness and the combination of white and yellow in Judaism which derives very specifically from the careful and detailed advice given in Leviticus regarding the regulation of leprosy. The Jews' attention to the condition of the skin flips into an attention to the condition of the skin of the Jews. Jews are made to wear stigmata on their skin as a turning back on them of their own cultural horror at the marked, cut or mottled skin. They are made into the principle of uncleanness their own religious regulations did so much to establish in Christian Europe.[62] Anti-semitic writers often referred to the sickly yellowish tint of the Jewish skin.[63]

The second has to do surprisingly with the links between colour and fringes. There is in Judaism a remarkable and highly formalized recognition of what might be called the power of the edge. This is apparent in the extraordinary attention paid to fringes, or marginal phenomena. The fringe is the point at which the skin curls on itself. The fringe both belongs and does not belong to the skin or shawl, just as the skin both does and does not belong to the body. Faithful Jews are subject to the demand given to Moses that they should wear a *tallith*, or tasselled shawl. The exposed or frayed edge is actually the sign of the body's wholeness or purity, guaranteed by the cut-without-a-cut that is circumcision. It makes a kind of sense of the simultaneous injunction to circumcision and the demand that Jews not cut or mark the body in mourning for the dead, in imitation of the practices of other people. Fringes must be open; this appears to be the logic that connects the prescription of circumcision, the word for which is associated etymologically with unblocking, or unloosing of the tongue, and the injunction not to cut earlocks. It is as though the prepuce lost from one edge of the body were retained and displayed at another edge. Related to this is the odd injunction in Leviticus 13 not to cut the corners of fields when reaping, in order that the poor may have something to glean.

In late medieval and pre-Enlightenment Europe, the prestige of the fringe is focused on a certain heightened attention paid to ornament and especially gold ornament. Jews were not permitted and equally did not permit themselves to wear extravagant ornament. Jewish sumptuary regulations and sumptuary regulation of Jews alike focus throughout this period on fringes, flounces, ribbons, trimmings, cuffs, linings and braid, as well as curls, ringlets, false hair, wigs and veils, and the materials of the edge, fur, lace, velvet. Sometimes seductive, curling or elaborated fringes are banned altogether: more often they are restricted in some way – one row of gold braid rather than two. This austerity goes along with a belief in the Jews' innate love of finery and especially the flaunting of gold, a fantasy that perhaps extends into the vengeful extraction of gold teeth from the bodies of murdered Jews by the Nazis. Gold seems to belong to this logic of ornament, the need to regulate the dangerously unnecessary. If a curl or fringe is where the skin doubles over on itself, the modest curtailing of the fringe equates to a regulation of the skin. In that fringes are often gold, and gold is the principle of the skin's radiance or emanation, the cutting back of fringes is equivalent to the muting or averting of gold by the colour yellow.

The associations of yellow both with meretricious gaudiness and with dimmed decadence come together in the idea of the 1890s, the 'Yellow Decade'. Undoubtedly, this has much to do with the coincidence of three, very different ways in which yellow was emphasized. The first, and, for subsequent decades, probably the most important, was *The Yellow Book*, John Lane's periodical which ran from 1894 to 1897. Borrowing from the 'Yellow Book', a collection of legal testimonies which provided the source for Browning's labyrinthine tale of Florentine betrayal and family murder in *The Ring and the Book*, the title and the lurid look of the magazine confirmed the parallels between sensuality, sexual decadence and yellowness. One of the first articles ever published in *The Yellow Book* was Max Beerbohm's Baudelairean 'A Defence of Cosmetics'.[64] The second form of yellowness which arose in this decade was the 'Yellow Press', the unprincipled use of scandal and sensation to sell newspapers. The third was the 'Yellow Peril', the fear of the growing military and commercial power of China and Japan, fuelled by diminishing British power from the mid-1890s onwards and large-scale immigration of Far Eastern populations into Britain, Canada and Australia following conflict and civil war in the regions.

Colours not only seem to have their tastes, textures and tangible qualities, they are also felt to have different speeds or kinetic potentials. Yellow is particularly ambivalent in this respect, since as the colour of light itself it appears to flash and flare out at enormous speed. But, as we have seen, yellow is also thought of as a slow, detaining colour. These ideas seep into violent anxieties about yellow or Asiatic peoples that developed at the end of the nineteenth century. The French race theorist Joseph Arthur de Gobineau represented black races as physically powerful and expressive and driven by the leaping desire of the body; yellow races, by contrast, were an old people, indolent, obese and decayed.[65] But the military expansion and economic migration of Eastern peoples at the end of the nineteenth century created a new amalgam of slowness and speed. The yellow peoples were represented as spreading and multiplying like a disease, and especially a skin disease, which was at once insidious, lingering and rampant. East Asian peoples walk into a long-established phantasmagoria of disgust attaching to epidermal yellow. The vicious terror of one anonymous writer warning in 1912 against the Yellow Peril in Canada was provoked in particular by the popularity of Chinese laundries. 'If it requires only one barrel of water', he sneered, 'for a Chinaman who doesn't know what a bath is, to "wash" the dirty linen of two hundred persons of all nationalities and habits, what is "Prairie Itch?"'[66] The popular novelist M. P. Shiel wrote no fewer than three novels about the Sino-Japanese military threat, *The Yellow Danger* (1898), *The Yellow Wave* (1905) and *The Dragon* (1913), reissued as *The Yellow Peril* (1929).[67] The insults traded between the Prince of Wales and the sinister Li Ku Yu at the beginning of *The Yellow Peril* indicate the disturbing intimacy of white-horror and yellow-horror:

'I should not wish the skin over it [my head] to be sickly, faded. Whose? The colour of decay! – and hair – the louse –'

'And yellow of death, of corruption, cholera, and tropical rottenness' – each speaking now with a bitterness that hissed, their faces leaning toward each other.

'Hence English hair yellow!' said Li Ku Yu: 'I have seen old Manchu women's hair turn yellow, too, like other plants in Autumn, their skins bleach. Yet the fair races not like that through age – freak of nature!'[68]

Another symptom of the *fin-de-siècle* sensitivity to yellowness is a remarkable essay published by Havelock Ellis in 1906 on 'The Psychology of Yellow'. Ellis's argument is that yellow has undergone a gradual discrediting in the West, and that this is part of a move along the spectrum towards the colour blue.[69] Michel Pastoureau has recently traced the gradual cooling of colour preferences in the West, in the steadily growing prestige of blue.[70] The fundamental determinant for this, thinks Ellis, is the Christian disavowal of the pleasures of nature and the body focused in the Greek world by the colours red and yellow. His argument is confirmed by the common idea, repeated, for example, by Nietzsche, that the Greeks did not see blue or green very well. Nietzsche argues that the Greeks saw deep brown instead of blue and yellow instead of green, a fact indicated, he says, by the fact that they used the same word for the greenness of plants and the colour of the skin, honey and yellow resins. The effect of this, according to Nietzsche, is a bond of reciprocity between the natural and the human that has been lost in the Christian cultures of the modern world: '[H]ow different and how much more like mankind nature must have appeared to them, since in their eyes the coloration of mankind also preponderated in nature and the latter as it were floated in the atmosphere of human coloration!'[71]

Ellis ends with a remarkable story of a man blind from birth whose sight is restored by an operation. One after another, he is shown the different colours of which he has heard so much. When he sees the colour yellow, he experiences an overwhelming desire to vomit.[72] Ellis leaves open the question of whether this is proof of the ingrained difficulty of yellow as a colour, or of the processes of cultural learning which make it possible (or perhaps rather impossible) to see colours at all.

A minor, but telling contribution to the culture of yellowness in the 1890s was Charlotte Perkins Gilman's remarkable and now celebrated story, 'The Yellow Wallpaper', published in *The New England Magazine* in 1892. The story tells of a woman, suffering perhaps from postpartum depression, who is confined to her bedroom by her over-solicitous doctor husband. Gradually, she grows obsessed with the ugly yellow wallpaper, with its clumsy and irregular patterns, eventually coming to believe that there is a woman trapped behind it.[73] When Gilman published an essay of explication about the story in 1913, entitled 'Why I Wrote "The Yellow Wallpaper"', she emphasized its moral: deny unhappy women the pleasures and vivifying power of work, and you will drive them to madness.[74] The message of the story has not escaped very many since. The scenery of the story, by contrast, is dismissed as unimportant, secondary, merely invention and embellishment. It might as well have been blue or green or pink wallpaper, and it might have been and would have been any kind of pattern on any kind of surface that took the print of the narrator's suffering, bewilderment and suffocated rage.

And yet there is much that ties the narrator and the narration to the specifics of the yellow wallpaper, in all its necessary arbitrariness. The wallpaper is a surface that is both bodily and literary. The narrator confesses that she would not be able to articulate her doubts about her treatment were it not for the fact that she is committing them to 'dead paper' (3). Her repeated acts of writing, which, she says begin to tire her more and more, gradually vanish from the story, to be replaced apparently by the obsessive attention to the paper on the wall, and the figure that she believes is confined behind it.

So there are two kinds of paper in the story, though both, alarmingly, are dead, or deathly: the wallpaper, and the paper on which it is described. The narrator seeks to liberate her other self by tearing away the wallpaper; but, having liberated that self, she is then imprisoned in identity with it. Having torn through the skin of the wall, she starts to circulate round and round it, cleaving close, as though to wear that skin back on again, or in enactment of the ambiguity of the word 'wear' (to take on and to wear out). The effect of breaking through one confining skin is to inhume her in another.

The story is only readable in that there is a contrary movement which tears the author out of this circuit of dead paper, this confining, crazy, grazed skin. The author says that she wrote this story, not to make people crazy, but to stop them going crazy. The story is made coherent, made to join up with itself, by the fact that the narrator breaks out of her own loop. For the narrated character, there is only the unintelligible surface of things: dead paper, incomprehensible, incomplete pattern, yellowness. The author lets us see what the narrator is too busy looking to be able to see of herself and what has been done to her. But perhaps this author is not quite able to trust to the fact that she is not, after all, this same woman, that she is not, after all, still in the room, not, after all, still in the paper, or, like her narrator's husband, 'sleeping under this paper' (16), rather than writing on it.

The story anticipates this act of re-enfolding. At two points in the story, before the woman's descent into madness, we read of marks on the wall. One is where the paper has been torn off at head height above her bed. The other is a circular mark or smudge that goes all round the room at a low level. By the end of the story, when she has herself torn off the paper in horizontal strips at head height (for there is now no furniture to help her reach higher) and has begun creeping stooped around the wall, like the woman of her fantasy, we get an explanation of what might have caused these marks. Perhaps some other hapless woman has been confined here. Or perhaps we have been seeing the traces of her future, disguised as another's past. Perhaps, then, the woman's narration is a kind of Möbius strip, the end of which takes us back to the beginning. All this would only apply to the narrator and not to the author, of course, who would somehow have got out of the labyrinth she constructs on, in, or out of paper, would she not?

There seem to be at least four discernible layers to the wallpaper. One is the paper itself, which can be worn, scored, pitted and torn. Another is the fungus-like design, billowing incomprehensibly and nauseatingly outwards but never sufficiently to stand clear, to achieve any kind of 'radiation' (9, 10). A third is the figure behind the design, the shifting, creeping shape of the confined woman, referring to all those stories of bricked-up nuns. And a fourth is the colour. It is not clear how the colour relates to the other layers. Yellow is the colour of the wall's stickiness, its introversion, the detention of its radiance. But the yellow of the wall also lifts off, stains, smirches, smooches. It is not just a colour, but also an atmosphere, an odour. The odour is the smell of the damp paper, 'hovering', 'skulking' (14) and 'hanging' (15), even getting into the narrator's hair. It has, it even is, a 'yellow smell' (15), the smell that is a second skin.

The yellowness is not so much a layer, locatable and distinguishable with respect to other layers. Perhaps in the end it is the colour of the paradoxical integument which makes it impossible to break through this paper to get the other side. The irresolution of the skin, the failure of the paper to add up to a skin, seems to make it capable of drawing everything up to its sickening surface. Its yellow is of the skin precisely in this billowing, enveloping failure of completeness.

The 1964 film of Ian Fleming's *Goldfinger* features a character, Jill Masterson, who is discovered dead by James Bond after deserting her master, Auric Goldfinger. The publicity images for the film, by Monty Norman, featuring the model Margaret Nolan painted gold, were very widely circulated and Shirley Eaton, the actress who played Jill Masterson, even appeared on the cover of *Life* magazine in gilded mode. This image reminds us of the capacity of that radiance which streams from the body to curdle or 'go off' into a kind of poison or excrement, in the particular kind of killing Midas touch possessed by the anally gold-obsessed villain of the film. In the film, Bond explains to his spymaster M that 'She died of skin suffocation. It's been known to happen to cabaret dancers. It's all right so long as you leave a small bare patch at the base of the spine to allow the skin to breathe.' Shirley Eaton's autobiography explains that the filmmakers believed their own script, for they left a patch of her abdomen unpainted.[75] In this, they anticipated and helped to form the urban legend that Shirley Eaton herself almost died of skin suffocation during the making of the film, a legend that was alive and well on a *Goldfinger* message board in December 2001.[76] The legend testifies to a willingness to believe in the skin's capacity to drown or suffocate in its own waste products, to which gold, the radiance of the body, can always revert. As we have seen, the colour yellow has a particularly powerful role in mediating between luminance and excrescence, the aura and the carapace. The book and film have now given their name to a fetish that involves the painting of women in gold, silver or metallic paints. The springs or satisfactions of this fetish seem to have to do with the extreme

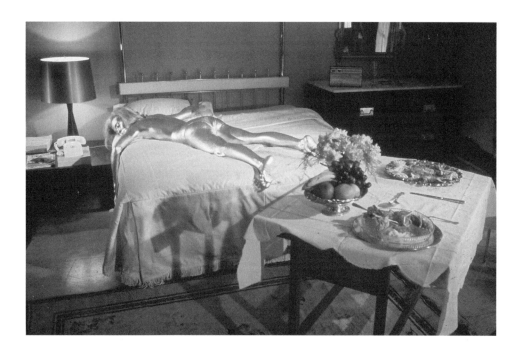

ambivalence of images that conjoin the radiance of a skin that is all aura and
effulgence with the suggestion of faecal daubing, thus either lifting faeces
into the condition of light or lowering light into shit. The images associated
with cacophilia often involve a similar painting of the body with excremental
products, imaging a sort of tonic exposure to the toxic. But such carapaces or
second skins are not always thought of as deadening or suffocating. As we will
see in the next chapter, the desire for the skin to be cleared of its dimming or
maculating excrescences is complemented and contradicted by a tradition of
covering, application and anointing, in which the skin is protected, nourished
and redoubled by its own excremental emanations.

Shirley Eaton lethally
gilded in a still from
the 1964 film
Goldfinger.

7 Unction

'What is the metaphysical coefficient of lemon, of water, of oil?'[1]

SACRED SUET

One of the favourite metaphors among the early Church Fathers for the process of taking on the new life of faith was the sloughing of the skin of the snake. St Augustine writes in *On Christian Doctrine* that

> the serpent gets rid of its old skin by squeezing itself through a narrow hole, and thus acquires new strength – how appropriately it fits in with the direction to imitate the wisdom of the serpent, and to put off the old man, as the apostle says, that we may put on the new; and to put it off, too, by coming through a narrow place, according to the saying of our Lord, 'Enter ye in at the strait gate!'[2]

Perhaps this way of making the body new survives in the popularity of contemporary dermabrasive and exfoliant treatments. A more austere version of this kind of excoriation takes the form of an entomo-oneirism, or dream of the insect, according to which a confining outer skin must be split in order to give room for the new body to emerge. The skin as imagined for the purposes of this emergence is toughened, and so must be split or burst open from within. The prominence of leathery, mineral or shell-like integuments in the fetishist costume that is currently mainstream, often incorporating rips or slashes which allow glimpses of tender, new flesh beneath, is a manifestation of this entomophilia. Entomology is from ἔντομος (*entomos*), 'cut up', so the insect, the English translating the Greek precisely, has section in its name.

But there is another, more emollient way in which the skin can be made new. This involves neither spoiling nor section, but unction, not the breaking out of new life from within, but the folding in, or applying of new life from without. Instead of being cast off, the skin can be doubled, renourished, refreshed, enhanced. This oneirism of unction is to be found at work in medicine in the history of plasters, poultices, cataplasms and other applications to the skin, a practice which has correspondences in other areas in cosmetics, in which indeed the dream of healing or nourishing the skin is at work within the

178

idea of enhancing beauty. It is also to be found in the religious and ceremonial practices of anointing, either for the purposes of restoring the sick, or for marking a passage from one life to another – from the condition of an ordinary man to that of a priest in ordination, for example, or the passage into the condition of king or queenship, in coronation.

Although the purpose of unction is the same as in the fantasy of flaying – the making of a new skin – the dreams and practices of unction have a different form and tone. Where the agent of flaying is the needle or the knife, and its action one of sewing (a joining made of repeated piercings, a joining which joins together joining with dissevering), unctuary actions involve the palpation of the hand, and the use of some intermediary substance which imitates and merges with the skin, rather than a tool which works it. The action of sewing is an action of sealing a form, drawing it together with itself; in any case, arresting its transformations. Salves, oils, unctions, unguents, lotions, liniments, embrocations all involve not an arresting of the state of matter into a skin, but a harnessing of the power of certain substances to change state.

Oil, the favoured material of human inunction, belongs to a group of ambivalent substances that includes wax, tallow, tar, grease, fat and pitch. Each of these substances itself exists in a variety of states at normal temperatures. The application of moderate heat can melt tallow and attenuate oil. The skin or film formed by any of these substances is a congelation occurring between liquid and solid. One can surmise that it is at such mid-points that the substance has its greatest virtue. Nevertheless, such a skin is always unstable, for the possibility of its alternative states seems to be immanent in it. There are thus chains of substance, through which one ascends or descends according to the action of heat. The candle shows all of these states or conditions at once: the solid wax or tallow, the translucent melting oil, the oil taken up into smoke and flame. Oil and wax are closely implicated in the ambivalence of the idea of spirit. A spirit can be both a fluid (alcoholic spirits, the animal spirits) and a vapour, something respired. It shows the same mobility or ambivalence in its liquid mode as it does in its solid. Perhaps it is for this reason that, in the Christian tradition of anointing, oil is specifically associated with the Holy Spirit. Oil's antipathy to water seems to make it natural that it should have an association with fire. Oil can be heated to very high temperatures before it evaporates, hence the culinary and military uses of boiling oil. There is the possibility of this burning in the soothing purity of any unction.

The fantasies of section exaggerate and intensify the skin's power to act as a barrier, to become as resistant as leather or horn or metal; for the most part, the oneirism of unction intensifies the dream of the transparent, transpirant skin, which is capable of changing its state by melting, liquefying, resolving into a dew or even a vapour. In such processes, the skin is doubled by the substances with which it merges, which can be applied to, rubbed or worked into it. Oils, liquids and humours have long been thought to constitute the life, or living process of the body, where the skin and bones are merely its case or shape. Contemporary aromatherapy stakes a great deal on what are tellingly called 'essential oils'. The

idea seems to be that at the essence of a living being is not something solid, but a powerful, viscous semi-liquid – in fact, an oil. (The French word for petrol, 'essence', preserves this association.) As we have also seen, the seventeenth century became progressively more sensitive to the skin's susceptibility to the action of liquids, which it lets out and, to a much more limited degree, absorbs. Considered as a membrane, the skin appears to enter into the condition of, or pass its substance across to, the substances which pass across it.

Comparative mythology and ritual afford innumerable instances of the religious, ceremonial, sexual and medicinal application of greases, fats and oils to the skin. At the root of these practices seems to be a vitalistic conception of fat as embodying, along with blood, the essential life of a creature. This life or sacred virtue of a being is held to consist in a hidden, interior skin, the form of which may be reconstituted by melting and cooling and may then be applied to another outside as a second skin. Many other cultures supply examples of the taking on of the vital powers of different creatures through smearing of their 'sacred suet'[3] on to the skin. Plutarch tells the story of a Spartan named Isidas who oiled himself prior to a battle with the Thebans and remained unharmed as a result.[4] W. Robertson Smith records that, in Australia, the kidney fat and caul fat of the victim of a blood revenge would be kept by an assassin, in order to lubricate himself with his victim's strength.[5] J. G. Frazer collects a number of instances of rituals designed to transmit power through anointing with fat, including the practice among East African Arabs of oiling the skin with the fat of a lion in order to take on the lion's boldness, and the magic ointment compounded from the ashes of venomous spiders, scorpions and snakes, with which priests of the god Tezcatlipoca in ancient Mexico would besmear themselves in order to harden themselves against the cruelty of human sacrifice.[6] These practices resemble the assumption of the skins of animals in order to achieve the same magical effect; indeed, the assumption of a skin of oil has the advantage that, as well as giving the subject a new skin, it also sinks into and renews his old one, blending with its substance rather than merely sitting on top of it. Edward Topsell reported in his *Historie of Four-Footed Beastes* of 1607 of the special powers attaching to the skin of a leopard. Not only does a leopard skin have the power to repel snakes and venomous insects, but its fat has sovereign powers to reconstitute the skin too:

> The same fat or sewet of a Leopard being mixed or mingled with the Oyle which proceedeth from the Bay-tree, and then mollified both together, and so annointed upon any one which is troubled with the scurfe or Mangy, the scabs whereof doth cut or pierce the skinne, doth presently and without any griefe or paine cure the same.[7]

W. Robertson Smith suggested in his *Lectures on Religion of the Semites* in 1889 that the belief among ancient Hebrews in the life concentrated in the fat of the kidneys led to a prohibition on consuming it and its sacrifice to the gods.[8] Smith's argument is elaborated by A. Smythe Palmer who in 1899 suggested that, for Akkadian peoples and the peoples of ancient Israel to whom they passed many of their ritual conceptions, fat and blood were both forbidden to humans to eat, because they constituted the life of a creature and therefore belonged properly to the gods. Being thus 'instinct with a certain spiritual potency' they could only be used externally, and so were smeared on to statues, altars and sacred stones, as an act of sacrifice and sanctification.[9]

Mary Douglas offers more complex reasons for associating the sacrificial fat of Hebrew sacrifice with the skin. In her *Leviticus as Literature*, she interprets the system of injunctions and prohibitions contained in the book in terms of an entire cosmic vision of analogical relations. Central to her reading is the suggestion that the precisely specified ordering of the elements of the sacrifice, suet, head, entrails and legs, is a topological reordering of the body's spatial logic to express its relationship with the sacred space of Mount Sinai and the tabernacle. In particular, it is suggested, '[T]he suet that divides the body at the diaphragm below the lower ribs is not just a covering. It corresponds in the body to the boundary of a forbidden sacred space on the mountain.'[10] The fat covering in the midriff area corresponds to the 'perimeter of dense cloud' that restricts access to Mount Sinai to Aaron and the elders, and the clouds of incense which help restrict access to the sanctuary to priests (79).

Douglas observes that the parallelism between the body and other kinds of space is doubled by a parallelism within the spaces of the body itself: 'The House-that-Jack-built model implies that the suet is a protective covering for the innermost parts as the skin is the covering for the whole body' (72). That is, the body's mirroring of itself mirrors the body's mirroring of social and ritual space. Douglas notes the importance of the idea of the many different kinds of skin-covering, as it were layered analogically one on another, of which the books of the Pentateuch speak, from the story of Adam and Eve onwards:

> The garments of skin that God sewed for them are the first of the coverings in the store of allusions on which Leviticus draws: in the inside of the body the soft innermost parts have solid covers, the thick layers of suet fat over the kidneys and liver; outside the body there is the hide of the animal or the skin of a person, the garment over the skin over the fat over the innermost parts, the house on the garment on the skin, and so on. (247)

This layering is also a feature of the rhetoric of the scriptures, which are similarly stacked in parallel layers or nested in Chinese boxes (70). Although Douglas does not quite go this far, the logic of her argument seems to be the suggestion that the skin, and its avatars, screens, coverings and layers of different kinds, is an autopoetic symbol of the structure of the analogical argument itself. The skin allows not just the recapitulation of the elements which make up the 'philosophy by enactment' (68), but also the imaging by enactment of the structure of the philosophy. It is skin that allows for the particular topology of that argument to occur, in which levels and layers are both distinguished and enfolded within each other.

SEALING

As well as having an affinity to the skin, oil has many features that make it apt to be considered as skin-like in itself. First of all, it has the property of spread; its natural tendency is to move evenly across a surface, forming a thin film upon it. If oil has the tendency to form skins, its tendency to spread also helps associate it with the spreading or transfer of virtues or properties between skins and across individual bodies. Practices of anointing borrow this power of spreading. Oil even seems to have the power to spread or disperse the light, in the rainbow effects which can be caused by thin films of oil. Unlike water, which scatters into droplets, oil can stretch, clinging to itself in its attenuation. According to Smythe Palmer, the smearing of the oil or fat of the victim on to the altar of the deity allows its vital power to pass across to the god. This virtue given up to the god is then available to be transferred back to the priest when he is anointed.[11] Liturgical forms for anointing in the Christian church often stress the symbolism and enactment of a partaking in the divine nature, parallel to the assimilation of the host. Only a small amount of oil is needed to form a coat, which gives rise to the possibility of replenishment through diminishment, in miraculous oil that lasts forever and never fails – as in the miracle of the magically eked-out lamp-oil that is recalled in the Jewish festival of Hanukkah. Unlike the body and blood of Christ, which are consumed and must be renewed, it is as if oil multiplies and renews itself as it is used, in illustration of the principle of inverse efficacy identified in chapter 6.

Another important property of oil is that it is waterproof, indeed repels water; oil-paper is paper that has been made transparent or waterproof by impregnation with oil, and an oilskin a waterproof garment. It is this capacity to act as a seal, combined with the fact that oils are less dense than water, which allows oil to calm agitated seas. Oil was used in Greece and Rome to form a preservative seal or plug across the top of liquid materials, such as wine.

The rituals of baptism, which were sometimes in the early Church associated with anointing, either after baptism or, in some traditions, before it, contain the practice or memory of a total immersion, or sealing. The oiling of the entire body was practised in the Syrian tradition. The Byzantine rite for the blessing of the oil to be applied to catechumens describes it as effecting 'an anointing of incorruption, an armour of righteousness, a renewal of soul and body, a defence against all the works of the Devil, and a deliverance from all evils, for those who in faith are anointed with it'.[12]

The widely spread practice of sealing with wax to indicate ownership or authority allows the idea of an oily, sealing skin to be combined with the idea of a mark. The idea of validation or ownership which is often associated with the application of a seal also seems to involve the suggestion of a metaphorical binding in of the thing sealed to the totality of the owner or sealing authority, as though the seal indicated a literal assimilation or enfolding of one flesh to another. The fourth-century ecclesiastical writer Theodore of Mopsuestia wrote of the ceremony of unction at baptism:

The sign[13] with which you are signed means that you have been stamped as a lamb of Christ and as a soldier of the heavenly King. Indeed, immediately we possess a lamb we stamp it with a stamp which shows to which master it belongs . . . in the same way you also, who have been chosen for the Kingdom of Heaven, and after examination been appointed a soldier to the heavenly King, are first stamped on your forehead, that part of your head which is higher than the rest of your body, which is placed above all your body and above your face.[14]

These ideas seem to be deployed in the frequent evocations of the metaphor of sealing during religious anointing. This is most emphatically visible in the Byzantine ritual for blessing of the chrism which takes place on Maundy Thursday:

So, Lord God Almighty, by the coming of your holy and adorable Spirit, make it a garment of immortality, a perfecting seal which imprints your

divine Name and that of your only-begotten Son, and that of your Holy
Spirit, on those who have received your divine washing.[15]

In Christian practices of anointing, the forehead may be signed with a cross
in oil. This practice seems intended to recall Ezekiel's vision of the righteous in
Jerusalem marked on their foreheads with what the Hebrew specifies as the
cross-shaped character *tov* (Ezekiel 9:4). In the Book of Revelation, the servants
of God are similarly 'sealed' with marks on their foreheads, to protect them
from the winds and locusts of destruction (Revelation 7:1–4 and 9:4). The cruciform mark inscribed both in baptism and in the practices of anointing sometimes associated with it may seem to recall these traditions, as well as to signify the 'chi' which is the first character of the Greek words χριστός (*christos*),
and χρῖσμα (*chrisma*). In this self-signification, the oil closes upon itself as it
seals up the body of the anointed one. The self-designation or crossing of the
oil over its own name in the χ also recalls a pun to be found in two places in
the Old Testament with respect to anointing. At the opening of The Song of
Songs the speaker calls to her lover: 'Thy name is as ointment poured forth'
(1:3). This is a rendering of what in the Hebrew is a play between *shem*, name
and *shemen*, oil. This play is found in an even more obviously chiasmatic form
in Ecclesiastes 7:1: 'a good name is better than precious ointment', the Hebrew
allowing the elements of 'good name' and 'good oil' to be run into each other:
tov shem mishemen tov. The ideas of opening and closing implied in naming
and anointing are emphasized in the second part of the verse: 'and the day of
death than the day of one's birth'; the good name (of the oil) may be what seals
the life that has opened with the anointing of birth. Sealing of this kind is a
softer version of the double incision of the cross discussed in chapter 3 in the
context of judicial and religious marking.

The practice of painting the face which became common among football
supporters and other sports fans during the 1990s, often with a design which
crosses or quarters the face with a national flag, seems to act out at the opposite extreme the logic of inviolability through identificatory marking. That the
whole of the face is made over into a shield or heraldic device – in which the
talismanic power of the cross is often, of course, also a governing feature –
indicates both a willing assimilation to the clan, and the sense of protection or
inclusion that this gives. It is an exposure – and no part of the skin can be as
exposed as the face, which one cannot see without a mirror – which is also an
aegis.

The association of the marking of the body with oil or sacred liquid makes
a localized act stand for the immersion or sealing off of the entire body: the
mark of oil is a kind of liquid knot or umbilicus. This, along with the magical
awareness of oil's dispersive powers, as when one oils a machine at certain key
points in order to ensure lubrication throughout the whole, starts to explain
the strange logic whereby the marking of specific portions of the body approximates to the making of a whole skin. The Catholic rite of Extreme Unction,
based on the *Rituale Romanum* of 1614, involves the anointing of the organs of

the five senses, the eyes, the ears, the nostrils, the mouth and the hands, accompanied by a prayer for forgiveness for the sins committed through each sense, in the following form:

> May the Lord forgive you by this holy + anointing and his most loving mercy whatever sins you have committed by the use of your sight [hearing/sense of smell/sense of taste and the power of speech/sense of touch].[16]

The senses seem here to be regarded as passages or gateways through which corruption can enter, but which are being redeemed by being sealed off by the cross of chrism (the lips are required to be kept closed while the oil is applied to them). It is hard not to be struck by the similarities with Egyptian practices of embalming. After having been embalmed and before being wrapped, the body seems to have been anointed with gum-resins such as frankincense and myrrh along with various other oils and fats. There may have been another anointing of the mummy and even the coffin at a later stage with a bituminous or pitchy substance, which would encourage grave-robbers to chop mummies up with hatchets and use them as fuel.[17] In contrast to the ritual of Extreme Unction, the Egyptian ceremony of anointing, with seven holy oils, was associated not just with the sealing of the body, but with the recital of the ceremony of the Opening of the Mouth over a corpse or mummy.[18] The ceremony was employed on statues as well as mummies, to enable them to be spiritually reanimated.

Earlier versions of the ritual of Extreme Unction also provided for the anointing of the feet and lower back, to ensure redemption from sins committed as a result of the power to walk and, until the abolition of this latter provision in 1916, *per lumborum delectationem*, through the delights of the loins.[19] We have seen that the loins and kidneys were often thought of as the seat of life, kidneys being thought to be involved in the production of semen and animal spirits. We have ceased to think of this area of the body as being generative, and therefore potentially culpable, though a certain contemporary vagueness about the relations between loins and groins perhaps testifies to its persistence.

The anointing of the hands is a particularly interesting feature of Extreme Unction, since here a higher or redeeming touch is being brought to bear upon the sins of touch itself. This moment seems to make it clear that the ritual sees touch as a mastersense; it is because all the other organs of sense are located in the skin that touching, or the application of a higher skin through anointing, has a particular efficacy at this dangerous moment for the soul. The two elements of the ritual, the spoken words, and the accompanying actions, are also blended in the form of a skin. William Dunne's manual for the use of the clergy explains that the oil should be removed from each organ before proceeding to the next, unless the organ is double, in which case the oil should be left in place until both eyes, ears, nostrils, etc. are anointed. Where there is danger of the oil being rubbed off, a danger which 'is more easily present in the unction of the ears', then it is suggested that the oil be removed from the first organ before proceeding to the second. 'By pronouncing the words slowly, the priest could do this without making any notable pause in the form', advises Dunne, adding in a footnote, 'It must be remembered that too long a pause would endanger its validity...an interval of one minute between two words would certainly invalidate the form. A less interval than this, if it be still notable, would render it doubtful.' [20] It is as though the intoned prayers were assisting in forming the skin being spread over the subject's body.

As we saw in chapter 1, Michel Serres has evoked a similar conjoining of the senses through the kinds of self-touching associated with the application of make-up and jewellery. A woman making up her face applies colour and jewels to the different organs of sense, eyes, ears and lips (the nose-rings of other cultures a sign of the insensitivity to odour in ours). In so doing, writes Serres, she paints on to the surface of her skin a picture of her real skin, in terms of the sensations it imparts.[21] What the 'cosmetography' of the skin achieves for Serres' self-adorning woman, the final, holy skin of unction does for the one receiving the rite; in both cases the sensitivities of the body are summed and summoned in a sealing second skin.

GIFT OF SCREWS

We have seen that, if oil repels water and spreads elastically across surfaces, it also sticks tenaciously to itself. Indeed, it is the self-adhesion of oil, combined with its dispersiveness, which helps give it its sealing character. But oil can also merge. Once it settles on and begins to mingle with another substance, it is very hard to remove. This adhesiveness is perhaps a reminder of the labour required to produce oil in the first place. As the essential principle of a thing, oil has the character of inaccessibility, and requires considerable effort of extraction; once it sinks into an absorbent substance or being, it once again seeks the depths and becomes inaccessible.

The binding, healing and annealing properties of oil relate closely to the awareness that oil is obtained as a result of painful or even violent processes; the slaughter and evisceration of the animal, the pressing of the grape or the olive. The last is often employed as an image for the passion of Christ's body, for example in Gerard Manley Hopkins's 'God's Grandeur', in its image of divine glory which 'gathers to a greatness, like the ooze of oil/Crushed.'[22] Emily Dickinson also deploys these traditional associations:

Essential oils – are wrung –
The Attar from the Rose
Be not expressed by Suns – alone
It is the gift of screws – [23]

The tradition that Christ sweated blood in the agony of Gethsemane, the Hebrew name of which means 'place of oil' or 'oil-press', often blends with the image of the pressed fruit, for example in the detailed meditations to be found in a long seventeenth-century poem called *Christes Bloodie Sweat*. Among the virtues of this agonistic substance is the power to cure corruptions manifesting on the skin. The poet imagines Christ's sweat as a sweetly healing river:

> *Christs bloody* sweate, was that distilling river,
> The comfortable *Iordan*, whose faire streames
> Did cleanse the *Syrian Naaman*, and deliver
> His bodie from the leprosies extreames:
>> We all are *Naamans* leprous, but more foule
>> Till in his bloody sweate he purge our soule.[24]

There is in fact an extraordinary tradition recorded in the apocryphal *Arabic Gospel of the Infancy of the Saviour* that Christ was himself anointed with a portion of his own skin, taken from him in circumcision and returned to him transfigured as an ointment:

> And the time of circumcision, that is, the eighth day, being at hand, the child was to be circumcised according to the law. Wherefore they circumcised Him in the cave. And the old Hebrew woman took the piece of skin; but some say that she took the navel-string, and laid it past in a jar of old oil of nard. And she had a son, a dealer in unguents, and she gave it to him, saying: See that thou do not sell this jar of unguent of nard, even although three hundred denarii should be offered thee for it. And this is that jar which Mary the sinner bought and poured upon the head and feet of our Lord.[25]

Cold-pressed extra virgin olive oil is thought to be the highest quality, since it is produced by a process of force, applied, we imagine, to the tenderest offspring of the olive tree, without, as it were, the anaesthetic of chemical processes. Somewhere in this wholesome vegetarian fantasy there is a residual gustatory sadism: the belief that anything which might have numbed the suffering of the pressing would dull the savour and the triumph of the palate. The olive was after all the fruit favoured by that most military and armoured of all virgins, Athena.

The pathic origin of oils seems to be an important part of the belief in their healing nature. Human fat, commonly derived from the bodies of executed criminals, and known as 'oil of man', was obtainable until the end of the eighteenth century. It was commonly employed as an ointment for shrunken limbs, and a contributor to *Notes and Queries* in 1896 reported having heard of a case of a respectable woman who endeavoured to obtain some for use as an aphrodisiac to win back her runaway husband.[26] The suffering that always seems to be involved in the extraction of oil, even from the earth or ocean bed, makes it precious, and passes as healing virtue into that to which it is reapplied. Oil is versatile; like a skin, it can be turned. Though oil is applied to surfaces, its power derives from the suggestion of a welling-up of what is deep or submerged. So, sitting on the surface as a sheen-like second skin, oil also provides a kind of hypodermis, a skin which comes from and sinks below the skin.

The insistence on purity in the oils of unction attaches in particular to oils of vegetable origin in which the guilty suggestions of violence and sacrifice are subdued and sublimated. The stress on the purity of oil will always, I think, have at its heart some lingering sense of guilty horror at the suffering associated with oil, a pathos that derives from the memory of its painful extraction from the body and its spitting and crackling on the sacrificial pyre. One of the ways in which the cosmetics industry persuades its customers of the healing, nourishing qualities of its various fats is to describe them as 'creams'. But the word 'cream', which suggests the free and unforced bounty of nature, retains its origins in painful sacrifice and the fat that is wrung from it; for it derives from *chrême*, the French version of the Greek χρῖσμα, the oil of unction which is itself a neutralized image of Palmer's 'sacred suet'. Sweating its holy oil, like the Virgin's milk, Christ's body is indeed, *la crème de la chrême*.

Let us propose two extreme forms of unction; anointing, in which the body is reskinned in the innocence of oil that has no animal origin; and the profane, or disfiguring skin of fat, or tar, in which the violent origin in the body is manifest, and the application of the new oil-skin itself brings, not new strength, as in the wearing of the bear's or lion's grease, but a skin of suffering. But in milk, and its derivatives, such as cream and butter, there is a third category of oil-skin, an oil which, because it is freely and spontaneously expressed from the body rather than extracted through the application of painful pressure, is thought of as beneficent and healing rather than appropriating or disfiguring. Milk is powerfully associated with the skin, firstly because it is exuded through it, and secondly because of its own aptness to form skins, as discussed in my last chapter. Other bodily liquids – tears, spittle, mucus, urine, sperm – are produced from specific orifices. The nipple is not an orifice, but a puckering, not a parting of the skin, but a gathering of it. Milk is therefore the sieved skin, the skin subtilized through its passage through the skin. There is perhaps a hint of this milkiness, or vital fat, contained within every sacred oil or unction. In Hindu culture, purifying functions are given to ghee, the refined oil produced from butter, itself the refined product of the sacred cow. The cow used to have a similar authority in the rural cultures of medieval Europe. A manuscript Latin life of the sixth-century St Ciaran from the *Codex Kilkeniensis* in Marsh's Library in Dublin relates that the young saint had a favourite cow who supplied all the pupils of the school he attended, St Finnion's at Cluan Iraid in Meath, with milk. When she died, the saint skinned her and placed the skin in the local church. Thereafter it was much in demand among the dying, for to die on the cow's skin was to be guaranteed eternal life in Christ.[27]

Milk represents the gift of skin, in two senses. It is first given through the skin; and then, in its epidermal qualities, it can also be thought of as giving the recipient a new skin, according to the logic of partitive association we have been observing, in which whatever passes through the skin carries something of the skin with it. The breasts sometimes stand as an image of the skin's vital, literally expressive power. A celebrated blazon and counterblazon written in 1535 and 1536 by Clément Marot, in praise and contempt of the breast respectively, picture the alternatives of the young and the depleted breast, in terms of the *cutis* and the *pellis*:

> *Tetin refect plus blanc qu'un oeuf*
> *Tetin du satin blanc tout neuf*
> *Tetin qui fais honte à la Rose*
> *Tetin plus beau que nulle chose . . .*

> *Tetin qui n'as rien que la peau*
> *Tetin flac, Tetin du drappeau*
> *Grand' Tetine, longue Tetasse,*
> *Tetin, doy je dire: bezasse?*[28]

> Breast, that's snowier than egg-white
> Breast of brand-new satin bright
> Breast that puts the rose to shame
> Breast more fair than any name . . .

> Breast now nothing more than skin
> Flagging, flat breast, flapping thin
> Great long titty, dangling dug
> Shall I compare thee to a beggar's bag?

The promise of the moist, delicate and burgeoning breast in the opening lines of the poem in praise of the 'beau Tetin' is answered by the desiccated, empty bag of the aged 'laid Tetin'. The living breast is transformative and self-transforming, its skin becoming and outshining in succession egg, satin, rose. The beautiful breast is swollen and convex; there is nothing to the evacuated breast but skin, and the reiterated names of skin ('peau', 'drappeau'), flapping indigently in the dry wind of speech. Alternative versions of the contreblazon give it the titles 'Le contre tetin' ('The Counter-teat') and 'Sur le tetin renverse', ('The Tit turned inside out').[29] If the breast is that part of the skin which becomes most skinny in age, then the principle of its recuperation may be the very milk which is the breast's product. The promise of creams and lotions which renew and nourish the skin is the covenant of the skin returned to itself, restored with its own vital principles. Skin and milk exude and renew each other ceaselessly.

SOUL-LIGHT

It is no surprise that the rendering of lifelike skin in painting, seemingly possessed of its own luminosity, depended upon the discovery of the powers of oil as a solvent of pigment. Oil, it appeared, could not only provide a carrier for colour, but was also a kind of envelope of light. We saw in chapter 1 that, as light made material, oil can act both to capture and avert the gaze, which has never ceased to seem important in cultures where the belief in the power of the eye to effect injury or damage survives. John Chrysostomos wrote that the seal marked on the forehead had the power not only to keep the Devil away, but also to force him to avert his eyes, for 'he does not dare to look at you directly because he sees the light blazing from your head and blinding your eyes.'[30]

The effulgent properties of oil are surely also reinforced by the fact that combustible oils, fats and waxes have also been used through so much of human history for illumination. That the fat of the body should have the power of furnishing light, rather than being rendered down into ash like the bones and the flesh, might seem to confirm the idea that fat contains the life of the body. A. Smythe Palmer suggests that the ritual coating of sacrificial victims with oil may have served more than the purposes of symbolic consecration, for the fat might often have ensured a vigorous immolation, and consequent assurance that the sacrifice was acceptable, where a more grudging, guttering flame would not.[31] Gaston Bachelard maintains that the burning candle is the sign of the alchemical elevation of matter, the refinement of matter into thought. The essence of the candle, he proclaims, is the movement whereby it lifts up and scatters light, transforming the oil into immaterial substance, and borrowing and generalizing its light-like powers of diffusion: 'oil is the very material of light; the beautiful yellow oil is condensed light, a condensed light that wants to spread out. Man has succeeded in liberating from this slight flame the force of light imprisoned in matter.'[32] Reminding his readers that 'petroleum' etymologically means 'petrified oil', Bachelard writes that the lamp 'makes light ascend from the depths of the earth'.[33] Oil is matter instinct with light, and the application of oil to the skin to make it shine makes the body participate in this cosmogony.

In a rather less rhapsodic vein, Naomi Wolf has denounced the way in which the new 'holy oil industry' of cosmetics 'offers to sell back to women in tubes and bottles the light of grace, to redeem women's bodies now that the cults of virginity and of motherhood can no longer offer to surround with consecrated light the female body whose sexuality has been yielded to others'.[34] Wolf compares the synthetic light of cosmetic effects with the natural radiance of living beings, arguing that this synthetic light reduces women to lustrous surface:

> Beauty's self-consciousness hovers at skin level in order to keep women from moving far inside to an erotic centre or far afield into the big space of the public realm … Indoors or out, women must make their beauty glitter because they are so hard for men to see . . . Real men are matt. Their surfaces must not distract attention from what it is they are saying. But women of every status glint . . . pyrotechnics of light and colour must accompany women's speech to beguile an attention span that wanders when women open their mouths.[35]

The synthetic glow is a betrayal of real soulfulness, for, says Wolf, 'people "light up" and objects don't'.[36] But this logic – of soul-light disfigured by skin-paint, of the skin which delays or detains the light – is part of a long-established Puritan pattern of denunciation of the artifices of the skin, the yellow sickness discussed in the last chapter. The Tertullianic zeal which governs Wolf's polemic emerges at the end of her book, where she evokes the full, radiant, being-in-the-body, freed from the demons of imperfection, that may await women once they give up their false holy oils:

> A woman-loving definition of beauty supplants desperation with play, narcissism with self-love, dismemberment with wholeness, absence with presence, stillness with animation. It admits radiance: light coming out of the face and the body, rather than spotlight on the body dimming the self.[37]

Wolf rages against the hijacking of religious forms and feelings in the marketing of cosmetics to women, but her grisly vision of wholeness and happiness is itself fundamentally religious in its ideal of the body wholly redeemed, in the magicking away of loss and pain and fear, all of these products of the Devil of corporate commodification. This is the same risen body, the body sublimated into the condition of light, which governs Christian dreams of redemption. Like the Puritans who recoiled with horror from the slippery impostures of Rome, it is lit by the fantasy of an unfalsifiable inner light which will shine steadily in place of demonic oil-light.

One of the strongest contemporary associations of oil and light is in the uses of oils, creams and butters to assist in the dangerous practice of suntanning. Such oils are marketed and, one imagines, experienced, as screens, filters and blocks, which maintain the freshness and youth of the skin through the long sessions of ultra-violet onslaught still willingly undergone by many women and, increasingly in recent years, men. The traditional associations of oils and fats with protective skins appear to be active in these practices. Fats and milks seem to be experienced as bilateral. On their inner surfaces, they cool, soothe, comfort and nourish as they sink into the skin; on the outside, they are thought to provide a tough barrier against the harmful rays of the sun. It is an ideal of 'soft strength' similar to that promised for a range of products, from toilet paper to cleaning products.

But the long association of oils with light and refining heat interferes productively with the marketing and consumption of sunscreens. For exposure to the sun seems designed to refine the thick and viscid smearings which block the light into a liquid skin of radiance, which draws light like a lens and holds it in the skin. Suntanners want more than the protective flooding of the skin with dark pigment; they want a darkness that gleams and glows, a light that shines in darkness, that seems furnished with its inner luminance. The phenomenological formula for this experience might be fat + heat = oil + light. Oil is a suntrap, which, as it is impregnated with light, allows the sunbather a solar anointing, just as cooking oil coats the sizzling sausage and distributes heat uniformly across it.

FLYING OINTMENT

The values of oil and unction that I have been examining so far are those that secure, nourish, protect, redeem, confirm and refine the skin. But the history of oil and unction is not all positive. Indeed, since the sixteenth century, oil has come to seem a highly ambivalent substance. One of the determinants in this shift in perspective towards oil is the belief in witches' ointment.

The traditions of the magical ointments used by witches may depend particularly on the powers of spreading and multiplying associated with oil. In Book 3 of Apuleius's *The Golden Ass*, Lucius watches in hiding as the witch Pamphile turns herself into an owl:

> First Pamphile completely stripped herself; then she opened a chest and took out a number of small boxes. From one of these she removed the lid and scooped out some ointment, which she rubbed between her hands for a long time before smearing herself with it all over from head to foot. Then there was a long muttered address to the lamp during which she shook her arms with a fluttering motion. As they gently flapped up and down there appeared on them a soft fluff, then a growth of strong feathers; her nose hardened into a hooked beak, her feet contracted into talons – and Pamphile was an owl.[38]

Here the emphasis seems to be on the total covering of the skin, for which the ointment needs to be warmed and thinned. Attempting to emulate Pamphile, Lucius applies the wrong ointment, and is turned into an ass, thus initiating the series of adventures that make up the rest of *The Golden Ass*. His transformation follows Pamphile's in being a topological transformation of his outer form:

> I tore off my clothes, and plunging my hands into it scooped out a generous portion of the ointment and rubbed it all over myself; then I flapped my arms up and down in imitation of a bird. But no down or feathers appeared; instead my hair became coarse and shaggy, my soft skin hardened into hide, my fingers and toes lost their separate identity and coalesced into hooves, and from the end of my spine there protruded a long tail. My face became enormous and my mouth widened; my nostrils dilated and my lips hung down; and my ears became monstrously long and hairy. The only redeeming feature of this catastrophic transformation was that my natural endowment had grown too – but how could I embrace Photis like this?[39]

In both cases the ointment brings about a thickening and hardening of the skin, the soft fluff developing into feathers, talons and beak for Pamphile and into the coarse skin and hooves of Lucius. The particular power of ointment seems to be that, having the power itself to move between hard and soft conditions, it encourages the conjoining of what would become the two fundamental principles of alchemy: *solve et coagula*. The story tells us that Lucius's unfortunate transformation is caused by the fact that his servant-lover Photis has given him the ass-ointment rather than the owl-ointment, but we may notice that two other features of Pamphile's transformation are neglected, the preparatory kneading of the ointment and the muttered charm. Perhaps there is the suggestion that, to achieve a form capable of flight, one needs to recruit the third aspect of the ointment, namely its volatility. It seems appropriate that applying the ass-lard in impetuous lumps should lead Lucius to take the grotesquely disproportioned and earth-bound shape he does. The antidote to the ointment takes a homely and ordinary form in both cases. Pamphile must bathe in and drink water soaked in dill and laurel, while Lucius must eat rose leaves; in both cases the substances seem to embody human softness.

Ointments were again to be given an aeronautic cast in the later medieval period in Europe, during which it was commonly alleged that witches anointed themselves with ointment in order to give themselves the power of flight. Most commonly, the magic ointment promises flight itself, rather than the metamorphic flight from form to form. One of the earliest references to the use of ointment to aid locomotion is in the record of the trial of Dame Alice Kyteler, who, it was said, had a staff 'on which she ambled and galloped through thick and thin, when and in what manner she listed, after having greased it with the ointment which was found in her possession'.[40] The witchfinders' and exorcists' manual of 1486, the *Malleus Maleficarum*, also reported on the use of oils and ointments by witches.[41] It appears that the image of the flying witch was much more common in mainland Europe than in England. During the sixteenth and seventeenth century, the use of oils and ointments to assist flight on a stick, stave or broom was routinely alleged of and confessed to by witches. Lambert Daneau, the Calvinist Professor of Theology at Geneva and Leiden, explained in his influential *A Dialogue of Witches* of 1564, an English version of which appeared in 1575, that the ointment was part of the taxi-service to the Sabbath provided by Satan for those who otherwise pleaded weakness or incapacity to travel, 'which many tymes he doth by meanes of a staffe or rod, which he delivereth unto them, or promiseth to doo it by force of a certen oyntment which he will geve them'.[42] Henri Boguet, a judge in the diocese of St Claude in Burgundy, wrote in his *Discours des sorciers* that ointment was used to assist those who did not already possess powers of sorcery to fly to the Devil's Sabbath:

> Some of them rubbed themselves with a certain grease and ointment; others did not rub themselves in any way. It seems moreover that those who were not sorcerers but were nevertheless anointed, were able to take flight through the chimney without delay, as if they were sorcerers.[43]

Some modern commentators on this tradition are at pains to show how little evidence there is that such liniments could not really have assisted flight. Even Montague Summers, who is quite prepared to believe in the possibility of miraculous levitation in certain, mostly saintly instances, proposes that the

idea of witches in flight must have been suggested by the sight of ritual
dances performed with hobbyhorses, though there is no evidence that such
dances formed part of Sabbath rituals.[44] Perhaps the only surprise here is that
the inefficacy of the ointment for inducing flight should have seemed worth-
while demonstrating. Much of the debate in the sixteenth and seventeenth
century also concerned the question of whether witches really could fly; even
those who thought it was possible, and they may not have been the majority,
did not think it was the ointment that did it. Daneau maintains that Satan
really employs the ointment as a kind of date-rape drug, to ease the appre-
hensions of neophytes not used to the rough and tumble of the Sabbath:

> [Y]ou must not think that Satan willeth all sorcerers to use those ointments.
> For he commaundeth but certen of them to doo that, whom he perceiveth
> to be either fearfull to venture or more deintie then that they can abide his
> horrible touching of them, like as are women, and certen men also. For by
> those confections wherewith he willeth them to bee oynted, he benummeth
> their senses, that they shall feele no payne while they are carried, or stand in
> horror of his handes, or of his bearing of them.[45]

The Spanish Jesuit Martin del Rio, whose huge and authoritative
Disquisitionum magicarum libri sex appeared in 1599, also doubted that the

ointment could really assist in the physical transport of bodies to the Sabbath, preferring the view that its principal purpose was to anaesthetize or stupefy those who are 'too timid to make the venture or too weak to bear the horrible contact with Satan via the body he assumes'.[46]

Daneau goes on to reassure his readers that the ointment itself has no magical powers to confer the power of flight:

> For these oyntments or oyles, are of no effect, nor any thing appertayning to the moving of them or to their iourney, but he commaundeth it to be done eyther by the meanes to detayne or keepe them from thinking how he handleth them: or surely if they avayle any thing, they availe in this respect, that by meanes thereof the bodily senses are layd a sleepe, and in the meane while Satan him selfe carrieth them.[47]

Boguet agreed that witches were enabled to fly not by means of the oil, or associated incantations, but through that ready standby of witch-scholars, the permission of God.[48]

Discussions of flying ointment since the 1930s have followed another path. Some recipes for flying ointments have survived, most of them involving the fat of a killed, boiled infant as a base, mingled with soot and poisonous plants, such as belladonna, aconite or henbane. In an appendix to Margaret Murray's *The Witch-Cult in Western Europe*, A. J. Clarke reports on his analysis of the components of ointments, concluding that it would be possible for the toxic properties of ingredients like belladonna and hemlock to produce delirium and irregularities of the pulse which could have been interpreted by witches themselves as the experience of flight.[49] In the recent revival of witchcraft in the milder, whiter form of Wicca, recipes for flying ointment abound. Most of them warn usefully, if also rather excitingly, against using its original poisonous ingredients, and promoting the idea that the flying that is involved will be in the form of a mild high, or astral projection. After the 1960s associated drug use and sexual experience as the supreme forms of transcendence, the assumption has been that the flying to which witches confessed must have been a form of chemically enhanced sexual ecstasy. Michael J. Harner set out an influential argument in 1973 for the hallucinogenic properties of the materials said to have been used in witches' ointments, and their power of penetrating the skin.[50] The hallucinogenic ointment hypothesis is accepted also by Ioan P. Couliano, who makes much of the fact that, in his *Quaestio de strigis*, of around 1470, Jordanes de Bergamo says that the witches either rode on a smeared stick or smeared the ointment on their armpits. Since, we are told, 'the most sensitive zones of the body are, precisely, the vulva in woman and the armpits', Couliano supposes this to be a clear indication that these substances were intended to be absorbed through the skin.[51] A footnote provides a glimpse of the pharmacology of the substances involved:

The alcaloids contained in the Solanaceae differ from the alcaloids contained in the hallucinogenic plants of Mexico and South America by virtue of their faculty of being absorbed by the skin. On the contrary, the latter are characterized by the presence, in their chemical structure, of a group called *indol*, which does not penetrate the skin. That explains the different customs of European sorcerers compared with the medicine men of Central and South America.[52]

Some have been unconvinced by the pharmacological reading of flying ointment. Brian P. Levack points out that many of the earliest recipes from the fifteenth century rely on non-hallucinogenic elements, like bat's blood and soot, and were said to be applied directly to the broom, rather than the body. He is supported by Murray, who suggests that 'in early times, the stick itself was greased, later it was the rider who was anointed'.[53] (This may be the case within the period with which she was dealing, though of course the example of Apuleius contradicts it.) Levack therefore concludes that '[t]he witches' unguents . . . should probably be viewed as products of either harmless folklore or demonological theory, and not as effective mind-altering substances'.[54] It is Michael Harner who seems to have suggested for the first time the use of the broomstick as applicator, allowing one recent writer, who attempts to represent the whole history of religious experience as the results of consuming fly agaric, or magic mushrooms, to aver confidently of the greased broomstick, 'now we know the witches were actually using their broomsticks and other devices to apply psychoactive ointments to their vulvas.'[55] Of course, the hypothesis that the broomstick was used as dildo-applicator may give an answer, but one wonders what daintiness prescribed the use of equipment of this kind at all – especially to apply the ointment to the armpit.

In fact, the pharmacological explanation, that the alleged witches were high rather than actually airborne, is anticipated in some contemporary commentators. The sceptical Dutch doctor Johann Weyer took the view that the ointment produced the illusion of flight by inducing a delirious trance.[56] Strikingly, and even rather sinisterly, such explanations of the ointments in terms of their psychopharmacological properties seem to imply that what mattered was the actual experiences or beliefs of witches, rather than the expectations of their torturers, or the background of belief within which both torturers and victims functioned. After spending several pages showing how accused witches would say anything and everything that was expected of them in order to bring their torments to an end, either temporarily, or through the judicially assisted suicide of the bonfire, Marvin Harris concludes nevertheless that 'most of the "genuine" sabbath meetings involved hallucinogenic experiences' and that '[h]allucinogenic ointments account for many of the specific features of witchcraft belief'.[57] There were plenty of contemporary commentators on witch trials, more sceptical about the reality of witchcraft even than some recent commentators, who suspected that the near-universal use of torture and intimidation mean that none of the testimonies or confessions of witches can be trusted at all. By contrast, contemporary pharmacological explanations suggest that there must have been some real basis to the accusations levelled at witches: that, in short, the inquisitors with their strappados and thumbscrews were actually *on to something*, and that the witches indeed had something to confess – if not sorcery exactly, then certainly the orgiastic consumption of mind-altering substances. It is not surprising, therefore, that the pharmacological explanation has come to have so much currency among those attempting to revive witchcraft in the contemporary world, who would also like witchcraft to have existed, though in the form of a misunderstood tradition of nature-wisdom and natural healing, rather than as baby-boiling, lycanthropy and sodomy with devils.

I may as well make my own position as clear as I can. There may have been some people who believed themselves to be witches, just as there are people who sincerely believe themselves to be mass murderers or Martians. There may also have been men and women whose skill in the decoction and administration of natural substances made them seem suspicious in the eyes of neighbours who were convinced of the reality of witches. And I suppose that some of these may have found that, in the right doses, poisons gave pleasurable effects. But, just as many sceptical commentators in the sixteenth and seventeenth centuries themselves suspected, there have never been any real *witches*, not ever, nor any actual witchcraft, white, black or candystriped. The numbers of those who thought they had a secret to confess before being driven insane by torture were vastly outnumbered by the women and men who were forced to endure rack, screw and faggot because they were a bit odd, or simple, or unpopular, or because a neighbour saw a chance of getting the last laugh in a squabble over a goat.

As so often, sex and chemistry are being used here to make a clean cut through culture and history. None of these explanations of flying ointment pay enough attention to structures of belief and feeling, and the powerful concentration of the material imagination around oils, ointments and the action of anointing. Relieving ourselves of the question of what the underlying pharmacological reality might have been of what 'witches' may or may not have done with their ointments leaves us, by contrast, free and able to examine the reality of the structures of belief that make witchcraft and its paraphernalia seem a powerful and alluring explanation of things. Whatever the psychotropic possibilities of the alleged ingredients of magic ointments, it is the complex cultural imagination of ointment that is the most powerful intoxication, not the ointment itself.

Indeed the belief in the intoxicating powers of ointment is an important part of its cultural power. It should also be clear that intoxication is no mere given, but has a cultural as well as a pharmacological history. The idea of intoxication is certainly also associated with greases and oils, as perhaps is the mixture of intoxication and lubrication produced by unctuary friction of all kinds. In 1672, Samuel Butler put into the mouth of his William Prynne, as part of his invective against Quakers, the statement that 'as *Witches* liquor their Staves and fly through the Air, even so do *Quakers* liquor their Throats with inchanted Potion.'[58] The peregrinations of the word 'liquor', here employed by Butler to mean grease or anoint, are an oblique contribution to the magical history of greases and oils. Up to the seventeenth century, the word 'liquor' referred not only to distilled extracts, but more to the products of melting processes, especially in cooking, to form tallow, lard, or shoeblack. Falstaff applies the term to his humiliation in *The Merry Wives of Windsor*, when he worries that 'If it should come to the ear of the court how I have been transformed . . . they would melt me out of my fat drop by drop, and liquor fishermen's boots with me' (*Merry Wives*, IV. v. 91–5, p. 881). Over following centuries, the liquoring of boots starts to coalesce with the lubricating and perhaps also insulating effects of alcohol. By 1785, Grose's *A Classical Dictionary of the Vulgar Tongue* is recording two slang meanings for the phrase 'to liquor one's boots': it could mean 'to drink before a journey' and, by metaphorical transfer, 'among Roman Catholicks to administer the extreme unction'.[59] The oily undertones of the word 'liquor' in its twentieth-century American usage preserve a sense that the pleasant poisoning offered by alcohol is something spread like an ointment rather than injected like a drug. The fact that the effects of alcohol are commonly said to 'wear off' indicates the survival of the idea of an effect that is applied to the body as a coating or varnish rather than being adjoined to or inserted into it. The other things that are most commonly said to 'wear off' are the effects of medications and enchantments and alcoholic intoxication is at the intersection of these two domains.

In a world in which the possibilities of surgical intervention were very limited, there was as much reliance on plasters, cataplasms, emplastrums, poultices and other devices applied to the skin to draw out distemper or infuse healing as there was on the swallowing of potions and elixirs. Indeed, in contrast to today, when we observe clearer distinctions between what is ingested and what is applied, many medicinal substances before the nineteenth century were intended for both internal and external application. In such a world, poison was thought of as something just as likely to be applied to the skin as administered *per buccam*. Indeed, the Latin *intoxicare* from which the English word derives means to smear with poison rather than to administer by mouth. Intoxication is the word used to describe the range of powers to harm possessed by witches and sorcerers in Daneau's *Dialogue of Witches*, in which sorcerers and others pledged to Satan are said to 'cast their divellish poysons and intoxications uppon men, or brute beastes', and this casting, which seems to evoke the scattering of seed, or the spreading of a net, clearly includes poisons that infiltrate the body through the operations of touch, and avenues other than the mouth.[60] Even ocular intoxication involved a kind of touch, the 'evil eye' of the fascinator being thought to be capable of emitting noxious particles which entered the eye or body of the victim, rather than having to be imbibed by them.

Another adjacent context in which the emphasis on salves and ointments may be understood is that of the religious uses of holy oil. Among the most explicit of English accounts of satanic unction is in the case of the Somerset witches, who were tried and condemned in 1664. Joseph Glanvill reports the wicked dealings over a long period of four women, Elizabeth Styles, Elizabeth Duke, Anne Bishop and Mary Penny, with a 'man in black'. According to the confession of Elizabeth Styles, 'before they are carried to their meetings, they anoint their Foreheads and Hand-wrists with an Oyl the Spirit brings them (which smells raw) and then they are carried in a very short time, using these words as they pass, *Thout, tout a tout, tout, throughout and about.*' Another of the women, Anne Bishop, said that her instantaneous conveyance to the Sabbath was secured by 'her Forehead being first anointed with a Feather dipt in Oyl'.[61] Most accounts of the Somerset witches follow Margaret Murray, who quotes only the passages dealing directly with the use of the ointment as a preparation for flight (though flight is not mentioned, but rather instantaneous passage).[62] But a striking fact about the pre-flight anointing of the Somerset witches is how closely it is echoed in the rituals they conducted once disembarked at the Sabbath. These involved the making of wax figures, or 'Pictures', which would first be anointed and then, in what has become the traditional witchly ritual established in European minds, pierced with thorns in order to bring about suffering to their victim in effigy by sympathetic magic.

Although Margaret Murray discusses the long history of making wax images in her *God of the Witches*, she does not put this discussion together with the practice of anointing. In part, the power of the idea of satanic anointing derives, like so much else in satanic behaviour, from the fact that it is a parody of religious practices of anointing with oil. Martin del Rio asserted that in using anointing, the Devil 'mimicks the holy sacraments instituted by God, and by these quasi-rituals imports a degree of reverence and veneration into his orgies'.[63] Boguet expressed the certainty that chrism was 'a sovereign antidote against the power of the Devil', proving it by reference to the confessions of sorcerers who had turned themselves into wolves, who 'when about to kill and eat certain infants, were unable to touch the part of the infant that had been anointed with Holy Chrism'. But the very inviolability of the chrism made it apt for travesty and mocking imitation. It was widely believed in the sixteenth and seventeenth centuries that Satan would leave his mark in secret places, such as the mucous membrane of the lips, nostrils or anus, or under the hair; but he was also sometimes said to put his finger on the most prominent place of all, the forehead, in the place where the chrism had been applied. Boguet reported that the Devil pretended in his ceremonies to lift off the protective sign of the oil left on the foreheads of his followers at Baptism.[64] So the anointings used by the Somerset witches seem to signify both the Devil's desire to make his followers compact with him, sealed into his black faith as though in a single, encompassing skin, and the capacity to double or multiply the skin, whether in order to effect translocation, or to transfer suffering between an effigy and its original.

We have seen that few if any of those who reported on the use of diabolic ointment believed in its powers to confer flight. Many, like those who currently trust in the uses of ointments to assist astral projection, believed that ointments might serve to induce a deep sleep during which the sleeper could be beguiled by grotesque and disordered visions. Although Johannes Weyer and others presented this as proof that the stories of the flight to the Sabbath and the lurid cavortings that took place there never in fact happened, others saw the trance as itself enabling a temporary dehiscence of body and soul. The English Neoplatonist Henry More accepted that the Devil did not transport his adherents in their habitual bodies, but rejected the arguments of sceptics like Weyer as 'slight Rhetorications, no sound Arguments', insisting that

> these *Sorceresses* so confidently pronouncing that they are *out of their Bodies* at such times, and see and doe such and such things, meet one another, bring messages, discover secrets and the like, it is more natural and easie to conclude that they be *really out of their Bodies* than *in* them . . . [T]heir *Ecstasies* are not mere *Dreams* and *Delusions* of the Devil, but are accompanied with *reall effects*.[65]

More offers the following intriguing explanation of the function of the oil, in preserving the sleeping body in a kind of suspended animation while its soul is disjoined from it:

> For the *life* of the Body is nothing else but that *fitness* to be actuated by the Soul. The conservation whereof is help'd, as I conceive, by the *anointing* of the Body before the *Ecstasie*; which ointment filling the pores, keeps out the cold, and keeps in the heat and spirits, that the frame and temper of the Body may continue in fit case to entertain the Soul again at her return. So the vital steams of the carcase being not yet spent, the pristine operations of Life are presently again kindled; as a Candle new blown out, and as yet reeking, suddenly catches fire from the flame of another, though at some distance, the light gliding down along the smoke.[66]

Defending the idea of the flight of witches, More's friend, Joseph Glanvill, agrees that 'the *Witches anointing* her self before she takes her flight, may perhaps serve to keep the Body *tenantable*, and in fit *disposition* to receive the *Spirit* at its return.' But he also suggests that ' 'tis easie to apprehend, that the *Soul* having left its gross and sluggish *body* behind it, and being cloath'd onely with its *immediate vehicle of Air*, or more *subtile matter*, may be quickly conducted to any place it would be at by those *officious Spirits* that attend it.'[67] The anointing is here both the seal which keeps the body from decomposition and the near-immaterial cloak of the soul, mimicking the mixed condition of oil, between the liquid and the volatile.

Others saw the ointment as having a penetrating rather than protective function. Reginald Scot reported that witches

> rubbe all parts of their bodies exceedinglie, till they looke red, and be verie hot, so as the pores may be opened, and their flesh soluble and loose. They joine herewithall either fat, or oile in steed thereof, that the force of the ointment maie the rather pearse inwardly, and so be more effectuall.[68]

Jean de Nynauld too emphasized the measures taken to ensure the penetration of the oil, rather than its sealing character, writing that 'they anoint all the parts of the body after having rubbed them until they were red, so that, with the pores opened and relaxed, the oil can penetrate more deeply.'[69] In fact, however, More also believes in the necessity of a diabolical penetration into the body for transformation:

> I conceive the Devil gets into their Body, and by his subtile substance, more operative and searching than any fire or putrefying liquor, melts the yielding *Compages* of the Body to such a consistency, and so much of it as is fit for his purpose, and makes it pliable to his Imagination; and then it is as easie for him to work it into what *shape* he pleaseth, as it is to work the Aire into such forms and figures as he ordinarily doth. Nor is it any more difficulty for him to mollifie what is hard, than it is to harden what is so soft and fluid as the Aire.[70]

More sees no operation of the ointment in this transformation, though he does seem to have, if not ointment, then wax figuratively at his fingers' ends as he evokes the powers of the Devil to make the bodies of his followers 'pliable to his Imagination'. As we have just seen, oil and wax come together in the metaphor of the candle relit by the smoke of another. Oil seems to be implicated in the idea of a subtle material, which can both maintain the contours of things, and slip through them, which can allow the soul to be reshaped, and dreams and visions to take on material form.

Ointment was associated for some writers with more literal kinds of metamorphosis, of man into wolf. Martin del Rio seems convinced that ointments provide some material assistance in the transformation of magicians into wolves:

> Sometimes (and this is a fact derived from a number of people's confessions), he wraps actual people very tightly in genuine animal skins, and in this case he gives them a wolf's pelt which they are supposed to keep hidden in the hollow of a tree. Sometimes, in accordance with the pact he has made with them, he manufactures from air the likeness of an animal, surrounding the magicians with it, and builds the copy round each part of their body, fitting head to head, mouth to mouth, belly to belly, foot to foot, and arm to arm. He usually does this when the magicians apply certain ointments to themselves with a view to effecting this change.[71]

Jean de Nynauld offers an extensive rebuttal of such claims in his *De la lycanthropie*, relying again on the theory that the ointment induces disordered dreams of transformation rather than the actuality.[72]

The middle years of the seventeenth century saw a debate about a different kind of volatililty with relation to oil, in the so-called 'weapon-salve' controversy. Here the claim was not for an ointment that conferred or even suggested transvection, but an ointment that itself had the power of flying magically from place to place. Paracelsus seems to have provided one of the earliest recipes for an ointment that could cure wounds by the power of sympathy. His *De summis naturae mysteriis* recommended that one collected the moss that grew on the skull or bones of a corpse, and ground it with human fat and blood. When a wounded person required treatment, a piece of wood was to be dipped in the blood of the wound and the unguent applied to it, rather than to the wound itself, which was merely to be kept covered and moist, preferably by means of the patient's own urine. Paracelsus claimed that wounds could be treated by this method at a distance of ten or twenty miles.[73] This claim was taken up in England by Sir Kenelm Digby, who reported curing a wound in a similar way; he had dissolved a powder ('Powder of Vitrioll') in a basin of water, and immersed in it a bloodsoaked garment taken from a man who had been gashed by a sword. The result for the patient was 'a pleasing kind of freshnesse, as it were a wet cold Napkin did spread over my hand'.[74] When the garment was taken from the basin and dried before the fire, however, it caused a burning sensation.

Digby provided a detailed set of physical arguments based on atomist theory to account for this phenomenon. His suggestion was that the atoms which were being continuously skimmed off the surface of bodies by abrasion and even the action of light not only maintained their skin-like consistency in themselves, as in the species theory of vision that we encountered in chapter 4, but also maintained a physical connection with their original body. This continuing physical community meant that any action applied to a remnant or offscouring of a body could induce effects upon the original body. Digby offers many stories in support of his theory, for example of wine that began to ferment in bottles at the time of the grape harvest, nursemaids who felt pain when the milk they had expressed was boiled, and a boy who developed a high fever after his faeces had been thrown on to the fire.[75]

Digby was only the most visible of a large number of writers who made similar claims for oils and ointments which were capable of effecting similar cures by the power of sympathy. The 'unguent war', as Carlos Camenietzki has called it, would last until the eighteenth century.[76] The occultist natural philosopher Robert Fludd described a similar substance that worked by means of magnetism; and, indeed, some of the theories of Anton Mesmer developed at the end of the following century would depend on a similar notion of action affected at a distance through the powers of a higher or magical touch. Many thought these therapies either ridiculous or impious. Fludd's weapon-salve was dismissed by William Foster, a parson from Buckingham, in a book entitled *Hoplocrisma-Spongus* in 1631, prompting an elaborate reply from Fludd in defence of his claims.[77] One of the most telling objections was offered by the moderate theologian John Hales, who pointed out that, if there really were some magical 'Eradiation and Emanation' connecting blood to the body from which it had spilt, and if harm as well as good could be done to the original through the power of sympathy, then we would need to maintain continuous vigilance over all such bodily products: 'what mean we then to be thus negligent of our *droppings*, as to let them fall at random into the *earth*, the *fire*, the *water*, and God knoweth where, since there is such *danger* depends from them?'[78] What Hales called the 'Volatile Balsam' of the weapon-salve represents the rendering into materialist form of the magical and religious belief in the universal continuity through contiguity of substances and beings.[79] The weapon-salve was a magical, volatile, ubiquitous skin that ensured the continuing intimacy of touch and contact cohering across every separation.

SMEARS

The epidermal associations of oil extend to usages such as the administering of birch oil, hazel oil, stirrup oil and strap oil, all of which refer ironically to the giving of floggings. Partridge adds 'oil of Baston', a topographical pun conjoining basting with Baston in Lincolnshire.[80] The fact that the use of oil for massage purposes, is a sign of mild decadence in sexual practices may itself be an indication of the median condition of the oleaginous, poised between luxury and disgust. As is often the case, the sexual arena maintains the balance between the shameful and the exalted powers of oil, as well as putting the section of the skin (flogging, flaying, pelting) in ironic contact with its unction. Tanning a hide involves a kind of negative unction, in the application of substance to a skin (tannin) to assist the process of leathering prior to its drying.

In fact, the history of oils and unction in modern Europe shows a growing suspicion of the oily and the greasy. While retaining associations of luxury and comfort, and virtues of purification and restoration, these substances have also gradually gathered a phobic crust. The word 'greasy' seems to have begun to be used as a term of discredit in English around the mid-sixteenth century. The very credit attached to the sacraments of anointing in Catholicism, about which there has been a long history of uneasiness in the Church of England, seems to have been a factor in the growing disgust with oil and oiliness. Writing in 1583, Philip Stubbes raged against the claims of the Pope to temporal as well as spiritual authority, when 'indeed he, being a greasie priest, and smered prelate, hath no more authority than other oiled shavelings have'.[81] The Catholic associations of oil and grease had still not abated a century later, when John Oldham's viciously anti-Catholic satire slithered together holy chrism and the lubrications of witches:

> That vessel consecrated Oyl contains,
> Kept sacred, as the fam'd *Ampoulle* of *France*;
> Which some profaner *Hereticks* would use
> For liquoring Wheels of Jacks, of Boots, and Shooes:
> This make the Chrism, which mix'd with Snot of Priests,
> Anoint young Cath'licks for the Church's lists;
> And when they're crost, confest, and die; by this
> Their lanching Souls slide off to endless Bliss:
> As *Lapland* Saints, when they on Broomsticks fly,
> By help of Magick Unctions mount the sky.[82]

The long memory of anti-Catholic disgust in Northern Europe may explain why it is that southern Mediterranean peoples and especially peoples of Latin or Hispanic origin, cultures identified strongly with Catholicism, came to be the targets of the racist insult 'greasy'. African and Asian peoples have less commonly been the target of this insult.

The shift in the values attached to greasiness is congruent with the shift in the value of the word 'smear'. An Old English glossary indicates that the word 'smeoru' was an equivalent to Latin *unguentum*.[83] In Middle English the words 'smyren' and 'smeren' were regularly used to describe the spreading of oil, chrism or medical preparations, without any negative connotations. In the Anglo-Saxon Gospel of St Matthew of about 1000, the words of Christ in the Sermon on the Mount which the Revised Standard Version gives as 'when thou fastest, anoint thy head, and wash thy face' (Matthew 6:17) are rendered as 'ponne du faeste, smyra pin heafod, and pweah pine ansyne'.[84] The Kentish *Ayenbite of Inwit* of 1340 uses smearing positively in its evocation of the oil of Christian bliss:

> Of pise oyle byep ysmered po pet god hep ymad kynges and lhordes of pe worlde and god zelf. And panne is pe man ziker cristen huanne he is ysmered myd pise holy crayme. Vor of crayme: is yzed crist: and of crist: cristendom. And huo pet is ysmered mid pise oynement: pet is pe blisse and pe loue of god.[85]

It is around the middle of the sixteenth century that smearing begins to be used in a contemptuous sense, to suggest dishonesty, fickleness or untrustworthiness. Robert Crowley, condemning the idleness of Catholic priests in 1550, warns that 'as long as ydle bealies [bellies] may come to the bishope and be smered for money . . . [t]hey shalle be called feedars of feedynge them selves, and not of fedyng the flock.'[86] The associations with superficiality are apparent in 1549 in the words of Erasmus as rendered by Coverdale and others: 'Why are you smeared with the vaine pleasures of this world, and set naught by the ioyes that never shal have end?'[87] In this last example, the word may have the sense not only of superficial decoration, but also of the liming of the superficial soul by pleasure. This mid-sixteenth-century shift in the values of oil and grease can be correlated with the abandonment of holy oil in the Anglican church, which can itself be dated between the 1549 Book of Common Prayer, in which anointing had formed part of the ceremony of baptism, and the 1552 version, in which anointing had vanished.[88]

By the beginning of the seventeenth century, the disapproval in the word had curdled unmistakably into disgust. Sending an enemy to prison in Marston's *Antonio's Revenge* (1601), the tyrant Piero Sforza says 'Lap him in rags and let him feed on slime/That smears the dungeon cheek.'[89] Smearing comes to suggest slovenly application that leaves the grease sitting on the skin unevenly or in undispersed clots. During the eighteenth century, the word also started to acquire its associations with acts of spoiling or erasure – with blurring, blearing and blotting. Finally, smearing becomes associated with the spreading of slurs, or discreditable rumours, perhaps with some influence from 'sneer'. That the idea of a physical substance should provide a figure for a verbal action is appropriate given the way in which the idea of spreading itself smears or spreads across these near-rhyming words: slur (a shortening of slurry, or churned-up mud), blur, sneer and blear.

The opposite of the exaltation associated with unction is tarring and feathering, a practice first imposed by an ordinance of Richard I in 1189 as a punishment for theft in the navy, in which the luminous oil is replaced by its sticky and stinking isotope. This becomes a degenerate second skin of disgrace rather than a second skin of rebirth. Sinking into the skin, the oil of unction also amplifies the skin's power of emanation and radiance. The tar of tarring and feathering puts stickiness in the place of luminosity. The tar is there to attract and retain whatever might touch or brush against the subject, the feathers perhaps functioning merely as a sign of this general susceptibility, as well as a more positive sign of cowardice, treachery or absurdity. The feathers signify a skin with no repelling powers, a promiscuously one-sided skin that that can pick up anything. H. G. Wells's Invisible Man finds himself subject to this condition of visibility in disgrace, when he reflects on the powers of the atmosphere to render him visible by reducing him to a greasy mucus of snow, rain or fog:

> [T]he snow had warned me of other dangers. I could not go abroad in snow – it would settle on me and expose me. Rain, too, would make me a watery outline, a glistening surface of a man – a bubble. And fog – I should be like a fainter bubble in a fog, a surface, a greasy glimmer of humanity. Moreover, as I went abroad – in the London air – I gathered dirt about my ankles, floating smuts and dust upon my skin. I did not know how long it would be before I should become visible from that cause also.[90]

We name this uneasy mixture of the sticky and the slimy the *viscous*. The Latin 'viscus' from which English 'viscous' derives means both mistletoe and birdlime. The mistletoe does not merely coil on the surface of the tree it colonizes, but literally grows through it; while birdlime is a glutinous substance obtained from the inner bark of the holly by a process of pulverizing, soaking and fermenting.

The first sustained philosophical articulation of the powers of horror attaching to unguent substances is to be found in Jean-Paul Sartre's *Being and Nothingness*. For Sartre, the *visqueux* is characterized by an epidermal in-betweenness, which is neither solid nor liquid, neither object nor subject, but greasy, slimy-sticky. Writing a couple of years before the practice of tarring and feathering would be revived as a punishment for female collaborators with the Germans, Sartre evokes the disgust induced by the viscous in terms of a loss of surface. For Sartre, the viscous must be understood as the refusal of a natural condition of things in which subjects choose their manner of being in the world through objects which as it were radiate a form of relation with the world. An object is chosen by a subject as the mode of its relation to the world 'depending on the mode in which it renders being, depending on the manner in which being springs forth from its surface'.[91] A viscous substance has none of this quality of springing forth. Rather than being emitted or reflected by the tar-skin, light is sluggishly hugged in by it. Thus, although tarring and feathering is an extreme act of stigmatization or marking out, it seems also to enforce a stripping away of distinctiveness, the refusal of any eminence or power of standing out from the inanimate world. Its hidden logic is that the one thus conspicuously coated must eventually vanish beneath a carapace of contingency; it will have to become its skin, a skin that will in fact be made up arbitrarily of whatever happens to touch or abut upon it. Long before roads were routinely finished with tarmacadam, a 'road' was a slang name for a prostitute, but there seems to be a continuity in the logic that makes the victim of tarring merely an object to be buffeted or traversed.

Oleaginous substances need to be understood in terms, not only of their capacity for transformation – congealing, melting, evaporation – but also in terms of the speed of that transformation. Where, for Sartre, being starts forth immediately, which is to say, faster than reflection, as a radiance from the surface of things, the congealing of radiance into substance is perceived as a slowing down, or a 'hysteresis', from Greek ὑστέρησις, signifying an afterness, or latecoming. Sartre conspicuously prefers objects that give him an immediate apprehension of the whole world through them, like his bike and his pipe, or substances which instantly reform and retain their form intact when he merges with them, like the sea in which he swims, or the snow across which he skis, to substances which have this quality of slow degradation: 'If I sink in the slimy, I feel that I am going to be lost in it; that is, that I may dissolve in the slime precisely because the slimy is in process of solidification'.[92] The victim of tarring is similarly reduced to the condition of slowing down, the process of hardening into an object.

WHICH INK?

We have seen that the marking of the skin is often designed to suggest a self-marking, the spontaneous appearance on the outside of a mark supposed to denote an inward condition. The victim of tarring is left in the median condition of slow congelation, to signify that a sticky surface is now all that they are. An intensified form of this oily self-figuring is to be found in the work of Dickens, work which is more driven by the material imagination, by the logic of substances and their different states, than that of almost any other writer. Grease and oil are by no means always negative for Dickens, and will often signify either honest industry or homely good humour. But in *Bleak House*, his most oleaginous novel, they are also embodiments of the corrupting and nauseating touch of social institutions.

There are two modes of dissolution in this novel, dry and wet. Dry dissolution involves explosion or slow wearing away into dust. In the slow rapacity of its delays, the law claws the skin off things, like Krook, who does a trade in skinning cats, or Mr Vholes, with his recurrent gesture of drawing off his gloves as though drawing off his own skin. But, compared to the operations of grease, there is a kind of rapture in this skinning, which belongs to the desiccant drift into dust. For this dissolution of skin is less threatening than the clouding, clammy, suffocating sweat of oil that stands ready to form on everything. Dust is perfected dissolution; grease is imperfect arrested dissolution, a dust only half-dead, or disgustingly half-revived. The novel begins with an evocation of 'Smoke lowering down from chimney-pots, making a soft black drizzle with flakes of soot in it as big as full-grown snowflakes', a greasy sleet, falling sluggishly through gelid light, which makes the narrator wonder 'if this day ever broke'.[93] Throughout the novel, light threatens to fail to break, to rise, to change state. Light coils, clots; brightness falls from the air, flatus itself collapses exhausted, into a sickeningly thin scum, a fat flatness.

The term 'unction' had been in use at least since the seventeenth century as a metaphor for the consoling and uplifting effects of preaching. Dickens brutally literalizes the metaphor in the person of Mr Chadband, the vain and unctuously self-righteous evangelical preacher, who is figured throughout as an engine for the production of oil. (In this, he seems a warmed-up version of the slippery Mr Slope in *Barchester Towers*, with whom Trollope tells us he 'never could endure to shake hands', on account of the 'cold, clammy perspiration [which] always exudes from him'.[94]) Chadband is introduced as 'a large yellow man, with a fat smile, and a general appearance of having a good deal of train oil in his system' (316). A little later, we learn how the oil is produced:

> The conversion of nutriment of any sort into oil of the quality already mentioned, appears to be a process so inseparable from the constitution of this exemplary vessel, that in beginning to eat and drink, he may be described as becoming a kind of considerable Oil Mills, or other large factory for the production of that article in a wholesale scale. (319)

Chadband's slithery, hypocritical, hysteretical discourse is no more than grease. The effect is redoubled by the fact that the scene of his first appearance in the novel also involves the appearance of little Jo, telling his improbable story of the mysterious veiled lady he has conducted to the grave of Captain Hawdon. While Chadband lays into the buttered comestibles, the law-clerk Guppy lays into Jo, 'patting him into this shape, that shape, and the other shape, like a butterman dealing with so much butter' (322). During the interrogation, Chadband subsides into gorging silence: 'the vessel Chadband, being merely engaged in the oil trade, gets aground, and waits to be floated off' (323). Meanwhile, Jo is at a different kind of sticking point: he 'sticks to it [his story] like cobbler's-wax', says Guppy (323).

If unction can be thought of as the drawing out of the vital fat of the body as an excremental humour, followed by the reapplication of this fat in redeemed and redeeming form, the oil of which Mr Chadband is composed and to which he gives rise in his manner and language never succeeds in leaving him. His oil is a kind of continuous, constipated flux. He is nothing but emanation, but an emanation that remains immanent, stuck to him, stuck to itself. Mr Chadband's oil participates closely in one of the systems of images which the book uses to designate itself and its world. It has its origin in the street mud evoked in the opening sentences of the novel. The mud is both slimy and sticky: foot passengers are 'slipping and sliding' in it, but their very slipping and sliding does not lessen or refine the mud, but merely adds 'new deposits to the crust upon crust of mud, sticking at those points tenaciously to the pavement, and accumulating at compound interest' (49). Like Jo, the passengers are both moved on and held back by this ambivalent, slippy-sticky element.

Everything, we are told repeatedly, is connected in this novel. What connects things up, though, are indistinct or aggregate substances, fog, dust, smoke, mud, gas, rain, which are all perhaps just variant states of one substance. Raining down, in a soft black drizzle, this primal substance creates connections by the action of coating everything with the same thin layer, creating a secondary skin or scum which blears and smears one thing into the next. The novel provides a perfect image of the oleaginous interlocking of lives in the table set up in the alehouse for the inquest of Nemo, which is described as 'ornamented with glutinous rings in endless involutions' (197). These rings are a sardonic comment on and flattening out of the image that occurs to Esther, of a chain or necklace of interconnections. Her situation, like that of everyone else in the novel, is more than a single ring; it is a chain of rings, though not forged with steel, but smeared with oil. Or, of course, ink, that other indeterminate, viscous substance in the novel. The inquest, or 'Inkwhich' as Jo calls it, is after all concerned to establish the cause of death of the anonymous lawwriter, the sight of whose handwriting causes Lady Dedlock such distress and precipitates the chain of investigations and their consequences that form the novel's plot. 'Which ink?' enquires the inquest. The glutinous circles are a kind of automatic writing in the grease of contingency of the logic of the book's own writing.

As it happens, the action of smearing passes across from scene to characters. Mr Jellyby leaves a small mark on the wall in the place where he rests his head. Jo's characteristic gesture is a smearing of a grimy tear-stained face with his sleeve, which doubles his sweeping away at the street. But, as in 'The Yellow Wallpaper', the connections established by this scummy skin do not go deep: by smearing one thing into another, they prevent anything being or residing in itself.

The fact that currency is greasy, that grease forms an economy, is indicated in many other Dickens novels, and perhaps most astonishingly in the money given to the young Pip in *Great Expectations* by the friend of the convict he has helped. The 'two fat sweltering one-pound notes, that seemed to have been on terms of the warmest intimacy with all the cattle markets in the country' are an image of the whole novel, with its central proposition that the abstract bond of money is also a bodily bond, a skin of swelter that collapses together labour and love and money in a greasy ring-a-roses of hands.[95] In *Bleak House*, by contrast, a novel in which there is so little circulation of money, or anything else, fat and grease form rather a sluggish ecology than an economy, governed by the alchemical principles of *solve et coagula*. Grease gathers in ever thicker deposits, causing sickness and sticky paralysis. Sometimes the congelation will offer the possibility of sublimation: a candle can be burnt to give light. But most of these sublimations fail. Mr Chadband consumes prodigious quantities of food, which is then converted into the oil which he exudes, not only in his considerable person, and his 'fat smile', but also in the oozing unction of his speech. He evokes the lamp of Truth, but his discourse is a lamp that produces oil rather than consuming it, producing a feeling of contamination rather than illumination. Dickens lingers on everything that Bachelard refines away in his phenomenology of the candle. The light in *Bleak House* is crepuscular and reluctant, and provided by feeble lamps and sick, guttering candles. The novel is larded with the creeping, cryptic slither of oil, and its air is impregnated with the reflux of fat rather than volatilized into flame, a fat that is always threatening to douse the fire it feeds. Instead of being refined or distilled, the tallow of candles stays semi-coagulate, as a skin immanent in the air, ready to precipitate over every surface like a loathsome dew or frost of fat, except that where frost sharpens things into scintillating singularity, grease blears what it coats into a continuous film of non-identity.

The death of Krook through explosion is the culmination of these image-sensations. It is presaged by the ghastly oil from which Guppy withdraws his fingers in the room above Krook's: 'A thick, yellow liquor defiles them, which is offensive to the touch and sight and more offensive to the smell. A stagnant, sickening oil, with some natural repulsion in it that makes them both shudder' (509). Krook is then discovered, diffused into a smouldering suffocating vapour in the room, and a dark greasy coating on the walls and ceiling' (511). The horror of Krook's death, in this novel in which so much seems to be staked on the hope of an explosion that will clear the air (an expression that derives from the practice of firing pistols and gunpowder to drive away the miasma of plague), is that it is explosion without partition, a dispersal of Krook's person which leaves him oilily intact. 'O Horror, he *is* here!', as the novel devilishly insists (511).

Dickens represents a particular kind of high point in the material imagination of slime or 'oil of man'. For the disgust and recoil from the slimy also represent a strange, perverse apotheosis, a vision of the slimy, not exactly lifted up or redeemed, but, as it were, acknowledged in all its oozing immanence. Dickens imagines a viscous universe, in which vision and words deliquesce into touch, contagion and contingency, consuming and transforming thought.

The adventures of grease by no means come to an end with Dickens. As Naomi Wolf has sardonically observed, the most powerful holy oils of our time are the extravagantly puffed creams and unguents of the cosmetic industry. These substances represent a secular resanctification of the idea of oil and the experience of unction. But just as Wolf was writing her scorching denunciation of the commodified cult of beauty in 1990, a new fantasy of holy oil was preparing, in the aromatherapy industry that gathered strength through the 1990s.

The idea that fragrances and aromas might have therapeutic properties derives from work on plant extracts undertaken during the 1920s and 1930s, but had to wait until the 1990s to be elaborated into a true alternative therapy. At the heart of aromatherapy is a complicated, cautious erotics of oil, and in particular the 'essential oils' which are believed to contain the essence of a plant. Aromas are to be found in essential oils, defined by Philippe Mailhebiau as the 'distilled essence' of a plant extracted by steam distillation, and therefore to be distinguished from the essences secreted by the plant itself.[96] Despite the fact that aromatherapy depends only marginally upon the application or inhalation of fragrance, its remarkable revival during the 1990s discloses the intimate co-operation between the actions of unction and the operations of odour.

Indeed, the association between oil and odour is another important factor in the growth of the ambivalence towards oil in modern European and American cultures; we are about to see that an important accessory to the horror of the greasy that reaches its apotheosis in Krook is the offence it offers to the nose.

8 Aroma

The beginnings of sensory history in recent years have been accompanied by a heightening of interest in the culture of odour and smell. Nevertheless, little has been written about the phenomenology or cultural inner side of odour. This may be an effect of the distance of the sense of smell from the allegedly more analytic and reasoning senses of sight and hearing and even touch, which seem to have a larger role in what might be called formative consciousness, the kinds of awareness and sensitivity that embody a rational image of the world and the self in it. It is often maintained that odour acts unconsciously on instincts and emotions. The kinds of awareness embodied in odour are fragile, delicate, evanescent, not easily to be captured in words, images, or ideas. But it is just this apparent irreducibility to image and concept which makes odour and the idea of odour so powerful, and has produced periods of great expertise in and sensitivity to it. The fact that the concepts of 'spirit' and 'essence' contain memories of the breath and aroma is an indication of the subliminal importance of olfaction in the phenomenology of culture.

The material imagination of oils and unguents is not easily distinguishable from that of aroma. In many cultures and at many times, the most important function of oil has been as a carrier or medium of fragrance, this being assisted by the fact that many of the fatty acids involved in the production of odour can be dissolved or suspended in oils. I wonder if we may think of oil as the body, and specifically the skin-body, of fragrance. 'Olfaction', the scientific term used in circumstances when the word 'smell' may seem too vulgar and too rankly vernacular, in fact preserves the link between the Latin *olere*, to give out a smell, and *oleo*, oil. What is the bodily meaning of an oil? It signifies above all a kind of immanent elasticity, a tendency to hang in sheets, skeins or skins, even when diffused in a volume of air.

The primary role of the sense of smell and the sense of taste which it supports is that of discrimination: of the ripe from the putrid, the attractive from the repulsive, the good from the bad. This makes smell the most ethically active sense, as well as the medium through which we are most powerfully, because involuntarily, acted upon. It is hard to be indifferent to a smell, in the way that one can be indifferent to something seen or heard. There are, perhaps, no neutral smells. Could a smell that evoked no response or carried no value be said to be smelled at all? To see or hear may be to examine, consider, discriminate, appraise; to smell is actively and intuitively to pass judgement, to say immediately yes or no. Smell acts as a gateway, or permeable membrane. When it says yes, the desired substance is approached and absorbed; when it says no, there is an immune response of recoil and repulsion. The sense of smell is the strongest discriminator of self from not-self. This is perhaps because commonly a great deal is at stake in smelling and tasting; after all, the decision whether or not to incorporate some foodstuff may be a matter of instant life and death. Although it is frequently said that odour is too subtle to be captured in the grids of language, the discriminatory role of olfaction impacts powerfully on language to produce a wide variety of olfactory terms, with subtle shadings of difference. Think of the finely differentiated spectrum that runs in English from stench, stink and reek, fetor, hum, niff and pong, all of which can only be used of bad smells, through smell and odour, which can be used of both good and bad smells, but have acquired a certain weighting towards the negative, to words like scent, fragrance, perfume and bouquet. Other words may temporarily be assigned to certain sources. Bouquet and aroma used to belong to things, especially flowers and foodstuffs, rather than persons; the rise of aromatherapy in recent years seems to have assisted a shift in the semantic spread of the latter to include persons.

It is for this reason that aroma was believed for so many centuries to be not only an indicator but also the very vehicle of disease. The miasma theory, which survived from the Hippocratic writings through to the development of the understanding of bacteria in the late nineteenth century, held that the minute particles of putrid matter which led to the sensations of smell were also responsible for illness. The theory probably survived as long as it did because of its considerable explanatory and predictive power; it was easy to read the processes of infection and contagion in terms of the passage of smells, and demonstrable that many of the hygienic measures employed to reduce smell also reduced disease. Where the miasma theory was a disaster was in the encouragement it offered to the idea that protecting oneself from odour, rather than bacteria, its unknown cause, was the key to health.

Even more unfortunate was the theory of the antagonism of odours, with the consequent reliance upon odour-antidotes, counter-aromas and prophylactic smells, in what Piero Camporesi calls 'a complicated game of odiferous affinity and antipathy'.[1] The Biblical injunctions to the burning of incense before the veil in front of the ark in the Holy of Holies (Exodus 30:6–9) formed 'an atmospheric curtain which protected the place of YHWH's revelation . . . against possible bad exhalations and fumes'.[2] It was common practice in ancient Greece to apply noxious fumes to the nose and sweet smells to the vagina of an hysterical woman, in order that the vagrant womb might be driven and inveigled respectively back to its correct position. During the centuries in which bubonic plague and other lethal epidemics raged in Europe, doctors ordered bonfires of sweet-smelling woods and herbs to be lit in streets and houses to clear the air. Houses infected with plague would be sealed off by circles of scented water. Doctors would protect themselves when visiting the sick with censers burning aromatic resins and by frequent application of perfumed handkerchiefs to the nose. The bench at the Old Bailey was strewn with sweet herbs to protect against the effluvium of the prisoners. Unpleasant odours were believed to be effective as well, the sharp tang of vinegar, coupled with the practical experience of its astringent properties, recommending it in particular. Others relied upon the principle of the affinity of like odours. Kenelm Digby suggested the following surprising method for sweetening bad breath:

> 'Tis an ordinary remedy, though a nasty one, that they who have ill breaths, hold their mouths open at the mouth of a Privy, as long as they can, and by the reiteration of this remedy, they find themselves cured at last, the greater stink of the Privy drawing unto it, and carrying away the lesse, which is that of the mouth.[3]

Aromatherapy reactivates this deep-rooted and long-lived sense of the power of smell. It seems extremely unlikely that odours alone can have significant antiseptic powers, though, of course, substances which possess certain distinctive qualities of smell may also have significant biochemical properties. The resin exuded by certain trees to form a protective skin when their bark is damaged is often mildly insecticidal, which provides an explanation for how sufferers from asthma may be helped by sleeping with bags of pine oil, which may deter somewhat the activities of the mites to which they are allergic. Yet the contemporary willingness to believe in the direct effectiveness of smell remains strong. One can encounter in more than one guide to aromatherapy the claim that 'plague and cholera swept through Europe wiping out entire communities except, in some cases, the local perfumers, who appeared to be immune to these diseases', though never with any historical documentation to support it.[4]

The idea that smell might form not just a discriminatory screen, but also a physical barrier to putridity and pestilence, involves an extension of the properties of the skin to the nose. Just as the skin is both sensitive and defensive, so too might one's nose be. James Manning's *I Am For You All Complexions Castle* of 1604 maintained that the relative insensibility to smell of humans when compared to animals meant that they were more protected from infection, since

> The putrified aire cannot passe so speedily to mans heart as the divers other creatures by the instrument of smelling, which is covered with a pellicle or filme, which is to be lifted up before he can smell by the ayre or fume: and that pellicle is grosser in man than in other creatures: and therefore requireth the hotter or stronger fume to moove it.[5]

Added to this is a transfer of powers between the nose and the odours that emanate from the skin. A smell, it sometimes seems, itself has the sense of smell. The doubling involved here seems closely related to the duality of the epidermis, which at any moment both feels and is felt: one feels an object touching one, and one feels the feeling of one's skin. In a parallel way, the power of the skin to give out smell creates the belief in the power of a smell to act as a skin.

Also implicated in this knot of beliefs and embodied fantasies is the doctrine of the respiratory skin, inherited from Hippocratic medicine. The skin could not only exhale odours, but also, it was believed, could inhale them too. A lost work of Heracleides known as *Apnous – On the Absence of Breath* is the source of a commonly repeated story of a woman apparently dead for three days who recovered, the explanation being that she continued to breathe through her skin.[6] Combined with humoral theory, this doctrine gave rise to complex explanations of the different degrees of vulnerability of different complexions. According to James Manning, for example, those of a sanguine complexion were most at risk of infection from the plague, because this complexion shared the hot and moist qualities of the air, and was therefore more apt to take the infection 'not at the nostrills or mouth . . . [but] . . . at the emunctorie places, and at the pores in the skin in other places, which are more large and readier to be opened, then in other complexions'.[7] As efforts to combat plague and infection increased, the heightened sense of the respiratory and absorptive powers of the skin led to an intense concern with the process of impregnation, along with an awareness of the powers of smell to sink into and then subsequently be exhaled from other skins or surfaces, especially bedsheets, clothing, curtains, hangings and even walls.

Here we might take a moment to reflect on the interesting fortunes of the word 'impregnate'. It originally meant to saturate, or permeate one substance with another. But impregnation has come to suggest a partial compounding, as in a liquid substance that has only partially penetrated a solid or semi-permeable substance, in precisely the way in which the skin can be partially penetrated by water, oil, dirt, etc. There is the same paradoxical principle of inverse efficacy here that we earlier found in the word 'tincture', and that is signalled in the expression 'soaked to the skin': for one might imagine that being thoroughly soaked would require the skin too to be penetrated. Usually, nowadays, the things we refer to as 'impregnated' are saturated surfaces or tissues. To be tainted is to be thoroughly spoiled: to be impregnated is to be thoroughly pervaded.

As Alain Corbin observes, 'the mephitism of walls and ceilings was sometimes astonishingly intense.'[8] Walls of prisons, hospitals and sickrooms were felt to be storehouses of infection, capable of soaking up, breeding and releasing miasma over a period of years. It is as though the emanatory power of odour was not only, as we have said, immanent with skin; exhaled by the skin, it also turned the inanimate surfaces upon which it precipitated into breathing skins. Among those concerned with mephitic walls in the years following the Revolution in France was Antoine-Alexis Cadet de Vaux, editor of the *Journal de Paris*, and a writer on chemistry and public hygiene, who warned that 'wherever men congregate together, whether in health or sickness, the walls are penetrated and insensibly surcharged with infected exhalations which, with atmospheric changes, these same walls re-exhale; aspiration and expiration really take place.'[9] He pointed to the successful purification of air obtained by the use of 'gaz muriatique oxygéné', a process in which, he said, the gas 'washes the atmosphere and strips it [*dépouille*] of miasmas', but observes that this processes is not effective against walls.[10] He proposed instead painting the walls with a solution of quicklime (calcium oxide) mixed with milk. His explanation of the necessity for the addition of oil makes explicit its epidermal purpose:

> the lime has no adhesion on the walls . . . By contrast, the addition of the oil, which imparts a soapy body to the lime, forms a dense and coherent layer, which is capable of retaining thickness; it is a kind of coat of varnish, which neutralises the porosity of the stone, plaster, brick and wood, and from which dust can be removed without exposing the painted portion.[11]

We seem somewhat less concerned today with the powers of walls to harbour evil, though we certainly have a lively concern with the bacterial perils and vulnerabilities of surfaces, especially in kitchens and bathrooms, along with a continuing faith in the power of astringent oils to attack and protect against them. The necessity for a substance that both burns and seals, that consumes putridity while itself retaining epidermal coherence and adhesion, is apparent in the thick, clinging gels marketed for use in lavatories. These, we are assured, have the power both of reaching into the hidden crevices of the lavatory bowl and preventing the escape or exhalation of miasma, which is therefore both scorched and asphyxiated. Meanwhile, the glutinous quality of the bleach, along with the 'freshness' of its odour, assures us, as only the nose can, of its gentleness. It is a piece of good skin applied to the bad skin of the toilet. The porcelain that it leaves behind gleams like the immaculately chrismated skin of the anointed.

The discriminatory role of olfaction, its role as a conveyor not of raw, sensory information about the world, but of the world's value and quality, assists the association between aroma and the soul. Many cultures have had a conception of the soul as essentially aromatic in nature. If one primary meaning of the unction of the body is a taking on of the life of a sacrificed victim, then the transformation of that vital fat into aroma is also closely involved in the sacrificial process. Perfume is so named because it is derived *per fuma*, through smoke. Incense and sweet odours come to be thought of as the most appropriate offering to the nostrils of the gods. Even Christianity, which began by turning its nose up fastidiously at the incenses used by Greeks and Jews, eventually developed its own traditions of the odour of sanctity, with its many stories of fragrant saints, and of bodies, like those of St Isidore and St Francis Xavier, miraculously preserved in a freshly laundered condition.[12] St Paul refers to the sweet fragrance ὀσμή (*osme*) of the diffused word of God.[13] Contemporary enthusiasts for aromatherapy are wont to recur to their belief that the essential oils which preserve the odours of plants and flowers also contain their life-principle: 'Every living thing has a life force, energy or "soul" which it is impossible to get hold of or see . . . It is the energy from the original life force of the plant that we introduce into the body by aromatherapy.'[14] Paracelsus is often cited as an authority for the belief that essential oils are so called because they contain the 'quinta essentia' of plants. One of the earliest and most emphatic proponents of this view is Marguerite Maury, one of the founders of the modern aromatherapy movement, who wrote of the 'vital creative energy' to be found concentrated in odorous substances: '[W]hen we are dealing with an essential oil and its odoriference, we are dealing directly with a vital force and entering to the very heart of the alchemy of creation', she writes. The aromatic essence is a source of energy: 'By inserting this energy force into our body, we can expect an efficacious and selective action on its part. The body will have at its disposal a vital and living element.'[15]

This idea of a force with a power to effect or confirm a shape runs through thinking about aromatic oils and incenses. This may seem counter-intuitive, since aromas represent a diffusion of the shape of the original substance, the sublimation of a grossly material substance into a more ethereal vapour. The higher nature of this vapour is indicated by the fact that it is scarcely apprehensible by the senses of sight, hearing or touch, which it can bypass or duck under to speak directly to the brain or spirit. Writers on aroma-therapy are fond of repeating the claim that the olfactory bulb, found behind and above the nostrils, offers a mainline deep into the limbic system, the most ancient part of the brain, which seems to be associated with emotion. By contrast, revolting smells are sometimes signified by the fact that they retain the suggestion of a gross bodily form, as in the Irish expression 'a hogo you could hang your hat on' for a particularly offensive reek.[16] Aromas are at once a concentration of living essence, and a volatile flight from shape: this is symbolized by the opaque, stoppered bottles in which per-fumed substances are kept. It is almost as though the very condensation of the essence were the reason for its pent-up desire for diffusion. That aromas are so commonly thought of as volatile may be a significant accessory to the tradition of flying ointments discussed in the last chapter. For ointments and aroma are closely associated, oil being used to secure and stabilize on the body the aromas that are to be released from it. If the oil that is the vehicle or carrier of the perfume were also regarded as sharing in its volatile aspect, then it might seem all the more possible for an ointment to lend perfume's powers of flight to the body. The diffusiveness of odour is probably also the reason that scent is so associated with time. The senses of sight and touch operate in space, but, in association with taste, the olfactory sense is able both to preserve memory and even, as in Proust's reveries, to redeem lost time. The Akkadian epic of Gilgamesh contains an episode that cinches the links between fragrance, skin and time. Gilgamesh is told of a precious rejuvenating sea-plant, Ur-shanabi. He dives successfully for the plant, but, as he stops on the way home to bathe, a snake, smelling the perfume of the plant, comes up and steals it, discovering in the process the power of metamorphosis through sloughing its skin, while Gilgamesh is left to weep at the loss of the chance of immortality.[17] Aroma is chronophoric, melancholic, allegorical, spectral.

However, even the most evanescent perfume always retains ghostly hints of bodily shape, or perhaps better, the compensatory desire for imagings of it. The most important function of the vital element concentrated in the essential oil, according to Marguerite Maury, is in shaping the 'definitive form' of the plant.[18] Richard le Gallienne articulates the nostalgia for shape and the hungry hinting at texture and tactile satisfaction that are imaged in the beauty and delicacy of perfume containers:

> the exquisite vessels, the fairy-like crystal bottles, the tiny phials of irides-
> cent glass, the quaint porcelain jars, the silken sachets, the dainty enamelled
> boxes, the carved and inlaid fancies, and all the dream-like *bijouterie*, in
> themselves 'a joy forever,' in which he [the perfumer] hoards his enchanted
> dews, his air-soft powders, and caressing pomades.[19]

But there are other devices for ensuring the durability of perfume than the bottle. One of these is the human skin itself. If aromatic substances can be persuaded to sink into the skin, then they can provide a nimbus of perfume, which helps to arrest, or mask the odoriferous processes of decomposition undergone daily by the skin. Perfumiers have developed complex techniques for holding evanescent scents, or slowing the release of perfume. One of the most important roles for oil, and especially olive oil, is to act as a fixative for perfume. Oil both gives the body a new, more refined, homogenous skin, and also acts as the skin or container for the perfume. Indeed, the principal means employed up until the twentieth century to extract the aromatic juices of flowers and plants, known as enfleurage, involved the repeated pressing of leaves and blossoms into a block of fat. The ladies of the sixteenth and seventeenth centuries who spent so much time concocting and blending their own perfumes would have been under no illusions as to the role of fats, and particularly animal fats, in providing a base for perfumes. Elizabeth I, who had her own still-room for the making of perfumes, invented a fragrance of her own, the principal constituents of which were apple blossom and the fat of a young dog.[20]

Just as the skin holds in the unseemly or disgusting odours imagined to be teeming on the inside of the body, so it also holds back the release of fragrance, like an inner skin. In Richard le Gallienne's evocation, there is always a secret and individual core to a woman's perfume, which is decorated by wispier, more teasingly dissimulative films: 'There will always be one perfume which is her inner, unchanging self; but she will know, too, how to select other perfumes, which will express the variable play, the lights and shades, the *nuances* of her being.'[21] It is perhaps this quality of fixing or slowing the release of aroma which gives oil the role of the phantasmal body, or visible form of aroma. When one wishes to sample a perfume quickly, it is spread on the wrist, firstly because the wrist can so easily be brought to the nose, but also, it is sometimes said, because there is so little fatty tissue there, and so the odour is not retained, but quickly released.

Perfumiers and aroma theorists work with an image of a musical body, just as medieval uroscopists used the image of a body of colour. A successful perfume is usually described as a complex chord, running from 'top' to 'base' (sic) notes. The top notes are immediate, subtle, evanescent, and usually consist of floral scents; they are described as stimulating and refreshing. Base notes are heavier and slower to diffuse; they are warmer, more animal and more likely to be described as heavy, sensual and comforting rather than arousing. Sometimes, the system of aroma is mapped more specifically on to the voice, with its imaginary distribution of resonance from head to diaphragm. 'Top notes are the head notes – the sharp clear aromas sensed by the nose . . . Middle notes are the heart notes. They are more stable than top notes and have a softer, more rounded scent . . . Base notes are the body notes and are deep, rich, strong, masculine and exotic scents.'[22] The musical analogy would lead one to expect the spelling 'bass', but 'base' seems to be universal. This spelling gives a topological hint; the base smell acts as a foundation, like the foundation cream that one applies before the rest of the make-up. Since its role is to restrain the release of the odour, it can be thought of as confirming a sense of aromatic contour, or body-shape. The spirituality of the aroma comes from the fact that it is an almost immaterial emanation from the body, but this emanation includes an emanation from another body as its *mis-en-abîme*. The deep, rich, bestial, baritone humus of the base notes (shit, sweat, sex) forms a corporeal hypostasis for the more refined layers that rise from it, first of all in a 'softer, more rounded' form, then in the shiveringly clear soprano sublime of the top notes.[23]

Where is the skin in all these airy laminations? In one sense, it appears to be the foundation, or basis for the aroma. In fact, though, the chthonic hints attaching to the masculine base direct attention to the foulness of the viscera enclosed within the skin. For post-classical and medieval Christians, it had been women who tended to be thought of as a fragile and perforated skin enclosing a cauldron of fermenting excrement. Writing in the early tenth century, Odon of Cluny had cautioned that

> The beauty of the body is no more than its skin. For if men were to see what lies beneath the skin, as one could see the insides of the lynx of Boeotia, women would turn their stomachs. Their charm amounts to nothing more than phlegm and blood and humours and bile. Anyone who stopped to think what lurked in the nostrils, the throat, or the belly, would realise it was all just filth. And if we cannot bear to touch phlegm or excrement even with a fingertip, why would we wish to embrace the very sack of excrements?[24]

Aroma inhabits a new space between the traditional alternatives of matter and form, namely that of subtlety. What counts most is neither density, nor clearly determinate shape, but the subtler values of discernment, refinement and delicacy. Its material correlative is neither mire nor iron, but smoke. The growing preference for these values in Western cultures has been tending for some time to encourage a view of the interior of men's bodies as a dangerous cesspit of slugs and snails. One might then say that the skin of aroma lies halfway up the scale from base to top, in the median position of the heart notes, with their softly veiled feminine curves. In truth, the skin seems to form and dissimulate veil-like at every level of the aroma, the very model of blended strata at work in this characterization of aroma implying a delicious caressing and confusion of impalpable cuticles. The skin is at work in the contemporary idealization of aroma therefore not as a barrier between body and circumambient air, but as a dynamic space of mingling between them.

There is a discreditable sense of the skin in perfumes. We affect to be disgusted by the fact that perfumes were used in earlier periods to mask sexual and excremental odours, rather than to suppress or replace them. The cosmetic rituals of cleaning, or that particularly refined form of it we know as 'cleansing', before applying new make-up has more affinities with the practices of the Greeks and Romans, who first stripped the body of its old smells – through a literal scraping, in the bracing action of the strigil – and then clothed it in new life, through the application of fragrant oils. But, in fact, nearly all perfumes effect such a masking or mixing of animal smells. Smells that 'stimulate' or 'refresh' or 'comfort' are often doing so through the hints of substances like musk or civet, obtained from the secretions of the excretory or sexual organs of mammals. Even fragrances that seem entirely floral or vegetable may be doing their work through substances that resemble the chemical form and mimic the effect of the steroidal sex pheromones in mammals.[25] So the base notes of perfumes point to another topology, in which animal smells, and especially those which associate sex with excretion, seem to lie – invisibly, but visualizably – underneath vegetable or floral smells, the dark, faecal mulch, churning with worms, beneath the pretty, odoriferous litter of leaf and blossom.

The history of odours is organized around this polarity between the animal smells of sex, excrement and death and the more spiritual fragrances of vegetable and floral matter. Perhaps because they give off so little odour, there is much less imaginative involvement in the smells of hard mineral substances. But there is one significant area of exception to this, in the pungent smells of sulphur and pitch associated with hell and demons. Pitch, a thick, dark, glutinous substance used to seal boats and vessels, is an organic substance obtained from the resin of trees (the word 'tar' may in fact derive ultimately from Old Teutonic *treow*, tree). But the fact that it, and allied substances, are also extractable from coal and petrified substances gives it a more dubious, because aged, or deathly vitality. The alchemical privilege accorded to mercury and sulphur, as agents of transformation and purification, led to both being used as preparations for the skin, with sulphur in particular being used as a remedy for scabies and other pruritic conditions. But the ambivalent mixture of the sluggish and the igneous in tar, pitch, bitumen, and other allied substances seems also to have enforced the negative associations of such substances. Alain Corbin has shown that there was great concern with the noxious emanations of the earth during the eighteenth century, focused especially on standing pools, swamps, bogs and graveyards.[26] But this is usually part of the 'excremental vigilance'[27] that grew up in this period, and therefore focused on the vegetable rather than the mineral earth. Indeed, sulphur was one of the materials used to fumigate insalubrious places like prisons and ships. The urban and industrial odours of the nineteenth and twentieth century, and what Richard Le Gallienne calls the 'new barbarism of gasoline' may represent a return of this troubling, infernal stench of the inorganic earth.[28] An anonymous reactionary text produced in France in 1877 spoke out against the destruction of traditional bonds of social responsibility in the era of what it called 'pétrolisation'. The title of the book presents the alternatives for the modern world starkly: Saint Chrême ou pétrol ('Holy Chrism or Petrol').[29]

Odour diffuses; but in the cultural imagination, it also rises. The move from earthy, mineral, excremental smells, through animal secretions, through to the more delicate or refined vegetable and floral smells, is a refinement and a movement upwards, as of smoke. But this movement of refinement never reaches the point of pure dissolution, for at this point the soul itself would lose its subtle adhesion to itself. Alain Corbin has described the process whereby the heavy animal-based perfumes of musk, civet and ambergris gave way from the late eighteenth century onwards to lighter, more delicate and, because more interfused, more individual floral scents. Women, he writes, were encouraged to think of themselves as floral, made out of odoriferous veils, leaves and layers. Rather than being enclosed within a gross and impermeable mask of scent, a woman was encouraged to develop and nurture her own natural atmosphere, with only the most inconspicuous applications of the perfumier's art to enhance it. 'What was important', he writes, 'was to tear off mask and plaster, air the skin, open the pores, and thus allow the woman's atmosphere to be diffused.'[30]

A delicate fragrance emphasized the tenderness and fragility of the self. It both discouraged the tactile invasion of the woman's atmospheric space and coyly encouraged the desire for it. Delicate fragrances obeyed the tactile rule of delicacy, in creating a bilateral sensitivity; the more delicate the touch that a substance enjoins, the more refined its own powers of touch will seem. In making women seem frail and tremulous, perfume seemed to extend their skins outwards, as though their aroma were itself a subtle, exploratory organ. This sense of aroma as possessing sensitivity as well as being detectable by it survives in the reference to the 'nose' of a wine. This sensitivity was a kind of innocent sentience. Screwed to the highest pitch of refinement, yet as unaware of itself as a lily or a rosebud, it was the airy mirror of the skin, so fine and sensitive that it could feel a pea jutting through half a dozen mattresses.

At different periods, perfumed substances have tended to be spread, not only on the skin, but on frail, spiritual second skins: on hair, wigs, and fans, in bouquets, sachets and the bags that would be worn between the breasts in Ancient Egypt, as well as by seventeenth-century French courtesans. By means of perfume, writes Richard le Gallienne, the very soul of a woman, her spiritual atmosphere, can be diffused around her in unmistakable emanations of fragrance. As surely as a rose tells us of its presence before our eyes have seen it, so it is with a woman who knows the art of perfume, whose very clothes thus become herself, whose dropped handkerchief is as much a love-letter of her writing as though she had signed it.[31]

During the sixteenth and seventeenth centuries in Europe, the commonest diffuser of personal atmosphere was the perfumed glove. The first perfumiers in modern Europe were glovemakers, and it was to the *gantiers-perfumiers* that Louis XIV granted his charter in 1656. Like the appearance of one's face, and the sound of one's voice, the odour of one's own skin cannot be fully apprehended by the individual. It is the individuating signature over which one does not have full ownership and control. The glove allows one to monitor and inhabit one's own aromatic atmosphere. It is a kind of odorous mirror, allowing the two senses of 'smelling', taking in a smell and giving one off, to be folded together. Perfumed gloves allowed one to assume and doff different envelopes of aroma during the day. Ordinarily, one diffuses aroma from one's skin in a sort of passive or involuntary emanation. The great advantage of the perfumed glove was that it allowed a more active control over perfume. This was a control of strength and reach and form as well as quality. The glove made perfume elastic rather than indifferently gaseous; it could seem to stretch, rarefy, condense, billow, wave, ripple, fold, rather than diffusing uniformly in all directions. The lady (or gentleman) wearing perfumed gloves could extend, and coyly retract, the tissue of her fragrance in more directions and further afield, recalling and diversifying the territorial functions of the urine-spray. The perfumed fan dissimulated and doubled this work of the hand in dynamically sculpting one's aroma in the air. Gloves were also reversible. One could be manipulated by another's fragrance as though one were a glove to their hand. During the heyday of perfumed gloves in the sixteenth and seventeenth century, toxic possibilities came to the fore. Catherine de Medici was believed to have murdered her enemies by sending them poisoned gloves. In 1572, during the reign of Catherine's son, Charles IX of France, a number of Protestants were invited to Paris to attend the marriage of the King of Navarre with Margaret, Catherine's daughter. There is a story that the queen dowager of Navarre was given a pair of gloves as a pledge of safe conduct which turned out to be poisoned. Her death unleashed the St Bartholomew's Day massacre of Protestants. The fear of poisoned gloves survived as long as 1871, when there was a scare in America about the wearing of green kid gloves that were found to have been dyed with arsenic. People were advised for a time to wear gloves of a less toxic colour.[32]

The revival of aromatherapy in recent years has brought with it the reawakened belief in the power of smell to convey the subtle ineffability of the unique self. Chrissie Wildwood assures her readers that no two people can blend an identical-smelling fragrance, even though they may use exactly the same blend of oils in exactly the same quantities from the same bottles. Amazingly, the oil will always take on an aspect of the blender's personality – their aromatic signature.[33]

Valerie Ann Worwood, the author of *The Fragrant Mind*, offers a typology of some odorous personalities, based on the different areas of the plant – florals, fruities, herbies, leafies, resinies, rooties, seedies, spicies, woodies, as well as sketches of 'the individual personalities of essential oils', such as the basil, fennel and frankincense personalities.[34]

If essential oils are easily impregnated with the unique souls of their users, it is because they are reflexes of these subtle souls. If essential oils can take the print of living beings, it is because they are themselves alive, dynamic, and, we are frequently assured, unanalysably complex. It has been claimed that essential oils have their own aura or energy field which can be disclosed by Kirlian photography.[35] In the more narcissistic regimes of contemporary aromatherapy, what matters is not the projection of an atmosphere for others, but the creation of an absorbent niche in which the self may be supported by itself, eked out by the virtues of gentle, friendly – and emphatically non-animal – aromatic powers. This is a power that does not cut, buffet, or crudely compel; its power lies in its subtle pervasiveness, which takes effect at the gentle osculation of surfaces:

> There is a common misconception that essential oils and water do not mix
> ... Even if you put, say, six drops of geranium essential oil in a bath, and can
> see that the essential oil floats on the top of the water, if you were to taste
> some of the water that seems untouched by it, the geranium is nevertheless
> evident. In some way, the aromatic molecule, or the vibration of the essen-
> tial oil, has managed to become imprinted in the water ... Water is ubiquit-
> ous in that it is everywhere, including our bodies . . . Water could be
> described as one long molecule, which would explain why an input at one
> end – an essential oil for example – can be detected at the other end. Next
> time you see essential oil floating on water, bear in mind that the entire
> body of water is imprinted with the properties of the essential oil.[36]

MANHANDLING

Aromatherapy is an interesting collection of different techniques and forms of application, absorption through the skin being only one way in which essential oils are believed to enter and affect the body. But massage is central to the prac-tice of aromatherapy, as it is to the earliest forms of ritual anointing, in which oil is vigorously worked or rubbed into the skin rather than merely applied to it. W. Robertson Smith suggests that, since the primary meaning of the Hebrew word meaning to anoint (*mashah*) is 'to wipe or stroke with the hand' the action of anointing a statue or sacred symbol 'is associated with the simpler form of hom-age common in Arabia, in which the hand was passed over the idol (*tamassah*)'.[37]

Religious ritual seems regularly to evolve away from the grosser or more obviously sexual kinds of contact implied in massage to more minimal or restrained forms of the application of oil, for example application of oil to the hair, or application by aspersion or sprinkling. The process of the minimization or withdrawal of touch accompanies and mirrors the sublimation of animal fat into vegetable oil. Nevertheless, the literal laying on of hands, and indeed the vigorous rubbing or kneading of the flesh, remains a horizon within actions of unction and, in movements of religious renewal, which often aim to return to the so-called pure and primitive origins of religion, or secularizations of religious ritual, such as aromatherapy massage, it will often be the subject of particular emphasis.

It would be easy to say that what at once powers such actions and is kept at bay within them is the erotic meeting of hand and body. But Gaston Bachelard has supposed that there is a different form of material imagination at work here, and with an equal claim to be considered primary. In his study of the actions of the will in relation to the materials of the earth, *La terre et les rêveries de la volonté* (1948), Bachelard sees the workings of oils, creams and doughs as derivatives from what he calls an ideal of primary paste, 'the perfect synthesis of stiffness and softness, a marvellous equilibrium of yielding and resisting forces'.[38] Bachelard's discussion of this primary paste occurs as the first in a series of discussions of dreams of terrene matter, as these are played out between the alternatives of the hard (rock, crystal, diamond, iron) and the soft (clay, putty, oil). It is the ideal of such a paste that allows Bachelard to posit the existence of a different kind of *cogito*, or sense of self. In between the neutral *cogito* of mere self-knowing and the more active kind of self-recognition which arises in the 'phenomenology of the *against*', the sense of straining or striving against things, and perhaps before both of them, there is 'a *cogito* of kneading', ('un *cogito* pétrisseur', *TRV*, 79).

The traction of the will which earth seems always to evoke for Bachelard is a dream of self-differentiation, a doubling of the growth through differentiation that is at work in all exercises of the imagination. Bachelard finds analogies to this primary paste in Sartre's concept of the *visqueux*. We have seen that the *visqueux* is the horror of being swamped within matter, its 'tactile fascination' a devious threat to the possibility of a subject's projective freedom.[39] Bachelard acknowledges the continuity between his concept of the primary paste and Sartre's horror of the *visqueux*, between the miry and the slimy, but argues that the *visqueux* can only be conceived as threat and nausea in the absence of the impulse to work against the resistance of things. But this impulse is always present in the dreamwork of the hand:

> In fact [the hand] thinks only in squeezing, in kneading, in being active. If it does not have the upper hand, if it becomes nervous in defeat, sinking, stickiness, then it is no longer a hand, but only a kind of envelope of skin. (*TRV*, 117)

Through the mediation of the hand, 'human being reveals itself as the counter-being of things' (*TRV*, 119). The being-there of existentialism is always shot through with the striving to be elsewhere of what Bachelard calls a 'sur-existentialism' (*TRV*, 121). For Bachelard, *devenir*, the work of becoming, seems always to approximate to *durcir* – forging, hardening (*TRV*, 108). He perhaps draws from Sartre the argument he bends against him, for he is here only re-emphasizing the optimistic side of Sartre's virile resiling against the threat of the *visqueux*.

Bachelard's evocation of the primary paste and the *cogito* of kneading seems to be the first stage in a graduated assertion of command, through a psycho-alchemical movement away from matter through the embodied dreams of matter and the progressively more worked induration of wood, stone, steel. Dreams of matter are a kind of alchemy, and alchemy itself a kind of magical education of matter. But the reflections on paste and the work of kneading lead in a different direction too, implying a movement not through a series leading from indifference to differentiation, but between states or tonalities of mixture leading from the inert to the quickened. Bachelard hints at this in his discussion of the variability of value of the idea of dough, paste or mucus in theories of alimentation. On the one hand, there is a virtue in vitriolic substances which cut through the cloying thickness of matter; on the other, the thickening power of matter is regarded as sovereign in reproduction, which is conceived well into the eighteenth century as a process of fermentation, in which the formless matter of the female seed is given shape and density by the male seed. Viscosity can therefore be thought of as a vital principle, becoming 'a symbol, a legendary force, a principle of union, of oneiric power. Now the viscous is copenetration, giving rise to the maxim *wed glue with glue in true matrimony*' (*TRV*, 125).

Bachelard's reference here is to C. G. Jung's discussion of the alchemical doctrine of a life force (*vis animans*), known alternatively as 'the resin of the wise', 'Arabic gum', 'viscous gold', '*acqua mercurialis*' or the glue of the world (*glutinum mundi*). Combining masculine and feminine in a self-fertilizing aggregate, it enables the compounding of all substances.[40] It seems therefore to be the opposite of the mythical universal solvent for which alchemists searched for so long. Kneading is an alternative order, in which it is not degrees of differentiation that count but the intensity of compounding. The highest principle is not the purest, but the most energetically mixed.

Kneading assists and mimics this life-giving process of fermentation. Kneading involves a kind of matter of the self, a manipulation of the world via a manipulation of the substance of the body. Bachelard evokes a 'dream of the hand', in which the dreamworker might murmur: 'Everything is paste for me, I am a paste for myself, my becoming is my own matter, my own matter is action and passion, I am indeed a primary paste' (*TRV*, 80). An important part of the calming and restoring effect of kneading is its onanistic echoing of one's own fabric, the dreamy merging of self in a substance that appears to be nothing but the self blanketed in its own extrusions. But this self-communing is always also instinct with community and the meeting of flesh with flesh. Most children learn versions of games that involve the sharing of the action of kneading or mingling or folding, for example in cat's-cradle, and the game of pat-a-cake, in which each participant is at once the other's patter and butter, pastrycook and paste.

One might see the hint of the action of kneading in many of the words which suggest an application of force and effort via the suggestion of bending and folding – bending or buckling to, plying, employing or deploying one's force. This primary paste is more than a groping preliminary to definite action, more than the vague stirrings of what will eventually result in the imposition of fixed shape. For the action of kneading or moulding does not have the definition of form as its aim or consummation, but rather the creation of a vital compound. The action of kneading is a process that turns slack mud, mire or waste into a dough or paste that is taut with potential, whether as nutriment or cement. 'Mixing in' is vital to this process, in particular the addition of oil, butter or other fatty substances to powder or flour. The aim of kneading is to blend together the joined and the disjoined, breadth and depth, the virtue of oil's smooth spread and the density of pulverized substance. In kneading, one repeatedly folds the outer skin of the substance inwards, until it is as it were crammed with skins, is saturated with its outside. The result is no mere mixture, but a *tonic mass*, full of tensile potential – as in the strudel dough that can be drawn out almost indefinitely.

The action of kneading makes the material alive because it invests it with energy. One literally puts work into kneading, inserting kinetic potential into the previously dead substance. When one kneads dough or clay, it is as if one were winding a spring. A lump of worked dough is a negentropic niche in things. Time has been folded into it along with work and air, and so, having undergone a transition from an in-itself to a for-itself, it has a future. Perhaps the most important feature of this enlivened substance is the third element which is added to the primary amalgam of water and earth. It is the addition of air, either through mechanical action, or through the addition of the yeast that will create gas as a byproduct of the chemical reactions it will induce in the paste, that contains the real promise of life in manipulated clay. Cooking is only the end of the process begun in kneading, which already cooks up new life in the dough. We saw in chapter 4 that the doctrine of maternal impressions depended upon a similar conception of the dough-like, kneadable fabric of the developing child.

The action of unction by rubbing and massage recapitulates this history, ritual, medical, horticultural, erotic, of the actions of kneading. It is an action that testifies to the skin's power to be turned from a layer, barrier or surface, into a mingled and mingling substance, into flesh and into more than flesh, into an ideal compounding of substances. If the application of oil constitutes an imaginary sealing, it also makes of the skin the possibility of interfusion or interchange. Kneaded dough, or shaped wax is frequently associated with the making of new life. It is surely for this reason that myths of the making of life so frequently seem to involve the kneading and cooking of clay into flesh. Just as clay is kneaded by the action of the spade or plough, digging in air along with fertilizing agents, so flesh is to be thought of as insufflated clay, a mud given breath, in which life has been compounded not by the action of shaping, but by the action of kneading. Adam is formed from clay and his Hebrew name has reference to the red of the earth. In the New Testament, Christ restores sight by working the dust into a paste with his spittle and applying it to the eyelids of the sufferer. No wonder then that the Christian sacrament of Eucharist should centre round the image of the body of Christ risen in the form of bread. The intended outcome of kneading, or digging, is always living flesh. But living flesh is flesh that retains this power to turn itself over, to knead and churn itself. A recent children's book, Susan Gates's *Revenge of the Toffee Monster*, shows that the imaginary links between moulding and surrogate life are still strong, the story concerning a young boy who stumbles on an old sweet factory in which he finds a toffee monster preserved in hundreds of frozen fragments, which is duly brought back to elastic life.[41] The emphasis of such stories is not only on the imitative relation between the outward or final form of the clay and its object. It is also on the analogy between a worked substance and the vital stuff that is living flesh. It is not the final shape of the model, but the shape-liness, the torque or tension of contour in it, the power of being given and retaining shape of the material of which it has been formed, that contains its inner virtue. The skin is the medium and the aim for the formation of this imaginary flesh, this worked and working transubstance. Aroma, which seems to lift up the soul into subtle atomization, is no spontaneous emanation; it is the product of work, the interchange of mass and manuality.

9 Itch

History, somebody says in T. S. Eliot's 'Gerontion' (it's hard to tell quite who), 'has many cunning passages, contrived corridors'.[1] I begin this chapter with one such; a miniature and sinuous intrigue in the history of dermatology. The condition reported and described since ancient times and known from the fifteenth century onwards simply as 'the itch', or sometimes, 'the seven-year itch' (not on account of its chronic recurrence, but its longevity) is now called scabies, from the Latin *scabere*, to scratch, or scrape. In French it bears the name *la gale*, though has also been known more familiarly as *la grattelle* and even, charmingly, *la charmante*, a name answered in English by the even more incongruously forgiving term 'the gentle stranger'. It is now known to be caused by the attentions of a small arachnid, a member of the *sarcoptis* or flesh-eating family, called *acarus scabiei*. It eats into the skin, boring out tunnels as it goes, operations which cause allergic reaction in the form of intense itching, leading to blisters or vesicles full of clear fluid, which, when scratched, produce scabbing and, often, secondary infection.

From the earliest times, the presence of tiny organisms at the sites of scabies had regularly been noted; Aristotle described the production of lice in the vesicles, as he presumed, by spontaneous generation, and many other physicians reported or assumed the existence of tiny worms or animals, including the medieval mystic and composer Hildegard of Bingen, who devoted a chapter of her *Pharmacy* to the description of what she called the *suren* involved in itch. None of these witnesses seem to have suspected that these tiny creatures might be a cause of the condition. It was not until 1687 that Cosimo Giovanni Bonomo wrote in a letter to his colleague Francesco Redi that, after watching women removing small insects on the end of a needle from the blisters of those suffering from scabies, he had thought to conduct his own investigations. Observing the extracted organisms through a microscope, he had seen 'a very minute Living Creature, in shape resembling a Tortoise, of whitish colour, a little dark upon the Back, with some thin and long Hairs, of nimble motion, with six Feet, a sharp Head, with two little Horns at the end of the Snout'.[2] He

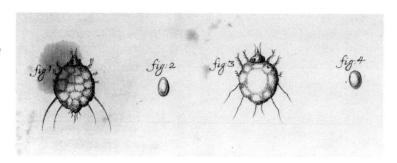

drew quite a good little picture of it. His observations led him roundly to reject the dominant explanations of itch as an expression on the skin of an imbalance of humours:

> From this Discovery it may be no difficult matter to give a more Rational account of the *Itch*, than Authors have hitherto delivered us. It being very probable that this contagious Disease owes its origin neither to the melancholy Humour of *Galen*, nor the corrosive acid of *Sylvius*, nor the particular ferment of *Van Helmont*, nor the irritating Salts in the *Serum* or *Lympha* of the Moderns, but is no other than the continual biting of these Animalcules in the Skin, by means of which some portion of the *Serum* ouzing out thro the small apertures of the Cutis, little watery Bladders are made, within which the Insects continuing to Gnaw, the infect are forced to scratch, and by scratching increase the Mischief, and thus renew the troublesom work, breaking not only the little Pustules, but the Skin too, and some little Blood Vessels, and so making Scabs, Crusty Sores, and such like filthy Symptoms.[3]

Bonomo got pretty much everything right about the itch-mite, most importantly the fact that it propagated, not by spontaneous generation, but through oviparous reproduction. Armed with these observations, Redi was subsequently to take a leading role in the demolition of the doctrine of spontaneous generation, with his experiments to show that, sealed off from the air and outside influence, no maggots were spontaneously generated from meat. As we will see later, the theory of spontaneous generation declined to stay demolished and began itself to be spontaneously regenerated at the beginning of the eighteenth century, not to be laid low for another hundred years. Of the two things Bonomo got wrong, one was trivial, the other was of great importance. First of all, he miscounted the number of legs the creature had; it is in reality no six-legged insect, but an eight-legged arachnid. We can easily have mercy on him and his watering eyes for this mistake, though both numbers and legs will also have importance in what follows. But he also claimed that the animal was to be found in the vesicles. This was a miniature disaster. Plenty of writers and observers were prepared to grant the probable truth of Bonomo's discovery, but it proved surprisingly difficult to replicate. Even though there are regular reports of keen-sighted peasant-women removing the mites on the end of a pin, scientists seemed to find it hard to winkle out the little creatures for themselves. There were probably two reasons for this. One was that the itch-mite is not to be found in the pus of blisters where Bonomo encouraged others to look for it, even if they had not already been so inclined by their assumptions about the affinity between corruption and 'worms'. Indeed, *contra* spontaneist presumption, pus is fatal to the itch-mite, which means that it is very hard to find in the most advanced and conspicuous cases of scabies. In fact the (female) itch-mite lives in the burrows where it lays its eggs. The other is that the numbers of mites required to constitute a serious infestation are anyway surprisingly low, and certainly typically in the dozens rather than the hundreds and the thousands.

The difficulty of confirming Bonomo's observations meant that, gradually, the humoral theory of itch which had dominated since the times of Cestus and Galen in the early centuries of the Christian era began to reassert itself over parasitological explanations. Once again, for more than a century, itch was down to salty choler, or acids rising to the surface of the body from corrupted blood.

It was not until 1812 that another serious claim came forward, this time from Jean-Chrysanthe Galès (who, colleagues observed, bore a name almost identical to the French name for scabies), to have identified the itch-mite. But once again, it was claimed that the mite had been harvested from vesicles and not burrows in the skin and others found it impossible to replicate Galès' discovery. This time the mite was able to go underground only for a couple of decades. In 1834, an undergraduate student named Simon-François Renucci, working at l'Hôpital Saint-Louis in Paris, once again used the technique he had seen employed by women in his native Corsica to extract the *acarus*, sliding a needle into one of the burrows in the skin and bringing out a single specimen on its tip. It became clear once and for all (once again) that this was a distinct organism, different from other mites such as the flour-mite and cheese-mite, and that it was the cause and not just the product of scabies. Although the existence of specific bacilli had been suspected and even assumed before this date, this was the first unequivocal demonstration of a single specific cause for a disease.

How was *sarcoptis scabiei*, the gentle stranger, able to keep its head down for so long (despite not really having a head at all, but only protrusive biting mouthparts)? Why did the itch-mite so come and go? How should one describe the rhythm of its appearances and concealments, and its long-deferred yet also abundantly anticipated explanation? Why was the seemingly obvious and uncomplicated parasitological explanation of scabies and itch resisted for so long? How could the presence of these animals have been so regularly reported over so many centuries without anyone being able to believe that they were the cause of the disease they accompanied? How could itch have been believed to be so extremely contagious without anyone ever trying the simple experiment of seeing whether acquaintance with an itch-mite were enough to infect a previously uninfected person?

Answers to these questions have been offered in some of the histories of this disease.[4] But there are more diffuse questions, of duration, periodicity and of rhythm, and of scale and number, which will come and go in what follows, which is in part the story of an intermittent coming and going between feeling and knowing, a history of the relations between what is sensed in the skin and what is seen and known of it. Surprisingly, the intermittence of itch will seem to shape an allegory of the kind of history, without steady progressions, visible passages, secure and absolute dates, that this study of the skin has enjoined.

CHARGING

And what has this story to do with the familiar, ordinary, universal, negligible, enigmatic and sometimes ecstatic sensation of itching?

Unlike pain, which is something inflicted on the skin, itching is something endogenously produced by the skin. I may say 'I have an itch', but am just as likely to say 'I itch'. It is an activity of the skin; a demand, an event, an action, pressing, imperative. In itch, the sense of touch demands the attentions of touch. No other organ of sense solicits its own attentions in this way, because no other organ exhibits the same two-sidedness as the skin. Itching discloses the importance for the skin of the nails, those hardened portions of the skin that allow the skin as it were to apply itself to itself.

Itching testifies to the variability of charge or tension in the skin. Didier Anzieu has pointed to the importance of this function of 'libidinal recharging', concentrating and diffusing sensation in the skin ego.[5] The experience of the skin is in great part this ceaseless fluctuation of excitations, the skin lived as a gusting curtain or aurora borealis of tickles and prickles and shimmers and quivers. Every time there is an itch, the skin presents itself as one pole of an energetic potential, to be completed by the scratching, or counter-irritation. Although itch and scratch appear to be complementary opposites, scratch countering and cancelling itch, they are also oddly isomorphic. The irritation or disturbance represented by itch is not countermanded but overwhelmed, by a corresponding but magnified form of irritation. The body which is subject to itch is inhabited by a need that, though it is on our periphery, is also as close as it can be. Itching and scratching involve a rising to the surface of ourselves, a centring of ourselves at our edges. Unlike pain, the intensity and tolerability of which are dependent upon its closeness to the centres of consciousness – making a pain in the arse much more tolerable than a toothache or sinusitis – itch is always exquisitely proximal, always, veritably, upon us. Itchiness calls for attention to the skin, but is also concentrated in those parts where the body touches on itself, between the toes and fingers and buttocks and in the armpits, as though to anticipate the corrective self-touching involved in scratching, as though a certain mimicry of the cure of itch were its cause. Unlike the ordinary sense-homunculus, in which the quality of the information imparted by lips, fingertips, and other especially sensitive parts of the body ensures their permanent enlargement, the itch-homunculus, if we could imagine such a thing, would have no regular, no permanent shape. Itches form and dissipate, like clouds in the sky, failing to join up into a continuous or coherent firmament. The itch-homunculus has the shape of a nest of ants, that comes and goes ceaselessly, never becoming one, never breaking apart.

TRANSPORTS

If one wonders why it is that human beings like to scratch themselves so much, one answer might be: because we so easily can. The dexterity of human beings means that they can reach into and scratch the different portions of themselves much more efficiently than, say, cows or dogs. Primates touch themselves and each other intensively, making constant journeys between mouth, nose, anus, penis, vulva, feet, armpits. Though making no reference to primate behaviour, Michel Serres has suggested that this contingency or aptitude for self-touching is constitutive of the embodied self. He answers Descartes' question 'where does the soul reside?' with the suggestion that the soul has no permanent seat anywhere, but rather arises at the fingers' ends, or wherever it is that one part of us touches, folds or crosses over another part. The metaphysics of the soul, he says, thus begin in gymnastics; wherever we can reach (and, when in health, we can reach nearly everywhere except between the shoulders) is a place where soul can arise in the simultaneous division and commerce between self and not-self. The important link between folding and the touching off of the soul has been beautifully proclaimed by Gilles Deleuze too, at the beginning of his book on Leibniz (a work that touches or folds over at many points upon Serres' own reading of Leibniz):

> The soul sings of the glory of God inasmuch as it follows its own folds, but without succeeding in entirely developing them ... A labyrinth is said, etymologically, to be multiple because it contains many folds . . . If Descartes did not know how to get through the labyrinth, it was because he sought the secret of continuity in rectilinear tracks, and the secret of liberty in a rectitude of the soul. He knew the inclension of the soul as little as he did the curvature of matter.[6]

For evolved primates, hygiene and health require the regulation of the passages between the different portions and passages of the human organism: channelling the contacts between mouth, hand, anus, penis, vulva, scalp, feet, armpit. The regularization of these self-contacts constitutes many of the codes of modern social politeness – slowing and conventionalizing the relationship between hand and mouth with eating implements, monitoring the flow of mucus and saliva, ensuring differences in posture; the military posture, for instance, which is defined in terms of the prohibition on self-touching, and religious postures, which contrastingly multiply self-touching and the conjugation of surfaces. This regularized flow marks out the cardinal points of *homo erectus*, barring certain passages and couplings, promoting others, in the approved manners of our 'autingency' or self-touching. Itching and scratching are the signs of disease and degradation partly because they belong to this alternative, eschewed order of carriages and connections and transactions.

Itching connects too with the secret history of masturbation, and the ridicule and disdain which it provokes. There is a close association of masturbation with disease, and in particular skin disease. For, like masturbation, itching makes us multiply, and copulate with ourselves. In masturbation and scratching, one strives to become two, just as in sexual relations, two strain to become one. In masturbation and scratching, the hand, attending to the body, multiplies both itself and the body. Masturbation has acquired since the nineteenth century a reputation for selfishness and closure. But masturbation and its relation to the itching-scratching machine also opens us out, creating of the skin a multiplicity. There is no etymological link between 'masturbation', from *manu sturbare*, to rub with the hand, and words like 'disturbance' and 'perturbation', which derive rather from different modalities of the agitation of the crowd, or *turba*. But there nevertheless seems to be the crowding in of some idea of the mass in the idea of masturbation, in which the self's one adds to itself the one-on-one of its self-attention, to form the three that is always a crowd.

Itching and scratching disclose the importance to the experience of the skin of its dead or insensitive areas, and in particular the nails. The fingernails are a tool. Though they are made of the same substance – keratin – as the top layer of the skin, they function as something we use on ourselves, a part of the world rather than a part of us. In fact, the horniness of the nails helps to associate them with inhuman existences which are nevertheless encrusted or encysted upon us: the horns of animals, the shells of crustaceans and insects. Nail polish plays with the possibility that fingernails and toenails might also be metallic or mechanical.

Michel Serres uses the fingernails to dramatize his notion of the contingency of the soul:

> I cut my nails.
> Where does the subject settle itself? Since I am left-handed, I take the implement in my left hand, and present the open blades to the end of my right index fingernail. I position myself in the handles of the scissors, the I situates itself there, and not at the tip of the right finger. The nail, awkward at the end of the thread of steel; the hand, fine and astute in its management of the cutting. The left hand subject works on the right hand object. The left hand participates in the I, suffused with subjectivity, the right hand is of the world.[7]

For Serres, the contact of the self with itself involved in cutting the nails brings about a meeting of the purely subjective, the radiant white light of the 'I', with the blackness or shadow of a surface that belongs to me but, for the moment at least, is part of the world, the realm of the not-I. These relations are both resumed and complicated in the action of scratching an itch. For, where the nail to be cut becomes an object, insensate, not-I, at the touch of the scissor blade, the itch which calls and compels the fingernail is not at all a part of the world but urgently and unarguably mine; nobody can feel my itch as I do, and only I can acknowledge my itch as my own. Where Serres brings his scissors to bear on his nails, in scratching, I bring my nails to bear like scissors. I wield myself like a tool or an implement, I impersonate an animal, surrendering the sensitivity of the fingertips for the insensitivity of the nail, or talon, or beak, in order to attend to the other modality of myself that is my itch. In the cutting of the nails the nominative 'I' encounters and passes over into the accusative 'me', as a current flows between positive and negative poles. But this current can flow only one way; even when Serres the left-hander switches hands, the left hand remains his subject hand, and the right hand doing the cutting remains stiffly objective. In the scratching of an itch, both poles are positive and negative at once. The active 'I' in the hand which scratches has already turned itself into a prosthesis, has taken on insensibility, in order to supply the stimulation which the patch of 'me' lit up by itch so craves, a stimulation which will soothe and sedate, restore the awakened 'me' to its insensibility.

There is a grotesque relationship between crucifixion and scratching. One of the fiendish things about crucifixion is not that the skin is laid open, but that the skin is made inaccessible to the victim himself. Crucifixion makes you an object and marks you as one, because it prevents you touching yourself. Christ is not hung on the cross so much as spread out or unfolded across it. Not to be able to touch yourself, to be an entirely explicated existence, would be the greatest excruciation, and it is no wonder that the crucifixion is remembered in the making of a sign upon the body which flutteringly undoes its torturing work. The multiple piercings of the skin in crucifixion, the scourging, the crown of thorns, and the piercing of hands and feet, themselves communicate ironically with the impossibility of scratching an itch. The fact that the hands which normally apply the consummating nails to one's itch are themselves nailed (for all the fact that, as we know, victims of crucifixions were usually not nailed but roped to crosses), cruelly highlights this non-communication between hand and body.

But, in scratching, the self is never merely two, or merely its own, solitary two-ness. Itch is the primary contagion, touching on ourselves, touching on others. Itching involves human transactions, or the possibility of them; you scratch my back and I'll scratch yours. All animals scratch, and some animals have evolved ecologies of itch and scratch involving other species. But there are no animals in which the meaning of this ecology is more marked, in which this ecology is more the occasioning of meaning itself, than higher primates. Because of the importance of scratching, squeezing, picking, combing and emunctive behaviour, as they are preserved in rituals of cosmetic application, grooming and combing, what we do to ourselves always implies the participation of others of the tribe or troop, even if scratching oneself has become for modern human beings a prickly and private affair. Itching and scratching always implicate a society of others, if only the others whose squinting eyes and wrinkled noses derogate the practice. Women, denied by codes of politeness in the cultures of the North the extraordinary range of self-pummellings and rowellings that men feel free to effect on themselves, resort to hand-mirrors and mascara brushes to touch themselves in public. The self delivered by the hand-mirror or compact mirror, in a jigsaw of topical glimpses rather than a total view, is like the intermittent sense of self delivered by itching and scratching.

Despite prohibitions, there are still overwhelming itching and scratching impulses that we cannot so easily disavow or distance ourselves from. Watch somebody struggling with a zip, or a knotted shoelace. Why can we never merely stand by to watch such an operation? Why do we itch to snatch the conundrum and ourselves accomplish its unloosing? Why is everyone sure that their fingers are more expert than another's? Itching and scratching are not just one action among many possible of the hand and fingers. They are the essence of a civility, a civilization that continues in large part to be handmade, the precipitate and solace of our fidgets. Our opposable thumbs – the very image of our capacity to close upon the world in a sort of self-touching – allows for our variability of scale, meaning that we can manipulate things that are much smaller than ourselves, allowing us not only to catch fleas, flies and mites, but also to ply needles (sometimes, as we have seen, for the purpose of skewering mites), count money, wield pens and turn pages like these.

Itching is the apprehension of the multiplicity of the skin. Itching is in continuity with other swarming sensations, in which the skin suddenly appears foreign to itself, and appears to have given up its singleness and entirety to pure multiplicity. Itching suggests irresistibly the passage of tiny creatures over, or, worse, actually in the skin, lice, mites, maggots, worms. We scratch in order to replace the touch of the imaginary insect with our own touch, or shudder to shake it off without the aid of hands. But creepiness also makes us one with, or coheres us with the multitude of, our congeners that creep and crawl. Goose bumps and gooseflesh transform us into another style of creature. Itching is therefore continuous with a host of sensations that seem to have to do with the skin becoming host to or intimate with other lives, lives that swarm and prickle and tingle and tickle, that cause shivers, shakings, and shudders. In English, we can hear that itching contains the word 'it'; itching is exposure to an 'it' or the 'i' in the I, as well as lots of other minimal denominations of the minute: mite; titch; tiny; nit; tick; titbit; midget.

Scratching literally involves the transaction of identities and passage of lives. Itching and scratching close the loop between the sexual and excretory organs and the mouth, a loop that is crucial for many of the organisms that live on and in and through us. Some parasites are reliant on the propensity of primates for scratching to conduct their episodic life cycles. One might take the pin-worm, for example. The pin-worm spends most of its time in the human gut, feeding plentifully off what it finds amenable in what its host has ingested.

Towards the end of her life, the pregnant female pin-worm migrates down the rectum to the anal ring, into which she burrows to deposit, one imagines with some relief, the best part of 30,000 eggs. Her burrowing causes intense itching, which is just as well for the eggs, for the resultant scratching scrapes them out of their shallow trench in the epidermis and transfers them via the fingernails, and the subsequent activity of eating, to their new host, or back into their old one, after their brief adventure of air. (The itch-mite and its eggs, by contrast, are vulnerable to scratching, and can often be removed from its burrow by the application of the nails.)

Codes of clothing have a crucial part to play in the regulation of itching and scratching. The development of underwear makes the itchiest portions of the body doubly inaccessible. I have never forgotten hearing that astronauts in the 1960s and 1970s had to ensure that their underclothing was completely unwrinkled before they were enclosed in their space suits, lest an unscratchable itch arise that should torment its victim unto madness. An example from the geo-cultural history of itch reinforces the association between costume and itch. Wales and Scotland were both known as 'Itchland' and 'Scratchland' from the eighteenth century onwards, to signify their infested condition. In Thomas D'Urfey's play *The Royalist*, a character known as 'Sawny Scrubham' is described as 'a red-hair'd *Scotchman*, that will engage upon his honour to give the Itch to a whole Army; and to that degree, that in a short time they shall scratch themselves to death'.[8] After the Jacobite uprising in 1745, this negative propaganda focused on the suppressed Scottish kilt, the imagined bare buttocks of the Scots being associated with their alleged propensity to display and attend to their itches publicly. Even a friend to the Scots like Tobias Smollett acknowledges this: in *The Expedition of Humphrey Clinker* (1771), a Welsh traveller to Scotland writes home that the natives of the country 'are scarce ever visited by any other disease than the smallpox and certain cutaneous evils, which are the effects of dirty living'.[9] Samuel Ireland paints the portrait of the typical Scot in 1814:

Come and illumine me J—cky Sc—tt,
Who cross'd the Tweed not worth a jot;
With scarce a kelt to shield poor breech,
Well armed with arrogance and itch.[10]

As late as 1875, a character in a poem entitled *Scotch Nationality* refers to 'the itch/The symptom national; which I deem the true cause and reason why/We ne'er stand still, or stay at home,/But scratch and boo, and fidge and roam'.[11] All of the jokes centring on the Scottish kilt funnel back to the fantasy of the pruritic condition of the Scots and their incapacity to leave themselves alone.

CATCHING

Scratching appears as a remedy for and cancellation of itch, but is continuous with it. Scratching only stimulates itching. In Scotland, 'itching' is used both of the stimulus and the response to it: you 'itch' an 'itch' rather than scratching it. When we say that we itch to do something, we transfer the sensation of itching to the fingers, which in the normal course of events are so involved in attending to itch that it is hard to think of them as being afflicted by it. In fact, scabies is often concentrated in the hands and between the fingers, perhaps precisely because the skin there is less sensitive and the burrowing of the *acarus* is less likely to cause an adverse reaction. Scratching and itching form a double-single, self-proliferating organism. At its heart, an itch, or a scratched itch, forms the most elementary ecology. An itch always multiplies itself. Who has ever scratched an itch once? Precisely because the scratching of an itch is so consummate a pleasure, it is in fact infinite, unfinishable. Once you begin to itch and scratch, there is no end to it.

Itch is proliferative in the sense that scratching an itch only makes it itch more, or produces another itch elsewhere. But itch is also transferential; it springs nimbly across to other areas of meaning. The Freudian association between itching and sexual desire is well established in medieval English. To itch means to have sexual feeling, and Partridge rescues from Florio's 1598 *A Worlde of Wordes* (via Farmer and Henley) the expression 'to play at itch-buttocks' and from D'Urfey's *Wit and Mirth* (1720) the phrase 'to have an itch in the belly'. The pleasant part known to blushing lexicographers as the female pudend was also known as an 'itcher', or 'itching Jenny'.[12] Later medical descriptions of itch, such as that of the condition of *prurigo pudendi muliebris* to be found in Robert Willan's *On Cutaneous Diseases* of 1808, maintain the association between itch and venery, while seeming to try to make it more adventitious:

> In this disease the itching is perpetual and almost intolerable, and induces the necessity of constant friction, with cooling applications, so that the patients are compelled to forego the pleasures of society, and to live in solitude. An excitement of venereal desires also takes place from the constant direction of the mind to the parts affected, as well as from the means employed to procure alleviation. The complicated distress thus arising renders existence almost insupportable, and often produces a state of mind bordering on frenzy.[13]

What Willan actually says is that it is the necessity of paying such extensive attention to the genital parts that brings on lustful thoughts. But what he also seems to harbour is the proto-Freudian suspicion that the itching is the occasion or excuse of an impulse to self-gratification that might otherwise find no means of expression.

A subtler interlacing of writing, itch and libido is established in Robert Herrick's verses 'To The Detractor'. The poem moves from complaint at being

the victim of the detractor's corrective thumb, to acquiescence in the correction
by pen rather than tongue:

> Where others love, and praise my Verses; still
> Thy long-black-Thumb-nail marks 'em out for ill:
> A fellon take it, or some Whit-flaw come
> For to unslate, or to untile that thumb!
> But cry thee Mercy: Exercise thy nailes
> To scratch or claw, so that thy tongue not railes:
> Some numbers prurient are, and some of these
> Are wanton with their itch; scratch, and 'twill please.[14]

The apparent simplicity of the sentiments here is complicated by the final
two lines, which allow us to suspect that, if there is a pleasure in the wantonness of metrical imperfection, there is an equally wanton pleasure in the attentions that will be paid to them in order to make them regular. The poetic incon-
gruities long to be scratched, making the detractor long to scratch them, as
though they were in his or her own skin. The cancellation or scratching out of
the wantonness is looked forward to with an intensity that is imperfectly concealed in that mild, telling intransitive phrase 'scratch and 'twill please'. It seems
likely that the pleasure will be halved or doubled between the reprover and
reproved.

The lubricity of itch seems to come to a head in the seventeenth and eighteenth centuries. Itch is thoroughly implicated, for example, in the portrait of
lustful womanhood provided by Nathaniel Richards, in a section entitled 'The
Flesh' which forms part of his little-known work *The Celestiall Publican: A
Sacred Poem* (1630):

> See how she tempts, with what a charming smile,
> Puts poison in her Eyes, eyes to beguile,
> Seducing eyes, aim'd at Eternall Light,
> From Heav'n, to looke on Hell, prurient delight,
> Deckt, timm'd, adorn'd, trickt up to pull men on
> With Pride of Eyes, to their confusion.
> Note the varietie of all her charmes,
> The Lazie, idle, stretching of the Armes;
> The Yawne, and then the Hey-ho, rolling eie,
> Sick stomacke for the Act; O Luxurie;
> Thy flames, in wanton women, strangely move,
> She that delights in Lust, can never Love.
> Observe each gesture, how she takes a pride
> To itch the Bumbe; to frisk from side to side,
> Mop, mew, bite Lip, and wriggle with the Taile,
> There's not a ioynt about her that shall faile
> To catch at Man; be Icie cold as stone,

Shee'l finde a Tricke to melt affection.
In each behaviour lives a Venome snare,
There's language in the curling of her haire,
Eyes, Cheeks, Lips, Hands, no motive Limme so weake
But serves to tempt; her very foot shall speake.
Shee'l part each other in such dall'ing sort
As if shee'd doe with th'Ayre for want of sport.
Crosse legges, and then with itching thighes & knees
Open and shut the passage by degrees.[15]

These verses connect looking with itching, and sexual display with claw-like 'catching'. The point of this poetic-pruritic display of itch is of course to relish and induce it, commuting the eye to the hand, the look to the tooth (the bitten lip) and the fingernail. The woman is all desire, her every 'motive Limme', her every 'behavior', a calling to her lookers-on to draw near to take part in her roaming self-satisfactions, and a casual lending of her fingers to us, or us to her fingers. The language of her gestures consists specifically in the different forms of her 'curling' upon herself. Perhaps the lalling of the glorious line 'There's language in the curling of her haire' will make some readers feel the oral self-touching, the languid crisping of the tongue over itself that is involved in the production of language, and that provides a reference for that later obscure suggestion that 'shee'd doe with th'Ayre for want of sport'. What might speaking be (the speaking out of these lines, for example), but a sportive doing or making do with air? The curling on herself extends even to her foot, which 'speaks' in the ways in which it doubles and doubles on itself, perhaps to scratch the other foot. That compressed and obscure phrase 'shee'l part each other' could be glossed as 'each will take part with the other', as well as anticipating the parting of the legs that might be a preliminary to scratching one foot with the other. Or perhaps it is meant to suggest the spreading of the toes of one foot by the toes of the other? Parting, in these lines, means spreading, laying oneself open, as well as partitioning or highlighting certain parts of oneself, and dividing oneself into two, in order to be able to supply oneself with one's own tender attentions.

We have seen, both in this poem and in Herrick's 'To The Detractor', early uses of the word 'prurient', to mean simply itchy, or provoking the desire to scratch. It was only during the eighteenth century that the word acquired its modern meaning of a peeping, prying, voyeuristic seeking after sexual arousal, but both Herrick and Richards anticipate this onanistic reflexivity of the modern use of the word. The one said to be prurient is always being suspected in part of putting the sex into the place where he aims to find it, bringing about through his own self-titillation the sexualization of that which is to provide the sexual interest, while probably concealing it even from himself. (There is always an element of hypocrisy in prurience.) To say that somebody is lascivious is to say straightforwardly that they have an itch they want scratched. To say that somebody is being prurient is to say that they are itching to find an itch to scratch. Criticizing the *OED* definitions of the word and getting his own improvement included in the third edition as a result, Christopher Ricks suggests in his brief discussion of the fortunes of the word 'prurient' in *Keats and Embarrassment* that 'the prurient is characterized by a particular attitude which it adopts towards its own impure imaginings, an attitude of cherishing, fondling, or slyly watching.'[16] He goes on to point out that there is also something itchily iterative about the attribution of prurience; to say that somebody else is being prurient in the modern sense, privily scratching their own sexual itch, is always itself a somewhat prurient act. This means that you are always at risk of falling prey to prurience when you catch other people out in it, as Ricks himself, for example, catches C. S. Lewis observing Milton's Satan:

> Like that other accusation which indicts the attitude with which a man contemplates his own thoughts, the accusation of complacency, prurience is an accusation not only very difficult to defend oneself against but also especially likely to rebound, since the accuser himself is up to some contemplation or other. Thus when C. S. Lewis speaks of Satan as 'leering and writhing with prurience', and when Milton's lines are seen to give no more warrant for 'writhing' than the words 'aside' and 'askance', one may legitimately wonder whether the watching Satan has not momentarily possessed his watching critic.[17]

Nathaniel Richards is certainly scratching his own itch in his writing of the alluring figure of the flesh, doing a perilously good job of turning himself and his readers on with his unpersuasive attempt to generate disgust. It certainly works on me, and, to be sure, I'm trying to make it work on you, and so, like Swift's fleas, ad infinitum. If this is prurience in me, then Ricks's point seems to be that it cannot but partly be in you too.

The fact that many pruritic conditions had already by the late seventeenth century been discovered to be caused by actual ectoparasitic infestation perhaps accounts for the suggestion of the parasitic which is essential to modern ideas of prurience as a state of mind rather than of body. You can quite comfortably call yourself lascivious, but you would have to be in a much more convoluted condition of what Joyce calls 'twosome twiminds' to call yourself prurient. You can't be simply, adjectivally 'prurient', since prurience is always to be found clinging secretly and illicitly on the back of other attitudes or purposes. Richards's interest in the young woman he conjures up is prurient because it is pretending to be appalled, and allowing its disgust to act as a cover for extended self-titillation, the itcher here producing his own itch.

Hence the twitch of the modern meaning in Smollett's couplet: 'Debauched from sense, let doubtful meanings run, The vague conundrum and the prurient pun', where the running of the sense from a bodily into a linguistic effect (one feels that the running here is effected with the smallest of feet) is an important part of the prurience.[18] The prurient pun is now a thing of words rather than of the body, of sense rather than sensation. But it is prurient because the play of meanings is a play between sense and sensation, since it is the quality of a prurient pun, as opposed to a bawdy joke, not to allow one either openly to accept or to set aside the bodily sense. A prurient pun, in fact, is itchy with the unexpressed. In letting the earlier meaning of bodily itch in the word 'prurient' sit alongside the metaphorical meaning which was beginning to become available by the mid-eighteenth century, Smollett himself effects a pun (a prurient one? it's got too smoky in here to tell) on the word 'prurient'.

Indeed, the peculiar flarings of parasitical other meanings in the idea of itch and prurience make it hard to be absolutely sure, and partly because of the projective structure we are uncovering in the very idea of prurience, that the more complex kinds of self-titillation are not sometimes incipient in much earlier uses of the word. When Robert Herrick invites his detractor to scratch out his 'prurient numbers', he seems to mean rather more by the invitation than a docile wish to be saved from error, since the pleasure in 'scratch and 'twill please' is also a pleasure in being attended to, and a pleasure in the thought of the bodily attentions involved in the action on the written skin shared between writer and reader. The teasing prospect of bodily gratification is therefore being, in the 'later' sense, pruriently twinned with another, more respectable pleasure. Another anticipation of the later meanings of the word 'prurient' given by the *OED* dates from 1589. It occurs in one of the satirical *Martin Mar-Prelate Tractates* which Thomas Nashe wrote against religious sects (which he called in his subtitle '*the scabbe that is bredde in England*'), especially the Puritans, whose extremism was endangering the newly established Anglican church. In *The Returne of the Renowned Cavaliero Pasquill*, Nashe gives us this exchange about Puritans between the traveller Pasquill and his interlocutor Marsorius:

> PAS. I frequented the Churches of the Pruritan Preachers, that leape into the Pulpet with a Pitchfork, to teach men, before they have either learning, iuggment, or wit enough to teach boyes. MARS. I pray you, Syr, why doe you call them Pruritans? PAS. They haue an itch in their eares, that would be clawed with new points of doctrine, never dreamed of; and an itch in their fingers, that woulde be nointed with the golden Æmulatum of the Church. I knowe they are commonly called Puritans, and not amisse: that tytle is one of the marks they beare about them. They have a marke in the heade, they are selfe conceited, *they take themselves to be pure*, when they are filthy in Gods sight.[19]

Here, the infection of pure motives with filthy longings, for the titillation of doctrine and the power and self-importance that it brings, makes the itchy ears attributed to the Puritans more than merely physically itchy. The transfer of the sense of itch to the ears and the sense of hearing would come to be very common in later centuries.

Itch strikes us as so particularly infectious, because it multiplies so obviously on the body of the individual sufferer, mimicking and anticipating its multiplication as it passes from person to person. As itch spreads over the sufferer's person, they are both parted from and rejoined with themselves. Scabies is not in fact very contagious, since prolonged physical contact – night-long sharing of a bed rather than sexual contact alone – is required for migration of the itch-mite to occur between persons. But it had and still has the reputation of being highly contagious. Thomas Spooner declared in 1714 that 'Certainly the Infection of no one Disease is more easily and certainly propagated (the Plague only excepted) than this of the *Itch*.'[20]

During the seventeenth century itchiness migrated energetically into metaphor, and skipped easily from metaphor to metaphor; from sex into other kinds of unmasterable impulse, such as curiosity, the desire for 'play' or gambling, the desire for fame and money (this one helped by the rhyme with 'rich') and the querulous instinct for theological dispute: in the infectious year of 1666, Pepys spotted an epitaph to Sir Henry Wotton in Eton College chapel which recorded him as the originator of the sentiment: 'Disputandi pruritus fit eccelesiae scabies' (the itch for disputation is the Church's scabies).[21]

These multiplications and running transformations of itch are expressions of the commutability of the fact and the thought of itch. If thinking is done with a thought-skin, a skin of thought, then itch is what we use to think this skin up.

Perhaps the commonest metaphorical passage of the idea of itch is the scribbling itch, or desire to write. A strong tradition connects the making of marks on surfaces – whether paper or canvas – with the action of scratching. In English, etching and sketching sound like cousins of itching and scratching, and scribbling (from *scribillare*, a diminutive form of *scribere*), through its seeming affinity to scraping and scrabbling, also has a relation to scratching. Scratching was the noise made by the pen for centuries before the typewriter and the ballpoint pen, and to 'scratch out' a line or a passage was to delete it – as in scratching from a race. Doing something from scratch, by contrast, means going back to the primary line, or crease, inscribed on the ground, to mark the beginning of a race, the division between before and after, beginning and sequel. The strangely long-lived libidinization of the marking of surfaces in human beings perhaps has as much to do with the reciprocal dynamism of the itch and the scratch as the desire for the making of permanent marks; itching and scratching are perhaps at work in every marking that implies an impression or incision as well as a deposit.

The itching-scratching apparatus at work in writing and drawing changes the metaphorical understanding of writing from expression to cooperation, from the imposition of signs on to an indifferently receptive surface to the idea of a collaboration of conversation of signs. We have seen already how Robert Herrick libidinizes this collaboration of hands.

With our surfaceless writing, which deposits letters in streams on an insubstantial or virtual screen, we seem perhaps to have got beyond inscription. And has not typing – the work of two hands and ten fingers, the touch of which has become lighter and lighter and further and further removed from the page or space which it touches – become an insect-like activity, a swarming and scurrying over a surface which it constitutes of itself? Not that the mechanization of communication has meant the complete abandonment of the itching-scratching relation. In the musical culture of turntabling or scratching, with its strange comminglings of the primitive manipulations of mud and earth of the potter at her wheel, with the technologies of bodiless inscription, and in extreme extensions of it such as those practised by the Australian performance artist Lucas Abel, who uses nails and knives to play gramophone records, the body is replayed in the circuits of technological itch and scratch.

The gambling itch is interestingly combined with the epistemophilic itch in contemporary scratch cards. As with many instances of itching and scratching, the scratch card connects the low and the exalted. The scratch card is a magical skin-fragment. Cards in general, charge cards and smart cards as we call them, are bits of skin that have indeed been charged up with magical potency. The scratch card is alive with our desire to scratch it: it has an itch (ours). In scratching the top off the wound, there will be a loss (we know that a repeatedly scratched or picked scab will never get better), but also a fund of pleasure which makes good the loss in compensation for the inevitable disappointment.

CREEPY-CRAWLY

Itching and the dispersal of the skin-schema that it signifies is at the greatest distance from the usual functions of the skin. Other transformations of the skin can be thought of as variations on its basic structures, or selective intensifications of certain of its qualities – its protectiveness in armour; its capacity to change appearance and to individuate in cosmetics and body painting; its power to heal itself in lesions. But itching seems to signify the possibility of the skin's absolute dissolution, the absolute identity of flesh and dust, in an identification with the skin's opposites. Itching evokes granularity; bits, flakes, dust, powder, sand, grit. Itching is not only the response to the irritation of such substances – like pepper and itching powder – it is also the temptation to become one with granularity's impossible life, the swarming insect-life of multiplicity, of ants and bees, and the fleas held for so long to be engendered by the mixture of sweat and dust. It is an association with the miniature, as alluded to, but unattended to by Gaston Bachelard, when he claims that '[o]ur animalized oneirism, which is so powerful as regards large animals, has not recorded the doings and gestures of tiny animals. In fact, in the domain of tininess, animalized oneirism is less developed than vegetal oneirism.'[22] He then acknowledges in a footnote that 'It should be noted, however, that certain neurotics insist that they can see the microbes that are consuming their organs.' Itch is the (usually) nonpsychotic form of this cultural dreamwork of the miniature.

The dream of worms does not destroy or deny the skin so much as reconstitute it, as a thing of holes, passages. If the skin were not a surface containing holes, but an imaginary tissue made up of holes with nothing to connect them to each other but the gaps between them, except perhaps the thought of their

Vivien Leigh as Cleopatra in a still from the 1945 film *Caesar and Cleopatra*, the puckerings of her head-dress mimicking her conspicuously pored skin.

connection – a skin made of air, made of nothing but thought, a dream skin – then skin would have become a swarm of malignant dust, which is made as much of gaps as particles. For Deleuze and Guattari, who have little to say about dust and powder, but plenty to say about sieves, pores and pockmarks, this bored littleness is the becoming of multiplicity itself, a multiplicity which is the form of the unconscious. Writing of Freud's Wolf Man, they declare that 'a wolf is a hole, they are both particles of the unconscious, nothing but particles, productions of particles, particulate paths, as elements of molecular multiplicities. It is not even enough to say that intense and moving particles pass through holes; a hole is just as much a particle as what passes through it.'[23] No contemporary authors have done more to broach the question of the life of multiplicity than Deleuze and Guattari. According to their own account, their own collaboration, the conjugation of their joined-up writing, was itself crowded, entomological:

> We are writing this book as a rhizome. It is composed of plateaus. We have given it a circular form, but only for laughs. Each morning we would wake

up, and each of us would ask himself what plateau he was going to tackle, writing five lines here, ten there. We had hallucinatory experiences, we watched lines leave one plateau and proceed to another like columns of tiny ants.[24]

Our fear is written over our skin, insofar as the skin is our first line of defence. When our skin bristles with horror, when we horripilate, becoming like a hedgehog, we are defending ourselves against some threat, some horror, that is itself horrent, whose skin can stand up, piercing rather than sustaining, like the inverted breast of the Iron Maiden. If we think of that threat in terms of a threat to the skin, the possibility of being torn or pierced, we mime becoming the kind of creature whose skin can become an armed host, can itself come to be made up of blades or needles or spears or knobs. When we shiver with horror, we defend ourselves against penetration not only by hardening, but by shattering or multiplication. The ants which pour out of the slit eyeball in Buñuel's *L'Age d'Or* replace the monocular singularity of our own gaze and of the screen which holds the scene in view with a scurrying that can no longer quite be seen or held steadily in place, but is nevertheless the model for another way of seeing, the seeing-feelingly of the swarming ant-mind, or of Bachelard's psychotic. When what horrifies us is the very existence of swarming, the possibility of being burrowed into and sieved, and turned into nothing more than a swarming, then the skin can take prophylactic refuge in the very pullulation that it dreads, borrowing a survival from the very kind of life it fears will carry it away piecemeal. The impulse to neurotic excoriation, and the desire to cleanse oneself of sebaceous material and other visible deposits in the skin which is indulged in a mild way by the makers of skin preparations, mutates, in the obsessives and psychotics described by Freud and Bion, into a horrified, but lingeringly libidinous identification with the worms that occupy the pores of the skin. (The long, thin extrusions of sebaceous matter were mistaken for dead worms by some earlier observers.)

The agency of invisible germs or animals had been adduced since at least the early Middle Ages as a cause of disease, especially for skin diseases.[25] Indeed, so attractive and satisfying was the hypothesis of the action of worms in particular that a large number of imaginary worms were identified to account for different medical conditions: these include the heart-worm; the echoing worm (which caused resonance in the belly when the patient spoke); eye-worms, ear-worms, and the tooth-worm. This consciousness is still alive in the grotesque airborne worm of Blake's Sick Rose, Blake being, as his famous vision of the satanic flea indicates, an *aficionado* of the verminous. In the way of such things, the strength of the nearly right theory both impeded microbiological understanding and assisted it once it arrived. One of the many secret passages running from the history of itch connects up with the history of worm-consciousness, both in terms of the teeming corruption that worms signify, and in terms of that avidity which Cleopatra's Clown calls the 'joy of the worm'.

Until the second half of the seventeenth century, there was a surprising casualness about the ways in which various poorly visible organisms were named. Particularly surprising to us now is the apparent vagueness about the distinctions between worms and insects. The distinction we make nowadays between a worm and an insect is remarkably firm, and seems to turn upon the nature of its relation to the ground or to surfaces. Put as simply as possible, an insect has legs, where a worm does not. Perhaps because human beings define themselves so much in terms of their uprightness, or distance from the ground, the distinction between creatures that have legs to hold themselves clear of the surfaces across which they move, however minimally, and creatures that maintain a continuous contact with their environments, like snakes, worms, snails, eels and fishes, is salient for us. We can even say that the possession of legs establishes a human, perpendicular orientation to the ground. A creature with legs stands 'on' and moves 'across' its ground. Not to have legs is to live against or in contact with one's environment, or even, like a fish or eel, amid it, with less suggestion of the vertical dimension. Creatures with legs have an attenuated and intermittent relation to the ground: they have, precisely, weight and 'relation' to a surface which supports them. They also have need of eyes. Vermicular creatures, by contrast, have so continuous a relation to the ground, or the surface from which they originate, that they are still partially of it; like the chthonic inhabitants glimpsed at the beginning of E. M. Forster's *A Passage to India*, they seem like mud moving, and so are never separate enough from their environment to need to see it. In one sense, worms and maggots are to be imagined as having a merely two-dimensional existence, never breaking contact with the surface or skin which is the whole of their world. In another sense, however, the fact that no breaking of contact is possible for the skin-dwelling vermicule means that the idea of the supporting skin becomes irrelevant to it. The idea that worms are bred from the skin, expressed out on to the surface of decaying bodies by the process of putrefaction, leads easily into the idea that they share in or even constitute the skin that is their habitat. Worms are creatures of the skin, whose lives express an apprehension of the skin as a formless, pullulating mass.

Our very word (one word or two?) 'creepy-crawly' seems to preserve this worm-insect ambivalence. Creeping is what worms and snakes and eels do, while crawling necessarily suggests the possibility of legs, if only of a vestigial kind. When humans crawl, the elbows and the knees must come into play. Though humans can easily creep in an upright position (like Macbeth's life, which 'creeps in its petty pace') the suggestion is of an approximation or approach to a sort of movement without legs. But the word 'creepy-crawly' also expresses the sense of the indistinction of the two kinds of movement, the two very different kinds of being, that it minimally distinguishes. A creepy-crawly is in fact an animal between a worm and an insect, of which the whole point is the uncertainty as to whether it moves on its belly or on legs, oozing or scurrying. The vision of the Ancient Mariner suggests the horrible ambivalence of this rot-life:

The very deep did rot: O Christ!
That ever this should be!
Yea, slimy things did crawl with legs
Upon the slimy sea.[26]

The rotting of the deep creates a skin, which is partly made up of slime. But the slimy things that participate in the sea's nature are also caught in the act of pulling away from it, and so are able to move 'upon' as well as 'amidst' it.

This distinction had not formed itself in the pre-microscopic era, and took some time to do so even after the regular differences between creeping and crawling things began to be tabulated. The word 'worm' was used, not only of serpents, dragons and monsters, as in references to sea-worms, and the ballad of the Lailly Worm, but also of anything of indefinite form and motion, including many of the creatures known to us as insects. The word 'vermin', as used still to refer to rats, pigeons and other strikingly non-wormy creatures, is an inheritance from the period when 'worm' could be used to refer to any creature of lowly and indefinite form. Perhaps the Edenic story of the abasement of the serpent, condemned to go on his belly after the Fall, provides a commentary on this pattern. Although in one sense the attaining of the upright posture in human beings meant the possibility of our becoming the itching and scratching animal par excellence, the human imagination of lowness is full of the possibilities of itching abrasion. The various associations between snakes, worms and mites not only implicate snakes with itch in a general way, but the squirminess of snakes, and the snakiness of squirm may give a sense of the lowliness and disgustingly onanistic manner of the snake's locomotion, which causes it to rub handlessly and leglessly against the ground, eventually, it appears, rubbing and scrubbing its skin off. To creep on the belly is to allow for no clear division between the animal and its environment. These associations between itch, creeping and the loathsome run through the ways in which diseases such as leprosy and syphilis were conceived from the late medieval period onwards. Leprosy is from Greek λεπρός (lepros), scaly, and 'herpes' is related to the Latin word that gives us 'serpent'.

Piero Camporesi has shown abundantly how the consciousness of the worminess of flesh was played out amid desperate and violent attempts to evacuate this corruption.[27] And this swarming, this prickling, this congregation or convocation of ants, or bees, or millipedes, this numberless fluttering as of moths or birds, is the source of some of our sweetest and most secret pleasures too.[28] Sometimes, it is magnified into a visible shudder, or shiver, or quivering, to enact the awed sense of imminence, of being in the vicinity of the god.

At such times the shudder transforms the skin into a kind of resonating membrane. Why should it be that a phrase of music, a cadence, or a figure, should be registered so immediately in this lifting, this shifting, this sizzling of the skin, as though they had not needed to be taken in and made intelligible by the ear at all? Is it that, at times like this, we are listening with our skins, which have become a sort of itching tympanum, an eerie, sifting, shifting, whispering, particulate formication, which can hear the passage of ants? And why is it that this sensation, that is so close to horror or apprehension, and that we may also describe as being 'moved' or 'touched', seems to depend upon sound? Is it because sound invades or comes upon us in a way that what we see does not, or not unless we apprehend it as something heard? The sensation of bristling always seems to come from behind, does it not, as though we had ears, rather than eyes in the back of our heads? (A. E. Housman insisted that it was the skin on the back of his neck that rose in the presence of poetry.) If a line of poetry makes our skin bristle, must we not have imagined it spoken, or whispered at our ears? A whisper makes us feel the tickling breath passing across our skin; it is a kind of talking to the skin.

Why do we say that things give us the creeps, or that they make our skin crawl, unless it is that we sense a commingling, a commensality, a mimetic charming or fascination of the skin by the movement that it finds so aversive? Sensing the crawling taking place over it, the skin itself begins to crawl: it squirms into the shape of an insect or a worm – or rather, the multiple form of the insect or worm – in order to escape the touch of insect or worm. At the beginning of the third century, Quintus Serenus Sammonicus, following the principle that like will cure like, recommended the application of what one would have thought the ultimate itching powder, the dust deposited by ants on the floors of their galleries, mixed with oil, for relief from scabies.[29] One should not smile too much: perhaps a mild suspension of formic acid was indeed dele- terious to the *acarus*, without risking the secondary dermatitis produced by so many more radical treatments. It is surely this losing of the skin's singularity or wholeness, this evasion of the economy of tegument and tear (the lesion in the skin always recruiting and being recruited to the story of the skin's lost and restored entirety) that constitutes the exhilaration of horror.

PROPAGATION

Michel Serres has observed that to tell the story of any scientific enquiry may be to rely on notions of time and space still at issue in that very enquiry. 'The classification of the sciences', he writes, 'orders them in a space and the history of science orders them in a time, as if we knew, in advance of those sciences themselves, what space and time consist of.'[30] A striking example of this paradoxical interference is provided by the history of the doctrine of the spon- taneous generation of the lower forms of creation. This doctrine, inherited from Aristotle and classical natural historians, was enthusiastically developed during the late medieval and early Renaissance periods. Lice were held to be bred from the putrefaction of sweat on the skin; eels and worms were bred from mud, and the carcasses of oxen and cows were believed to produce bees. The arrival of tadpoles and frogs in showers of rain was regularly reported.

The story of the long argument between the spontaneists and those who attempted to show that all life came from reproduction has been told by Caroline Wilson and Edward G. Ruestow.[31] Whence and how did the understanding arise of whence and how life arose? Is this understanding to be thought of as a long-deferred but necessary unfolding of a buried truth? As given birth to out of previous embryonic conceptions? Or as a coming together of different contingent possibilities, just like the way in which spontaneists conceived the chemical processes resulting the formation of insects and worms? We might wonder if there are any ways at all in which we might imagine the arrival (and retreat) of the understanding of the processes of life in the seventeenth and eighteenth centuries which would not be predicted by and implicated in the ways in which these periods told themselves about birth and life.

It might seem an easier task to tell the story of how the invention of the microscope – or at least, perhaps, the invention of ways to use it, for these occurred a century or so later than the actual invention – made visible for the first time the reproductive processes of those tiny creatures who had been suspected of being formed directly out of processes of putrefaction and decay. Everything, from now on, one might think, would have to be accepted as coming from something, and something of its own kind: as seemed to be affirmed by the frontispiece to William Harvey's *Exercitationes de generatione animalium* (1651), which shows crocodiles, insects and men all issuing from a split egg on which is written *ex ovo omnia*.[32] The discovery of the itch-mite by Bonomo would play, and indeed has played, a central part in that story, for, as we have seen, it was Bonomo's letter of 1687 that seems to have spurred Francesco Redi into his campaign to demonstrate the origins of all life in reproductive processes familiar from the world visible to the naked eye. (Why this expression: the naked eye? What makes the microscope or telescope a clothing of the eye? Why the suggestion of vulnerability and powerlessness in the unassisted eye? Why the suggestion that the eye needs a covering? What assails it? Did anyone ever think of the eye as naked before the apprehension of what might be assailing it invisibly, against which one might need some protection?)

The microscope allowed individual examples to be studied and described of organisms, such as *sarcoptis scabiei*, that had previously only been apprehensible in vague masses and multiples. The study and illustration of individual examples reinforced and was itself reinforced by the assumption that all examples of an individual organism would follow the patterns observed in a single specimen. The demonstration of the regularity of form and life cycle in the representative organisms disclosed by the microscope ought to have been more decisive than it was in discouraging belief in spontaneous generation. The doctrine of spontaneous generation encouraged the idea that the organisms produced out of putrefaction – maggots engendered from rotting meat, eels engendered in mud, fleas formed from drops of sweat or urine in dust – were imperfect, *ad hoc* organisms, whose formation from putrefaction was the very opposite of the divinely driven work of creation that resulted in men and the higher animals, but, as its opposite, had its place in a universe in which the two principles of generation and corruption were supreme. The mites, worms and insects produced by spontaneous generation were both supernumerary, and a kind of half-life. The experience of itch belongs to this sense of the multi-plicity of half-formed creatures as it is lived on the skin, and itch seems to mean excrescence, the extra, the exception.

Sexuality and the supernumerary breeding of monsters come together in the mid-eighteenth century in 'The Mollies' Club', a homophobic poem by Edmund Ward. Wondering why it is that, in a country so full of female beauty, 'Men should on each other doat,/And quit the charming Petticoat', Ward spins out a scabrous creation myth for lovers of the same sex:

Sure the curs'd Father of this Race,
That does both Sexes thus disgrace,
Must be a Master, mad or drunk,
Who bedding some prepost'rous Punk,
Mistook the downy Seat of Love,
And got them in the Sink above;
So that at first a T—d and They
Were born the very self-same Way;
From whence they drew this cursed Itch
Not to the Belly, but the Breech.[33]

Birth through the anus is itself a kind of spontaneous generation, which then produces the itch to reproduce itself in similar ways.

Far from adjusting human beings to the scale of the microscopic, the inven-tion newly acquainted human flesh with the apprehension of the limits of the eye. Where does life come from? The microscope seemed to confirm that it came from that new frontier of the eye, the realm of the micro-invisible, which was at once far beyond the ordinary reach of the senses, so that it could be apprehended only by reason, and, because it reached so deep into the heart of the matter of which the observing animal was composed, it was also as close as it was possible to be – as close as an itch. If the experience of the body can be lifted up into discourse and knowledge, then the process can occur in the oppos-ite direction as well. One of the reasons that the parasitological theory of the origins of itch took so long to be verified, or had to be verified over and over again, was the inveterate attractiveness of the idea of the fecundity of itch, and the belief that worms, ticks, lice and the like were bred from itch and its associated corruptions by spontaneous generation, rather than causing them.

Itch may be thought of as the tenacious residue or sinking back on to the body and its sense of itself of a conviction of the link between corruption and generation, and between impulse and the dissolution of entirety. Itch represents the continuing unconscious and affective life of the doctrine of spontaneous generation. That itch does not comprehend itself, that it reaches out into other forms of impulsive or irresistible reaching out, seems an appropriate enough redoubling. If the experience of itch is an experience of displacement, of the dislocation of an organism from itself, then the displacement of bodily itch into other less obviously corporeal impulses and affections is the form of itch's continuity in discontinuity. The impulses that get categorized as itches – the itch for fame, money, knowledge – are as self-generating and self-sustaining as Aristotle believed lice to be. They come from and feed on themselves, arising from no need of the organism they impel. It is almost as though itch were the affective form of the idea of infection; the way that infection makes itself felt, the skin's way of knowing it.

One of the more powerful counters to the idea of spontaneous generation was that of *emboîtement*, or encapsulated preformation. This doctrine, which had its origin in the work of Augustine, proposed that seeds or eggs contained a miniaturized form of the creatures that would develop from them. When a creature was born and developed, this theory suggested, it was nothing more than the enlargement and unfolding of a creature already contained in miniature form inside the egg. Of course, this must mean that the egg must also contain miniature forms of the eggs carried in the body of the creature from which its children will be born, and inside those, the eggs of successive generations. Time in this conception is inner, rather than outer, and grows from its middle rather than from its edges, from the kernel rather than the rind. The living world, according to this conception, is an unfolding or outering of what was created as a infinite series of insides, in a biological anticipation of the Big Bang theory. The doctrine of spontaneous generation suggested by contrast that there could be radical newness in the world, and a newness that came, not from within, but from without, in a process of creation-on-creation, or 'epigenesis' from the merely fortuitous meeting or folding together of pre-existing elements. Creatures formed of spontaneous generation were, as it were, creatures entirely of the surface; they bred in particular on the skin, because they were nothing but the accidental outside of matter: they were a birth from the surface, or extrusion from the surface of things rather than as the opening out or unfolding of an inner principle or potential. But this breeding from the skin also represented the dissolution of the skin, or a conception of the skin as incapable of maintaining distinctions between the inner and the outer, the self and the other. It would suggest to Cyrano de Bergerac in his *L'Autre monde* of 1656–61 the idea of the whole of human flesh and blood as a swarming, formless skin or *tissure* of other existences.[34] If the microscope had done much to suggest the regularity of living process even beyond the domain of the visible, it also, as Caroline Wilson has suggested, 'takes away the privilege of the surface', since what is inside or beneath the surface bears no structural relationship to how it looks on the outside.[35] The more closely one looked at the skin, in particular, the more internally complex, dynamic and densely populated it seemed. The discovery of the amazing freshwater hydra (or polyp) by Abraham Trembley in 1740 seemed to literalize this new notion of the skin's powers to symbolize the powers of generation and regeneration over the constraints of inner-originating form. Trembley discovered that it was possible to cut this polyp in two, or three, and generate new animals from each of the severed portions. The animal appeared (at first, mistaken, sight) to have no mouth or internal organs and seemed to be capable of extraordinary stretchings and contractions.[36] Charles Bonnet, who originated the term *emboîtement* to describe the theory of encapsulated preformation, wrote in amazement to his friend Gabriel Cramer in 1742:

> Oh sir, pray tell me, what can this be? An animal which can be propagated by cuttings, an animal whose young issue from its body as a branch issues from a stem, and on top of everything, an animal which one can do nothing less than turn inside out like a glove or a stocking, yet it continues to live, to eat and to reproduce. These are the marvels, the prodigies we owe to M. Trembley.[37]

ORDERS OF MAGNITUDE

Always at work in the sensuous and experimental apprehension of itch was the pressure of number. Those who saw spontaneous generation were seeing the numberless or innumerable multitude of tiny things; they were encountering the limits of their capacity to distinguish items with the eye. Although the microscope played a large part in the argument against doctrines of spontaneous generation, for example by revealing the eggs and reproductive organs of tiny creatures, it was also capable of encouraging the spontaneous reversion to spontaneism, as experimenters looked into drops of rainwater and saw them teeming with uncountable and unaccountable animalcules and infusoria. When the eye met its limit, an imaginary skin seemed to take over the function of registering the delight, disgust or horror, a skin that both formed a screen or surface on which this teeming could be projected, and was itself dissolved into a pure teeming. The microscope accelerated the demonstration that the skin itself was not a simple surface or covering, but had thickness and complex interiority.

But, as both magnification and techniques for the preparation of specimens improved during the seventeenth century, it proved increasingly possible to examine individual examples of these creatures. Books such as Robert Hooke's *Micrographia* (though Hooke himself assumed the spontaneous generation of insects) focused on individual specimens of organisms, engraved with extraordinary detail. This examination revealed a number of things. First of all, it showed the staggering intricacy of these 'living atoms', including and especially the complexity of their inner organs (many of them being conveniently transparent). Secondly it confirmed observations such as those of Bonomo that small insects reproduced, whether by oviparous (in the case of mites) or viviparous (in the case of lice) means. Both of these demonstrations tended to discountenance the prejudice that organisms produced by spontaneous generation were of no fixed form, or tended to be of monstrous or imperfect form, by showing that, even at the microscopic level, the rules of reproduction and the preservation of the autonomy of different species applied. Nothing came from nowhere and there was sameness and regularity throughout this teeming multi-plicity of the microscopic world. The examination of individual specimens went along with efforts to calculate more and more precisely their scale. The calibration of number, and the growing focus on the representative individual of a species took the place of the itchy apprehension of the numberless and the measureless.

The sensation of swarming, in what one can call the entomological apprehension of the skin, is closely related to questions of scale and magnitude. The attention of mathematicians like Leibniz was drawn to the doctrine of encapsulated preformation because of the ticklish problems of infinite divisibility it raised. Physicians in the early modern period sought to describe and predict the patterns of multiplication and iterative transmission of infections on and across the individual body, as well as the patterns of transmission between bodies in populations, and their interactions with populations of nonhuman organisms. But this intimation of the infinitesimally large or small found expression in actual human bodies, and, in particular, on the skin. The skin offered a specialized form of the bodily apprehension – through itch, prurience and the other modes of horror – of swarming and the mutative interchange of lives.

Skin diseases involving itch were known and accurately described by classical physicians. But the skin could not appear as a viable and visible subject in its own right, rather than as the expression of other kinds of disturbance of the body's complexion, until the development of lenses at the end of the fifteenth century and of the microscope during the seventeenth and eighteenth centuries. The skin was the first and the defining arena of microbiology, though not just because the skin was often the first object to be examined. Unlike any other organ, the skin allowed the exploration of the invisibly tiny. The workings of the skin, the very visibility of the body, were revealed by the new optics to be invisible to the naked eye. Medicine had long relied upon hypotheses about the agency of principles that it was impossible to see; but microbiology opened up a new kind of invisibility – not the invisibility of spiritual orders and influences, but the invisibility of what we may as well call the *minifold*: the multitudinous tiny. If it was the eye that measured the immeasurability and ungraspability of nature in theories of the sublime, it was the skin that first registered the tiny ticklings, bitings and swarmings of the miniature sublime presented to the entomological apprehension.

Large and small interpenetrate in the history of conflict too, in which skin complaints have often been very influential factors. The institutionalization of mass warfare was also a gift to the student of skin diseases, since skin diseases flourish under the conditions of mass concentration, poor hygiene and systematic deprivation that were increasingly characteristic of warfare. (Napoleon was one of the most famous sufferers from scabies.)[38] Michel Serres has suggested that, in every battle, every warlike encounter, there are not two but four participants: the antagonists, the cause over which they are fighting, which provides its stabilizing context or 'channel', and the sluggish or stagnant weight of the noise, or interference that impedes and diffuses the struggle. Both antagonists struggle to maintain the integrity and the possibility of the struggle against the remorseless entropic force of fatigue, demoralization, hunger, disease, rumour (trench whispers) and broken communications. Serres emblematizes this struggle in the Goya painting of the two giants who toil against each other while they sink slowly into the mud.[39] It is a desperate affair, this struggle between war and noise; in the end, the noise, the mud, the snow, the lice, will always win, since in the end war itself will have to surrender, exhausted. Serres has characterized this noise as 'parasitic'; and the case of the itch-mite which has been so intimately involved with military matters is a narrowing into literalness of Serres' metaphor.[40] The itch and its progenitors are the symptoms and beneficiaries of war, even as they are its adversaries. In 1634, Thomas Moffett's description of the operations of the 'wheal-worms' led him to warn 'let proud despicable mankinde learn, that they are not only worms but worms-meat; and let us fear the power of that great God, who can with so contemptible an army confound all pride, haughtiness, daintiness, and beauty, and conquer the greatest enemy.'[41] As the dermatological historian Reuben Friedman has remarked: 'It may be said of the itch-mite that ever since wars began, its role always has been that of a voraciously belligerent neutral, getting under the skin of and making life miserable for the soldiers of both sides, with fine impartiality.'[42]

The intimate participation of *sarcoptis scabiei* in the massing of men's bodies for military purposes is a representative example of the commingling of the minute and the multitudinous, the inconsiderable and the massive, that has come to characterize the modern world, and slowly, latterly, its science. As Michel Serres has argued, parasitism works both to restore and strengthen equilibrium through almost negligible adjustments of the host organism and to bring about huge effects in human life and history:

A small difference and a return to a reinforced stability; a small difference, and there is unbelievable multiplication and uncountable destruction. Plague and flood. Endemic and epidemic diseases; variations of virulence, always small causes for either almost inexistent or immense effects, on the left or on the right. The third that is excluded, when such logics are excluded, is quite simply, history.

It multiplies wildly with its smallness; it occupies space with its imperceptibility.[43]

If it seems inevitable according to one theory of scientific emergence and the growth of knowledge that the itch-mite should at last have come to light, the fact that it needed to come to light many times before it could be seen is testimony to the difficulty of acknowledging and accounting for the small and invisibly multitudinous. In one sense, this is a problem of optics; it was difficult to get close enough to the itch-mite to be able to make it out. But this is contradicted by the fact that so many had seen *sarcoptis scabiei* with their own eyes, perhaps with the casual assistance of the lenses that had been available since the late Middle Ages, or the flea-mirrors which Descartes reports were in common use in the mid-seventeenth century. Perhaps it is because the itch-mite, like itch itself, is on a borderline between visibility and invisibility, or marks the (always mobile) limits of the visible. Telling the story of the beginnings of miscoscopical investigation, Charles Singer observes that

> The itch-mite is frequently mentioned by early writers as illustrating the extreme complexity of minute nature and as representing the smallest possible living form, indivisible in its minuteness and a veritable 'living atom', a term often applied to these minute organisms by sixteenth and seventeenth-century writers. It is interesting in this connexion to observe that the word 'mite' is probably derived from a Gothic root *mei*, to cut or divide; thus the words mite and atom, which in the seventeenth century were interchangeable, have really a similar connotation. Both words imply a fragment of matter so far broken up that its further division is impossible.[44]

It seems to have been this reputation as the smallest possible unit that gave the itch-mite its homeopathic power. In his *History and Adventures of an Atom* (1769) Tobias Smollett describes just this power of inflicting itch. The story is a satirical recasting of contemporary British politics during what the fictional publisher's address to the reader describes as 'ticklish times', as an account of a Japanese empire of a thousand years previously.[45] The Rabelaisian satire of British political life is driven by a Pythagorean conception of the incessant passage not only of atoms, but of souls and spiritual qualities from body to body. The first-person narrator is an atom, endowed with the capacity of reason and speech, which is currently lodged fortuitously in the pineal gland of Nathaniel Peacock, but has himself formed part of and moved between the bodies of the characters in his story. At the beginning of his adventures, he is lodged in the big toe of the Emperor Got-hama-baba (George II), which is employed daily in the ceremonial office of kicking the breech of his prime minister Fika-kika (the Duke of Newcastle, and prime minister for much of George II's reign). Fika-kika himself suffers from an 'itching of the podex', or arse, caused, as Nathaniel's tutelary atom explains, by 'the juxta position of two atoms quarrelling for precedency, in this the Cuboy's seat of honour. Their pressing and squeezing and elbowing and jostling, tho' of no effect in discomposing one another, occasioned all this irritation and titillation in the posteriors of Fika-kika.'[46] One day a particularly violent kick causes the narrating atom to be dislodged from his position in the imperial toenail and to be propelled to a position between the two dissenting atoms, thus affording Fika-kika an orgasmic moment of relief, but also promoting in him a lubricious desire for the repetition of the pleasure of this 'pedestrian digitation', which he brings about by surrounding himself with bearded sycophants who are employed to apply their deliciously bristling faces to the daily kissing of his arse. The fidgeting indecisiveness of Fika-kika is ascribed to this permanent condition of semi-arousal.[47] Smollett takes pleasure in showing that the large and abstract realm of political life is merely amplification and exemplification of the minute.

WHAT TIME IS IT?

The question of scale that makes itch an intrigue of the visible relates to another problem of visibility, the problem of registering and rendering historical passage. How is one to tell the story of itch in history, in a way that does not simply tell it off as a gradual passage of a tormenting but misunderstood bodily phenomenon into a form of understanding? Although it is possible to tell the story of the discovery and adjustment to the entomological apprehension, its bringing to consciousness and understanding, in a way that accords with traditional sorts of intellectual history – whether progressive, as in liberal histories of science and medicine, or epochist, as in the equally positivist Foucauldian way of reading history that claims to displace it – there is something about this history which suggests the inadequacy of these fundamentally Euclidean ways of modelling the movements of history, the monotony of all those topologies of boundary, territory, inside and outside. Although parasites have their highly recognizable effects on individual human bodies, it was obscurely recognized that they would require something like an epidemiological awareness, which would be able to take account of multiplicities and patterns. Is there a way of telling this story, imagining being able to tell it, which would preserve the entomological apprehension of its coming-and-going becoming, resisting the desire to explain history as an unfolding sequence of explanations: an itchy history?

Perhaps the itch-mite, the 'gentle stranger', as it was known, was too close, too much the familiar and accomplice of our days. As a result, it does not belong to our history of growth and lineages and irreversible, once-and-for-all emergences, or not only to it. In folklore, itch has marked associations with nonlinear temporality, often being regarded as premonitory. The pricking of the thumbs in *Macbeth* signifies the approach of wickedness. When we shiver with the apprehension of what is described as 'somebody walking over our grave', it is to anticipate in our living bodies the dissolute condition in which we will be able to be walked over by ant, maggot and man alike. The tingling or the burning of the ears is still associated with an apprehension that one is being talked about, in the kind of long-range hearing with the skin that I evoked earlier in this chapter. Itching in other places was often taken as a happier augury. A robber in D'Urfey's *The Banditti* (1686) says of an approaching victim, 'Methinks I have him in my Clutches already, the palm of my hand itches; we shall have good luck to day.'[48] A character in the same dramatist's *The Rise and Fall of Massaniello* sees another itch as anticipating a rise in his social fortunes: 'the Crown of my Head has itch'd damnably of late, a certain Sign of aproaching Dignity.'[49] In such tickling, tingling premonitions, it is as though the homogeneous fabric of time were folded over or pleated up in the skin.

As I suggested in chapter 1, the time of the skin and its epiphenomenal tingles and titillations is like the time of the weather; a matter of quantities, of the swarming life of numbers, and epidemics, which are always changing, but changing into themselves, always on the surface, but a surface that is folded into knots, tori and chasms. Although the history of itch does suggest links to different local contexts and determining circumstances (the new perceptual order opened up by the microscope, the growth of parasitological understanding, changing protocols of bodily deportment, the geopolitics and gendering of insult and disgust), telling the story of itch from the viewpoint of these things will probably only ever tell us what we already abundantly think we know. Itch seems never to rise to the status of historical event or subject, but to exist as a stubborn, low-grade, unshiftable, parasitic accompaniment to historical events, of which it is impossible to say for sure at any one time whether it is old or new, context or occurrence, a residual infection or a reinfection, whether, in other words, it really is of any one time in particular. Because it is so diffusely present, so intermittently continuous in human affairs, and because it is so biotrophic a phenomenon, that cannot live or reproduce without its host, itch never comes into focus and has no obviously large-scale and determinate effects. Because itch is everywhere, it is everywhere and at every moment being linked up differently to different things; it does not even exhibit the continuous temporal contour of diseases like typhus or leprosy, or epilepsy, the stories of which it has latterly proved possible to tell in terms somewhat other than the traditional ones of 'The Battle Against . . .' (As we have seen battling is itself what itch and associated parasitic conditions are mostly against.)

This order of time and temporal change is not only more closely related to the weather than the kinds of history we construct which are indifferent to the mere comings and goings of rain and cold, fog and sun, wind and frost, it is also meteorological in its form. The history of the itch-mite, whose own history is the history largely of what it has been mistaken for, and therefore not even its own, belongs to a climate of multiplications and diminutions, epidemic flarings up and fallings back, insinuations and extirpations, and other seemingly irrational and undetermined fluctuations which nevertheless exhibit a kind of complex order, and in which the tiny and the large are strangely looped into each other, a climate that modern mathematics has been trying for some time to understand. The Euclidean history which depends so much on the line or the plane cannot see the topologies or strangely looped and inclensive life-cycles and life-stories that biomathematics now invites us to think of and imagine with. Michel Serres' twenty-year-old lament still applies: 'In the human sciences, at least, the old mechanical model still dominates, even among those whose discourse talks of rejecting it.'[50] This order, the order of variable and intercommunicating intensities rather than simple causative extensions, is the order of the French *temps* which allows one to ask what time it is in asking what the weather is like. It is currently as complex and refractory to our understanding as the weather, which we can still only predict for a matter of a week at most, largely because of the ungraspably complex relations between tiny, iterative fluctuations and large resultant effects. But we have our part in this time, nevertheless, as it takes part in us. Can we take the measure, the temperature, of this epidermal time, as it rises and falls, gathers and recedes, between the endemic and the epidemic, going everywhere without ever getting anywhere, living itself out through what we take to have been our time?

10 The Light Touch

'"A light touch" – but "a heavy hand". Is that because touch cannot by defini-tion be heavy. But then is not "a light touch" a tautology?'[1] Gabriel Josipovici's speculation is the hint for the concluding investigation this chapter conducts into lightness of touch.

This book has described a course that runs from the skin's duress towards the many kinds of finesse that are associated with the skin. The skin is subjected both to immoderate assault and to exacting regimes of care. Because we perhaps fear the loss of what Heidegger saw as the relation of care towards the world in a world of distant and abstract commodities, there seem to be energetic attempts to recuperate these relations among advertisers and marketers. Nowhere is this more paradoxical than in cleaning agents, whether they are detergents, or the multifarious forms of tissue with which the world is thronged. There is, for example, the Persil website, which glories in the subtitle 'For Love, Life and Laundry'.[2] A surprisingly large proportion of the site is devoted to the care and protection of the skin. A team of dermatologists has been recruited to offer advice about eczema and blackheads. These are no anonymous boffins: they are all visible, all female, and all themselves appear to have perfect skin. Like the products they are endorsing, seemingly, experts must be both strong and soft, fortepiano. The site is divided into two parts: 'Time In' ('because clothes can't look after themselves') and 'Time Out' ('because there's more to life than laundry'). The Time Out section is divided into 'Time With Your Kids', which contains tips on what to do with your children (in the gaps between looking after their clothes), and 'Time For Yourself'. It is quite clear what Persil believes you should do when you are not caring for your children, because your time for yourself is to be lavished on your skin, that other problem child. The 'Time Out' section yields three further links, headed 'Healthy Skin', 'Relaxation' and 'Healthy Diet'. The 'Healthy Skin' click takes you to a section that offers to help you 'listen to your skin': 'You can hear . . . but are you listening? Your skin is talk-ing to you non-stop – why not make it a two-way exchange! Your inner voice has a few opinions, too – how do you tune into those?'. Your nattering skin turns out

Lisa Deanne Smith, *itch (Frog)*, 1997, dermographic drawing.

to be adept at dropping hints about the dangerous harshness of scrubs, exfoliants and other products, as well as advising consumers to look out for the kind of helpful, healing ingredients that no doubt abound in Proctor and Gamble products. There are also Instant Skin Tips. The page with which you are served when you click as I did on '45 and over' is candidly headed 'Problem Skin', and its menu reads like a bizarre dermatological weather forecast for the less-than-roaring forties: 'Dry and Tight; Flaky in Parts; Oily; Lumpy and Bumpy' and, most alarmingly, 'Dry in some areas, Oily in others'. There are plenty of emollients and unguents on offer for this group, though the bottom line comes elsewhere in the site with a sort of shrug: 'Sleep is vital at this stage in life'. The skin is there even in the page on Relaxation, which advises retreat to a quiet room and repetition of a mantra 'repeated over and over, so that it gradually replaces the many jangled and disconnected thoughts, which are darting through our busy minds'. The advice is plainly to surround yourself in the smooth entirety of the acoustic envelope defined by Didier Anzieu. You are not to think of it as wasted time. You must think of it instead as 'a precious few moments in each day when all that you are concerned with is yourself. And of course, that insistent little voice within . . .' And what is the voice saying? It is nagging you with bulletins from cosmetic dermatologists about alcohol overconsumption, smoking and eating cheesecake. Click on 'Healthy Diet', and you are taken to a page called, what else, 'Feed Your Skin'. Now this is full of wonders for the observer of delicacy. For, as we are about to see, delicacy concerns that which is and is not touched, and more specifically that which is not consumed. 'Some of the foods we buy are so healthy, it's almost a pity to eat them.' Instead, put them on your face: lemon, olive oil, avocado, oats. The section offers 'one word of warning' (as it must, in order to be properly strong and soft): 'these natural beauty recipes are only effective when completely fresh. You must never try to store homemade preparations, since these contain no preservatives. The trick is to make them and then use them up at once – while they're still almost good enough to eat!'

Lisa Deanne Smith,
*itch (Tea Roses
in Bowl')*, 1997,
dermographic
drawing.

The extraordinary thing about this opulent, unsolicited address is that it should have so little to do with cleaning clothes, and so much to do with the urgent pleasure, the pleasant urgency, of caring for the skin. Who could not care about this care? Don't care, it seems, must be made to care. What it seems to want, what we seem to want to be confirmed in by it, is the delight of care, two words that, shunted together, might deliver the keyword for what follows: delicacy.

I have tried to show in this book that the awareness of the skin is a matter not just of forms, ideas and conceptions of the skin, but also of the work of sensations in cultural forms. The sensation of delicacy is perhaps the most pervasive of the ways in which touch informs and inflects thinking, values, ideals and attitudes. The values of tact, 'touch', subtlety, refinement and so on, all depend upon and ramify from the thought of the sensation of its particular kind of lightness of touch. I looked in the last chapter at the powers of itch, shudder and horror. One might at first think that delicacy was the opposite of these rougher types of handling and stronger kinds of response, but in fact they are parallel, lightness of touch being implicated in both. The fact that 'delicacy' is often used as a synonym for 'sensitivity' is evidence of the traditional propensity to see touch as the substrate or shared medium of all the senses.

What I offer here is one way of taking seriously Deleuze and Guattari's suggestion that it is possible to make out and even make something of 'blocs of sensation', such a bloc being defined as '*a compound of percepts and affects*'. Percepts and affects, forms of seeing and feeling, 'are independent of a state of those who experience them . . . go beyond the strength of those who undergo them'.[3] Although it seems to me that Deleuze and Guattari become frankly mythical when they say that 'Sensations, percepts and affects are beings, whose validity lies in themselves and exceeds any lived',[4] as well as in assuming that art offers a privileged way of preserving such affects, they may help to identify a mythical impulse within the history of affects and sensations. Though there is in the Western pantheon no god of itch, or goddess of delicacy, there is at least one example of a god who has become identified so closely with a sensation as to have given it his name: panic. I will go far enough in taking Deleuze and Guattari seriously as to try allowing that delicacy is not just adjectival but also substantial, not just a predicate but a form, a kind of being, with a sort of history and a power not only to persist but also to organize things in its image, or taking its print.

I mean by delicacy a certain touch that is not quite a touch, a touch that does not take hold, that holds back. I mean the lightness of touch that we intuitively identify with touch as such. There is a disorientation in this touch, which is partly a disorientation of touch itself. Why should the most characteristic form of a sense be the form in which it dims and diminishes, rather than prolongs and perfects itself? Sight is not sight unless it is lucid, nor hearing properly itself unless it is sound as a bell (however, taste and smell also thrive on marginality and the minimal, on hints and wafts). The diminishment in question may be glossed by Derrida's discussions of the possibility or difficulty of diminishing dissimulation at the beginning of *Veils*, his antiphonic text written with Hélène Cixous. At the end of a lifetime which, as it seems to him, he has spent discussing veils, he would like to find a way of hitting on the thing itself, the truth revealed. To do this requires, not an undoing but a mysterious kind of 'diminution' that he remembers hearing of from the women weavers of his family: 'Interminable diminution . . . Diminish the infinite, diminish *ad infinitum*, why not?'. This reduction or narrowing down will take the form of a reflection on the delicate but undiminishable touch of various kinds of fabric, the veil of the temple, the veilings enjoined by St Paul, the veiling mist of Cixous' myopia, the fringes of his own tallith, inherited from his father. And yet, 'finishing with the veil will always have been the very movement of the veil: un-veiling, unveiling oneself, reaffirming the veil in unveiling. It finishes with itself in unveiling, does the veil.'5

SURFACE TENSION

Lay your palm flat on a surface. Now close your eyes and, as slowly as you can, lift your palm away, so that the sense of pressure becomes concentrated on the base of the thumb, the balls at the bottom of the fingers. Keep slowly withdrawing the pressure, until you are touching the surface only with the pads of your four fingers and the outward edge of your thumb. You can do this with a photocopier, which by photographing only what is pressed against its surface, can act as a sort of tactile camera. First photograph the whole hand; then patches of it, then the fingertips alone, then the ridges of the fingerprints, the rest of the hand receding into ghostliness.

You may be able to find the point of equilibrium at which the pressure imparted by your fingertips is answered exactly by the pressure of the surface upon which it rests. Just at the point before the fingers detach from the surface, it will not be certain whether they have in fact detached. A sort of restraining second skin will seem to have arisen between fingers and world, like the pianist's finger that coaxes the most subtle withdrawing sound, not by depressing the

Brooke Davis, *Peel II*, 2002, polaroid emulsion transfer.

key, but by lifting the finger away from it. This skin will apprehend, not sensation, but its trace, or the merest thought of that trace. At this point, if the mind can mute the cacophony of other sensations which ordinarily compete with and complete the sense of touch, we may seem to be able to sense, not the object of sensation, but our sensing itself, which we ordinarily see or feel straight through. Practice will allow us to identify what seems to be the exact point at which sensation interposes itself between contact and non-contact, as a glaze or patina, which is indeed so fine and so intangible that it is not certain whether it is being felt or remembered. This is the paradox about this interface; there is an exact point, neither in contact nor out of contact, at which exactitude becomes impossible, because it is not possible to distinguish the actuality of touch from its phantasm or aura, nor to detach the thought of the touch, or the image of the touch impressed on our thought, from the touch itself. The quality of this touch will be like a breath, indeed, the magnification of the quivering of the fingers caused by the intake of breath will need to be controlled in order to keep this imaginary skin intact; experiment will show you what is already known to archers, snipers and threaders of needles, that the fingers are steadier on the out-breath. (In fact, the fingers cannot be entirely motionless, for in this condition, they feel nothing. There needs to be a minimal level of tremor to ensure the continued friction that gives sensation of touch and texture.) It does not seem possible to evoke the same sensation when bringing fingers toward their object. The minimal stickiness, the detention of the skin in its touching, seems only to be achievable in the action of withdrawing the touch, withdrawing from touch.

The principle on which this all depends seems to be that which has risen to the surface in different ways throughout this book, of the unbroken continuity between things and thinking; the idea, in contradiction to our most fundamental philosophical principles, that things and the way we think of them, are woven of the same stuff. The little boy who strips away the *folie de grandeur* of the Emperor in his non-existent New Clothes is usually assumed to be the hero of the fable. But the nakedness which is all he can see with his naively naked eye asserts a simple distinction between the naked and the clothed which coarsens the finer and maturer apprehension that there might be fabrics too finely woven for our sensory apprehension, fabrics in which the work of the hand would shade off into the work of thought. At the point at which the subtlety of this body comes close to its absolute limit, thought must take over from the senses. But, just at this impalpable limit, just as the equilibrium of thought and sense begins to over-balance, and thought takes over from sense, the thought of the limit suddenly becomes palpable to itself as a kind of fold or crease of touch within the thought. When every layer has melted away in the X-ray gaze of thought, there is always a last, infinitesimal film of tact, a surface tension in the mind to which thought has recourse, to veil things in the thought of them, to protect things from their nakedness before thought. There is thought and there are things; and there is also the milieu, the mid-place, in which they encounter each other.

As we have seen in discussions of the simulacrum and of aroma, the idea of the perfect, self-sustaining skin is always retained in ideas of subtlety or ideal tenuity. For tenuity, tendency, tenderness and tension all derive from a Greek root τείνειν (teinein), meaning stretch or draw out, with a paradoxical relation to words radiating out from tenire, which signify transformations of touching or holding: content, intention, attention. The word 'subtle' is from Latin subtelis, signifying either an underweb or that which lies beneath a web, and so perhaps signifies something woven with extreme fineness. The subtle is on the boundary between materiality and thought: the subtle is the thought of a substance too tenuous and rarefied for the actual senses, that requires a subtle, or virtual body to apprehend it. Subtlety of action, or strategy, or thought, involves the capacity to discriminate between layers, to thin one's thinking to the point where it can be insinuated into a reality that is already finer than fine.

HOLDING BACK

We are accustomed to distinguishing between sensation and thought, but this delicacy consists of the fragile interfusion of sense and thinking, even as delic-acy feels as though it consisted of the tiniest holding back from touch. Names for this class of sensation – subtlety, tenderness, delicacy, grace, refinement, tact – retain different aspects of this ambivalent intangibility. In all of them, there appears to be the thought of the sensation that holds back, or restrains itself, the tact of a tactility that retracts itself, but not fully, just enough to invent this infinitesimal meniscus between touching and non-touching. The daintiness of lace, the fineness of tissue-paper, speak to us of their own skin-like weakness, of the thinness of the skin which arises between them and our imaginary (never quite imaginary) touch. Delicate and subtle things have a life of their own, and call, not for grasping or prodding or palpation, but for caress.

In the caress, a further element is added to the milieu opened up by the retreating touch, for in the caress, there is an approach or address to another skin capable of sensation, capable of its own experience of the borderline

Cheryl Casteen,
'Safe Stretch', 2003,
photo lightbox.

between thought and feeling. To caress an object in the world is to treat it as though it possessed such a sensitive skin.

For touch is unlike the other senses in this, that it acts upon the world as well as registering the action of the world on you. When you touch something, your touch may result in the sensation of its touch on you, but need not. I can, after all, touch somebody or something with gloves on, or with my skin anaesthetized, so that I do not feel their answering touch. Although looking is to seeing, and listening is to hearing as active touching is to passive being-touched, it is hard to imagine looking without seeing, or listening without hearing in the same way. The distinguishability of touching and being touched results from the fact that touching is an action in a way that looking and listening are not. Although looking can be thought of as an invasive action, it is surely significant that the sense of invasion is often if not usually expressed by the victim in terms of touch or contact: I felt

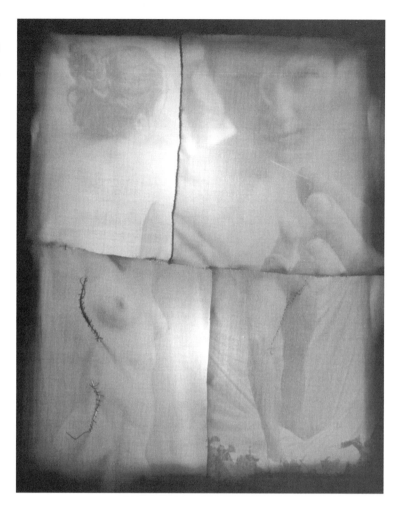

Tamara Sadlo,
'Stitches & Scars:
I don't know why, but I
know why not', 2002,
photo emulsion, linen,
lightbox and thread.

her eyes roving over me; his gaze bored into me. The very fact that touching forms a continuum with grasping and all the other modes of manipulation and that every touch exists within the horizon of the grasp, the wrench, the twist, the buffet, makes for the special kind of poignancy that attaches to the blow that is undelivered, the grasp that is not one. In rendering something ready-to-hand, in using it as a tool, I may seem to take it into myself, make it part of my substance, my repertoire of possibilities. Delicacy, by contrast, prescribes a touch that is not quite one, a touch that refrains from the vulgarity of grasping or handling.

Even though delicacy always involves a reflexive relation between the act of touching and that which is touched, delicacy is also embodied in objects, or not-quite-objects. Like many designations of tactile quality, delicacy shimmers between the object touched and the touch itself. That which is delicate calls for delicate handling: a delicate matter, a ticklish situation, around which one may tiptoe. What characterizes the delicate object? Delicate objects tend to reproduce in themselves the presence and absence which is part of the experience of delicate touch. Perhaps the representative delicate substance is lace, the characteristic of which is that it is full of holes; one of the earliest techniques of lacemaking is known as 'punto in aria', meaning 'a stitch in air'. The idea of mixture is involved in every text or textile, a word that refers to woven fabrics. But a network includes a third element, namely vacancy itself. A network is made up largely of what it is not. The fineness of the network is at work in many other kinds of delicate substance or structure.

Delicacy and tactile subtlety both partake in and amplify the perversely feeble power of the tip, the fringe, the edge, the hem, a power that goes beyond being a symbolic space in which to negotiate 'anxieties about actual and symbolic limits, borders and boundaries', as Elaine Reedgood has suggested in a recent article on Victorian fringes.[6] Delicacy belongs to that which trails, hangs or floats. Perhaps the most important of the tips in the body are the fingertips, but they communicate with the tip of the tongue and tiptoes, to suggest reach and the delicacy of that which is almost touched, touched and not touched at once. We have met powerful edges in myth and religion through this book. Athena is the opposite of the Gorgon whose head she nevertheless wears in or on her aegis. Where the Gorgon is all swarming edginess, repulsive because she draws the viewer in, Athena is all containment, greaved and cuirassed, repelling all borders. But the aegis that Athena wears is fringed by the snakes that are a reminder of the Gorgon's hair. Christ's healing similarly issued out from his hem. It is as though the power, itself imaged as a sort of issue, were thought of as most concentrated, not in the middle, but at the edge.

The French word for lace, *dentelle*, arose from just this attention to the edge. The usual word for lace in France during most of the sixteenth century was 'passement', and the term 'passement dentelé' was used to designate the typical pointed or toothed edge that was so popular for collars and cuffs: by the late sixteenth century 'dentelle' had come to designate any kind of lace.[7] Lace itself evolved from a technique known as 'cutwork', which involved the fraying of a fabric at the edges by removal of threads and the building up of designs by button-stitch. The development in Italy of the elaborate form of cutwork embroidery known as 'reticella' led to the discovery that it was possible to make patterns with a needle without using any foundation.

The delicate is modest, moderate, tempered. But the taste for the delicate can also become excessive. During the heyday of lace, during the seventeenth century, lace gained a reputation for being at once subtle and sumptuous. Certain kinds of subtlety became gross or coarse, hence, perhaps, in its degraded survival, the association of lace with pornography or the tackily erotic.

SCALES

Delicacy often suggests that which approaches the edge of the sensation of touch itself, often because the details of what are touched are too small to be apprehended by the skin, even the sensitive skin of the fingertips, unaided.

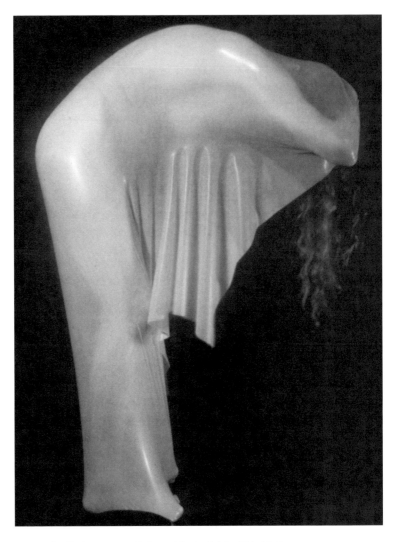

Cheryl Casteen 'Classical Latex', 2003, photo lightbox.

The baffled narrator of Flann O'Brien's *The Third Policeman* encounters an honest descendant of the rascally tailors of 'The Emperor's New Clothes'. The mysterious Policeman MacCruiskeen is an engineer of the intangible. He first shows him a spear with a point which is so fine it is invisible, yet capable never-theless of pricking his skin. His next artefact is an elaborately decorated box, containing 22 other boxes, which decline in size as they approach and then pass beyond invisibility into thought:

> 'Number Twenty-Two,' he said, 'I manufactured fifteen years ago and I have made another different one every year since with any amount of night-work and overtime and piecework and time-and-a-half incidentally.'
> 'I understand you clearly.' I said.

'Six years ago they began to get invisible, glass or no glass. Nobody has ever seen the last five I made because no glass is strong enough to make them big enough to be regarded truly as the smallest things ever made. Nobody can see me making them because my little tools are invisible into the same bargain. The one I am making now is nearly as small as nothing. Number One would hold a million of them at the same time and there would be room left over for a pair of woman's horse-breeches if they were rolled up. The dear knows where it will stop and terminate.'

'Such work must be hard on the eyes,' I said, determined to pretend that everybody was an ordinary person like myself.[8]

The idea of the skin seems itself to have shrunk down almost to nothing, though this is the end of a process of serial diminution from touch to sight to thought. The third box in the sequence is still apprehensible with the hand:

I went over to it and gave it a close examination with my hand, feeling the same identical wrinkles, the same proportions and the same completely perfect brasswork on a smaller scale. It was all so faultless and delightful that it reminded me forcibly, strange and foolish as it may seem, of something I did not understand and had never even heard of.[9]

Encountering the thought of this infinite littleness produces shrinkage in the one who contemplates it, a tightening, a pulling back and looking away, as though to reassert the membrane between possible and impossible things. It is wrinkling, the miniature perturbation of the surface, which asserts the persistence of a surface through the descriptions in this passage:

All my senses were now strained so tensely watching the policeman's movements that I could almost hear my brain rattling in my head when I gave a shake as if it was drying up into a wrinkled pea . . . He took two wrinkled cigarettes from his fob and lit the two at the same time and handed me one of them.[10]

If delicacy and subtlety involve the retreat or abstention of the hand, they never entirely surrender the idea of a material that has been worked into shape, by fingers or their surrogates: the gold leaf beaten with hammers, the hay spun into gold, the elf fingers sewing shoes, the fine striations of the engraver. Delicacy involves work on a scale that makes it a matter of the mind, work that approaches the condition of weightlessness. The aim is to produce a work that seems untouched by human hand, a hand shaped purely by the mind. The work involved in shaping such half-imaginary objects is a refined work, a work that refines the idea of work.

Lightness is one of the most important features of delicacy. But the lesson of Policeman MacCruiskeen's work is that delicacy also involves the apprehension of altered scale. In the early nineteenth century, E. H. Weber devised a method for measuring the sensitivity of different areas of the skin. This involved applying to the skin pairs of points, the distance between which could be varied. Where the skin was densely provided with receptors of touch, such as the lips and fingertips, the two points of the needles could still be clearly felt even when they were set closely together. In other areas, the points would have to be set further apart before they could be distinguished. The 'two-point threshold' determinable for different areas of the skin by means of this simple device allowed Weber to measure and map the variable sensitivity of different portions of the body.[11] Weber demonstrated the physiological basis for the principle that had been apparent in thinking about the question of sensitivity, namely that it involves variation in scale. Apprehended from the inside, the sensation of touching something intricate, tender or finely worked, seems to involve a bringing together of scales into consonance, a magnification or shrinking back of the body itself, as though to come up close were to grow larger. 'Body size', David Appelbaum has grandly affirmed, 'is an index of touch . . . no one body size fits the varying magnanimity with which we salute the world.'[12] The adjustment of the sense of bodily scale and sensitivity to which the microscope gave rise has been noted by Ann Jessie Van Sant, who draws a parallel between Smollett's Matthew Bramble, a man of excessive sensibility who is 'as tender as a man without a skin; who cannot bear the slightest touch without flinching', and Swift's Gulliver, exposed by dint of his shrunken size in Brobdignag to the skin in revolting close-up. 'Delicacy of the nervous system', Van Sant concludes, 'does for all the senses what the microscope does for vision.'[13]

Delicacy involves more than a simple adjustment of scale or focus, or the simple matching or homing in of the body's attention to its object. In objects and conditions we think of as delicate, there is either a movement of approach, as the relatively gross body moves in, or a movement of recession, as that body holds or moves back. This is to say that one is never quite in touch with something one touches delicately, or that seems to require such a delicate touch. There is always a balancing of the large and small.

Delicacy belongs to the nondualistic conception of the relations between mind and body argued, as we saw in chapter 4, by Gassendi and others in the seventeenth century, a conception of the universe as divided not between matter and form, but between different states of matter, conceived in a continuous scale rather than in terms of binary contrasts. At one end of the scale is gross, dense, dark matter. At the other end of the scale is fine or subtle matter, scarcely, it seems, to be apprehended by human senses tuned to the needs of our slow and gross existence, but nevertheless material in its nature. Delicacy comes about not at a certain point in the scale, as gross beings give way to delicate beings, but rather in the rucking or wrinkling of the scale of measurement itself, as a grosser sensibility meets with and minimally recoils from, a more refined object. This is perhaps why delicacy always involves the condition of tremulous adjustment, with the delicate point being the unstable meeting point of two alternatives.

There are two kinds of equilibrium, the first inert, the second dynamic. In the first kind of equilibrium, the two sides are completely and exactly balanced. The equality is stable, robust and unbudgeable. The scales stand still, locked in the exactitude of their equilibrium. This is the balance of masses found in a building supported by columns at its four corners. There is another kind of equilibrium, the kind signalled when we speak of a 'delicate balance', in which the equilibrium is unstable, inhabited and defined by tremor. This is the balance of equipoise, of the dancer *en pointe*, of the liquid that quivers on the point of boiling, or of crystallizing.

Delicacy always involves the thought of such a zone of tremulous delay, or complex equilibrium. A delicate question is one the outcome of which will be forced if one treats it too crudely or forcefully. Delicate negotiations are those in which competing pressures must be held in balance, without tipping over to favour the interests of one or another party.

It is the skin which is the index of the balance of a constitution. One's complexion is a mixture of internal propensities and external influences. Indeed, since one's internal propensities were held themselves to be a combination held in a delicate balance, one's skin is a mixture of mixtures.

In fact, the word 'scale' has in it a buried allusion to the epidermal. The scales on the surfaces of fish or snakes derive from the OE *-scealu* and Teutonic cognates like OHG *-scala*, and Danish and Swedish *-skal*, all words which mean a shell, skin or paring. The scale in which things are weighed is perhaps related to this in that it has the form of a dish or hollow shell, as in the Danish *-skaal*, which also yields the word 'skull', the brain-pan. Just as we measure the weight of things through the sense of pressure given by the skin, so shells are in requisition for the measurement of things relative to each other. The word 'test' has a similar etymology, for it derives from the skull- or head-shaped bowl or *teste* in which metals would be subject to the proving effects of fire in alchemy. In both testing and scaling, there is the lingering thought of a head that has been scooped out into a skin, or that which, itself weightless, weighs.

DELICATESSEN

One cannot understand the history of delicacy without thinking about the specific kind of eating and foodstuff designated by the word. Perhaps all everyday touch consumes what it touches; when we learn to grasp, we do it first of all in order to convey the objects to our mouths, which is to say, out of sight and out of mind. The delicacy is a food that solicits lingering contemplation – delicatessen, rather than rapid ingestion. The delicacy may have a subtle, evanescent, short-lived flavour, a savour that is like the desire or the aromatic ghost of a taste. A delicacy is something that resists eating, something that is too good, too fine for eating, and thus all the more delectable. There is delight behind both delicacy and delicatessen. The kiss involves the extremes of a fluttering touch light as breath (touching with the mouth without touch) and touch as greedy consumption.

Hunger and need swallow, consume, ravening the food in as a dog does, gulping it down without touching it ('without touching the sides' as one says of a first, thirsty swig), and as though to gobble up the very time taken to eat it. The socialization of eating induces delay, lingering, the savouring of the pleasure of consummation, which requires that consummation be put off in order to be intensified. The child who eventually learns that sucking a sweet gives more pleasure than the ecstasy of crunch and gulp is learning culture's great lesson of delayed gratification, that longer of less is better than shorter of more. Perhaps this is in fact a recalling of what the infant at the breast (or bottle), seems already to know, or be able quickly to teach itself, in spinning out delight in its dilatory, dabbling play with the nipple. We tell children not to play with their food, but the whole of the civility attached to eating is a kind of play with food: shaping it, circling it, keeping it at bay, finding it out by indirections.

The author of a nineteenth-century philological fantasy on the linguistic idea of the delectable notes that words like English 'smack', which signifies 'a sounding blow with the open hand, a loud kiss, and the taste of food' and German *Geschmack*, enact a smacking of the lips, a sort of transposition into tactile sound, or sonorous sensation, of the pleasure and desire of eating.[14] The fact that one smacks one's lips while eating, in order to prolong and amplify its pleasures, is presumably what leads to the use of sounds and words which recall or anticipate that pleasure in the absence of the food. I have no idea what merit might still attach, if any ever did, to Hensleigh Wedgwood's further suggestion that the family of Latin words *deliciae*, *delicatus* and *delectare* and *dulcis* derive from the Greek γλυκύς, 'sweet', a word which itself includes reference to the idea of licking, and yields words like English 'click' and French *claquer*, *claquer la langue*. He explains the 'de' sound at the beginning of the Latin words denoting the varieties of the delectable as a drawing out of the ugly sound *dl-* deriving from Greek *gl-* into the more congenial *del-* (slyly, Wedgwood describes the syllable as 'exploded by the Latin taste'[15]). Whatever its extravagance, there does seem a kind of neatness in making out the clicks and smacks of linguistic pleasure as the pleasure of licking made audible. Language allows, even arises in the kind of lingering and prolonging (Latin *ligurio*, to lick one's lips, long for) comprised in licking. The *OED* suggests that the word 'delicate' becomes associated in English with delight and the delicious. How miraculous were there also to be some link with the rare Latin word *delice*, which means weaned, or put away from the breast!

Understanding the history of delicacy requires us to recognize the long, close affinity between *delicatesse* and *delicatessen*. A sixteenth-century Italian treatise on politeness translated into English in 1774 identifies a number of indelicate behaviours which are an affront to social life, most of which involve the disturbance or ruffling of the smooth outside of the body, such as coughing, yawning, scratching, paring of nails, spitting or public emunction, adjustment of the dress and inelegant shuffling or waddling. The other infractions of which the treatise speaks, such as mockery of others and telling people your dreams at length, seem to be sublimated forms of the same disturbance of integrity. One of the problems for the culture of politeness is how to regulate itself with a lightness of touch commensurate with its own ideals. One example of how to do this is given in the story of a cavalier who, having dined with a bishop, is lent a servant by his host to accompany him on part of his journey. His mission is to explain, in the most delicate way possible, that the cavalier has an eating disorder:

[I]n one particular action of yours, there appeared some little imperfection: which is, that when you are eating at table, the motion of your lips and mouth causes an uncommon smacking kind of sound, which is rather offensive to those who have the honour to sit at table with you.[16]

The maintaining of the smooth and interrupted skin of social life is particularly under threat at times of eating, when the two principal functions of the mouth, taking in nourishment, and exchanging speech, may interfere with each other. The point of the story is to show how the indelicacy of the smacking lips may be, as we tellingly say, smoothed over by a speech which diffuses and distances it.

From the sixteenth to the eighteenth centuries the play between *delicatesse* and *delicatessen* can be seen embodied in the fortunes of the word 'cates', meaning victuals, fare or provender (it survives in modern English only in the word 'cater'), which became conventionally associated with the word 'delicate'. The word 'cates' is sometimes qualified with the twinning adjective 'delicate', though its more usual partner is the word 'dainty', as in the 'cates and dainties' set out in Keats's 'Eve of St Agnes'. Cates are often 'curious', as in the 'costly Cates and curious carowses, that Marke Anthony received of love-sicke Cleopatra for a welcome' spoken of in Robert Kittowe's *Love's Load-starre* (1600).[17] The word 'curious' is like the word 'delicate', in naming both the quality of an object and the quality of the apprehension of it. A delicate object requires careful handling, just as a curious object makes us inquisitive. The word 'cates' retains its association with ethereal food as late as 1861, in the evocation of a repast spread by a beautiful woman known as the 'Rose of Goshen' in Edward Atherstone's poem *Israel in Egypt*:

Refection elegant; rich fruits, and wine,
And cates, for lightness, that might snow-flakes seem,
And yet substantial. But so exquisite,
touched by her hands, were they,—that more like feast
Of mingled odours, breath of flowers, it seemed,
Than food material.[18]

However, the growing assumption that cates were particularly subtle and delicate forms of foodstuff created an irony: for as with the pleasure in fine fabrics, the desire to consume delicate food can itself come to seem anything but delicate, and can turn immoderate, gross and lustful. Although cates and delicacies are tiny and exquisite (titbits rather than more substantial or 'wholesome'), they are associated with gorging, sating and cloying of the palate, or with the attempt to refresh decadent appetites. The figure of 'Sensuality' in Thomas Nabbes's 'morall maske' *Microcosmus* (1637) calls for 'all th'Ambrosian cates,/Art can devise for wanton appetite'.[19] The dedication to James Mabbe's *Spanish Bawd* (1631) urges his friend Sir Thomas Richardson to 'take a little of this coorse and sowre bread; it may be, your stomack being glutted with more delicate Cates, may take some pleasure to restore your appetite with this homely, though not altogether unsavoury food.'[20] Edward Benlowes associates cates with the increased yield that comes from moderated appetite, in celebrating the habits of the just man who 'Scanted abroad, within dost feast,/Hast CHRIST Himself for Cates, The Holy GHOST for Guest'.[21] Joseph Beaumont has Eve tempt her partner to taste of the apple with these words:

> O wellcom wellcom, since I now have here
> A banquet fit to entertain my Dear.
> Soul-fatning Cates, seeds of *Divinity*,
> Edible Wisdom, and a mystic feast
> Of high Illuminations. Ask not why
> Our jealous *God* injoin'd us not to taste
> Of that whose most refining energy
> Would raise us to be Gods as well as He.[22]

By the eighteenth century, the pursuit of a balanced diet resulted in the suspicion of food that was either too gross or too airily insubstantial. Henry Baker's 1726 'Invocation of Health' begins with the blessings of the one who lives

> not in Palaces, where dainty Cates
> Are variously compounded, to stir up
> Cloy'd Appetite . . . [but]
>   in some lowly *Cot*,
> Where humble Food, the *Rasher* from the Coals,
> Sav'ry Repast! on homely Lunchion cut,
> Affords delicious Banquet; not *Ragoût*,
> Or *Fricassy*, or Second-Course to cloy
> The *Stomach* fill'd before.[23]

Another versified guide to health of 1770, by John Armstrong, similarly cautions its reader to 'Avoid the cates/That lull the sicken'd appetite too long'.[24] And Mark Akenside praises the wholesomeness of the nymph Hygeia who 'saves,/From poisonous cates and cups of pleasing bane,/The wretch devoted to the intangling snares/Of Bacchus and of Comus'.[25]

There is a parallel between the coarsening involved in developing an appetite for delicacy and the complex concern with moral delicacy which arose during the eighteenth century. C. J. Rawson has shown how central the terms 'delicate' and 'delicacy' are to the eighteenth-century culture of sensibility. Delicacy can mean sensibility itself, a heightened susceptibility to feelings of all kinds. However, as Rawson observes, insofar as an excess of sensibility can be dangerous, leading to libidinality and emotional libertarianism, the demand for the sensual gratification over the demands and duties of society, delicacy can also act as a 'regulator of sensibility'.[26] Delicacy is one way of holding the balance between sense and sensibility. But, as Rawson shrewdly observes, the impulse to check excesses of feeling is not itself simply on the side of sense against sensibility. It can, indeed, in order for it to be integrated naturally and gracefully into life and manners, it must, be experienced as itself a feeling. Thus, says Rawson, '[t]he difficulty of reconciling delicacy, which restrains the feelings, with sensibility, which indulges them, is only apparent. For it was possible to see the restraint itself as a feeling in its own right, and a "sensibility".'[27] But the balance between feeling and judgement represented in the instinct for social delicacy is not as stable as Rawson's words might imply. For, as is suggested by his own discussion of Hugh Kelly's comedy *False Delicacy*, a play which enjoys the comic complexities that arise from too extreme an exercise of scruple, the feeling of delicacy, which exists to restrain excess of feeling, can itself become excessive.[28] Delicacy means having no skin, or too thin a skin. But false delicacy, the pretence of scruple or the elaborate exhibition of modesty and coy retiringness, implies that one makes a false or insensible skin out of the idea of one's thin skin.

David Hume suggests a similar kind of recoil in his essay on delicacy of judgement, in which he proposes that delicacy has two forms: the passive delicacy of passion which leaves one at the mercy of strong feeling, and the more discriminating delicacy of taste, which allows one both to appreciate a wide variety of pleasures and sensations without succumbing to any one of them. Once again, there is a kind of screening of feeling, a feeling without quite feeling.[29]

During the course of the eighteenth century, the continuing popularity of the figure of the delicate heroine, who acts as a sounding board and amplifier of sensation while keeping it at a distance, is matched by a growing concern about delicate constitutions and delicate children. Delicacy was both a fashionable desideratum and a disease; indeed the distempers expressive of extreme sensitivity – the vapours, nervousness – became fashionable accessories. In the nineteenth century delicacy became steadily more pathological, even as the delicate heroine remained a staple of fiction. Where delicacy was a way of being, and a mode of social action during the eighteenth century, delicacy was accompanied more and more by passivity during the nineteenth, as doing became the opposite of feeling.[30] By the middle of the century, delicacy had come to be a delicate euphemism for degenerate feebleness, sometimes with suggestions of sexual perversity. J. Compton Burnett recommended an eccentrically robust therapy for delicate children in 1895, suggesting that puniness, and accompanying pathologies such as the desire to masturbate, could be corrected by the vigorous 'inrubbing of oil' – he recommended cod-liver oil or salad oil – into the skins of such young children. He claims that he rubbed oil in this way into the skins of four out of five children, all of whom were puny and stunted at birth. He reported that the one who was not rubbed because he appeared the most robust was now the most delicate of the five.[31]

Feminist reaction against the cult of passive delicacy in women shared in this new heartiness. In an article published in the *Century Magazine* in 1915, Amy Louise Reed used the programmes of physical training introduced at Vassar College for women to launch an unflinching assault on the mid-Victorian conception of the delicate woman, whose modesty and feebleness were the outward signs of an 'ethereal spiritual nature [and] moral sensitive-ness and purity superior to man's'. The article ends with an unregretful farewell to a mid-Victorian conception of delicacy:

> Gone, gone forever, is the delicate female of the sixties! Gone are her wasp waist and her billowing skirts and her sweeping train and ringlets with which her dainty fingers played. Gone, too, are her futile little sketch-book, the framed mottoes she embroidered and the sentimental songs she sang to her guitar, which made up the sum of her accomplishments. And if with these have passed away a certain fairy grace, an evanescent perfume, a charm without a name, shall we repine, we who have emerged into the liberty to walk and run and tramp the hills, and draw deep breaths, and look our interlocutor in the face, and even, if we happen to have thoughts, to utter them like other human beings?[32]

FINESSE

Delicacy is a striking feature of phenomenological and post-phenomenological appropriations of the sense of touch. It is to be associated with the protection or preservation of the other; with the nonconsuming lightness of touch evoked in their different ways by Sartre, Merleau-Ponty, Levinas, Irigaray and, in a range of recent works culminating in his recent reflections of the status of touch in Western philosophy, Derrida.[33]

One of the most powerful and influential attempts to form a philosophy around lightness of touch is to be found in Luce Irigaray's *An Ethics of Sexual Difference*. In this book, Irigaray reads the whole of the philosophical tradition, from Aristotle through to Merleau-Ponty and Levinas, as the attempt of male knowledge to put itself back in the world, to make of the world a home. This home is always a recapture of the first home, the first, absolute proximity of the womb, in which the world and we were absolutely intimate, absolute familiars. Finding his place in the world for the male philosopher means finding the unacknowledged female as his place, placing himself in the place of the place that originally exceeded him, getting on the outside of the inside that was his original and enduring home. Philosophy makes itself at home in the world by putting the female in her place as his place. By occupying the place of place, by becoming the world, woman becomes absent from it.

The last two chapters of the book respond to two philosophical attempts, those of Merleau-Ponty and Levinas, to open vision to the powers of touch. The first of these works with Merleau-Ponty's arguments about the relations of sight and touch in *The Visible and the Invisible*. Rumours and assumptions to the contrary,

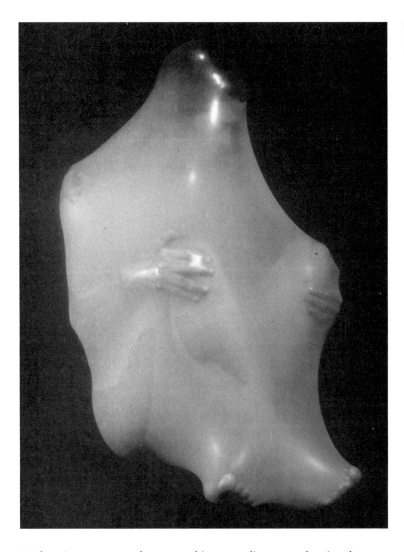

Cheryl Casteen,
'Amnio', 2003,
photo lightbox.

Merleau-Ponty says, we do not see things at a distance, and seeing does not merely distance us from the world. Seeing is not merely a fixing and grasping, it is also a sort of reaching, touching, bringing and palpation. We see within a world that seems hospitable to our seeing. Colour which is never a mere object in the world, and can never be seen immediately and in itself, is represented as the strongest indication that things seen and their seers participate in each other's natures. Vision and the invisible form together an atmosphere, which guarantees their contact without itself ever becoming visible, just as one sees by means of light without being able to see light itself. Merleau-Ponty renders this participation, the condition of the world's visibility which cannot itself be seen, in terms of touch. Irigaray loses no time in identifying this tactile or atmospheric ground for the figurings of sight, as female, indeed matricial. Responding to Merleau-

Ponty's claim that between colours and the visible 'we would find anew the tissue that lines them, sustains them, nourishes them, and which, for its part is not a thing, but a possibility, a latency, and a *flesh* of things',[34] Irigaray asks:

> Where does this tissue come from? How is it nourished? Who or what gives it consistency? My body? My flesh? Or a maternal, maternalizing flesh, reproduction, subsistence there of the amniotic, placental tissue, which enveloped subject and things prior to birth, of tenderness and the milieu that constituted the atmosphere of the nursling, the infant, still of the adult.[35]

The world in which the philosophy of touch makes itself once more at home, after the painful exile inaugurated by Descartes, is the body of the female, which is that which, enclosing everything, cannot touch itself. Irigaray accepts and even admires the way in which Merleau-Ponty opens the phenomenology of vision to the phenomenology of touch. But she also finds a kind of narcissism or even autism in it. One makes oneself at home in the world by sealing oneself up in it, as in a skin of touch perfected by vision:

> Merleau-Ponty would want it to be vision which closes – and works – my body, including the reversibility of the visible. And for the horizon to perfect me in a network, a garment, a skin, which we give to ourselves, which we weave unceasingly in order to live, to be born. (*Ethics*, 175)

Merleau-Ponty solves the Cartesian dichotomy between world and thing by dissolving all distance and difference, such that 'All that remains to be said is that the world is isomorphic with the subject and vice versa, and the whole is sealed up in a circle. Nothing new happens, only this permanent weaving between the world and the subject' (*Ethics*, 182).

Touch, however, is not fixed and finite for Irigaray, as she says it is finitizing and perfecting in Merleau-Ponty. Merleau-Ponty finds a guarantee of the aptness of the world for vision in the two-sidedness of touch, which expresses the 'alliance between looking and being looked at' (*Ethics*, 159–60). The hand can feel things from within, but can also feel itself as a hand from without. But Irigaray will not accept this tactile figure (modelled on the Möbius strip) of the reversible implication of world and self, in which '[m]y hand and its "other side," and the universe and its "other side" would be inscribed on the same horizon, would mingle their knowledges, their assimilations, in the same cycle or orbit, each one putting the other within-without, without-within' (*Ethics*, 160), or rather will suggest that it is not the only way to read the figure of tactility. In place of the hand which clasps itself as its own other, as in an Escher drawing, she suggests another figure of self-touching, 'a touching more intimate than that of one hand taking hold of the other'. This touching is that of prayer – 'The hands joined, palms together, fingers outstretched . . . A gesture often reserved for women (at least in the West) and which evokes, doubles, the touching of the lips silently applied upon one another' (*Ethics*, 161).

Touch is imaged for Irigaray in the face, that portion of the body which, because it can never close over on itself, touch itself as a hand can touch itself, 'is always in darkness' and is 'never born' (*Ethics*, 171). It is also expressed in the mucous membranes, those portions of the skin which mark a different kind of boundary between the visible and the invisible, and which can equally never quite be seen. Merleau-Ponty recruits touch to the enclosures of sight, making them into what Irigarary calls a chiasmus. Irigaray seeks the delicacy of a seeing that would see, without hoping to be able to see round, the world's partiality, a seeing with holes in it, these holes the hollowings of vision by touch. It would be a seeing in which touch had assuredly entered in, but a delicate touch that did not complete, hold itself in its own hands: 'The joined hands, not those that take hold one of the other, grasp each other, but the hands that touch without taking hold – like the lips. The joined hands perhaps represent this memory of the intimacy of the mucous' (*Ethics*, 170).

Like so many other post 1960s philosophers, Irigaray's real, unspoken inter-locutor here is not Merleau-Ponty, but Sartre, who provides a very different view of the caress and the erotic emulsion provided by the mucous membrane. For Sartre, always so sensitive and sometimes phobically so, to the contact and movement of surfaces over one another, the caress is a mutual fascination, a reduction of a free body in action to the inertia of fleshliness:

> [T]he caress is not a simple stroking: it is a *shaping*. In caressing the Other, I cause her flesh to be born beneath my caress, under my fingers . . . If I extend my hand, remove it, or clasp it, then it becomes again body in action; but by the same stroke I make my hand disappear as flesh. To let it run indifferently over the length of her body, to reduce my hand to a soft brushing almost stripped of meaning, to a pure existence, to a pure matter, slightly silky, slightly satiny, slightly rough – this is to give up for oneself being the one who establishes references and unfolds distances; it is to be made pure mucous membrane.[36]

The reaction against Sartre may also provide an impetus to Emmanuel Levinas, in his reflections in *Totality and Infinity* on the weight of the light touch and the erotics of the caress. Tenderness, writes Levinas, is the 'profane' exposure or exhibitionism of the Other, or rather, it is the approach to the always withdrawn not-yet of its inviolability. Tenderness has to do with an alternation of violation and inviolablity, which is why Levinas can say that '[t]he simultaneity of the clandestine and the exposed precisely defines a pro-fanation.'[37] At this point, Levinas suddenly and somewhat mysteriously says that tenderness is to be distinguished – by 'this depth in the subterranean dimension of the tender' – from 'the graceful, which it nevertheless resembles' (*Totality*, 257). We have to wait six pages for some more light to break on this distinction, when Levinas evokes the way in which the artist converts beauty into 'weightless grace' (*Totality*, 263). As so often in Levinas, art stands for fix-ation, appropriation, fetishization, fascination, the turning of ethical events into dead simulacra. Art 'substitutes an image for the troubling depth of the future . . . It presents a beautiful form reduced to itself in flight, deprived of its depth' (*Totality*, 263). And Levinas will have nothing numb or arrest ethical exposure. In order to protect the possibility of exposure, he will in fact have no contact, no coming together of separated entities. Tenderness must be rawness, swoon, agony, abyss, or it will be nothing, or rather just a *thing* like any other.

But delicacy seems to belong more to Levinas's deprecated category of grace than to the tenderness he hymns, hoardingly and yet trying all the time to keep his hands off it. Delicacy in fact always is a work, the case of a perturbation rather than the perturbation itself. It is a mediation, a transformation, a place of arrest, a detention: a *skin*. The skin is important for Levinas only in its exposure, which is what he seems to mean by its 'depth', and not in its capacity to hold or arrest.

Irigaray's reading of Levinas takes the form of a subtle doubling. Her essay begins with a kind of caress of Levinas's notion of the caress, which follows its contours without ever actually breaking into paraphrase. Without even mentioning Levinas, we are told of the powers and the delicacy of his caress. But, where Levinas insists on depth, Irigaray insists on threshold:

> *Eros* can arrive at that innocence which has never taken place with the other as other. At that nonregressive infinity of empathy with the other. At that appetite of all the senses which is irreducible to any obligatory consumption or consummation. At that indefinable taste of an attraction to the other which will never be satisfied. Which will always remain on the threshold, even after entering into the house. (*Ethics*, 185–6)

The caress is not that which delivers up the other as object or animal of touch. (How well all children learn the lesson that animals, like children, exist to be *stroked*.) The caress is a way of bringing into being that which one touches. As defined by Irigaray, the touch of the caress 'weds without consum(mat)ing . . . perfects while abiding by the outlines of the other' (*Ethics*, 186).

Irigaray's charge is that Levinas in fact never allows this encounter, and as a result never moves across from or breaks out of the dream of male self-transcendence. His voluptuous exposure is construed as a kind of recoil from contact. It is as though a hand were to reach out in a dark place and touch, where it had expected an object, another hand, or the twitching fur of an animal. One recoils from such a touch, not necessarily with revulsion, or with a revulsion that has in it something of Levinas's sense of extreme exposure. Where Levinas recoils from the danger of betraying the flesh into the carapace of an outline, the outline is precisely what is produced in Irigaray's caress:

> The most subtly necessary guardian of my life is the other's flesh. Approaching and speaking to me with his hands. Bringing me back to life more intimately than any regenerative nourishment, the other's hands, these palms with which he approaches without going through me, give me back the borders of my body. (*Ethics*, 187)

Against Levinas's revulsion from the idea that the other might be captured in the dream of similitude, that one might kill the other in making it comparable with oneself, Irigaray proposes the exchange of similitudes, in the reciprocal making out of a shape which remains, as it were, open to futurity and therefore immune from the ossifying touch of art, fantasy, representation:

> To give or give back to the other the possible site of his identity, of his intimacy: a second birth that returns one to innocence. A garment that isn't one, a kind of envelopment that keeps continual watch over a space for birth – becoming other than a return to self. A becoming in which the other gives of a space-time that is still free. (*Ethics*, 206–7)

This will involve a touch that is 'more modest than the caress'. In order to allow for the porous encounter of self and other, this touch must hang back even more than the caress. It appears to be the shape or feint of the caress, the caress, so to speak, caressed in air:

> A caress that precedes every caress, it opens up to the other the possible space of his respiration, his conception. Greeting him as other, encountering him with respect for what surrounds him – that subtle, palpable space that envelops each of us like a necessary border, an irradiation of our presence that overflows the limits of the body. (*Ethics*, 207)

Irigaray has a serious point to make, that, in seeking to protect himself and his ethics from the violence of appropriation, Levinas recoils into the violence of noncontact, which allows him his dream of a voluptuous identification with 'the son' as an image of self-distancing that is really a self-containment, an occultation of woman. Rather than the transcendence in contact, the caress which 'seeks out the not yet of the female lover's blossoming' (*Ethics*, 211), there is the selfish transcendence of the one who holds back so far and so completely, forgetting the 'vital threshold – the tactile' (*Ethics*, 214) that it is as though he has raped 'without a trace' (*Ethics*, 210). Indeed, it is the very lack of any trace, track, imprint, mark of the coming together of bodies, that is the rape, and conviction thereby assured. Irigaray recoils at this revulsion from contact. Finally, it is Levinas's own protocol that is turned about him, namely that he has substituted dream for real encounter, when 'the other cannot be transformed into discourse, fantasies, or dreams' (*Ethics*, 216). Convicted at the bar of his own tribunal, Levinas will die by his own hand, without the need for sentence. This is the double of the caress, the touch that kills without a touch, without ever coming close.

Michel Serres has also elaborated a kind of ethics of the delicate touch in a number of his works. In the last chapter of his *Le tiers-instruit* (*The Troubadour of Knowledge*), this delicacy is defined openly in terms of a holding back. The law of physical objects, or of animal existence, is that of propagation or unchecked spread. Things take up, and take over space. Serres names this compound evil of the propagating singular, evil itself:

By themselves, gases occupy the volume that is offered before their expansive pressure. No one has ever seen a gas show proof of restraint in order to leave a part of the space empty. Barbarism follows the single law. The law of expansion. That of gases. They propagate themselves. The barbarian spreads. Violence spreads blood, which spreads out. Pestilence, epidemics, microbes, are propagated. Noise, ruckus, rumours, spread. In the same way, force, power, kings spread. In the same way, ambition spreads. In the same way, advertising spreads. The rubric of all that things that spread, as amply as a gas, of all the things that expand, that take up space, that occupy volume, must be named. Evil gets around, that is its definition: it exceeds its limits.[38]

The human has often been distinguished from the nonhuman in terms of that which expands into its possibility, as opposed to that which remains closed inertly in itself. But, for Serres 'To persevere unceasingly in its being or in its power characterizes the physics of the inert and the instinct of animals' (117). Where others have seen it as necessary for the human to obviate or absent itself entirely, in order to indemnify the other against annihilation or objectification by knowledge, Serres distinguishes the human from the nonhuman in terms of its capacity to restrain itself: '[H]umanity begins with holding back.' Not an absolute, self-immolating abstention, but the attempt to 'invest a part of our power in softening our power' (120). Reason and science need to hold back in order not to fall into madness, need to be incomplete in order to be entire. Even the solar inferno of the One in Jewish, Christian and Muslim monotheism needs and permits a little chiaroscuro, the partial absconding from creation that allows evil to come about: 'We have God to thank for having held back a good deal short of monotheism' (118). A name for this principle of reserve might be delicacy.

Is there a way, first of all, of accounting for the particular touch or feel of this concern with the light touch among these writers in terms of our new conditions of life, our new forms of material imagination: and, secondly, of turning it to account?

We have, I think, to recognize that delicacy has in part changed its place and its value. It is true that the delicate still harbours dreams of the fragile and evanescent, of that which, in the human and beyond it, is vulnerable to the human, and is powerful in its very vulnerability. The embrace of delicacy has to do with a desire to pull back from the power of the human, newly experienced as destructive, and a new kind of self-relation in this holding back. It is as though the human had crossed to the side of the other, of that which needs to be protected from itself. The human now appears to be vulnerable most of all to itself. To be human is to be balanced between humanity's self and its other.

But power is not merely mitigated in delicacy. We must recognize that our world is one in which delicacy itself has become a modality of power. We saw in the last chapter that the exploration of the microscopic during the seventeenth century established a new borderline between the visible and the invisible. The skin became, not the visible outline or outside of things, the contour where bodies entered into the sphere of the visible, but that which marked the intimate horizon between the visible and the invisible, a horizon not at the edge of sight, but within it. While remaining the outward sign of the body, the body's shell of visibility, the skin became impossible to see with the naked eye. With its many tenants and fellow-travellers, the skin itself has become, more and more, a manifold. This new sense of the delicacy of the skin, of the skin as the harbinger of a sort of higher, more ideal touch, and also of an increased vulnerability, has reappeared in the age of cinema, which allows us to see into the gaps between things and to manipulate the world at a distance. The ideal of delicacy is perhaps already in operation in Virilio's tele-contact, or touch at a distance.

It is certainly apparent in the most marked change wrought by technologies of communication over the last two centuries, which is a change, not in the absolute terms of space, time and speed – how fast bodies may be transported, or how far forms transmitted – but in terms of the topology of scaling, or the meeting and interpenetration of different scales. We still think in terms of linear functions, of large causes having proportionately large effects. But we live in a world (have always, despite ourselves, lived in such a world) in which very small causes can have very large effects, and in which the small and the large are bent and blent together in ways that our languages have some difficulty adjusting to. The prehension of the delicate belongs to this paradoxical, quasi-chaotic inter-mingling of large and small. Sensitivity used to be at the opposite end of the scale from power, which needed to make itself blunt and insensible to maintain its power. The rise of biopower means that power involves, no longer the brute manipulation of life, but insinuation into it, infiltration and manipulation of the minuscule balances that maintain systems.

Power used to be *applied*. That is to say, it needed to be brought up against its object, which would either resist, buckle, or be displaced by the pressure. Such meetings, impressions or collisions take place on the outside of things, and so we protect ourselves against accidents and enemies by armoured defences. Now, it is not that there are no comings together, no bearings down, no adversity any more. It is that it is no longer quite clear where the outside of things is to be found. In the age of interface which is now upon us, an age which has been much less sudden and longer in preparation than we might imagine, everything is at once inside and outside everything else. Our skins are mingled skins, our skins the milieux of mixed bodies.

The culture of trauma is a nostalgia for adversity, for that which would have struck us and left its mark. There is, as far as I know, no history of the crash, the impact, the explosion in the cinema, even though cinema, the most repres-entative modern art, seems to exist in order to celebrate and contain just this extreme jeopardy of the surface. Everything that happens in cinema seems to take place between the extremes of the light touch and the heavy hand, on a scale that runs from the kiss, through the punch and the shot to the explosion. For cinema is itself the art of the light touch, which touches and moves its audi-ences without laying a finger on them. The skies used to shake with the roars of the Saturn rockets, according to some, the loudest sounds ever produced by man, which tore themselves away from the pull of gravitation by means of massive effort, as though boring through some mountain of resistance. But there is in fact very little resistance in the universe, in which dense clumpings of matter like the earth are amazingly rare and the average density is the equivalent of between five and fifteen molecules of hydrogen per cubic metre, a condition of vacuum that has never been achieved on earth. To traverse great distances, one must change the equation: not great expenditure of effort, enormous space-craft the size of conurbations powered by combustible fuels pushing against gravity, but spacecraft of unimaginable lightness and tininess, to ski the solar winds and loop gravitational loops. If one wants sacks of rocks from the moon, then one will need quarrypit contrivances, picks, shovels and rockets. But what if one wants to collect matter in the fantastically dispersed condition that is the norm in the universe? All the matter in the tail of a comet can be contained in an average-sized jam-jar. In order to collect this material, the Stardust project proposes to use a Policeman MacCruiskeen kind of apparatus, in the form of an aerogel, among the lightest substances ever produced: a kind of 'frozen smoke' an ounce of which contains the area of several football fields folded into it. Only the multiple internal foldings of a foam like this will be adequate to catch the cometary particles travelling at 14,000 miles an hour.[39]

So, in one sense, ours is a world of delicacy, a world in which there is an impossible, obscene continuity between the pedagogy of the delicate, of that which touches almost without touching and what we used to hear called the school of hard knocks, to distinguish it from the useless velleities of abstract speculation. The ethics and erotics of delicacy arose in and still belong to a world in which the scales were still secure and consistent, in which lightness of touch could be distinguished against density, weight and mass, in order to be rescued or secured from it. But the particular kind of delicacy, touch that is not a touch, that is abroad today, is not an impossible, utopian dream of tender-ness, but is necessary to our constitution, to our adjustment to the shape of things, and what it may still mean to be life-size. In this diversification of the light touch, the thought of the skin will continue to discover new kinds of salience; but the skin understood, not in the fixated terms of surface, bound-ary or container, holding apart self and world, space and time, extension and intensity, maximum and minimum, and those holding them in adversary place, but rather as a milieu, mingling and manifold.

References

Pregression: A Skin That Walks

1 Antonin Artaud, *The Peyote Dance*, trans. Helen Weaver (New York, 1976), pp. 37–8.
2 Didier Anzieu, 'The Nomad Skin', *L'Epiderme nomade et la peau psychique* (Paris, 1990), p. 26.

1 Complexion

1 *James Joyce in Padua*, trans. and ed. Louis Berrone (New York, 1977), p. 21.
2 *Diodorus of Sicily*, with an English translation by C. H. Oldfather (Cambridge, MA and London, 1968), I.91.4, vol. I, p. 311.
3 Aristotle, *De Generatione Animalium* (*On The Generation of Animals*), trans. Arthur Platt, in J. A. Smith and W. D. Ross eds, *The Works of Aristotle* (Oxford, 1967), vol. V, II.6.743b.
4 Job of Edessa, *Encyclopaedia of Philosophical and Natural Sciences, As Taught in Baghdad About AD 817, or Book of Treasures*, trans. A. Mingana (Cambridge, 1935), p. 54.
5 Alessandro Benedetti, *Anatomice: Or The History of the Human Body*, in L. R. Lind, *Studies in Pre-Vesalian Anatomy: Biography, Translations, Documents* (Philadelphia, 1975), p. 88.
6 St Thomas Aquinas, *Summa Theologica*, translated by the Fathers of the English Dominican Province (Westminster, MD, 1981), Supplement, question 80.3, vol. V, p. 2883.
7 St Augustine of Hippo, *The City of God Against the Pagans*, ed. and trans. R. W. Dyson (Cambridge, 1998), p. 626.
8 *Galen on Anatomical Procedures*, trans. Charles Singer (Oxford, 1999), pp. 5, 63–5.
9 Avicenna (Abu Ali al-Hussain Ibn Abdallah Ibn Sina), *The Canon of Medicine*, trans. Laleh Bakhtiar, O. Cameron Gruner and Mazar H. Shah (Chicago, 1999).
10 *The Middle English Translation of Guy de Chauliac's Anatomy*, ed. Björn Wallner (Lund, 1964), p. 67.
11 Thomas Bartholin, *Anatomia Reformata* (Lugduni [Leiden], 1651); Johann Remmelin, *Catoptron Microcosmicum: A Survey of the Microcosme: or, The anatomy of the bodies of man and woman: Wherein the skin, veins, arteries, nerves, muscles, viscera, bones, and ligaments thereof are accurately delineated, and so disposed by pasting, as that all the parts of the said bodies, both internal and external, are exactly represented in their proper site* (London, 1695).
12 Andreas Vesalius, *On the Fabric of the Human Body: Book II: The Ligaments and Muscles*, trans. W. F. Richardson and J. B. Carman (San Francisco, 1998), pp. 143, 144.
13 Aristotle, *Historia Animalium*, trans. D'Arcy Wentworth Thompson, in Smith and Ross, eds, *The Works of Aristotle*, vol. IV, III.11.518a.
14 Benedetti, *Anatomice*, p. 88.
15 Vesalius, *On The Fabric of the Human Body: Book II*, p. 142.
16 Marie-Christine Pouchelle, *The Body and Surgery in the Middle Ages*, trans. Rosemary Morris (Cambridge, 1990), pp. 125–59.
17 See, for instance, George McClelland Foster, *Hippocrates' Latin American Legacy: Humoral Medicine in the New World* (Langhorne, PA, 1994).
18 Vivian Nutton, 'Humoralism', in W. F. Bynum and Roy Porter, eds, *Columbia Encyclopaedia of Medicine* (London and New York, 1993), vol. I, pp. 281–91.
19 John Gower, *Confessio Amantis*, in G. C. Macaulay, ed., *The English Works of John Gower* (London, 1979) 7.388, vol. II, p. 243.
20 Ben Jonson, *The English Grammar*, in *Workes of Benjamin Jonson* (London, 1641), vol. III, p. 52.
21 Henry Wotton, *A Courtlie Controuersie of*

Cupids Cautels, Connteyning Fiue Tragicall Histories, very pithie, pleasant, pitiful and profitable. . .Translated out of French... by H.VV. (London, 1578), p. 222.

22 My phrase 'implicate order' alludes to the work of the physicist David Bohm, whose *Wholeness and the Implicate Order* (London, 1980), is an important contribution to the variegated thought of the fold which has become so conspicuous in the last two decades.

23 *The Historie of the World: Commonly Called, The Naturall Historie of C. Plinius Secundus*, trans. Philémon Holland (London, 1601), vol. II, sig. Aiiij^v.

24 William Sclater, *An Exposition With Notes Upon the First Epistle to the Thessalonians* (London, 1619), p. 136.

25 Margaret Cavendish, Duchess of Newcastle, *The Description of a New World, Called The Blazing World* (1666), in Kate Lilley, ed., *The Blazing World and Other Writings* (Harmondsworth, 1994), p. 133.

26 Barbara Duden, *The Woman Beneath the Skin: A Doctor's Patients in Eighteenth-Century Germany*, trans. Thomas Dunlap (Cambridge, MA, 1991), p. 121.

27 *Ibid.*, p. 123.

28 In his essay 'Cold, Disease and Birth', Ernest Jones attributes these beliefs to memories of the exposure to cold air in the trauma of birth; *Papers on Psycho-Analysis*, 5th edn (London, 1977), pp. 320–24. The meanings of heat and cold may be at once more complex and more cultural than this explanation allows.

29 Lawrence Wright, *Clean and Decent: The History of the Bath and Loo and of Sundry Habits, Fashions and Accessories of the Toilet, Principally in Great Britain, France and America* (London, Boston and Henley, 1980); Steve Dobell, *Down the Plughole: An Irreverent History of the Bath* (London, 1996); Claude Bouillon, *La peau: une enveloppe de vie* (Paris, 2002), ch. 1 'L'eau sur la peau', pp. 12–39.

30 Quoted without source in John Dowson, *An Essay on Warm and Cold Bathing, For the Preservation of Health* (Whitby, 1857), p. 4.

31 Philip Myers, *The Importance of Bathing, With Directions How to Practice It to the Greatest Advantage* (Nottingham, 1836), p. 14.

32 Girolamo Mercurialis, *De morbis cutaneis et omnibus corporis humani excrementis tractatus* (Venice, 1572); *A Sixteenth-Century Physician and His Methods: Mercurialis on Diseases of the Skin, The First Book on the Subject (1572)*, ed. and trans. Richard L. Sutton Jr (Kansas City, MO, 1986).

33 Daniel Turner, *De morbis cutaneis: A Treatise of Diseases Incident to the Skin* (London, 1714).

34 Anne Charles Lorry, *Tractatus de morbis cutaneis* (Paris, 1777).

35 Joseph Jacob Plenck, *Doctrina de morbis cutaneis qua hi morbi in suas classes, genera & species rediguntur* (Vienna, 1776).

36 Elizabeth Liebmann, 'The Age of Reason', in Barbara Maria Stafford et al., 'Depth Studies: Illustrated Anatomies From Vesalius to Vicq d'Azyr', *Caduceus*, VIII (1992), pp. 45–7.

37 Robert Willan, *On Cutaneous Diseases*, vol. I (London, 1808).

38 Thomas Bateman, *A Practical Synopsis of Cutaneous Diseases According to the Arrangement of Dr. Willan, Exhibiting a Concise View of the Diagnostic Symptoms and the Method of Treatment* (London, 1813); *Delineations of Cutaneous Diseases: Exhibiting the Characteristic Appearances of the Principal Genera and Species Comprised in the Classification of the Late Dr. Willan; and Completing the Series of Engravings Begun by That Author* (London, 1817).

39 Noah Worcester, *Synopsis of the Symptoms, Diagnosis and Treatment of the Most Common and Important Diseases of the Skin* (Philadelphia, 1845).

40 Michel Serres, *Les cinq sens* (Paris, 1998), p. 59. References hereafter in my text.

41 Paul Valéry, *L'Idée Fixe, Collected Works of Paul Valéry*, vol. V, ed. Jackson Matthews, trans. David Paul (London, 1965), p. 33.

42 Michel Serres, *The Troubadour of Knowledge*, trans. Sheila Faria Glaser and William Paulson (Ann Arbor, 1997), p. 31.

43 *The Complete Grimm's Fairy Tales* (London, 1975), pp. 94–7.

44 Maurice Canney, 'The Skin of Re-Birth', *Man*, XXIX (1939), pp. 105–6. The theme of transformation in the representation of flaying between the fifteenth and nineteenth centuries in Europe is explored by Jacques Gélis, 'L'homme «dépouillé»: Pour une anthropologie de la peau', in André Burguière, Joseph Goy and Marie-Jeanne Tits-Dieuaide, eds, *L'Histoire grande ouverte: hommages à Emmanuel Le Roy Ladurie* (Paris, 1997), pp. 326–36.

45 Marina Warner, *The Leto Bundle* (London, 2001).

46 Samuel Beckett, *Footfalls*, in *Complete Dramatic Works* (London, 1986), p. 402.

47 Ewa Kuryluk, *Veronica and Her Cloth: History, Symbolism and Structure of a 'True' Image* (Oxford, 1991), p. 197.

48 Quoted in Ian Wilson, *The Turin Shroud* (London, 1978), pp. 76, 145.

49 Paul Schilder, *The Image and Appearance of*

the *Human Body: Studies in the Constructive Energies of the Psyche* (New York, 1970), p. 86.

50 *Ibid.*, p. 123.

51 Pliny, *Natural History* (Cambridge, MA and London, 1938–42) vol. III (Books 8–11) with a translation by H. Rackham, VIII.liv.126, p. 91; Samuel Butler, *Hudibras*, ed. John Wilders (Oxford, 1967), p. 97.

52 Didier Houzel, 'The Concept of Psychic Envelope', in Didier Anzieu *et al.*, *Psychic Envelopes*, trans. Daphne Nash (London, 1990), p. 45.

53 *Ibid.*, p. 46.

54 *Ibid.*, pp. 44–5.

55 Dider Anzieu, 'Formal Signifiers', in Didier Anzieu *et al.*, *Psychic Envelopes*, p. 8.

56 Michel Serres, *Atlas* (Paris, 1994), p. 45.

57 Michael Joyce, *Afternoon: A Story*, electronic hypertext (Watertown, MA, 1987).

58 Juliet Fleming, 'The Renaissance Tattoo', in Jane Caplan, ed., *Written on the Body: The Tattoo in European and American History* (London, 2000), p. 66 and J. Curtis, *An Authentic and Faithful History of the Mysterious Murder of Maria Marten* (London, 1828).

59 Lawrence S. Thompson, 'Religatum de Pelle Humana', *Bibliologia Comica: Or Humorous Aspects of the Caparisoning and Conservation of Books* (Hamden, CT, 1968), pp. 119–60 (135). References hereafter in the text.

60 Walter Hart Blumenthal, *Bookmen's Bedlam: An Olio of Literary Curiosities* (New Brunswick, 1955), pp. 77–8. References hereafter in the text.

61 Percy H. Fitzgerald, *The Book Fancier: Or, The Romance of Book Collecting* (London, 1886), p. 122.

62 Keith A. Smith, *Structure of the Visual Book* (Fairport, NY, 1992), p. 225.

63 See, for instance, John Thorne Crissey and Lawrence Charles Parish, *The Dermatology and Syphilology of the Nineteenth Century* (New York, 1981); Gérard Tilles, *La naissance de la dermatologie (1776–1880)* (Paris, 1989) and John Thorne Crissey, Lawrence Charles Parish and Karl Holubar, *Historical Atlas of Dermatology and Dermatologists* (London, 2001). The more philosophically and culturally inflected histories of the skin provided by François Dagognet, *La peau découverte* (Le Plessis-Robinson, 1993) and Claudia Benthien, *Skin: On the Cultural Border Between Self and World*, trans. Thomas Dunlap (New York, Chichester, 2002) are closer to the ways in which I try to make sense of the skin in this book.

64 Michel Serres and Bruno Latour, *Conversations on Science, Culture, and Time*, trans. Roxanne Lapidus (Ann Arbor, 1995), p. 60.

2 Exposition

1 Didier Anzieu, *A Skin for Thought: Interviews With Gilbert Tarrab on Psychology and Psychoanalysis*, trans. Daphne Nash Briggs (London, 1990), p. 63.

2 Didier Anzieu, *The Skin Ego*, trans. Chris Turner (New Haven, 1989), p. 40. References hereafter in the text, abbreviated to SE.

3 Ashley Montagu, *Touching: The Human Significance of the Skin*, 3rd edn (New York, 1986), p. 19.

4 Didier Anzieu, *Le moi-peau*, 2nd edn (Paris, 1995), pp. 129–31.

5 W. B. Yeats, 'Crazy Jane and the Bishop', *Complete Poems of W. B. Yeats*, (London, 1979), p. 295.

6 Roland Barthes, *The Pleasure of the Text*, trans. Richard Miller (Oxford, 1990), p. 9.

7 *Ibid.*, pp. 11–12.

8 Klaus Theweleit, *Male Fantasies: Vol. 1. Women, Floods, Bodies, History*, trans. Stephen Conway, Erica Carter and Chris Turner (Cambridge, 1987), p. 242.

9 Barrie M. Biven, 'The Role of Skin in Normal and Abnormal Development, With a Note on the Poet Sylvia Plath', *International Review of Psychoanalysis*, IX (1982), p. 224.

10 Armando R. Favazza, *Bodies Under Siege: Self-Mutilation and Body Modification in Culture and Psychiatry*, 2nd edn (Baltimore and London, 1996), p. 148.

11 Roland Barthes, *Camera Lucida: Reflections on Photography*, trans. Richard Howard (New York, 1981), pp. 80–1.

12 Bertram D. Lewin, 'Sleep, the Mouth, and the Dream Screen', *Psychoanalytic Quarterly*, XV (1946), pp. 419–34, and 'Reconsideration of the Dream Screen', *Psychoanalytic Quarterly*, XXII (1953), pp. 174–99. I discuss the skin function of the dream screen in my 'Fascination, the Skin and the Screen', *Critical Quarterly*, XL (1998), pp. 9–24, esp. pp. 15–17.

13 Philip Larkin, 'Sunny Prestatyn', *The Whitsun Weddings* (London, 1986), p. 35.

14 Michel Serres, *Les cinq sens* (Paris, 1988), pp. 35–6.

15 *Bob Flanagan, Supermasochist* (San Francisco, 1993), p. 61.

16 Anzieu, *A Skin For Thought*, p. 66.

17 Susan Buck-Morss, 'Aesthetics and Anaesthetics: Walter Benjamin's Artwork Essay Reconsidered', *October*, LXII (1992), pp. 3–41.

18 Marshall McLuhan, *Understanding Media:*

The Extensions of Man (London, 1967), p. 57.

19 Randy Shilts, *And the Band Played On: Politics, People, and the AIDS Epidemic* (Harmondsworth, 1988), pp. 64–6, 75–8.

20 Paul Virilio, *Open Sky*, trans. Julie Rose (London, 1997), pp. 35–45.

21 Gilles Deleuze, *The Logic of Sense*, trans. Mark Lester and Charles Stivale (London, 1990), pp. 86–7.

22 *Ibid.*, p. 87.

23 Jacques Derrida, *Spurs: Nietzsche's Styles*, trans. Barbara Harlow (Chicago, 1979), p. 37.

24 Friedrich Kittler, *Discourse Networks, 1800/1900*, trans. Michael Metteer and Chris Cullens (Stanford, 1990), p. 224.

25 Virilio, *Open Sky*, p. 45.

26 Salman Rushdie, *The Ground Beneath Her Feet* (London, 1999), p. 485.

27 *Ibid.*, pp. 339, 253.

28 *Ibid.*, p. 437.

29 *Ibid.*, p. 343.

30 Samuel Beckett, *Molloy, Malone Dies, The Unnamable* (London, 1959), p. 307.

31 Susan Sheftel et. al. 'A Case of Radical Facial Self-Mutilation: An Unprecedented Event and Its Impact', *Bulletin of the Menninger Clinic*, L (1986), pp. 525–40. The case is described in Kathy O'Dell, *Contract With the Skin: Masochism, Performance Art and the 1970s* (Minneapolis and London, 1998), p. 96, n.26.

32 Jacques Derrida, 'La parole soufflée', *Writing and Difference*, trans. Alan Bass (London, 1978), p. 187.

33 Antonin Artaud, *The Peyote Dance*, trans. Helen Weaver (New York, 1976), pp. 37–8.

34 Richey Edwards's response to the doubts of the journalist Steve Lamacq that he and the band were 'for real', was to roll up his sleeve and cut the words '4 REAL' into his arm with a razor blade; Simon Price, *Everything: A Book About Manic Street Preachers* (London, 1999), p. 51.

35 *Modern Primitives*, ed. Andrea Juno and Vivian Vale (San Francisco, 1989).

3 Disfiguring

1 Joe Nickell, *Looking for a Miracle: Weeping Icons, Relics, Stigmata, Visions, and Healing Cures* (Buffalo, NY, 1993), pp. 93–7.

2 C. P. Jones, 'Stigma and Tattoo', in Jane Caplan, ed., *Written on the Body: The Tattoo in European and American History* (London, 2000), p. 8.

3 *Ibid.*

4 James Joyce, *Ulysses: The Corrected Text*, ed. Hans Walter Gabler, Wolfhard Steppe and Claus Melchior (Harmondsworth, 1986), p. 66.

5 Otto Meinardus, 'Tattoo and Name: A Study on the Marks of Identification of the Egyptian Christians', *Wiener Zeitschrift für die Kunde des Morgenlandes*, LXIII/LXIV (1972), p. 30.

6 Athenaeus, *The Deipnosophists: or Banquet of the Learned*, trans. C. D. Yonge (London, 1854), XIV.2, vol. III, p. 840.

7 Hamish Maxwell-Stewart and Ian Duffield, 'Skin Deep Devotions: Religious Tattoos and Convict Transportation to Australia', in Caplan, ed., *Written on the Body*, p. 113.

8 Michel Serres, *Les cinq sens* (Paris, 1988), pp. 141–9.

9 Michel Serres, *Hominescence: Essais* (Paris, 2001), pp. 75–83.

10 Paul Virilio, *Open Sky*, trans. Julie Rose (London, 1997), pp. 3, 28.

11 Jones, 'Stigma and Tattoo', p. 9.

12 Franz Kafka, 'In The Penal Settlement', trans. Willa and Edwin Muir, *Metamorphosis and Other Stories* (Harmondsworth, 1971), pp. 167–200.

13 Jean-François Lyotard, 'Prescription', *L'Esprit créateur*, XXXI (1991), p. 18.

14 Jean-François Lyotard, *The Inhuman: Reflections on Time*, trans. Geoffrey Bennington and Rachel Bowlby (Cambridge, 1991), p. 158.

15 *Ibid.*, p. 158.

16 Emmanuel Levinas, *Collected Philosophical Papers*, trans. Alphonso Lingis (Dordrecht, Boston and Lancaster, 1987), p. 116.

17 *Ibid.*, p. 121.

18 Lyotard, *The Inhuman*, p. 190.

19 Piero Camporesi, *The Incorruptible Flesh: Bodily Mutilation and Mortification in Religion and Folklore*, trans. Tania Croft-Murray and Helen Elsom (Cambridge, 1988) and Caroline Walker Bynum, *Fragmentation and Redemption: Essays on Gender and the Human Body in Medieval Religion* (New York, 1991) and *The Resurrection of the Body in Western Christianity 200–1336* (New York, 1995).

20 See, for example, Anita Phillips, *In Defence of Masochism* (London, 1998) and Jay Prosser, *Second Skins: The Body Narratives of Transexuality* (New York, 1998).

21 François Dagognet, *La peau découverte* (Le Plessis-Robinson, 1993), p. 33.

22 Michel Serres, *The Troubadour of Knowledge*, trans. Sheila Faria Glaser and William Paulson (Ann Arbor, 1997), p. 139.

23 Jones, 'Stigma and Tattoo', p. 7.

4 Impression

1 Barbara Maria Stafford, *Body Criticism: Imaging the Unseen in Enlightenment Art and*

Medicine (Cambridge, MA, 1991), pp. 281–39.

2 Edmund Spenser, *The Fairie Queene*, ed.
Thomas P. Roche, Jr and C. Patrick
O'Donnell, Jr. (Harmondsworth, 1984),
v.xii, 37.7, p. 873, vi.i.7.1, p. 879.

3 *A Book of Knowledge, In Four Parts . . .*
(London, 1696).

4 *Dreams and Moles, With Their
Interpretation and Signification* (London,
n.d. [1750?]), p. 16.

5 *Book of Knowledge*, p. 42.

6 *The Spaewife, Or Universal Fortune-Teller:
Wherein Your Future Welfare May Be
Known , By Physiognomy, Cards, Palmistry
and Coffee Grounds. Also, a Distinct Treatise
on Moles* (Belfast, 1845), p. 10.

7 *Book of Knowledge*, p. 9.

8 *The New School of Love; Being the True Art
of Courtship: Shewing How Every One May
Know Their Partner's Disposition and
Temper by the Hair, Eyes and Nose, &c.
With the Signification of Moles in any Part
of the Body; and the Interpretation of
Dreams, &c, &c* (Glasgow, 1793), p. 3.

9 Thomas Borman, *Love's True Oracle, or a
New and Curious Fortune-Book for Men,
Maids, Wifes and Widows . . . To Which Is
Added, The Signification of Dreams and Moles*
(Newcastle, n.d. [1810?]), pp. 13–14.

10 *Partridge and Flamsted's New and Well
Experienced Fortune-Book . . . [with] The
Signification of MOLES in any part of the
Body; and the Interpretations of DREAMS as
they relate to good or bad Fortune* (London,
n.d. [1710?]), p. 13.

11 Borman, *Love's True Oracle*, p. 14.

12 *The Golden Dreamer: or, Dreamer's
Interpreter, Clearly Showing How All Things,
Past, Present, and to Come, May Be
Ascertained By Means of Dreams; to which is
Added a Correct Signification of Moles*
(Newcastle on Tyne, 1840), p. 24.

13 *Ibid.*, p. 24.

14 *Dreams and Moles*, p. 18.

15 *Book of Knowledge*, p. 42.

16 *Ibid.*, pp. 42–3.

17 *Partridge and Flamsted*, p. 13.

18 *The Spaewife*, p. 8.

19 *Ibid.*, p. 9.

20 *Book of Knowledge*, p. 42.

21 Borman, *Love's True Oracle*, pp. 12–13.

22 On the history of the relationship between
moles and melanoma see John P. Bennett
and Per Hall, 'Moles and Melanoma: A
History', *Annals of the Royal College of
Surgeons of England*, LXXVI (1994),
pp. 373–80.

23 *Dreams and Moles*, p. 16.

24 Borman, *Love's True Oracle*, p. 12.

25 I discuss the meanings of dots and spots in
'Maculate Conceptions', *Textile: The Journal
of Cloth and Culture*, I (2003), pp. 1–11.

26 Chris Sizemore and Elen Pittillo, *Eve*
(London, 1978), p. 432.

27 Daniel Turner, *De Morbis Cutaneis: A
Treatise of Diseases Incident to the Skin*
(London, 1714). References hereafter to *De
Morbis Cutaneis* in text.

28 Thomas Fienus, *De viribus imaginationis
tractatus* (Lovanii, 1608).

29 *The Strength of Imagination in Pregnant
Women Examin'd: and the opinion that
marks and deformities in children arise
from thence, demonstrated to be a vulgar
error. By a member of the College of
Physicians* (London, 1727).

30 *A Discourse Concerning Gleets, Their Cause
and Cure . . . To which is added, a defence of
the 12th chapter of the first part of a treatise
de Morbis Cutaneis, in respect to the spots
and marks impressed upon the skin of the
foetus, by the force of the mother's Fancy,
containing some remarks upon a discourse
lately printed, and intitled, the Strength of
Imagination in Pregnant Women
Examined, etc.* (London, 1729).

31 James Blondel, *The Power of the Mother's
Imagination Over the Foetus Examin'd. In
answer to Dr. Turner's book, intitled, A
Defence of the XIIth Chapter of the First Part
of a Treatise, De morbis cutaneis* (London,
1729).

32 Daniel Turner, *The Force of the Mother's
Imagination Upon Her Foetus In Utero,
Still Farther Consider'd: In the way of a
reply to Dr. Blondel's last book, entitled,
The Power of the Mother's Imagination
Over the Foetus Examined . . .* (London,
1730), p. 144.

33 The theological dimensions of the
Turner–Blondel debate are convincingly
demonstrated in Philip K. Wilson's '"Out
of Sight, Out of Mind?": The Daniel
Turner–James Blondel Dispute Over the
Power of the Maternal Imagination',
Annals of Science, XLIX (1992), pp. 63–85.
More recently, Wilson has connected the
Enlightenment discussion of maternal
impressions to more modern concerns
with heredity and deviance, in
'Eighteenth-Century "Monsters" and
Nineteenth-Century "Freaks": Reading the
Maternally-Marked Child', *Literature and
Medicine*, XXI (2002), pp. 1–25.

34 J. W. Ballantyne, *Manual of Antenatal
Pathology and Hygiene: The Embryo*
(Edinburgh, 1904), pp. 105–6.

35 Ambroise Paré, *On Monsters and Marvels*,
trans. Janis Pallister (Chicago and London,
1982), pp. 41–2.

36 Jacques Gélis, *History of Childbirth: Fertility, Pregnancy and Birth in Early Modern Europe*, trans. Rosemary Morris (Cambridge, 1991), p. 57.

37 Turner, *Discourse Concerning Gleets*, pp. 74–5.

38 John Maubray, *The Female Physician: Containing All the Diseases Incident to That Sex, In Virgins, Wives, and Widows . . .* (London, 1724).

39 *Libellus qui inscribitur de formatione hominis in utero materno, vel ut notiori titulo, secreta mulierum* (Antwerp, 1538), sig E2ᵛ.

40 Levinus Lemnius, *The Secret Miracles of Nature . . . In Four Books . . .* (London, 1658), p. 16.

41 Maubray, *Female Physician*, pp. 62–3.

42 George M. Gould and Walter L. Pyle, *Anomalies and Curiosities of Medicine* (Philadelphia, 1897), p. 85.

43 Johannes Swammerdam, *Miraculum naturae sive uteri mulieribus fabrica* (Lugduni Batavorum, 1672); Blondel, *Power of the Mother's Imagination Examin'd*, p. 24.

44 Samuel Taylor Coleridge, *Biographia Literaria, or Biographical Sketches of My Literary Life and Opinions*, ed. James Engell and W. Jackson Bate, 2 vols (London and Princeton, 1983), vol. I, p. 168.

45 Robert Plot, *The Natural History of Stafford-shire* (Oxford, 1686), p. 269.

46 *Le Siècle*, 7 November 1862, reported in Laisnel de la Salle, *Croyances et légendes du centre de la France* (Paris, 1875), vol. II, p. 2.

47 Francis Mauriceau, *The Accomplisht Midwife, Treating of the Diseases of Women With Child, and in Child-bed*, trans. Hugh Chamberlen (London, 1673), p. 53.

48 Maubray, *Female Physician*, pp. 355, 361.

49 *Ibid.*, pp. 364–5.

50 *Ibid.*, p. 365.

51 Claude Quillet, *Callipaedia: seu de pulchrae prolis habendae rationae* (Lugduni Batavorum, 1655).

52 *Callipaediae: or An Art to Have Handsome Children* (London, 1710); *Callipaedia: or The Art of Getting Pretty Children*, trans 'by various hands' [in fact, principally William Oldesworth] (London, 1710); *Callipaedia: A Poem in Four Books . . . Made English By N. Rowe* (London, 1712). *The Conjugal Directory; or the Joys of Hymen: a Poem in Three Books*, a pirated translation based with tiny variations on the 1710 Oldesworth translation of *Callipaedia*, first appeared in 1768, but was reprinted by John Lowndes in 1825. Later in the century, L. Noirot borrowed Quillet's title for his attempt to provide more up-to-date advice to parents, in his *La Callipédie Contemporaine, ou l'art d'avoir des enfants sains de corps et d'esprit* (Paris, 1869); though it offers to put Quillet's advice on a more scientific basis, the third chapter of the book on the influence of the mother's imagination during maternity recycles some of the classical stories alluded to by Quillet alongside cases allegedly from his own clinical experience. Noirot's explanation of the phenomenon is that the soul of the mother, 'est grosse aussi de la pensée de ce même embryon', is engrossed with the thought of the embryo that fills out her body (p. 102).

53 I follow Andrew Pyle's description of the transformation of Aristotelian species theory into mechanistic theories during the seventeenth century: Andrew Pyle, *Atomism and Its Critics: Problem Areas Associated With the Development of the Atomic Theory of Matter From Democritus to Newton* (Bristol, 1995), pp. 359–75.

54 Quillet, *Callipaedia*, p. 33.

55 *Titi Lucreti Cari De rerum natura, libri sex*, ed. and trans. Cyril Bailey (Oxford, 1947), IV.54–64, vol. I, pp. 364–5.

56 The discussion of simulacra is to be found in Pierre Gassendi's *Animadversiones in decimum librum diogenis laertii* (Lugduni, 1649), pp. 236–60; the corresponding discussion is to be found in Walter Charleton, *Physiologia Epicuro-Gassendo-Carltoniana: or A Fabrick of Science Natural, Upon the Hypothesis of Atoms* (London, 1654), pp. 136–81.

57 Charleton, *Physiologia*, p. 137.

58 *Ibid.*, p. 141.

59 David Sedley, *Lucretius and the Transformation of Greek Wisdom* (Cambridge, 1998), pp. 39–42.

60 Quillet, *Callipaedia*, p. 33.

61 *Callipaediae: or The Art of Getting Pretty Children*, p. 39.

62 *Callipaedia: A Poem in Four Books*, p. 26.

63 *Callipaediae: or An Art to Have Handsome Children*, pp. 83–4.

64 'Metaphysical Colloquy, Or Doubts and Rebuttals Concerning The Metaphysics of René Descartes, With His Replies', *The Selected Works of Pierre Gassendi*, ed. and trans. Craig B. Brush (New York and London, 1972), p. 273.

65 *De rerum natura*, ed. Bailey, vol. I, p. 190.

66 Gassendi, 'Metaphysical Colloquy', p. 274.

67 Nicolas Malebranche, *The Search After Truth and Elucidations of the Search After Truth*, trans. Thomas M. Lennon and Paul J. Olscamp (Cambridge, 1997), p. 87. References hereafter in my text.

68 Kenelm Digby, *Two Treatises. In the One of Which, The Nature of Bodies; In the Other, The Nature of Man's Soule; Is Looked Into . . .* (Paris, 1643), pp. 329–30.

69 *Ibid.*, p. 330.
70 *Ibid.*, p. 336.

5 Stigmata

1   Elizabeth Bronfen, *The Knotted Subject: Hysteria and Its Discontents* (Princeton, 1998).
2   *Ibid.*, p. 35.
3   Etienne Trillat, *Histoire de l'hystérie* (Paris, 1986), p. 54.
4   *Soeur Jeanne des Anges, supérieure des Ursulines de Loudun: autobiographie d'une hystérique possédée, d'après le manuscrit inédit de la Bibliothèque de Tours*, ed. Gabriel Legué and Georges Gilles de la Tourette (Paris, 1886).
5   Jean-Martin Charcot and Paul Richer, *Les démoniaques dans l'art* (Paris, 1887).
6   Christopher G. Goetz, Michel Bonduelle and Toby Gelfand, *Charcot: Constructing Neurology* (New York and Oxford, 1995), pp. 192–6.
7   Jacques Maître, *Une inconnu célèbre: la Madeleine Lebouc de Janet* (Paris, 1993), pp. 49–77.
8   The most comprehensive modern account of religious stigmatization is to be found in Ian Wilson's *The Bleeding Mind: An Investigation Into the Mysterious Phenomenon of Stigmata* (London, 1991). Its appendix, 'Stigmatic Biographies' (pp. 131–48), gathers and summarizes the forms taken by the phenomenon from the fourteenth century to the present. F. A. Whitlock and J. V. Hynes provide a judicious overview of the history and literature of the phenomenon in 'Religious Stigmatization: An Historical and Psychophysiological Enquiry', *Psychological Medicine*, VIII (1978), pp. 185–202.
9   Pierre Janet, *The Mental State of Hystericals: A Study of Mental Stigmata and Mental Accidents*, trans. Caroline Rollin Corson (New York and London, 1901).
10 William James, *Psychological Review*, I (1894), p. 199.
11 Maurice Apte, *Les Stigmatisés: étude historique et critique sur les troubles vaso-moteurs chez les mystiques* (Paris, 1903), pp. 172–3.
12 See Schlomo G. Shoham, *The Mark of Cain: The Stigma Theory of Crime and Social Deviation* (Jerusalem, 1970).
13 Erwin J. Haeberle, '"Stigmata of Degeneration": Prisoner Markings in Nazi Concentration Camps', *Journal of Homosexuality*, VI (1980–1), pp. 135–40.
14 Sander Gilman, 'The Image of the Hysteric', in Sander Gilman et al., *Hysteria Before Freud* (Berkeley and London, 1993), pp. 386–9.
15 Thomas D. Savill, *Lectures on Hysteria and Allied Vaso-Motor Conditions* (London, 1909), pp. 46, 49. References hereafter in text.
16 *The Complete Poems and Plays of T. S. Eliot* (London, 1973), p. 16
17 Victor Burq, *Métallothérapie: traitement des maladies nerveuses, paralysies, rhumatisme chronique, spasmes, névralgies, chlorose, hystérie, hypochondrie, délire, monomanie, etc; des convulsions de l'enfance, du choléra, des crampes des cholériques, etc.; par les applications métalliques: abrégé historique, théorique et pratique* (Paris, 1853).
18 Paul Richer, *Etudes cliniques sur l'hystérie-epilepsie ou grand hystérie* (Paris, 1881), p. 539.
19 Gustave Alquier, *De l'anesthésie cutanée et de sa valeur sémiologique* (Paris, 1873), p. 44.
20 Georges Gilles de la Tourette, *Traité clinique et thérapeutique de l'hystérie* (Paris, 1891–5), vol. I, pp. 128–33.
21 Jacques Fontaine, *Des marques des sorciers et da la réelle possession que le diable prend sur le corps des hommes* (Paris, 1611), pp. 6–7. References hereafter in my text.
22 Michel Pastoureau, *The Devil's Cloth: A History of Stripes and Striped Fabric*, trans. Jody Gladding (New York, 2001), p. 27.
23 Nineteenth-century studies of dermographism in hysteria include the following: Ernest Mesnet, 'Autographisme et Stigmates', *Revue de l'hypnotisme et de la psychologie physiologique*, IV (1889–90), pp. 321–35; Charles Féré and Henri Lamy, 'La dermographie', *Nouvelle Iconographie de la Salpêtrière*, II (1889), pp. 283–9; Arthur Ducamp, *Dermographie chez un hystérique* (Montpellier, 1890); Henri Guimbail, *La dermographie, son rôle dans l'histoire, le mécanisme de sa production* (Clermont, 1891); V. Cornu, *Contribution à l'étude de la dermographie (urticaire graphique, provoquée)* (Paris, 1890); Toussaint Barthélemy, *Etude sur le dermographisme: ou dermoneurose toxivasomotrice* (Paris, 1893); Maurice Lannois, 'Dermographisme ches des épileptiques atteints d'helminthiase intestinale', *Nouvelle Iconographie de la Salpêtrière*, XIV (1901), pp. 213–37; Louis Trepsat, 'Un cas de démence précoce catatonique avec pseudo-oedème compliqué de purpura', *Nouvelle Iconographie de la Salpêtrière*, XVII (1904), pp. 193–9.
24 Janet Beizer, *Ventriloquized Bodies: Narratives of Hysteria in Nineteenth-Century France* (Ithaca and London, 1994), p. 26.
25 *Ibid.*, p. 29.
26 Charles Baudouin, *Suggestion and Autosuggestion: A Psychological and*

Pedagogical Study Based Upon the Investigations Made by the New Nancy School, trans. Eden and Cedar Paul (London, 1920), p. 100.

27   Edmond Duchâtel and René Warcollier, *Les miracles de la volonté: sa force plastique dans le corps et hors du corps humain* (Paris, 1914), pp. 60–1, 211–14.

28   H. P. Blavatsky, *Isis Unveiled: A Master-Key to the Mysteries of Ancient and Modern Science and Theology* (New York, 1877), vol. I, p. 396. References hereafter in the text.

29   Sigmund Freud, 'Charcot', *Collected Papers* (London, 1948), p. 14.

30   Georges Didi-Huberman, 'Une notion de "corps-cliché" au XIXe siècle', *Parachute*, XXXV (1984), pp. 8–14.

31   Goetz *et al.*, *Charcot*, p. 143.

32   *Ibid.*, p. 144.

33   Alison Winter, *Mesmerized: Powers of the Mind in Victorian Britain* (Chicago, 1998), pp. 306–20.

34   Michel Serres, *Genesis*, trans. Geneviève James and James Nielson (Ann Arbor, 1995), p. 34.

35   Georges Didi-Hubermann, *Invention de l'hystérie: Charcot et l'iconographie photographique de la Salpêtrière* (Paris, 1982), pp. 51–2.

36   Montague Summers, *The Physical Phenomena of Mysticism: With Special Reference to the Stigmata, Divine and Diabolic* (New York, 1950), pp. 129–30.

37   *Ibid.*, p. 130.

38   Sigmund Freud, 'Fragment of an Analysis of a Case of Hysteria', *The Standard Edition of the Complete Psychological Works of Sigmund Freud*, trans. James Strachey *et al.* (London, 1995), vol. VII (trans. Alix and James Strachey), p. 24.

39   Sigmund Freud and Joseph Breuer, *Studies on Hysteria*, Standard Edition, vol. II, pp. 206–7. References hereafter in text.

40   Sigmund Freud, 'A Note Upon the "Mystic Writing Pad"', *Standard Edition*, vol. XIX, pp. 227–32.

41   Jacques Derrida, *The Post Card: From Socrates to Freud and Beyond*, trans. Alan Bass (Chicago and London, 1987), p. 441.

42   Didi-Hubermann, *Invention de l'hystérie*, p. 90.

6 Off-Colour

1   The literature on colour, which is very substantial, tends to fall into three groups: colour theory and the philosophy and psychology of colour perception; the history of colouristic style and technique in painting; and archetypalist claims for the experience of colour, often combined with claims for its healing properties. Informative and stimulating though they may be for the cultural historian, Faber Birren's many works on the experience of colour belong in the third category. Even John Gage's superb, wideranging *Colour and Culture: The Practice and Meaning of Colour From Antiquity to Abstraction* (London, 1993) demonstrates a very restricted understanding of colour outside the sphere of art. The materials for a properly cultural history of colour are scattered and intermittent, but would certainly include the works of Manlio Brusatin, David Batchelor, Jacqueline Lichtenstein and Michel Pastoureau cited in what follows.

2   B. Berlin and P. Kay, *Basic Color Terms: Their Understanding and Evolution* (Berkeley, 1969).

3   Illuminating as it is in other ways, the reading of blackness and whiteness in Adam Lively, *Masks: Blackness, Race and the Imagination* (London, 1998), pp. 20–42, is an example of this limitation.

4   David Batchelor, *Chromophobia* (London, 2000), p. 22.

5   *Ibid.*, p. 52.

6   Jacqueline Lichtenstein, *The Eloquence of Color: Rhetoric and Painting in the French Classical Age*, trans. Emily McVarish (Berkeley, Los Angeles and Oxford, 1993), p. 52.

7   *Titi Lucreti Cari De Rerum Natura, Libri Sex*, ed. and trans. Cyril Bailey (Oxford, 1947), IV.72–86, vol. I, pp. 365–7.

8   Lichtenstein, *Eloquence of Color*, pp. 62–3.

9   *Chambers' Dictionary of Etymology*, ed. Robert Barnhart (London, 1988), p. 170; Julius Pokorny, *Indogermanisches Etymologishes Wörterbuch* (Berne and Munich, 1959–69), vol. I, p. 460.

10   Tertullian, 'On The Ascetics' Mantle', *The Writings of Quintus Sept. Flor. Tertullianus*, 3 vols, trans. Revd Sydney Thelwall and Revd Dr Holmes (Edinburgh, 1869); vol. III, p. 188, *De pallio, Patrologia latina cursus completus*, ed. Jacques-Paul Migne (Paris, 1844–65), vol. II (1844), pp. 1037–8.

11   Michel Pastoureau, *Jésus chez le teinturier: couleurs et teintures dans l'Occident médiéval* (Paris, 1997), p. 86.

12   Benjamin Keach, *The Progress of Sin: Or the Travels of the Ungodly . . .* (London, 1684), p. 148.

13   Richard Brathwait, *Panthalia: or the Royal Romance . . .* (London, 1659), p. 86; Thomas D' Urfey *The Virtuous Wife: A Critical Edition*, ed. William E. Carpenter (New York and London, 1987), II.i, p. 89.

14   *Virtuous Wife*, ed. Carpenter, III.i, p. 113.

15 Christopher Harvey, 'The Church', *The Synagogue, or, The shadow of The Temple: sacred poems and private ejaculations, in imitation of Mr. George Herbert* (London, 1640), p. 5.

16 Mark Haeffner, *The Dictionary of Alchemy: From Maria Prophetissa to Isaac Newton* (London, 1991), pp. 200–201.

17 Patrick Ker, 'Carolismus, or, The *Loyal Patient*, on the *Sovereign* touch', *Flosculum Poeticum: Poems Divine and Humane, Panegyrical, Satyrical, Ironical* (London, 1684), p. 24.

18 Samuel Pordage, *Mundorum Explicatio: or, the explanation of an hieroglyphical figure: wherein are couched the mysteries of the external, internal, and eternal worlds: . . . a sacred poem* (London, 1661), p. 193.

19 *Ibid.*, p. 300

20 John Donne, 'To Sir Edward Herbert, at Julyers', *Poems, by J.D.: With Elegies on the Authors Death* (London, 1633), p. 83.

21 John Reynolds, *The Triumphes of Gods Revenge against . . . Murther or His miraculous discoveries and severe punishments thereof. . .* (London, 1635), p. 434.

22 The discovery was reported in January 2002 by astronomers Ivan Baldry and Karl Glazebrook to a meeting of the American Astronomical Society meeting in Washington DC. See http://news.bbc.co.uk/1/hi/sci/tech/1754900.stm.

23 Lichtenstein, *Eloquence of Color*, p. 185.

24 Plutarch, 'Concerning the Face Which Appears in the Orb of the Moon', *Moralia, In 16 Volumes* (Cambridge, MA and London, 1927–69), vol. XII, with translation by Harold Cherniss and William C. Humbold, pp. 34–223.

25 Dante Alighieri, *The Divine Comedy*, with translation by Charles S. Singleton (Princeton, 1971–5), *Paradiso*, vol. I (1975), Canto 2, ll. 49–148, pp. 18–25.

26 The most comprehensive discussion of theories of lunar spots is still the chapter entitled 'The Spot on the Lunar Disk' in Pierre Duhem's *Medieval Cosmology: Theories of Infinity, Place, Time, Void, and the Plurality of Worlds*, ed. and trans. Roger Ariew (Chicago and London, 1985), pp. 479–98.

27 *The Questions of Bartholomew and the Book of the Resurrection of Christ*, 4.4 in *The Apocryphal New Testament: A Collection of Apocryphal Christian Literature in an English Translation*, trans. J. K. Elliott (Oxford, 1993), p. 661.

28 Ewa Kuryluk, *Veronica and Her Cloth: History, Symbolism and Structure of a "True" Image* (Oxford, 1991), p. 184.

29 Quoted in Steven Runciman, *Byzantine Style and Civilisation* (Harmondsworth, 1975), p. 87. Gage's chapter 'Light From the East' (*Colour and Culture*, pp. 39–68), deals in great detail with the artistic representation of divine light in Byzantine and European medieval culture.

30 Zohar, 1.15a, quoted in Gerschom Scholem, 'Colours and Their Symbolism in Jewish Tradition and Mysticism', *Diogenes*, CVIII (1979), p. 104.

31 Lorenz Oken, *Elements of Physiophilosophy*, trans. Alfred Tulk (London, 1847), p. 79.

32 *Virgil: Eclogues, Georgics, Aeneid I–VI*, with a translation by H. Rushton Fairclough revised by G. P. Goold (Cambridge, MA, 1999), 2.616, p. 356.

33 Gilbert J. French, *Notes on the Nimbus* (Bolton, 1854); Franz Xavier Kraus, *Geschichte der Christlichen Kunst* (Freiburg im Breisgau, 1896), vol. I, pp. 220–2; Adolf Krücke, *Der Nimbus und verwandte Attribute in der frühchristlichen Kunst* (Strasburg, 1905); Marthe Collinet-Guérin, *Histoire du nimbe: des origines aux temps modernes* (Paris, 1961).

34 Edwin D. Babbitt, *The Principles of Light and Color: Including Among Other Things the Harmonic Laws of the Universe, the Etherio-atomic Philosophy of Force, Chromo Chemistry, Chromo Therapeutics, and the General Philosophy of the Fine Forces, Together with Numerous Discoveries and Practical Applications* (New York, 1878).

35 A. Marques, *The Human Aura: A Study* (San Francisco, 1896); William Wilberforce Colville, *The Human Aura and the Significance of Color: Three Lectures* (London, 1905); Walter J. Kilner, *The Human Atmosphere* (New York, 1911).

36 Stanley Krippner and Daniel Rubin, eds, *Galaxies of Life: The Human Aura in Acupuncture and Kirlian Photography* (New York, 1973).

37 Richard Bentley, *The Folly of Atheism, and (What is Now Called) Deism, Even With Respect to the Present Life* (London, 1692), p. 8.

38 Frederick Lees, 'Modern Saints and Modern Miracles: An Interview With Joris Karl Huysmans', *The Humanitarian*, XIV (1899), p. 82.

39 Batchelor, *Chromophobia*, p. 106.

40 Lichtenstein, *Eloquence of Color*, p. 165.

41 Fenja Gunn, *The Artificial Face: Cosmetics in Antiquity* (Newton Abbot, 1973), p. 80.

42 Frantz Fanon, *Black Skin, White Masks*, trans. Charles Lam Markmann (London and Sydney, 1986), pp. 111, 112.

43 Barbara Maria Stafford, *Body Criticism:*

Imaging the Unseen in Enlightenment Art and Medicine (Cambridge, MA and London, 1991), pp. 310–11.

44 *The Code of Maimonides. Book Ten: The Book of Cleanness*, trans. Herbert Danby (New Haven, 1954), p. 150.

45 E.V. Hulse, 'The Nature of Biblical "Leprosy" and the Use of Alternative Medical Terms in Modern Translations of the Bible', *Palestine Exploration Quarterly*, CVII (1975), pp. 87–105; John Wilkinson, 'Leprosy and Leviticus: The Problem of Description and Identification', *Scottish Journal of Theology*, XXX (1977), pp. 153–66.

46 *Coleridge: Selected Poems*, ed. Richard Holmes (London, 1996), p. 87.

47 Michel Pastoureau, 'Une histoire des couleurs est-il possible?', *Ethnologie française*, XX (1990), p. 371.

48 Joannitius (Hunayn ibn Ishaq al-'Ibadi), *Isagoge Johannitii in Tegni Galeni*, trans. H.P. Cholmeley in *John of Gaddesdon and the Rosa Medicinae* (Oxford, 1912), p.142; repr. in *A Source Book of Medieval Science*, ed. Edward Grant (Cambridge, MA, 1974), p. 707.

49 Michel Pastoureau, 'Formes et couleurs du désordre: le jaune avec le vert', *Médiévales*, IV (1983), pp. 62–73.

50 *The Yellow Sash; or H[anover] Beshit An Excellent New Ballad To the Old Tune, of Lillibullero* (London, 1743).

51 John Gage, *Colour and Culture*, p. 171.

52 Robert Fludd, *Medicina Catholica: seu mysticum artis medicandi sacrarium* (Frankfurt, 1629–31), vol. II, p. 60.

53 Manlio Brusatin, *A History of Colors*, trans. Robert H. Hopcke and Paul Schwartz (Boston and London, 1991), pp. 29–30.

54 *Poems of Gerard Manley Hopkins*, ed. W. H. Gardner and N. H. MacKenzie, 4th edn (London, New York and Toronto, 1970), p. 69.

55 Pastoureau, 'Formes et couleurs du désordre', p. 69.

56 Oken, *Physiophilosophy*, p. 79

57 *Ibid.*, p. 78.

58 Kuryluk, *Veronica and Her Cloth*, p. 196.

59 Julia Kristeva, *Powers of Horror: An Essay on Abjection*, trans. Leon S. Roudiez (New York, 1982), pp. 2–3.

60 J. W. von Goethe, *Theory of Colours*, trans. Charles L. Eastlake (London, 1967), p. 308.

61 Robert Weltsch, 'Wear It With Pride, The Yellow Badge', *Jüdische Rundschau*, XXVII (4 April 1933); translated at www.yad-vashem.org.il/about_holocaust/documents/part1/doc14.html. Consulted 19 December 2002.

62 For further discussion of the skin in Nazism see James M. Glass, 'The Skin Ego

and Purification Ritual: Psychodynamics Behind the Nazi Final Solution', *Journal for the Psychoanalysis of Culture and Society*, II (1997), pp. 45–54.

63 Klaus Hödl, 'Der jüdische Körper als Stigma', *Österreichische Zeitschrift für Geschichtswissenschaften*, VIII (1997), pp. 222–3.

64 Max Beerbohm, 'A Defence of Cosmetics', *The Yellow Book*, I (1894), pp. 65–82.

65 Gregory Blue, 'Gobineau on China: Race Theory, the "Yellow Peril," and the Critique of Modernity', *Journal of World History*, X (1999), p. 100.

66 'The Oriental Canker' or 'The Yellow Peril in Canada' (1912), p. 53.

67 M. P. Shiel, *The Yellow Danger* (London, 1898), *The Yellow Wave* (London, 1905), *The Yellow Peril* (London, 1929).

68 Shiel, *Yellow Peril*, pp. 19–20.

69 Havelock Ellis, 'The Psychology of Yellow', *Popular Science Monthly*, LXVIII (1906), pp. 456–63.

70 Michel Pastoureau, *Blue: The History of a Color*, trans. Markus I. Cruse (Princeton, 2001).

71 Friedrich Nietzsche, *Daybreak: Thoughts on the Prejudices of Morality*, trans. R. J. Hollingdale (Cambridge, 1982), pp. 182–3.

72 Ellis, 'Psychology of Yellow', p. 463.

73 'The Yellow Wallpaper', *The Charlotte Perkins Gilman Reader: 'The Yellow Wallpaper' and Other Fiction*, ed. Ann J. Lane (London, 1980), pp. 3–19. References hereafter in my text.

74 *Ibid.*, pp. 19–20.

75 Shirley Eaton, *Golden Girl* (London, 1999), p. 12.

76 http://www.allwatchers.com/Board.asp?BoardID=3554. For a debunking of the legend, see the 'Urban Legends Reference Pages' website: http://www.snopes.com/movies/films/golding.htm, and dermatologist Val Reese's comprehensive 'Skinema' site about dermatology in the cinema: http://itsb.ucsf.edu/~vcr/BondGirlEaton.html. Consulted 21 December 2002.

7 Unction

1 Jean-Paul Sartre, *Being and Nothingness: An Essay on Phenomenological Ontology*, trans. Hazel E. Barnes (London, 1984), p. 604.

2 St Augustine, *On Christian Doctrine*, trans. J. F. Shaw, in *The Confessions, The City of God, On Christian Doctrine*, trans. R. S. Pine-Coffin et al. (Chicago, 1990), 2.16, p. 726.

3 W. Robertson Smith, *Lectures on the Religion of the Semites. First Series: The*

Fundamental Institutions (Edinburgh, 1889), pp. 359–60.

4 A. Smythe Palmer, *Jacob at Bethel: The Vision – The Stone – The Anointing* (London, 1899), p. 146.

5 Mary Douglas, *Leviticus as Literature* (Oxford, 1999), p. 79. References hereafter in my text.

6 Smythe Palmer, *Jacob at Bethel*, p. 148.

7 'Agesilaus', in *Plutarch's Lives*, with a translation by Bernadotte Perrin, vol. v (Cambridge, MA and London, 1990), pp. 97–9.

8 Smith, *Religion of the Semites*, p. 360.

9 J. G. Frazer, *The Golden Bough: A Study in Magic and Religion* (London, 1936), (*Part V:2 Spirits of the Corn and Wild*) vol. VIII, pp. 162–6.

10 Edward Topsell, *The Historie of Four-Footed Beastes* (London, 1607), p. 586.

11 Smythe Palmer, *Jacob at Bethel*, p. 150.

12 W. Jardine Grisbrooke, 'Blessings of Oil and Anointings: The Byzantine Rite', in *The Oil of Gladness: Anointing in the Christian Tradition*, ed. Martin Dudley and Geoffrey Rowell (London and Collegeville, 1993), p. 214.

13 Edward Yarnold translates this word as 'seal', noting its origin in 'Syriac *rushma*, underlying Greek *sphragis*': Edward Yarnold, *The Awe-Inspiring Rites of Initiation: Baptismal Homilies of the Fourth Century* (Slough, 1971), p. 186, n.25.

14 *Commentary of Theodore of Mopsuestia on the Lord's Prayer and on the Sacraments of Baptism and the Eucharist*, trans. A. Mingana, Woodbrooke Studies: Christian Documents Edited and Translated With a Critical Apparatus: vol. VI (Cambridge, 1933) p. 46.

15 Grisbrooke, 'The Byzantine Rite', p. 212.

16 Martin Dudley, 'Rites for the Blessing of Oils and Anointing: The Western Tradition', in *Oil of Gladness*, pp. 186–7.

17 A. Lucas, *Ancient Egyptian Materials and Industries*, 3rd edn (London, 1948), pp. 359–64; E. A. Wallis Budge, *The Mummy: A Handbook of Egyptian Funerary Archaeology* (London and New York, 1987), p. 212.

18 Budge, *The Mummy*, p. 238.

19 Dudley, 'Rites for the Blessing of Oils', p. 187.

20 William Dunne, *The Ritual Explained: A Manual for the Use of the Clergy, With Special Reference to the Clergy in England*, 5th edn (Ambleside and London, 1941), p. 68.

21 Michel Serres, *Les cinq sens* (Paris, 1998), pp. 35–6.

22 *The Poems of Gerard Manley Hopkins*, 4th edn, ed. W. H. Gardner and Norman MacKenzie (London, 1970), p. 66.

23 *Emily Dickinson: The Complete Poems*, ed. Thomas H. Johnson (London, 1984), p. 335.

24 L. F., *Christs Bloodie Sweat, or The Sonne of God In His Agonie* (London, 1616), p. 19.

25 *The Arabic Gospel of the Infancy of the Saviour*, in *New Testament Apocrypha: Apocryphal Gospels, Acts and Revelations*, trans. Alexander Walker (Edinburgh, 1870), pp. 101–2.

26 C.C.B., 'Oil of Man', *Notes and Queries*, 8th series, x (1896), pp. 314–15.

27 *Dictionary of National Biography*, ed. Leslie Stephen and Sidney Lee (London, 1885–1900), vol. x, p. 350.

28 Clément Marot, *Les Epigrammes*, ed. C. A. Mayer (London, 1970), pp. 156, 158.

29 *Ibid.*, p. 158.

30 John Chrysostomos, *Baptismal Homilies* 2.24, quoted in John Halliburton, 'Anointing in the Early Church', *Oil of Gladness*, p. 79.

31 Smythe Palmer, *Jacob at Bethel*, p. 181.

32 Gaston Bachelard, *The Flame of a Candle*, trans. Joni Caldwell (Dallas, 1988), p. 66.

33 *Ibid.*, p. 66.

34 Naomi Wolf, *The Beauty Myth* (London, 1990), p. 81.

35 *Ibid.*, p. 82.

36 *Ibid.*, p. 80.

37 *Ibid.*, p. 241.

38 Apuleius, *The Golden Ass: Or Metamorphoses*, trans. E.J. Kenney (Harmondsworth, 1998), 3.21, pp. 50–51.

39 *Ibid.*, 3.24, p. 52.

40 Holinshed's *Chronicle of Ireland* (1587), p. 69, quoted in Margaret Murray, *The God of the Witches* (London, 1952), p. 88.

41 Jacobus Sprenger and Heinrich Kramer, *Malleus Maleficarum: The Hammer of Witchcraft*, trans. Montague Summers, ed. Pennethorne Hughes (London, 1968), p. 68.

42 Lambert Daneau, *A Dialogue of Witches, in foretime named Lot-tellers, and now commonly called sorcerers . . .* (London, 1575), sig. F7^r.

43 Henri Boguet, *Discours des sorciers: avec dis advis en faict de sorcelerie.et une instruction povr un Juge en semblable matiere*, 2nd edn (Lyon, 1608), pp. 104–5.

44 Montague Summers, *The History of Witchcraft* (London, 1994), p. 5.

45 Daneau, *Dialogue of Witches*, sig. H6^r.

46 Martin del Rio, *Investigations Into Magic*, ed. and trans. P. G. Maxwell-Stuart (Manchester, 2000), p. 94.

47 Daneau, *Dialogue of Witches*, sig. H6^r.

48 Boguet, *Discours des sorciers*, p. 105.

49 Margaret Murray, *The Witch-Cult in*

Western Europe: A Study in Anthropology (Oxford, 1921) pp. 279–80.

50 Michael J. Harner, 'The Role of Hallucinogenic Plants in European Witchcraft', in *Hallucinogens and Shamanism*, ed. Michael J. Harner (New York, 1973), pp. 127–50.

51 Ioan P. Couliano, *Eros and Magic in the Renaissance*, trans. Margaret Cook (Chicago and London, 1987), p. 153.

52 *Ibid.*, p. 245, n. 34.

53 Murray, *God of the Witches*, p. 91.

54 Brian P. Levack, *The Witch-Hunt in Early Modern Europe* (London and New York, 1987), p. 45

55 Clark Heinrich, *Strange Fruit: Alchemy, Religion and Magical Foods: A Speculative History* (London, 1996), p. 123.

56 Johann Weyer, *De praestigiis daemonum* (1583), trans. John Shea as *Witches, Devils, and Doctors in the Renaissance* (Binghamton, NY, 1991), 3.17, pp. 225–8.

57 Marvin Harris, *Cows, Pigs, Wars and Witches: The Riddles of Culture* (London, 1975), pp. 220, 221.

58 Samuel Butler, 'John Audland's Letter to William Prynne, and William Prynne's Answer', *The Genuine Remains In Prose and Verse of Mr Samuel Butler* (London, 1759), vol. I, p. 388.

59 Francis Grose, *A Classical Dictionary of the Vulgar Tongue* (London, 1785), no page numbering.

60 Daneau, *Dialogue of Witches*, sig. C3ᵛ.

61 Joseph Glanvill, *Saducismus Triumphatus: or full and plain evidence concerning witch-craft and apparitions, in two parts, the first part treating of their possibility, the second of their real existence* (London, 1681), vol. II, p. 139, 148.

62 Murray, *Witch-Cult*, p. 101, *God of the Witches*, p.101–2.

63 Del Rio, *Investigations Into Magic*, p. 94.

64 Boguet, *Discours des sorciers*, pp. 51–2, 53.

65 Henry More, *An Antidote Against Atheism: Or, An Appeal to the Natural Faculties of the Mind of Man, Whether There Be Not a God*, 3rd edn (London, 1662), in *A Collection of Several Philosophical Writings of Dr Henry More*, 2nd edn (London, 1662), pp. 123–4.

66 *Ibid.*, p. 123

67 Glanvill, *Saducismus Triumphatus*, vol. I, pp. 14, 13.

68 Reginald Scot, *The Discoverie of Witchcraft*, ed. Brinsley Nicholson (Wakefield, 1973), 10.8, p. 148.

69 Jean de Nynauld, *De la lycanthropie, trans-formation, et extase des sorciers . . .* (Paris, 1615), p. 26.

70 More, *Antidote*, pp. 122–3.

71 Del Rio, *Investigations Into Magic*, p. 100.

72 Nynauld, *De la lycanthropie*, pp. 50–3.

73 A.P.T.B. von Hohenheim (Paracelsus), *De summis naturae mysteriis libri tres, lectu perquam utiles atque iucundi*, trans. (from German) Gerard Dorn (Basle, 1570), pp. 127–9.

74 Kenelm Digby, *A Late Discourse Made in a Solemne Assembly of Noble and Learned Men at Montpellier in France . . . Touching the Cure of Wounds By the Power of Sympathy*, trans. B. White, 2nd edn (London, 1658), p. 9.

75 *Ibid.*, pp. 79, 123, 124–6.

76 Carlos Ziller Camenietzki, 'Jesuits and Alchemy in the Early Seventeenth Century: Father Johannes Roberti and the Weapon-Salve Controversy', *Ambix*, XLVIII (2001), p. 97.

77 William Foster *Hoplocrisma-Spongus: or, a Sponge to wipe away the Weapon-Salve. A Treatise, wherein is proved, that the Cure late-taken up amongst us, by applying the Salve to the Weapon, is Magicall and Unlawfull* (London, 1631); Robert Fludd, *Dr Fludd's Answer Unto M. Foster, or the Squeezing of Parson Foster's Sponge, Ordained by his for the Wiping Away of the Weapon-Salve* (London, 1631). An account of the arguments is provided in Lynn Thorndike, *A History of Magic and Experimental Science* (New York, 1923–58), vol. VIII, pp. 503–7.

78 John Hales, 'A Letter to an Honourable Person, Concerning the *Weapon-Salve*' (1630), in *Golden Remains, Of the Ever-Memorable Mr. John Hales, of Eaton-Colledge* (London, 1673), pp. 288, 290.

79 *Ibid.*, p. 284.

80 Eric Partridge, *A Dictionary of Slang and Unconventional English, Colloquialisms and Catch Phrases, Fossilised Jokes and Puns, General Nicknames, Vulgarisms and Such Americanisms As Have Been Naturalised*, ed. Paul Beale (London and New York, 1991), p. 820.

81 *Phillip Stubbes's Anatomy of the Abuses in England in Shakespere's Youth AD 1583. Part II: The Display of Corruptions Requiring Correction*, ed. Frederick J. Furnivall (London, 1882), p. 70.

82 John Oldham, 'Satyr IV: S. Ignatius His Image Brought In, Discovering the Rogueries of the Jesuits, and Ridiculous Superstitions of the Church of Rome', *The Works of Mr. John Oldham, Together With His Remains* (London, 1684), Bk 1, p. 80.

83 'Epinal-Erfurt Corpus', *The Oldest English Texts*, ed. Henry Sweet (London, 1885), p. 107.

84 *The Holy Gospels in Anglo-Saxon,*

Northumbrian, and Old Mercian Versions, ed. W. W. Skeat (Cambridge, 1871–87), The Gospel According to St. Matthew (1887), p. 56.

85 Dan Michel's Ayenbite of Inwyt or, Remorse of Conscience, ed. Richard Morris, vol. I. Text (London, 1965), p. 93.

86 Robert Crowley, An Informacion and Peticion, Against the Oppressours of the Pore Commons of This Realme (1550), repr. in Select Works of Robert Crowley, ed. J. M. Cowper (London, 1872), pp. 154–5.

87 'The Paraphrase of Erasmus Upon the Epistle of Sainct James thapostle', in The Second Tome or Volume of the Paraphrase of Erasmus Upon the Newe Testament, trans. Miles Coverdale et al. (London, 1549), fol. 37 (sig. C.G.i).

88 The Booke of the Common Prayer and Administracion of the Sacramentes, and Other Rites and Ceremonies of the Churche: After the Use of the Churche of England (London, 1549), facsimile reprint as The Book of Common Prayer Printed By Whitchurch March 1549: Commonly Called the First Book of Edward VI (London, 1844), fol. cxvi, sig. Ff2ʳ; The Booke of the Common Prayer and Administracion of the Sacramentes, and Other Rites and Ceremonies in the Churche of Englande (London, 1552), facsimile reprint as The Book of Common Prayer Printed By Whitchurch 1552: Commonly Called the Second Book of Edward VI (London, 1844), sig. X3ʳ.

89 John Marston, Antonio's Revenge, ed. W. Reaveley Gair (Manchester, 1999), iv.iii, p. 134.

90 H. G. Wells, The Invisible Man (London, 1996), p. 92.

91 Sartre, Being and Nothingness, p. 602.

92 Ibid., p. 610.

93 Charles Dickens, Bleak House, ed. Norman Page (Harmondsworth, 1971), p. 49. References hereafter in my text.

94 Anthony Trollope, Barchester Towers, ed. Michael Sadleir and Frederick Page (Oxford, 1980), p. 29.

95 Charles Dickens, Great Expectations, ed. Angus Calder (Harmondsworth, 1970), p. 107.

96 Philippe Mailhebiau, Portraits in Oils: The Personality of Aromatherapy Oils and Their Link With Human Temperaments (La Nouvelle Aromathérapie), trans. Susan Y. Chalkley (Saffron Walden, 1995) p. 4.

8 Aroma

1 Piero Camporesi, The Incorruptible Flesh: Bodily Mutation and Mortification in Religion and Folklore, trans. Tania Croft-Murray and Helen Elsom (Cambridge, 1988), p. 210.

2 Cornelis Houtman, 'On the Function of the Holy Incense (Exodus xxx 34–8) and the Sacred Anointing Oil (Exodus xxx 22–33)', Vetus Testamentum, XLII (1992), pp. 463–4.

3 Kenelm Digby, A Late Discourse Made in a Solemne Assembly of Noble and Learned Men at Montpellier in France . . . Touching the Cure of Wounds By the Power of Sympathy, trans. B. White, 2nd edn (London, 1658), p. 76.

4 June Thornton, Beautiful Skin With Aromatherapy (London, 1998), pp. 8–9.

5 James Manning, A New Booke, Intituled, I Am For You All Complexions Castle: as well as in the time of pestilence, as other times, out of the which you may learne your complexion, your disease incident to the same, and the remedies for the same (Cambridge, 1604), p. 9.

6 Helen King, Hippocrates' Women: Reading the Female Body in Ancient Greece (London and New York, 1998), pp. 225–8.

7 Manning, Complexions Castle, p. 10.

8 Alain Corbin, The Foul and the Fragrant: Odour and the Social Imagination, no translator named (London, 1994), p. 26.

9 Antoine-Alexis Cadet de Vaux, Moyen de prévenir et de détruire le méphitisme des murs (Paris, 1798 [an IX]), p. 4.

10 Ibid., p. 5.

11 Ibid., p. 7.

12 See Constance Classen, David Howes and Anthony Synott, Aroma: The Cultural History of Smell (London and New York, 1993), pp. 52–3; Constance Classen, The Color of Angels: Cosmology, Gender and the Aesthetic Imagination (London and New York, 1998), pp. 36–60.

13 1 Corinthians 2:15, Novum testamentum graece, ed. Constaninus Tischendorf (Leipzig, 1869–72), vol. II, p. 579.

14 Shirley Price, Practical Aromatherapy: How To Use Essential Oils To Restore Health and Vitality, 3rd edn (London, 1994), pp. 9–10.

15 Marguerite Maury, Le Capital 'Jeunesse', trans. Mervyn Saville as The Secret of Life and Youth: Regeneration Through Essential Oils – A Modern Alchemy (London, 1964), pp. 80–1.

16 James Joyce, Ulysses: The Corrected Text, ed. Hans Walter Gabler, Wolfhard Steppe and Claus Melchior (Harmondsworth, 1986), p. 307.

17 The Epic of Gilgamesh, trans. Andrew George (London, 1999) p. 99.

18 Maury, Secret, p. 80.

19 Richard le Gallienne, The Romance of

Perfume (New York and Paris, 1928), p. 46.

20 *Ibid.*, p. 29.

21 *Ibid.*, p. 43.

22 Thornton, *Beautiful Skin With Aromatherapy*, p. 24.

23 *Ibid.*

24 Odon of Cluny, *Collationum libri tres*, *Patrologia Latina Cursus Completus*, ed. Jacques-Paul Migne (Paris, 1844–65), II.9, vol. CXXXIII (1853), p. 556.

25 D. Michael Stoddart, *The Scented Ape: The Biology and Culture of Human Odour* (Cambridge, 1990), pp. 161–7.

26 Corbin, *Foul and the Fragrant*, pp. 22–6.

27 *Ibid.*, p. 20.

28 Le Gallienne, *Romance of Perfume*, p. 46.

29 Anon, *Saint Chrême ou pétrole: thèse philosophique sur l'idéal des sociétés* (Paris, 1877).

30 Corbin, *Foul and the Fragrant*, p. 182.

31 Le Gallienne, *Romance of Perfume*, p. 45.

32 'Poisoned Gloves', *The Manufacturer and Builder*, III (September 1871), p. 212.

33 Chrissie Wildwood, *The Bloomsbury Encyclopedia of Aromatherapy* (London, 1996), p. 47.

34 Valerie Ann Worwood, *The Fragrant Mind* (London and New York, 1995), pp. 279–303, 308.

35 Mandy Aftel, *Essence and Alchemy: A Book of Perfume* (London, 2001), p. 49.

36 Worwood, *Fragrant Mind*, pp. 30–1.

37 W. Robertson Smith, *Lectures on the Religion of the Semites. First Series: The Fundamental Institutions* (Edinburgh, 1889), p. 215.

38 Gaston Bachelard, *La terre et les rêveries de la volonté* (Paris, 1948), p. 78. References, to *TRV*, in my text hereafter.

39 Jean-Paul Sartre, *Being and Nothingness: An Essay on Phenomenological Ontology*, trans. Hazel E. Barnes (London, 1984), p. 609.

40 C. G. Jung, *The Collected Works of C. G. Jung*, ed. Herbert Read, Michael Fordham, Gerhard Adler, William McGuire, vol. XII, *Psychology and Alchemy*, 2nd edn (London, 1980), pp. 160–1.

41 Susan Gates, *Revenge of the Toffee Monster* (London, 1999).

9 Itch

1 *The Complete Poems and Plays of T. S. Eliot* (London, 1973), p. 38.

2 'An Abstract of Part of a Letter From Dr Bonomo to Signior Redi, containing some Observations concerning the Worms of Humane Bodies' by Richard Mead, *Philosophical Transactions*, XXIII (Jan, Feb 1703), p. 1296. Bonomo's letter first appeared twenty years previously as *Osservazioni intorno a pellicelli del corpo umano* (Florence, 1687). The letter is also translated in J. E. Lane, 'Bonomo's Letter to Redi', *Archives of Dermatology and Syphilology*, XVIII (1928), pp. 1–25.

3 *Ibid.*, pp. 1297–8.

4 See, for example Michel Janier, 'Histoire du sarcopte de la gale', *Histoire des sciences médicales*, XXVIII (1994), pp. 365–79 and Danièle Ghesquier, 'A Gallic Affair: The Case of the Missing Itch-Mite in French Medicine in the Early Nineteenth Century', *Medical History*, XLIII (1999), pp. 26–54.

5 Didier Anzieu, *The Skin Ego*, trans. Chris Turner (New Haven, 1989), p. 105.

6 Gilles Deleuze, *The Fold: Leibniz and the Baroque*, trans. Tom Conley (London, 1993), p. 3.

7 Michel Serres, *Les cinq sens* (Paris, 1998), p. 19.

8 Thomas D'Urfey, *The Royalist* (London, 1682), p. 48.

9 Tobias Smollett, *The Expedition of Humphrey Clinker*, ed. Angus Ross (Harmondsworth, 1985), p. 188.

10 Samuel Ireland, *Chalcographimania or the Portrait Collector and Printseller's Chronicle* (London, 1814), p. 19.

11 Ebenezer Elliott, *Scotch Nationality: A Vision, in Three Books* (Sheffield, 1875).

12 Eric Partridge, *A Dictionary of Slang and Unconventional English*, 8th edn (London and New York, 1991), p. 603; John Florio, *A Worlde of Wordes, Or Most copious, and exact Dictionarie in Italian and English* (London, 1598), p. 149, where the phrase 'to play at itch-buttocks' is given as a translation of 'giocar' a leva culo, *to play at levell coile*'; John S. Farmer and W. E. Henley, *Slang And Its Analogues Past and Present* (New York, 1965), vol. IV, p. 17; Thomas D'Urfey, *Wit and Mirth: Or Pills to Purge Melancholy* (London, 1719–20), vol. VI, p. 324.

13 Robert Willan, *On Cutaneous Diseases* (London, 1808), p. 96.

14 Robert Herrick, 'To The Detractor', *Herrick: Poems*, ed. L. C. Martin (London, 1965), p. 66.

15 Nathaniel Richards, *The Celestiall Publican: A Sacred Poem: lively describing the Birth, Progresse, Bloudy Passion, and glorious Resurection of our Saviour, The Spirituall Sea-Fight, The Mischievous Deceites of the World, the Flesh, The Vicious Courtier, The Jesuite, The Divell,' &c*, 2nd edn (London, 1630), sigs. F8ʳ–F8ᵛ.

16 Christopher Ricks, *Keats and Embarrassment* (Oxford, 1984), p. 15.

17 *Ibid.*

18 Tobias Smollett, 'Reproof: A Satire', *Plays and Poems Written by T. Smollett* (London, 1777), p. 234.

19 Thomas Nashe, *The Returne of the Renowned Cavaliero Pasquill of England, from the other side the Seas, and his meeting with Marsorius at London upon the Royall Exchange: Where they encounter with a little household take of Martin and Martinisme, discovering the scabbe that is bredde in England: and conferring together about the speedie dispersing of the golden Legende of the lives of the Saints* (London, 1589), repr. in the *Complete Works of Thomas Nashe*, ed. Alexander B. Grosart (London, 1883–4), vol. I, pp. 94–5.

20 Thomas Spooner, *A Short Account of the Itch, Inveterate Itching Humours, Scabbiness and Leprosie* (London, 1714), p. 4.

21 *The Diary of Samuel Pepys*, ed. Robert Latham and William Matthews (London, 1983), 26 February 1666, vol. VII, p. 60.

22 Gaston Bachelard, *The Poetics of Space*, trans. Marie Jolas (Boston, 1994), p. 164.

23 Gilles Deleuze and Félix Guattari, *A Thousand Plateaus: Capitalism and Schizophrenia*, trans. Brian Massumi (London, 1988), p. 32.

24 *Ibid.*, p. 22.

25 Audrey Meaney, 'The Anglo-Saxon View of the Causes of Disease', in *Health, Disease and Healing in Medieval Culture*, ed. Sheila Campbell, Bert Hal and David Klausner (Basingstoke, 1992), p. 14.

26 Samuel Taylor Coleridge, 'The Ancient Mariner', ll. 123–6, in *Selected Poems*, ed. Richard Holmes (London, 1996), p. 85.

27 Piero Camporesi, *The Incorruptible Flesh: Bodily Mutilation and Mortification in Religion and Folklore*, trans. Tania Croft-Murray and Helen Elsom (Cambridge, 1988), pp. 90–105.

28 The pleasures of itching and scratching are celebrated in Matthaeus Czanakius's Latin poem, *Nobile scabiei encomium. Ad nobilis-simos scabianæ reipublicæ scabinos* (1627). See too Frans Meulenberg, 'The Hidden Delight of Psoriasis', *British Medical Journal*, CCCXV (1997), pp. 1709–11.

29 Quintus Serenus Sammonicus, *Liber medic-inalis*, in *Corpus Medicorum Latinorum*, vol. II, Fasc. 3, ed. Friedrich Völlmer (Leipzig, 1916), VI.71–80, p. 8.

30 Michel Serres, *Hermès V: Le Passage du nord-ouest*, (Paris, 1980), p. 23.

31 Caroline Wilson, *The Invisible World: Early Modern Philosophy and the Invention of the Microscope* (Princeton, 1995), pp. 140–75, and Edward G. Ruestow, *The Microscope in The Dutch Republic: The Shaping of Discovery* (Cambridge, 1996), pp. 201–59.

32 William Harvey, *Exercitationes de genera-tione animalium, quibus accedunt quaedam de partu, de membranis ac humoribus uteri & de concpetione* (London, 1651).

33 Edmund Ward, 'The Mollies' Club', *A Compleat and Humorous Account of All The Remarkable Clubs and Societies in the Cities of London and Westminster* (London, 1756), p. 268.

34 Cyrano de Bergerac, *L'Autre monde, ou les états et empires de la lune et du soleil* (Paris, 1968), p. 127.

35 Wilson, *Invisible World*, p. 62.

36 Abraham Trembley, *Mémoires, pour servir à l'histoire d'un genre de polypes d'eau douce à bras en forme de cornes* (Leiden, 1744).

37 Unpublished letter, Manuscrits Bonnet, vol. I 1740–59, Bibliothèque publique et univer-sitaire de Genève, quoted in John R. Baker, *Abraham Trembley of Geneva: Scientist and Philosopher 1710–1784* (London, 1952), p. 25.

38 Reuben Friedman, *The Emperor's Itch: The Legend Concerning Napoleon's Affliction With Scabies* (New York, 1940).

39 Michel Serres, *The Natural Contract*, trans. Elizabeth Macarthur and William Paulson (Ann Arbor, 1995), p. 3.

40 Michel Serres, *The Parasite*, trans. Lawrence R. Schehr (Baltimore, 1982).

41 Thomas Moffett, *The Theater of Insects: or Lesser Living Creatures* in Edward Topsell, *The History of Four-Footed Beasts and Serpents . . . Collected Out of the Writings of Conradus Gesner and Other Authors* (London, 1658), p. 1095.

42 Reuben Friedman, *The Story of Scabies*, vol. I (New York, 1947), p. 81.

43 Serres, *Parasite*, p. 194.

44 Charles Singer, 'The Dawn of Microscopical Discovery', *Journal of the Royal Microscopical Society*, IV (1915), p. 325, quoted in Friedman, *Story of Scabies*, vol. I, p. 200.

45 Tobias Smollett, *The History and Adventures of An Atom*, ed. O. M. Brack and Robert Adams Day (Athens and London, 1989), p. 3.

46 *Ibid.*, p. 15.

47 *Ibid.*, pp. 15–17.

48 Thomas D'Urfey, *The Banditti: or, A Lady's Distress* (London, 1686), p. 21.

49 Thomas D'Urfey, *The Rise and Fall of Massaniello, Part 1* (London, 1700), p. 9.

50 Serres, *Parasite*, p. 194.

10 The Light Touch

1 Gabriel Josipovici, *Touch* (New Haven and London, 1996), p. 141.

2 http://www.persil.com/. Consulted 23

December 2002.

3 Gilles Deleuze and Félix Guattari, *What Is Philosophy?*, trans. Graham Burchell and Hugh Tomlinson (London and New York, 1994), p. 164.

4 *Ibid.*

5 Jacques Derrida, 'A Silkworm of One's Own: Points of View Stitched On The Other Veil', in Hélène Cixous and Jacques Derrida, *Veils*, trans. Geoffrey Bennington (Stanford, 2001), pp. 24, 25.

6 Elaine Freedgood, 'Fringe', *Victorian Literature and Culture*, xxx (2002), p. 262.

7 Margaret Simeon, *The History of Lace* (London, 1979), p. 3.

8 Flann O'Brien, *The Third Policeman* (London, 1974), p. 65

9 *Ibid.*, p. 63.

10 *Ibid.*, pp. 64–5.

11 E. H. Weber, *De Tactu* and *Der Tastsinn*, trans. Helen E. Ross and David Murray, in *E. H. Weber on the Tactile Senses*, 2nd edn (Hove, 1996).

12 David Appelbaum, *The Interpenetrating Reality: Bringing the Body to Touch* (New York, 1988), p. 69.

13 Tobias Smollett, *The Expedition of Humphrey Clinker*, ed. Angus Ross (Harmondsworth, 1985), p. 79; Ann Jessie Van Sant, *Eighteenth-Century Sensibility and the Novel: The Senses in Social Context* (Cambridge, 1993), p. 104.

14 Hensleigh Wedgwood, 'On The Connection of the Latin *Dulcis* With *Deliciae, Delicatus, Delectare*', *Transactions of the Philological Society* (1860–1), p. 151.

15 *Ibid.*, p. 153.

16 *Galateo: or a Treatise on Politeness and Delicacy of Manners. From the Italian of Monsig. Giovanni de la Casa* (London, 1774), p. 22.

17 Robert Kittowe, *Loues Load-starre. Lively Deciphered in a Historie no lesse commendable than comfortable* . . . (London, 1600), sig D2ᵛ.

18 Edward Atherstone, *Israel in Egypt: A Poem* (London, 1861), p. 165.

19 Thomas Nabbes, *Microcosmus: A Morall Maske* (London, 1637), Act IV (unpaginated).

20 James Mabbe, *The Spanish Bawd, Represented in Celestina: or the Tragicke-comedy of Calisto and Melibea* . . . (London, 1631) (unpaginated [p. i]).

21 Edward Benlowes, *The Summary of Wisedome* (London, 1657) (unpaginated), stanza 88.

22 'Psyche: In XXIV Cantos: The Humiliation', *Complete Poems of Dr. Joseph Beaumont,* ed. Revd Alexander B. Grosart (Blackburn, 1880), p. 117.

23 Henry Baker, *The Second Part of Original Poems: Serious and Humorous* (London, 1726) p. 88.

24 John Armstrong, 'The Art of Preserving Health', in *Miscellanies* (London, 1770), vol. I, p. 29.

25 'Hymn to the Naiads', *The Poems of Mark Akenside* (London, 1771), p. 356.

26 C. J. Rawson, 'Some Remarks on Eighteenth-Century "Delicacy," With a Note on Hugh Kelly's *False Delicacy* (1768)', *Journal of English and Germanic Philology*, LXI (1962), p. 3.

27 *Ibid.*

28 Hugh Kelly, *False Delicacy: A Comedy* (London, 1768).

29 David Hume, 'Of the Delicacy of Taste and Passion' (1741), in *Selected Essays*, ed. Stephen Copley and Andrew Edgar (Oxford, 1998), pp. 10–13.

30 Elizabeth MacAndrew and Susan Gorky, 'Why Do They Faint and Die?: The Birth of the Delicate Heroine', *Journal of Popular Culture*, VIII (1974), pp. 735–45.

31 J. Compton Burnett, *Delicate, Backward, Puny, and Stunted Children: Their Developmental Defects, and Physical, Mental, and Moral Peculiarities Considered As Ailments Amenable to Treatment By Medicines* (London, 1895), pp. 12–13.

32 Amy Louise Reed, 'Female Delicacy in the Sixties', *Century Magazine*, XC (1915), p. 864.

33 Jacques Derrida, *Le Toucher: Jean-Luc Nancy* (Paris, 2000).

34 Maurice Merleau-Ponty, *The Visible and the Invisible*, trans. Alphonso Lingis (Evanston, 1968), pp. 132–3.

35 Luce Irigaray, *An Ethics of Sexual Difference*, trans. Carolyn Burke and Gillian C. Gill (London, 1993), p. 159. References hereafter, abbreviated to *Ethics*, in my text.

36 Jean-Paul Sartre, *Being and Nothingness: An Essay on Phenomenological Ontology* trans. Hazel E. Barnes (London, 1984), pp. 390, 396.

37 Emmanuel Levinas, *Totality and Infinity: An Essay on Exteriority*, trans. Alphonso Lingis (Dordrecht, Boston and London, 1993), p. 257. References hereafter, abbreviated to *Totality*, in my text.

38 Michel Serres, *The Troubadour of Knowledge*, trans. Sheila Faria Glaser and William Paulson (Ann Arbor, 1997), pp. 108–10. References hereafter in my text.

39 Sidney Perkowitz, *Universal Foam: The Story of Bubbles From Cappuccino to the Cosmos* (London, 2001), pp. 77–80, 150–56.

Index